MW01110142

Minnesota State Parks:
A Camper's Guide

By Michael Keigan

AuthorHouse™
1663 Liberty Drive
Bloomington, IN 47403
www.authorhouse.com
Phone: 1-800-839-8640

First published by AuthorHouse 3/28/2011

ISBN: 978-1-4567-5059-6 (sc)
ISBN: 978-1-4567-5058-9 (dj)
ISBN: 978-1-4567-5060-2 (e)

Library of Congress Control Number: 2011903410

Printed in the United States of America

This book is printed on acid-free paper.

Table of Contents

Forward

First, I would like to thank you for taking the time to look at this book. It is our hope that this will become a tool for you to use when you are planning to stay at any of the fabulous state parks here in Minnesota.

This book is only meant to be used as an enhancement to all of the rest of the information that can be found through the Parks Department for the state of Minnesota and the Department of Natural Resources. I strongly recommend to anyone who is reading this to use the same resources we did when planning trips to the various parks.

The most frequent way we used to access any information was to visit the following DNR web site: www.dnr.state.mn.us/state_parks/map.html. When you arrive at this map, you can click on any site location for the parks and the next page that comes up will give you synapses' of what can be found at the parks, maps of the parks, and the telephone numbers for contacting the reservation line. This is a great site, I am sure it will become one of your favorites when time comes to make any plans for visiting a state park.

Here are the telephone numbers to use if you plan on staying at a state park: Reservation Line - 1.866.857.2757 or Minnesota State Parks at 1.888.MINNDNR (1.888.646.6367).

Julie and I had many, great adventures during the two plus years that we spent driving all over this state trying to complete this work. There were long hours of driving and many, many miles covered in trying to get to every park. But, don't get me wrong, we had a great time. Right here at the beginning, I would like to tell you that I am no stranger to camping and canoeing - I have been involved with these activities for most of my life. I used to do a lot of tent camping. I own two tents and all of the associated gear to go along with them. But, after I turned forty, I found that I really didn't enjoy sleeping on the ground anymore. In the mornings, after struggling to sleep on an air mattress or cushion, I would awake to discover all sorts of new aches and pains that I had to deal with. As a resolution to this problem, I designed and built my own small sleeper camper. In 2002, I became very interested in 'teardrop' trailers; but, the more I looked into their design and size, I knew they wouldn't be a good fit for me. (No pun intended.) Our little trailer is just the right size so that it trails nicely behind the pickup; yet, if we do get stuck inside due to weather, it is not claustrophobic. We have traveled to all sorts of places and this little rig suits us just fine. It has been with us out west in Wyoming and Montana, it has been south, and it has been east into Wisconsin and Michigan. But, most of all, it has kept us high and dry during the wet times in our journey around the state and has been a wonderful help in keeping us from getting eaten alive by the other state bird - the mosquito.

The first part of this book is the story of our travels. It is in this section that I try to convey some of the history and interesting facts about the parks. Anyone who knows me, they know that I love to tell stories. I really had to hold myself back in this section and not get too verbose because every trip we made had a little adventure in it.

The second section of this book is the portion that describes what is available for use at the parks and I try to relay to you information about the campsites at each park that Julie and I felt would offer the best stay for us. Included in the second part of the book, along with the little section of descriptors for each park, you will find maps of the campgrounds for each of the parks and a map of the entire park. These have been included so that you will be able to see first hand what we are describing as you are reading. It was through the graciousness of the State of Minnesota and the Department of Natural Resources that they have allowed me to include these documents in the book. Without the maps, I fear that this book would not be as valuable a resource for you, the reader, when you are making decisions as to where to stay at a Minnesota state park. I owe the Parks Department and the Department of Natural Resources a great thank you.

Every camper who visit's a park does so with their own interests in mind. So, I tried to be very factual and straight forward about what each park had to offer for us. You will have to make your own decisions when you are out on your own adventure.

Mike Keigan

The Journey

Visiting Minnesota's State Parks

In the summer of my 48th year, my wife and I were traveling around the state of Minnesota. We were visiting the state parks. At the beginning, when the idea first came into my head, it was to be trips to the four corners of the state. We were going to take the little camper that I had built, and we were going to camp at the various state parks that can be found at the corners of this state. That was the original plan. As the summer progressed, that plan blossomed into an even bigger idea.

The first park that we visited was The Blue Mounds State Park, which can be found a couple of miles north of the city of Luverne. This is a very pretty state park and definitely qualifies as being in the corner of the state. South Dakota is just a few miles to the west and Iowa is just a short drive to the south. Blue Mounds State Park was created to help preserve a very unique feature that is found there in the area of Luverne. In that entire southwest corner, especially around and south of Pipestone, the bedrock comes up very shallow under the surface soils and in many parts – this bedrock pokes up through the ground. The rock formation that I am talking about is referred to as Sioux Quartzite. At the state park, there is a line of this rock formation that faces to the east. It has been heaved upward for 50 to 60 feet creating a large cliff in the middle of the prairie. It is a beautiful site. From a distance, these cliffs do have a color to them; so much so, that even the native tribes in the area referred to the site as the Blue Mounds in their language. The park has a small dam and this creates a small lake for the campers to use. After getting home from this little trip, we started to work on developing our plan to get to the other parks at the corners of the state.

Julie, my lovely wife, likes to do all sorts of crafts and she likes to cook. She is a great cook and I love eating whatever she makes for our meals. One of the hobbies or crafts she likes to do is quilting. It was this hobby of hers that would take us on our next leg of the journey. In August, in the state of Minnesota, quilting shops and stores all over the state sponsor an event that is referred to as – The Minnesota Quilt Shop Hop. The whole event is designed to bring in people to all of these little fabric stores and quilt shops. The owners of the shops get together and offer prizes and little give-aways that help to get the people motivated to come to see the stores.

In past years, Julie, with me tagging along sometimes, attempted to visit a minimum of 8 or 9 shops in each of the separate regions of the state. Doing this would get her qualified for what ever grand prize was being offered for that year. Attempting to get to 8 or 9 shops in each of the separate regions, in the time allowed by the event, would make this a difficult task; trying to do it while working around work schedules and other family events would turn this into a major adventure. Quilters from all over would travel many, many miles across the state for the possibility of winning some of these prizes. Now, those prizes – yes, some of them are really grand – but, she wasn't winning any of them. When the time for the quilt shop hop started to approach in the middle of July 2009, we saw an excellent opportunity to combine these three things we were doing and get them done at the same time – visit the four corners of the state, staying at the state parks, and doing the quilt shop hop.

So ---- the next area of the state that we were heading towards was the northwest corner. Julie had been studying the information concerning the quilt hop for that year and she had made the decision that trying to make it to all the different regions in the state and to try and visit all of these different quilt stores was out of the question. The constraints of time and cost of gas helped to make the decision to skip trying to visit all the shops in the southern third of the state. So, she decided that she wanted to visit the shops of the northeast, northwest, the central east, and the central west regions. Well, this would fit well into my original plans to visit the corners of the state. We were going to head to the northwest corner of the state; so, we might as well go visit these quilt shops along the way during the trip. It was a good idea; however, we had no idea just how big a trip we were getting ourselves into.

Before going any further with the story, I have to point out that I work as a Registered Nurse. I have to work weekends. Julie works at a job that is secretarial in nature and she works Monday through Friday. On those weekends that I would have off, Julie and I would hook up our little trailer to the truck and off we would go. So, there were some limitations to our little adventurous trips – they had to be completed in the course of a single weekend. Sometimes, we were able to plan slightly longer trips if we both had a Friday off.

I should explain a little about our camper trailer. I have a wood shop set up in our large pole barn/garage. I enjoy creating many different things in the shop for friends and family. About eight years ago I became very interested in a type of trailer that many people own and use. These small trailers fall into a category referred to as "teardrops."

Teardrop trailers are small sleeper trailers that are not very large but still allow the owners to sleep in a more comfortable situation, up off of the ground, and if it rains – all your equipment doesn't end up soaked. I really liked this idea and since about the time that I had turned 40 years old, I really don't enjoy sleeping on the ground anymore. So, I built my own version of a small sleeper camper. It is slightly larger than a "teardrop", it has a queen-sized futon mattress in it and Julie and I can be very comfortable in it. It is able to carry all the equipment that we need when out camping and is still less than seven feet tall and only twelve feet long. We are able to pull into a camp site and be all set up in just a matter of a few minutes. The same applies to when we want to get ready to pull out from our campsite; just a few minutes and we have everything buttoned up and are ready to hit the road.

So, let's get back to the original story line. There sometimes happens in corporations and large organizations that the left hand doesn't know what the right hand is doing, and vice verse. Well, like a corporation, sometimes we would be making plans for a trip – it was just that we weren't doing it together. She would have an itinerary set up for all the shops she wanted to visit in the region. I would have a separate itinerary set up for the different parks and sites that I wanted to visit. This did lead to some friction at times; but, with a little effort and a few changes in direction along the highways and byways – we would get it worked out.

Leaving from our little cabin in the woods to drive to the northwest corner of the state would be a daunting single day trip all on its own.

However, you throw in six or seven stops along the way to visit a quilt shop or a park, the stops to get snacks and fill the truck with gas caused this daunting trip to become a monster. From Bay Lake, we drove to Perham, from Perham to Detroit Lakes, down to Fergus Falls, up to Moorhead, further north still to East Grand Forks, then finally head to our ultimate destination – Lake Bronson State Park. Yes, it was an exhausting trip to say the least. The weather wasn't working in our favor either. Julie and I have both come to the agreement that the states of Minnesota, North Dakota and South Dakota should pay us a fee for whenever we hook up our trailer to the back of our truck. It seems that each time we go on one of our little excursions, especially if we are heading towards the Dakotas – it starts to rain. There we were that Friday afternoon, driving all over God's creation and a huge part of Minnesota, dodging rain storms and squalls – all in an effort to make it to another very unique area of the state. During our stop at East Grand Forks, we visited a new recreational area – The Red River State Recreational Area. This area was set up after the big floods that occurred there during 1997. This park sits along the shores of the river, right in the middle of town. It is situated inside the berms and walls that were erected to help protect the cities. It has very nice camp sites and great facilities, a trail that follows along the river – but, it is right in the middle of town.

The northwest corner of the state of Minnesota is a region that is heavily affected by the yearly flooding on the Red River of the North. This, however, is just a mere pittance compared to the affect that an earlier epoch had on this region.

What we know today as the northwest corner of the state of Minnesota, most of eastern North Dakota, a huge part of Manitoba and western Ontario were once covered by a huge glacial lake known as Lake Agassiz. This lake existed as the glaciers were receding from the continent northward some 10,000 years ago. With the lake covering all of the aforementioned area, it had enormous effects on what the area would look like after the lake was gone. One of those effects was that there was huge deposition of salts and minerals into the sub-soils in the area. These salts, then, continued to leech down through the soil over the thousands of years since the lake has drained away. These salts and minerals made it all the way down to the ground water.

When the first settlers moved up into the area of the Red River and started to hack out a living in the region, they tried to sink wells down and get to a fresh water source. They didn't find one. What they found was salt water. How improbable was that? Salt water in the ground water and you are in an area that is nearly smack dab in the middle of the continent – about as far away from any ocean as you can get. It was the salt deposits and minerals from the ancient lake that had leeched all the way down and caused the ground water to become salty – not very useful for those poor settlers. So, they had to come up with a different source for their fresh water.

For many decades, the people living in the area were resigned to using surface water sources for their fresh water: the local lakes, streams, or potholes. Back during the Great Depression, President Franklin D. Roosevelt had created many agencies to try and help get the American population back to work. One of those organizations was the WPA – the Works Progress Administration.

This organization helped to put men and women back to work, created jobs and in the end helped to find solutions to this area's water problem. Dams were built on many of the streams and rivers in the region and this made for easier access to fresh water supplies. Cities like Hallock, Lancaster, and Lake Bronson now had a very large and abundant supply of water. Later, the state of Minnesota would create a state park around the lake that one of those projects had created. This place was the ultimate destination for all the driving we had done.

Lake Bronson, Minnesota, is a small town on the roadside heading to the very northwest corner of the state. The lake, and the community that shares its name, is located in an ecological area called - the tall grass/aspen zone. This is the zone of vegetation that exists between the thicker forests to the north and east and the flat prairie to the west.

The state park sits along the shores of Lake Bronson and is nestled among scrub oaks, aspen and other varieties of trees. Even though this state park is in an area of the state that is lightly populated, it was surprising to see how busy the park was. When we arrived at the park, we parked along the roadside near the main office. While sitting there, we were treated to an impromptu car show. Earlier in the day, at the community of Lake Bronson, there had been a gathering of owners of classic cars. For some reason they had decided to do a drive through the park with their classic cars. There were Chevelles, Novas, Mustangs and one very nice Thunderbird that went rolling slowly past us. This little spectacle just added to the ambiance of the scene and the park.

The park has a wonderful open picnic area with many tables spread out beneath the canopy of oaks and aspens. Just across the road from the picnic area, there stands a large stone tower that is listed on the National Registry of Historic Sites. The tower was constructed by those men of the WPA during the time that they were building the dam that formed the lake. The tower was erected to enclose a 5000 gallon water holding tank that was used to hold fresh water as the lake and dam were being constructed. The very unique design of this tower with its roofed-over deck on the top, and an interior staircase that follows the walls around to the top, allows visitors to get a good view from up around the tops of the trees. Another reason that the park is so busy is the fish that can be found in the lake. Even though Minnesota is known for its multitude of lakes, the northwest corner is an area of the state where this isn't so. Lake Bronson, therefore, draws a lot of visitors who use the water for boating, skiing, and fishing. After spending a comfortable night at Lake Bronson, we broke camp and headed to our next destination.

We drove to a small spot at the very northwest corner of the state. This little town is known as Noyes. A number of years ago it was quite the busy little border crossing. There was a duty free shop there, a bar, a café, and several other businesses and homes. There is a major railroad line that crosses the border between the United States and Canada right there. However, as has happened to many small towns across the state, the town of Noyes is nearly a ghost of its former self. Many of the businesses that were once there have closed and the population of the town has dwindled through the years. We were driving up the road looking at some of the buildings that were beginning to become overgrown with weeds and small shrubs when we suddenly realized that we were crossing the border into Canada. I looked ahead of us as I was driving and I saw the Canadian Customs building ahead on the left side of the road. I looked in the side mirror and saw the large sign pronouncing entrance into Canada. I immediately realized our error. But there was another problem - we had no passports. So, there in the wide spot of the road just south of the Customs Building, we did a big U-turn and headed back past the sign welcoming us to the United States. I can only imagine that the Canadian Official inside of the building, drinking his morning cup of coffee, must have wondered what we were doing. This, then, was the northwest corner of the state.

The next destination happened to be another small state park that is a short distance south of Lake Bronson – Old Mill State Park. This little park is small and set back off the beaten path. It is an absolute jewel for those of us who, when camping, want to get away from the hustle, the bustle, and the crowds. The park only has 25 to 30 sites and none of the sites has access to electrical hook-ups. There are vault toilets, no showers, and some spigots to get fresh water from and this also helps to keep some of the congestion down. Old Mill is built on the site where a family of Swedish immigrants - the Larson's - had settled. They had started a flour mill on their property to process the grains of the farmers in the area. After a time, a tradition had developed about camping at the Larson's while waiting for the mill to finish with the grain. The state park was built to continue this tradition. Each year as a tribute to the family – a group of re-enactors comes to the park in the late summer and they have a weekend long celebration where they try to bring back the flavor of that bygone era.

Julie and I both agreed that this is a lovely park and that we would return in the future to spend more time there. This park is also located in the tall grass/aspen zone and there is nice cover from the oaks and other trees that are around the campsites. On the way to this small state park, we traveled through the town of Karlstad – The Moose Capital of Minnesota.

From Old Mill, we continued on our trek east. The next stop was Hayes Lake State Park. This park is about 20 miles south of the city of Roseau, MN. The park exists in an area that is different than the area of the state we had been traveling through earlier. Now, the forest areas we were driving past were thicker and there was more mix to the tree species. Now, you could see a lot more pines in the woods. Hayes Lake State Park has an abundance of pines. The entire park sits in rows and rows of Red Pines, White Pines, and spruces. This park owes its existence to those men that were building the parks and other facilities back in the 1930's, too. However, this park differs from Lake Bronson because this park was built by the men of the CCC – Civilian Conservation Corps. There is a dam at this park, too. This dam was built for the same reason as Lake Bronson - the need for a fresh water source, in large amounts, for the farmers. Now, it is used for canoeing, boating, swimming, and fishing. Hayes Lake has all the usual species of fish that can be found in a Minnesota lake. Crappies, bass, and northern pike are there for the catching. As long as you, the angler, can prove that you are smarter than a fish.

From Hayes Lake, we headed north, back to Roseau. I couldn't remember if I had ever been to Roseau before in my life. If I had, I don't recall. Hockey is big in the state of Minnesota, duh! Hockey is huge in Roseau. Just driving down the city streets, I could feel it and I am not a big hockey fan.

Roseau also had one of the quilt shops that Julie wanted to visit. So, we stopped, she went to the quilt shop, I got out of the truck to stretch my legs. On our little treks around the state, we have started to take a third companion along with us – our little Mini Schnauzer – Bo. He is nearly the perfect sized dog for traveling. He fits easily on the seat between Julie and me as we are driving along. He gets by on a little dog food and some water and if you let him out to run around and try and kick over a tree or two, he is happy. So, when we stopped at Roseau, it wasn't just me that was stretching his legs.

After Julie finished her business at the quilt shop, we headed back up the road and traveled to the shores of Lake of the Woods and the town of Warroad. Like Roseau, Warroad is another one of those cities that lives and breaths hockey. We stopped for just a short time in order to take some pictures of the lake. Then, it was on to the next park – Zipple Bay State Park.

Zipple Bay State Park is literally hacked out of a Red Pine forest on the south shore of Lake of the Woods. There are many remote campsites here in this park and there is an excellent boat access in the bay on the west side of the park. Once the boats are in the water of the bay, it is a no-brainer to get to the lake. Many fishermen come to use the park facilities for its good docks and the bay.

All most all of the campsites in this park are surrounded by pines and there are beautiful picnic areas and a swim beach right along the sandy shore of the lake.

When we left Roseau, we were driving along Minnesota Highway 11. This is one of, if not the most northern highways in the state. After we had made our little excursion through Warroad and Zipple Bay, we drove through the town of Baudette. This city sits along the route on MN Hwy. 11 and completes the trifecta of big hockey towns near Lake of the Woods. We drove on through Baudette and continued east to the next stop in the journey and that was at a small state park along the shores of the Rainy River. This is a wonderful drive, it isn't the greatest roadway in the world - but, I have been on worse. Besides, there was also evidence along the way the state is attempting to make the road a nicer drive. You are basically following along the banks of the river, heading east and then every once in awhile taking a couple of sharp turns to the right and then the left to account for the river's slight bend to the southeast as it heads toward International Falls. There is a very remote, small state park that sits next to one of the river landings on the Rainy River. It is about half way along the road between Baudette and Falls/Ft. Francis. Franz Jevne State Park is a beautiful and remote park that allows for the wonderful seclusion that I enjoy and at some of the campsites - you can literally fish the river right from your picnic table.

It is a strange thing to look across the river from the park and realize that you are looking at a completely different country. What is the difference between the spot on the north shore verses this spot I was standing on there on the south shore? Not much. The types of trees over there were the same types of trees that are found on this side. The grasses are the same. The weather and the seasons are the same - all the same; yet, a completely different country. That's kind of weird.

From that little park we continued on the eastward tack towards the city that is easily recognized as the "Icebox of the U.S." - International Falls. This city on the border leading into Canada is quite a town. Back in the mid 1990's, my father, myself and our good friend Doug found ourselves stranded in International Falls when we were trying to get to Canada. We spent four or five days waiting for a vehicle to get repaired at one of the local auto dealers; so, while we waited, we went fishing on the Rainy. I remember that we had a great time and I remember that the local ice cream place in town made the best chocolate malts. Now, my memory and my taste buds may have been a little biased at the time because we got stranded in International Falls on a weekend that registered the hottest summer time temps ever recorded in the city. Regardless, we had a good time.

Well, that was back in the mid 90's. Now it was 2009 and we, in our little rig, were dodging rain showers again - much the same as we had done on the day before. International Falls has a real love affair going with Smokey the Bear. There is a huge statue of the bear right in the middle of the town. We took pictures. Julie went to the quilt shop there in town and then it was back to the roadway and this time we were heading south-southwest. We were headed toward Blackduck, MN, and the final quilt shop we were going to be able to visit that day. It was getting on toward the late part of the afternoon and it was going to be close trying to get to Blackduck before the shop closed - but, we made it. Thank God that the speed limits on U.S. highways are 60 miles per hour, rather than 55. It gave us just the edge in order to make it on time. Once the visit to the quilt shop was done there in Blackduck, the next place we headed to was a small state park on the eastern shore of Upper Red Lake, Big Bog State Park.

Big Bog State Park is a small park sitting next to an inlet of water that leads out into Upper Red Lake. As you can imagine, this is a very popular park for those sportsman who want to use it as the base of operations as they fish Red Lake. The sites had very good tree cover but as with many parks it is wide open under the trees and little brush or undergrowth. Ultimately, you could sit at your campsite on one end of the small campground and just about see what everybody else was doing at their camp sites. This did not detract however from how nice the park was. It had the absolute best toilets and showers that we have visited in any of the state parks so far. The bathrooms were large and well kept. The showers were set aside in individual rooms. There was an actual changing area to stand comfortably in before and after your shower - and you were in there all by yourself, very nice.

There are camper cabins available at Big Bog and, according to the staff at the park office; those cabins are very popular during the winter when the ice fishermen come up to Red Lake. This is a very family oriented park with fishing piers, a swimming beach and grocery facilities just a mile or two away. The confusing thing about the park is that the feature of the park, the thing that it is named for, is not there at the place where the campsites are. Now, the site where the bog is has a beautiful, aluminum boardwalk built out into the bog and you can walk along and see the wide variety of species of plant, animal, and birds that call a northern bog home. The bog and the boardwalk are about nine miles north on the highway from the campground area.

From Big Bog, we traveled east again to visit two other state parks that are located up in that region. Actually, these two state parks aren't in that region at all because they are just north and west of Grand Rapids, Minnesota. I think they would qualify more as parks located in the north central region; but, I am not going to quibble over those little details. We were on the road, we had some time - so, we headed in that direction. The first park we got to that morning was a park located near the town of Big Fork - Scenic State Park.

Minnesota has 72 State Parks and 6 or 7 State Wayside areas. Each of these areas brings its own special features and beauty to people who visit them. There is Itasca State Park - the grand daddy of all parks here in Minnesota and the headwaters of one of the greatest rivers in the world. There is the awesome beauty of the waterfalls along the North Shore of Lake Superior at Gooseberry, Temperance River, Cascade and Grand Portage. The miles and miles of hiking trails and the wild and scenic river that can be found at St. Croix State Park, Wild River, and Interstate State Park. The vistas and scenery that can be observed when visiting Glacial Lakes, Great River Bluffs, or Camden are fantastic.

So, there we were, once again dodging rainstorms, and driving through the entrance into Scenic State Park. What a lovely surprise was in store for us. I am not sure if it was the over cast skies and the low hanging clouds, the heavy moisture that was in the air and because it was so wet out that everything around had a sort of muffled quality; but, Scenic State Park struck me as one of the most beautiful parks I have ever visited. There are huge old growth Red and White Pines in the park. Two or three lakes are within the borders of the park and can be used for fishing, canoeing, swimming, or whatever else you are looking for. Hiking trails and picnic areas and great camping sites rounded out the facilities available to campers at this great state park. As is most of the northeastern region of the state, the area around Scenic State park is closely tied to the logging the occurred in the state in the mid 1800's. After the logging was complete, settlers moved in and attempted to farm the area. They, however, had a very difficult time. In 1921, residents in the area lobbied the state to turn the area into a state park to help preserve its natural beauty.

We were very hesitant to leave Scenic State Park; but we had many miles to go ahead of us and we couldn't afford to let too much of the day slip by us. We left Scenic and headed south toward Grand Rapids. From there, slightly southwest to the state park that sits along the shores of the Mississippi River - Schoolcraft State Park.

Henry Rowe Schoolcraft was one of the early explorers of the northern parts of Minnesota and was one of the many explorers who searched for the headwaters of the Mississippi River. This park sits along the shores of that river and is named in his honor. It is a nice park with just the bare essentials for camping - fresh water, vault toilets, and nice level campsites with lots of shade from hardwoods and pines. It has a nice boat landing and dock that go out into the river for the fishermen to use. There is a nice picnic area that is along the shore and according to the staff at the park there is a white pine in the picnic area that is over three hundred years old. During the time we spent at the park, I got the impression that this would be a nice park to come and stay at for Julie and me. It is relatively close to our home. It is a quiet park and off the beaten path; yet, it is still close to a major city area where the campers can re-supply.

After we were done visiting Schoolcraft, we pointed the truck northwest and followed U.S. Hwy 2 until it brought us back to Bemidji. On the north shore of Lake Bemidji is - Lake Bemidji State Park. This is a nice state park that allows its campers the ability to access the lake right from the two or three boat access points in the park. It is a nice family oriented park that sits on some rolling, hilly terrain. It was surprising to see how well the park staff had managed to get level camping spots created in some parts of the park. There are a lot of camping sites in this park and all of them are grouped into the one main area, so...you could find yourself a little crowded with neighbors all around. Everything is there within the park for a great camping experience and the city of Bemidji is just a few miles to the southwest. Lake Bemidji has been an important resource to all peoples who have lived along its shores for many hundreds of years now. The region was inhabited by the Eastern bands of the Dakota who fished the waters and hunted the plentiful game in the region until the middle of the 1700's. This was when the Anishinabe (the Ojibwe) pushed them further out into the Great Plains and they took over the region as their new home. The name given to the lake by the Ojibwe was – Bemidjigumaug. The word means 'cross water'. Early white settlers in the area had a difficult time pronouncing the word and shortened it to the word we use today.

We left Bemidji that afternoon and headed south to get to Park Rapids because that was where the next quilt shop was for Julie to visit. We got to Park Rapids without difficulty and after doing the stop over there - we went further on our trek. The next stop was the quilt shop in Walker. We pulled into the shop and Julie ran in and exited as fast as she could because we had to hit the road again. Time for us was starting to close in. There were two shops left to get to on this great adventure - that was in Pine River and Pequot Lakes. However, that was a few miles further south on Hwy. 371. It was Sunday afternoon, moving on into the evening, and we were on Hwy. 371, heading south. Anyone who knows that stretch of highway can then understand what my concern was. TRAFFIC, and lots of it. The ebb and flow of traffic in and out of the Twin Cities metro area on Friday and Sunday afternoons can be very daunting. Well, the traffic was bad; but, we made it. Pine River went smoothly and when we pulled into Pequot Lakes, it was just a few minutes before the owner was going to close. Julie had made it to all the shops she needed to get to with not a moment to spare.

We left Pequot Lakes, took the long way around Brainerd to avoid all of the traffic that was going to be there and within an hour we found ourselves back at home at the little cabin in the woods. It was quite the adventure. The part of the story about traveling to Blue Mound by Luverne, Minnesota, happened in the earlier part of the summer. But, it is ultimately included as one of the four corners of the state. So, we had driven over 1400 miles in just over three and a half days. We had started out at our home and had been all over the northwest corner and north central portion of Minnesota and except for one accidental excursion of about 100 feet into Canada - we had never left the state of Minnesota. The state of Minnesota is only 400 miles long, north to south. So, if you drive 1400 miles anywhere - you have seen a lot of Minnesota.

This is not the end of the story. The quilt shop hop was done, but the epic journey continues with us moving further on our journey to travel to the four corners of the state. But, in a moment of inspiration, while visiting the small state park at Hayes Lake, I asked Julie what she thought about the idea of visiting all of the state parks and then writing a book about our experience. She thought it was a good idea and thus was born the start of our epic journey. We had been to some of the state parks and there were many more yet to see.

Prior to developing the idea for our journey around the state, Julie and I had been to a couple of other state parks and special places in and around Minnesota. We certainly don't want to skip them in this tale.

Itasca State Park as mentioned earlier in the story is the grand-daddy of all the state parks. It was the first place to receive the distinction of becoming a state park here in Minnesota. It is a large park with many beautiful sites to see. Lake Itasca is the headwaters of the Mississippi River and the spot where the water cascades through some small rocks and boulders to create a small creek is a 'must see' destination within the park. There are miles of hiking trails and miles of roadways to take a car or pickup on in order to see some of the other pretty lakes and marshes of the park. There are old growth pine species that exist here too, and a very, very large white pine. There are excellent facilities available within the park and this park would easily accommodate any and all members of a family. There are no other places in this country where you can see the Mississippi River where it is only about 8 feet wide and about 1.5 feet deep. Itasca State Park should be on the short list for anyone's list of the best places to see in Minnesota.

Earlier in the story, I talked about the state park located just north of Luverne. Blue Mounds State Park is a great place to go visit. There are lots of things to keep you busy at the park and we just happen to be there when Luverne was celebrating "Buffalo Days". This is an annual celebration of the history of the area and its residents. The reason I wanted to talk some more about the southwest corner of the state is because I would be remiss if I did not talk about another very special spot down in that region. The city of Pipestone is a location on the North American continent where people have continually resided for many hundreds, if not thousands of years. When I was talking about the bedrock that came up to the surface of the land at Blue Mounds State Park, it is that same phenomena that led to the significance of the area around Pipestone. The Pipestone National Monument was created by the Federal Government in order to try and preserve these sites in the region of the southwest corner of the state where very dark red shale comes close to the surface of the ground. Prior to white settlers coming to this area, the tribes of Plains Indians that resided in the region always kept a small community located near where the city of Pipestone currently sits. They mined this shale and used it for their own purposes and for trade. There is abundant evidence showing that other tribes traveled great distances to get to the area to trade for the special stone. If you are in the vicinity of Pipestone, you must stop and see this special historic site.

Now, we will leave the southwest corner for later, and travel back to the north and east. I was born in Minnesota and have spent a majority of my adult years living in this state, but I grew up in northwestern and North-central Wisconsin. Through the years of living there, my family became very attached to three small parks that are very close to the border of Minnesota. In fact, two of the parks are just across the St. Croix River.

In the northwest corner of Wisconsin lies the city of Superior - one of the cities referred to when someone says "The Twin Ports". The city of Superior is a large city when compared to other cities in that region of Wisconsin. If a person where to start traveling south out of Superior, you would be driving down Wisconsin Hwy 35. This Hwy 35 fairly mimics Interstate 35 which is just a short distance to the west inside of Minnesota. About 10 to 12 miles south of Superior on this highway there is a sudden and very abrupt point at which the roadway starts to climb a steep slope. The road winds back and forth just a couple of times until you reach the top and see to the left a sign that you are driving through Pattison State Park. This is a small state park and there are about 60 campsites available and there are miles of hiking trails that are well used by the residents of the area. There is a small dam near the highway that creates a lovely little lake to the east. But, what is unknown to many people as they speed by this quaint little park is that they had just driven by the tallest waterfall in the state. Big Manitou Falls is a waterfall that has developed along a fracture in the bedrock that was up-thrust in this area. The Black River flows west-northwest through this area, on its way to empty into the St. Louis River. When the Black River reaches the area of the park, it pitches over the edge of the escarpment and down a couple of steps to a total of over 160 feet of drop. The ravine and the valley that stretches out to the west is a lovely site. There are 'overlook' spots for viewing and taking pictures on both sides of the ravine. This is called Big Manitou Falls because further up stream beyond the dam and lake and about one half miles further down Highway 35 is Little Manitou Falls. At this locale, the Black River drops over a ledge about 30 feet high. All things considered, this is a lovely, small park and would be a site to see if you have some extra time on your hands while visiting up in the area of Duluth.

Next, we travel further down into the northwest part of Wisconsin. This area of the state is that which is so distinctive when looking at it on a map. The western border of the state, which follows the course of the St. Croix River, creates a recognizable form of an Indian head - thus the reason it is referred to as the Indianhead Region. As the river flows and winds its way south to its confluence with the Mississippi, it cuts a path through land forms and regions that were very active millions of years ago. At the tip of the nose of the Indianhead, there is a community of approximately 2500 people - Grantsburg. Just north of that city is a large wetland that has been preserved by the DNR of Wisconsin and is called 'Crex Meadows'. It is a wildlife preserve and serves as the home to a multitude of different bird, animal and vegetative species. This area of open meadows and marshland was first used as a source of natural pigments used in dyes and paint. It was in the midst of the 1800's shortly after the town of Grantsburg was founded that the first ditches and dikes were built to help in draining and maintaining water levels in the marshes and meadows. The mining for those natural pigments continued for many years until the industry replaced natural pigments by ones that were created chemically. The interwoven system of ditches and dikes in the area helped to create a very diverse habitat for many different birds and animals. The Department of Natural Resources in the state of Wisconsin ultimately took over the management of the area and then designated it a 'Wildlife Refuge' in order to help protect it.

I was only a young child of about 6 or 7 years old when my family first visited this lovely little spot. On the north side of the preserve, there is a small campground that was built atop a small sand and gravelly ridge. This campground is a very nice spot to camp at; but, bring your binoculars and/or a spotting telescope, because you can see many of the birds and animals of the preserve right there from your campsite as you look southward into the swamps and marshes.

The next little spot that I would like to talk about is also very close to

Grantsburg, Wisconsin. Along the St. Croix River as it travels southward are many areas where it splits into numerous channels and backwater oxbows. There is just such a small channel that cuts into the Wisconsin side of the river just south of a spot known as the Soderbeck Ferryboat Landing. This small channel cuts its way through deposits of sandstone that had been left from ancient geologic times creating what the locals in the area call "The Sandrock Cliffs". I have been at "The Sandrock" so many times I couldn't even begin to count them. I used to hunt whitetail deer in the area with friends who owned property there. There is a tall stand of Red Pines that sits on top of the cliffs as they overlook the channel. During the mid-summer, when river levels are at their lowest, the channel passing by "The Sandrock" can be dry. A small island that is west of the cliffs usually can't be reached unless you are willing to get wet; but, as I said, on dry years - you can walk to the island. Tucked among the Red Pines on the top of the cliffs are about one half dozen small campsites where you can set a tent. These are remote sites with a small water spigot at the base of the cliff by the parking area and a couple of vault toilets. If you are camping here, you will definitely get the feeling of being in a very isolated and remote locale. When standing or walking among the tall red pines, on top of the fallen pine needles - it is eerily quiet. You can easily hear the wind blowing through the tops of the pines. It is a lovely and wonderful place that holds a special spot in the hearts of my family.

Another little trip that Julie and I took was to visit several of the nice parks that are just a short drive south and east of where we live. The first park that this trip took us to was Mille Lacs Kathio State Park. This is a park that is located about seven miles north of Onamia on Hwy. 169. There is a lot of history for this park and the area, not the least of which is the tribal lands that are located all around the park and on the west side of the lake. The area around Mille Lacs Kathio has had humans living there for many thousands of years. The productivity of the area for fish and for wild rice has always been prime sources of foods for the local natives. The park entrance is located off of Highway 169 about ½ mile west on County Road 26. This park has over 10,000 acres and ranks as the fourth largest of all of the state parks.

The Dakota, or Sioux, Indians had lived in the region for many hundreds of years prior to white settlers moving in. The name given to the tribes of the area was Mdewakanton, which was a reference to their living near Mdewakan, the Spirit Lake (Mille Lacs). They ultimately started to migrate to areas of the open prairie and oak savanna of southern and western Minnesota when the pressure of white settlements in the east pushed other rival Indian tribes westward. One of those tribes was the Ojibwe. They had moved west in answer to the continuing pressure of white settlers in their previous homelands in Eastern Wisconsin and Michigan. A large battle occurred in 1750 between the Ojibwe and Dakota tribes and it was this battle that forced the Dakota out of their ancestral homelands among the lakes and trees and out onto the prairies. This was the Battle of Kathio.

One of the first white men to make it into this area of the state was Daniel Greysolon, Sieur duLhut. He traveled to the area as one of the first explorers and in July of 1679, he raised the flag of France at the headwaters of the Rum River, on the banks of Mille Lacs Lake. The word 'Kathio' in the name of the park is attributed to Greysolon. He had used a Dakota word – Izatys – in his journals as a reference to the local native settlements. Somehow, in the translating of his journals later, the word was misspelled and became – Kathio. These terms, Izatys and Kathio, became the oldest references to settlements in Minnesota's history.

The second white man of influence to reach the area was Father Louis Hennepin as he traveled up the Mississippi and stayed with many of the tribes along the way. He stayed at the villages in the area for six months around the year 1680. He references this stay in a book published in 1683 called – Description of Louisiana.

In the 1850's, after the logging boom had started in the state, this area was affected as well. Within 50 years, the region's stands of White and Red Pines had all been logged off. Saw mills were located all along the shores of Mille Lacs and down the Rum River. Logging continues to this day in the region but it is managed much more carefully.

There is a wonderful Interpretive Center and museum located about three miles north of the state park. It is located on the east side of Hwy.169 as you approach Grand Casino, Mille Lacs, on the highway. Much of the history of the area and the tribes can be found there.

From Mille Lacs Kathio, we moved further east following the roads that traveled around the big lake. We went through the small towns of

Cove and Wahkon which sit on the south shore of the lake. Then, we entered the east side of Isle, Minnesota, and there on the left side of the road is the entrance to Father Hennepin State Park. The park was established to protect and to preserve the beautiful west side of the Isle Bay area of Mille Lacs Lake. However, historically, the park also carries an association to the incident where Father Hennepin and two of his companions were held captive by the local tribe. It is said that the small rocky outcrop that pokes up from beneath the waters of Mille Lacs Lake, about 1 mile east of the state park, is the spot where the Indians kept the priest and his two friends. Ultimately, the French, in order to help secure the release of the prisoners, sent Daniel Greysolon back into the area from where he was stationed at a French fort near Grand Portage.

Father Hennepin State Park is a small state park and the sites at the park are sometimes a little close together; however, it is still a lovely place that offers a lot of recreational opportunities for all the members of a family to enjoy.

The next stop along our route on this trip would take us to St. Croix State Park. Driving east on MN Hwy. 48, out of Hinckley, will take you to the intersection of Hwy. 48 and Hwy. 22. You turn south and take the lovely drive down to the headquarters for the park. As you drive down this highway, you will be passing by the mixed pines and hardwoods that can be found throughout the park. This is the largest state park in Minnesota. This park encompasses over 33,000 acres. There are miles and miles of trails for hiking, skiing, and riding. There are 80 miles of groomed snowmobile trails in the winter. The west bank of the river sits along the east side of the park. When we stayed at the park, there was some barrier tape placed along the edge of the grass to warn people to go no further toward the edge. There had been a little mud slide in the area and there were about a dozen trees and all the soil that had collapsed down on to the sand below.

The park offers all sorts of activities for any one who comes to visit. There is an Interpretive Center, a Horse Camp area, many remote campsites along the trails, boat and canoe landings, and more miles of trails for any kind of activity than you shake a stick at.

This state park even has a small store on the grounds between the two main camping areas. It has all sorts of small grocery items available for purchase, plus lots and lots of souvenir items. When we stayed at the camp, we thought that the little store was a very unique feature because St. Croix State Park is at least 15 miles from Hinkley and around ten miles east of Danbury, Wisconsin. If you had run out of some necessity at your campsite, there is a good possibility the item needed may be at the store and negate the need for a long drive to one of these towns.

I had never stayed at St. Croix State Park before, even though I had known about it almost all my life. When my sisters and I were young, still in junior high and high school, our parents would take us on canoe trips all over during the summers. And for many years, there was always the annual float down the St. Croix. We would put the canoes in at the bridge just west of Danbury and then float the canoes down all the way to Soderbeck Landing or down to the bridge crossing on Highway 70, 5 miles west of Grantsburg, Wisconsin. This usually meant that there was one night spent camping in one of the many sites set up along the river. We would always be floating down stream and passing the signs that indicated that it was state park property we were passing.

When we had finished our stay at St. Croix State Park, it was time to head to the next park. An interesting thing about the trip to that next park we were going to is that its a park that is upriver from St. Croix; but, not up river on the St. Croix. It is up river on the Kettle River. The Kettle River converges with the St. Croix at a point near the southern tip of St. Croix State Park. During our many trips in a canoe down that section of river, I can remember that at that spot where the two rivers converge is a very nice and exciting rapid.

The next park we were going to was Banning State Park. It sits along the north side of the Kettle River and this section of the river is very popular for canoeists and people with kayaks. The Kettle River drops quite far along its path through the center of the park and this leads to exciting rapids to try and navigate through.

Julie and I were impressed with Banning because of the camping area. It has nice sites and there is a lot of undergrowth that is present between each of the camp sites. I told Julie that it looked like they had literally hacked out the space for each campsite. All of this undergrowth really allows for a lot of seclusion at each campsite. You may be able to hear your neighbors; but, you can't see them. Banning State Park is very close to some of the Minnesota State Trail system. The Willard Munger Trail is just 2 miles from the park; so, this park is popular for those persons looking to walk or ride on some trails. Besides the rapids for the canoe and kayak crowd, there is also a water fall called Big Spring Falls that is located at the very southern end of the park, down by the town of Sandstone. There are also remnants of the buildings that were used to quarry the sandstone that can be found down by the river. Prior to the state park being formed around the turn of the 20th century, there was actually a small village called Banning that was located in this area near the river. Unfortunately, the village didn't survive into the modern day; but, the park is named for the village and its founder –William L. Banning, who was president of the St. Paul and Duluth Railroad. Getting to Banning State Park is not a problem because it is easily accessed on I-35, heading east at the off ramp for the town of Finlayson.

The next stop on this trip was to be at the next state park up I-35, Moose Lake State Park. This state park is a wonderful spot to come and stay. The terrain around the park is very much the same as in Banning State Park. There is a lot of undergrowth between the sites and allows for good seclusion. The lake that sits within the park, Echo Lake, is a good lake for fishing with the variety of species normally found in our Minnesota lakes. A nice boat launch, fishing pier, and a swimming beach are also available for use at the park.

In my opinion, the one absolute best reason to come and visit this nice little spot is because of the interpretive center that is attached to the main office for the park. In that building is a fabulous collection of Lake Superior agates and there are displays that are set up that help to explain the 'how-to's' of the creation of Lake Superior agates and the geology of Minnesota. The park entrance for Moose Lake State Park is located just one third of a mile east from the #214 exit on I-35. So - easy to get to; a very nice educational display; secluded camping – this is and would be a great place to get away from it all.

After we were done visiting Moose Lake State Park and seeing the sites there, we continued on our little trek up I-35. The next stop was just outside the tiny little town of Thomson, Minnesota. Jay Cooke State Park is located about 3 miles east of Carlton, Minnesota. You take the Carlton exit off of I-35 and then drive through Carlton and onto Thomson. Staying on Hwy. 210, you drive through Thomson and pass by the Thomson Dam and the reservoir it creates. There is a nice scenic overlook spot set up near the dam and allows visitors to watch the river and anyone who is brave enough to be attempting to run some of the whitewater in the area. The dam stands very tall and impressive from the spot at the over look site. When we stopped in at the overlook that day, it was the middle part of summer and there wasn't any great torrent of water coming over the dam. So, we were able to see a couple of people with kayaks attempting to maneuver their way among the rocks and water. The river, however, it is completely different in the spring and after heavy rains when the runoff is increased. At the height of the runoff in the spring, the gorge below the dam and through the park thunders with the sound of the flowing water.

The area around the park is also a spot where the bedrock comes up very shallow under the surface soil and in many spots – there simply isn't any surface soil, just the bedrock. When I was attending the University of Wisconsin, completing my work in soil science and resource management, our professor took the class on a field trip up to this park just to see the interesting landforms and the bedrock in the area. The park is wonderful and has many miles of trail for hiking, cross country skiing, and snowmobiling. The beauty of the river, the picnic areas and the campground in the park create a great camping experience. The campsites in the park are situated along a shallow hillside on the north side of Hwy 210; but, they are fairly level and there are lots of trees for shade. The swing bridge that crosses the river near the location of the office and interpretive center is a wonderful spot to get a good view of the river as it winds down from the dam. Then, turning and facing the east, you can look down river and see the gorge as it opens up and the waters disappear over the edge of the escarpment about a half mile down stream. The park is also a good spot to learn about some of the history of the region and how this area was used 300 hundred years ago for fur trading.

The park is only about twelve miles from Duluth and the access from I-35 makes this an easy park to get to and anyone in the family would enjoy a stay at this state park.

The next state park that we visited is a park located on the east side of Big Sandy Lake – Savanna Portage State Park. If you ever find yourself traveling on MN Hwy. 65 and you find yourself passing the west shoreline of Big Sandy, then you aren't far from this state park. The small town of

McGregor, Minnesota, is located at the intersection of Hwy. 65 and Hwy 210. Traveling north on Hwy. 65 from this crossroad approximately seven miles will bring you to the spot where County Road 14 branches to the east. This road will lead you around the south shore of the lake and then up the east side. After ten miles, you will get to the entrance into Savanna Portage State Park.

The area around Big Sandy Lake and Lake Minnewawa is a very popular vacationing spot and there are many people who own cabins and second homes in the region. When I was a small child, I remember coming up to visit relatives at a cabin on the shores of Big Sandy. My father told me that some of the best walleye fishing on all of Big Sandy was right in front of the dock at this small piece of property.

Savanna Portage State Park will allow you the opportunity to really get away from it all. There are four or five small lakes within the park, miles of hiking and biking trails, fishing, swimming, boating and canoeing are all available activities to participate in at the park. From the Ranger's office at the entrance, you can take one road that will lead you north until you reach a small isolated lake. This lake, Wolf Lake, is a beautiful lake with nice clear water. There is a small picnic area and a boat landing at the lake. When we were visiting the spot, we were the only people there at the time. It was very quiet and peaceful. The history of Savanna Portage State Park is woven throughout the long history of the man living in the area. The natives had created the trail and series of portages leading from the small creeks and rivers in the east to the Prairie River and Big Sandy Lake in the west. At one spot in the park along the side of the paved road is a marker that signifies the place at which this ancient trail runs through the park.

The small creeks and rivers to the east lead to the St. Louis River and ultimately – Lake Superior. The Prairie River leads to Big Sandy and then a small portage over to the Mississippi River. The trail created and used by the native tribes connected the watershed of the Lake Superior Basin to that of the Upper Mississippi River. It was this trail navigating through marshes, swamps, small creeks and rivers that the first voyagers used to access the upper Mississippi River. They traded beads, knives, blankets, and alcohol to the Indians for the huge bounty of furs from animals like the beaver, marten, muskrat, fox, and otter. When the voyagers first started using it, the trail was already hundreds of years old and easy to follow due to it being used so frequently by the natives.

This is a lovely state park and allows for very nice secluded and remote camping for visitors.

There are two parks that are located very close to where we have our little cabin in the woods. The first of these two parks is actually a 'recreational area' located north of Highway 210 between Brainerd and Ironton. This is the Cuyuna State Recreational Area. This recreation area is made up of many small lakes that are located between the towns of Ironton, Tromwald, and Riverton. These small lakes didn't always exist in the locations they are at. These bodies of water were created by the mining industry.

The first major industry to come to the lakes region of Crow Wing County was fur trading. When the first explorers made their way through the region they discovered the bounty of wild animals, the natives, and the possibility of opening up trading for pelts and furs. The second industry was when the logging industry made it up the rivers into the north country of Minnesota and started to harvest the millions and millions of acres of pines and hardwoods. When the Railroads made their way into the northland, the face of commerce and the lifestyles of everyone were affected. Towns and cities that had been important at one time due to their location along the rivers, now found themselves being bypassed by the railroad. The railroad represented the next step up in moving trade goods and resources from region to region and those towns and cities along the railroad survived, while others didn't. One of the first towns to spring up along the rails as they were being laid out was a small town that developed between Reno and Serpent Lakes – Withington. This small settlement continued to grow and soon changed its name to Deerwood. Brainerd and Deerwood were the two main towns of Crow Wing County at that time late in the 1800's.

Then, the third industry to develop in the region was discovered in the 1890's when one of the most famous people from this area of Minnesota, Cuyler Adams, discovered iron ore on the surface of the ground on his property near Deerwood. The mining industry hit the region like a tidal wave. The hunger of the growing nation was demanding more and more material to build and grow. Iron ore and taconite were two of the items that helped to feed that demand. Mining companies sprung up in the area and excavation of the ore began and flourished for decades. Dozens of small mining pits were dug during that period. Mining continued to be a strong industry that brought thousands more people into the region. The city of Crosby, Minnesota, owes its creation to the mining industry. After a period of time, the mining started to slow and the pits weren't developing the same tonnage as in the early 1900's. One by one many of the companies moved on to different areas where new ore had been found. One area in particular was just 70 miles north where the huge deposits of iron ore were discovered north of Grand Rapids, by Hibbing, Virginia, and all the way to Tower/Soudan.

When the mining industry left, they left the large gaping holes in the ground – a testament to the end of that industry in the lakes region. But, soon these gaping holes filled in with the fresh water that is so abundant in the region. In many cases, the mining pits were deep enough that they had dug into the level of the underlying aquifer – so, these pits were filling with natural ground water and this made them a prime resource for fishing. The DNR came to the area and started to work on developing the lakes and with Mother Nature's helping hand started to reclaim the area from the spoils of mining. Today, the Cuyuna State Recreational Area has more than a dozen deep lakes within its borders that have clean, cool waters that are home to rainbow, brown, and brook trout.

The Recreational Area is just a mile from Ironton and Crosby and any visitors would be able to find what they might need for fishing or camping at the merchants in these towns. There is a small campground with nice level sites, vault toilets, water, and electricity available to campers. There are several public landings situated on the lakes in the park and several picnic areas. One of the picnic areas is situated along side of the shore of Portsmouth Mine and you could literally fish in the lake from your seat at the picnic table. Thus, we have moved into the fourth industry that has come to affect this area – tourism. Deerwood, Riverton, and many of the other communities in the area owe much of their existence to the importance of tourism and the thousands of people who come each year to visit the area.

For those that are interested and are not familiar with how the name of the state recreation area came about, I will tell you. We have to go back to that fateful time in the 1890's when Cuyler Adams was trying to calculate the size of the discovery he had made. He was discussing with his wife many of the details of what would be happening in the area once the mining companies came to retrieve the ore. One of his predicaments was naming his discovery. At the suggestion of his wife, he created a word by combining the first part of his name with the name of the Adam's family dog – Una. Thus was created – CuyUna, or the Cuyuna Range. With the end of the mining in the area, the name 'Cuyuna' continued to stick. Ultimately, the residents of the area have adopted the term to reference the region – Cuyuna Country. The Cuyuna Recreational Area is a lovely quiet place that any one would find enjoyable to visit and stay awhile.

The next state park to talk about is one that is situated just south of Brainerd on Highway 371. This park is unique from several standpoints and its ties with the history of Minnesota can not be understated. This is Crow Wing State Park.

About five miles south of Brainerd on Highway 371, there is as large wayside and visitor center which was created by a cooperative of the businesses in the Central Lakes region. On the west side of this wayside is the entrance to Crow Wing State Park. The park sits on top of mostly flat, sandy soils on the east side of the Mississippi River. It is nestled amongst groves of scrub oak and red pine plantations. This type of topography is predominant south of Brainerd and the Mississippi meanders back and forth as it travels south to Little Falls and further south to St. Cloud. At one of the large 'S' shaped meanders, the Crow Wing River flows into the Mississippi. It was at this spot along the Mississippi that one of the first towns to exist in north-central Minnesota was established. As the first white explorers and settlers moved into the area, it was only natural for them to settle near the spot where this state park now sits. People had been living at this junction of the two rivers for hundreds of years. Prior to the 1750's, the Wahpeton and Mdewakanton Sioux resided in the region. After the Sioux were pushed further south and west by the Ojibwe, the new tribe took over many of the sites that the Sioux had been living at and one of those was the one that was here at Crow Wing State Park.

The Indian village that was at this location was the home to many great Ojibwe leaders; one of which was Chief Hole-in-the Day. William

Alexander Aitkin and Clement Beaulieu may have been the fur traders that were responsible for building the fur trading post at the town of Crow Wing; but, the first white settler to take up permanent residence in the area was Allan Morrison. He built a small trading post just south of the mouth of the Crow Wing River in 1823.

The town of Crow Wing thrived during the early years, the 1850's and 1860's. The site was a river crossing for one of the major trails leading up into the northwestern part of the young state. When the fur trading industry started to wane, forestry and logging took its place. At its peak, the town of Crow Wing had nearly 700 people living in it. The Ojibwe had their village on an island in the river across from the town. Crow Wing was so important in this northern part of the young state that in the 1860's there were two members of the State House of Representatives that were elected from the Crow Wing area. When the railroad arrived in northern Minnesota, Northern Pacific chose a river crossing site about 6 miles up river from the town of Crow Wing. A small community sprung up at that site and today we know this place as Brainerd. With the railroad running to the town, Brainerd became a more influential spot and Crow Wing started to fade from existence.

Crow Wing ceased to exist as a town and was only remembered in the history books and the memories of those families that had lived there. After the big timber had been logged off in the region, the land started to be used for farming. Much of the evidence for the existence of the community disappeared under the furrows that were plowed. The area today is managed with respect to the continuing harvest of agricultural and forestry products.

We have been discussing how this area was important with regard to the humans that chose to live here; but, another important thing about this are is that this is where three different bio-regions in the state all come together. The rolling, open prairie comes in from the west and southwest. The pine and boreal forests come down from the north and the mixed deciduous forests of the east and southeast all meet in this area. The state park is loaded with a wide diverse population of plant and animal species. Deer, bear, fox, raccoon, coyote, and dozens of other animal species make their homes in the area. Native prairie grasses, pines and other evergreen species, hardwoods and other deciduous trees make up the forests in the area. The Mississippi, the Crow Wing, and the Nokasippi Rivers and about a thousand other lakes and streams make this central lakes region of the state a wonderful place to spend some time.

The sites for camping in the park are set among the oaks and pines and this allows good shading from the mid-day sun. There are several picnic areas and a boat landing site down on the river. An amphitheater near the camping area, boat/canoe rentals down by the river, and miles of trails for hiking and cross-country skiing add to the recreational opportunities for the park. Finally, in my opinion the nicest part of the park is taking the hike down the trail that leads to the old Crow Wing Town site. At the old town site, you can see the home of Clement Beaulieu. The building, through the efforts of many volunteers, has been rebuilt and stands on the spot where it was located back in the 1860's. It is wonderful example of the type of architecture that was popular at the time that Clement and his family still lived in Crow Wing. Down the hill from the house, near the river, is a long board walk that has been built to replicate the one that existed there when the town was booming. As you walk down the board walk, you can listen to the sounds of the birds and other wildlife all around you and gaze at 'the mighty Mississippi' as it winds toward the Gulf of Mexico fifteen hundred miles away.

There is one last item I want to mention about Crow Wing State Park and it has to do with the thousands of wild raspberry plants that sit along the roadways and trails in the park and under the shade of the scrub oaks. It would be amazing to try and be at the park right at the time when those plants and their berries become ripe.

My sister Katherine and her husband own some property along Hwy 169 on the way to Ely. Their property sits along some hills south of Burntside Lake. They had invited Julie and me up to the property to spend the 4th of July weekend in the summer of 2009. We had a good time. Kathy's husband Mike and I went fishing on Burntside Lake and had a very enjoyable morning. Julie and Kathy had gone in to Ely to see some sites and do some hiking around the lake.

After our stay there at the property, we left and were able to stop by and visit a state park that is also along the highway between Ely and Tower.

Bear Head Lake State Park is situated about 6 miles south of Hwy

169 and is the historical site of an old logging mill. The mill closed many years ago and the site was then turned into a beautiful state park. Many tall pine tree species are there in the park and this park definitely fit's the description of - "off the beaten path". A beautiful lake for fishing and boating, many miles of trails for hiking and cross country skiing make this a fine place to stay regardless of what the season of the year is.

From Bear Head Lake, we moved on down the road and found ourselves in the town of Soudan. There is a lot of history around this little town. It is not hard to find the point in town where all of this history was focused - you just need to look up hill. The Soudan Mine has a long history in the area and it started out as an open pit mine and then changed over into the deep shaft mine that exists there now. When the mine shut down so many years ago, it was almost too much for the town of Soudan. As did so many other towns in the state, mining was an integral part of the lives of these little towns - without the mine, there wasn't much need for a town.

Soudan has hung on. With Lake Vermillion just a few miles away, the mine being turned into a state park, and the continuing flow of people through the area heading to and from the Boundary Waters, helps to keep the town going. Now, in 2010, we found out that the state government has finally finished the negotiations in the acquisition of property around Lake Vermillion. The deal that was made allows the state to purchase thousands of acres of land on the east side of Lake Vermillion. The plans have not been finalized quite yet; but, it looks as though the park will have over 5 miles of shoreline on Vermillion and the park will encompass land that stretches from the Soudan Mine Park and all the way to the border of the Boundary Waters Canoe Area. This will become – Vermillion State Park.

Now, let's get back to the Soudan Mine site. The mine which is situated at the top of a large hill on the north end of town is a site to see. The large structure of the winching system that was built to raise and lower the crews into the darkness of the subterranean levels can be seen from almost all the areas around town. There are mine tours that are offered to people who come to visit the park. These tours are very informative and can give a person a new perspective on what it is to live above ground. I believed them, I didn't need to go on the tour. I, personally, have my feet firmly planted on the <u>surface</u> soil. I just don't think that I could get comfortable knowing that there was more than a thousand feet of rock hanging over my head and I already know that I am not thrilled about being in tight, confining places. For me, the tour was out.

However, up on the topside, you can walk around the grounds, around the buildings, and go right up to the fence that is placed around the edge of the old open pit mine. You can look down into the pit and get a good perspective of what the miners of those days had to go through and the danger involved in working the mines.

Today, the Soudan Mine has found some new life in the form of being a site for scientific research. There are a couple of organizations that are performing physics experiments at the bottom of the mine.

We had an enjoyable time wondering around the park and watching the films about the mine. The next port-of-call for us was further down the road toward home and it happened to be at another mine site.

We went to the Hill Annex Mine and had a look around. The mine is located in the small town of Calumet, this is a short distance south of Nashwauk, and not far from Hibbing. The Hill Annex Park is not a park that you can stay at. It is what is referred to as a 'day-park'. The main office of the park, which is situated just a stones throw from the edge of the pit, is set up like a museum of sorts and you are able to see many photos and items that are associated with the mine. While we were there visiting, there was a small emergency down in the mine with the tour that had been going on. There was a lady who was riding along on the tour - she had become a little 'overcome'. An ambulance had been called to assist and while we were there, we watched as they drove up and then left the park to go to the local emergency room. If we would have budgeted a little more time, it would have been interesting to go on the tour. Julie and I will have to save that for another day and another trip. As I have mentioned before, all these little camping trips that we are going on all occur over the course of a single weekend. It was time to head back to the little cabin in the woods and start planning for the next trip.

The next trip corresponded with a family event. My niece was involved in a scholarship opportunity which included a beauty contest and she was awarded a spot as one of the princesses. Yes, we are very proud of her. Anyway, once our obligations were done back in the Clearwater area, we hit the road again and headed west to visit another group of parks. The first place we went to visit is a small state park located just a few miles south and west of the city of Monticello, MN. Lake Maria State Park is a park that is devoted to those people who want to do some remote tent camping. All of the sites within the park can only be reached by hiking trail. It is a beautiful park that is set way back off the roadway. The park is set in an area of rolling terrain and there are fields and woods spread throughout the park. Miles and miles of hiking and cross country skiing trails are in the park. My brother-in-law, Mike Williams, makes use of the trails in this park frequently. It is a beautiful drive through this park and we were able to view lots of different animals and birds during the short time we were there. We even saw a very large owl fly over our truck as we drove around near the boat landing. We believe it was a Great-Horned Owl; not certain, but it was big. After we were finished in the Clearwater area, the next park that we headed towards was a park situated just a few miles south of the town of Starbuck, Minnesota. Glacial Lakes State Park is a fantastic little park that is nestled in the hills, ridges and valleys of that area south of Starbuck. The soils that can be found here is what has developed since the retreat of the glaciers 10,000 years ago. The park has a great fishing lake, many miles of trails and the nice shading of the oaks, ash and iron wood that are growing in the area. If there is anyone out there with an interest in geology, this is a great place to come to in order to see kames, eskers, kettles, and end moraines.

I just love driving in this area. The hills and rolling terrain which was left by the glaciers are now populated by many farm fields and pastures. I have always enjoyed driving over to the area of Glenwood, Lake Miniwaska and Starbuck. The moraine that was left by the glacier so many thousands of years ago is the feature that helps to create Lake Miniwaska. When driving the north/south bound roads that crest over this moraine - can nearly take your breath away as you look southward and see so much of Minnesota laid out in front of you.

So, once we left Glacial Lakes, we headed east and followed a State Scenic Trail – the Glacial Lakes Scenic Byway. This afforded us the opportunity to continue driving around on the lesser used highways and county roads and see more of the countryside. The next destination for our journey was a state park near the small town of Sunburg, Minnesota. Monson Lake State Park is located in between two lakes and is the site of an Indian massacre that occurred back in 1862, during the Sioux Uprising. While we were driving out to this park, as I said before, we were traveling along some of the back roads and then we looked above us and saw that there was a flock of about ten to twelve pelicans flying toward the same spot to which we were heading. It was a fun seeing those large birds wheeling around in the air, not too far up but still high enough that they were able to catch the thermals in the atmosphere that made their job of flying easier. We arrived at Monson Lake to find a wonderful little park. There were tall oaks and cottonwoods that gave lots of shade to the park area. There are just a small number of sites at this park and we were assured that it would be a good idea to call ahead in advance to reserve a site for camping because the park was popular and the sites filled up fast. One of the reasons that the park fills with visitors so fast is that the fishing on the two lakes is very good. Those fish are the normal species that can be found on Minnesota lakes and there seems to be an abundance of them in these two lakes. Monson Lake doesn't have all the amenities of a larger park, but it makes up for it in other areas. Julie and I agreed that this small park would also be a park that we would come back to visit in the future.

Our next stop – Sibley State Park. Sibley is a huge state park and has all the amenities available for family camping. It is located just a few miles from the city of New London. This makes for easy access to the park for any and all visitors. Minnesota Highway 23 between Willmar and St. Cloud is fast becoming a main artery for traffic flow. This nice large state park is just a few miles west of that roadway. Sibley State Park is in the same category of parks as you would find at Itasca and St. Croix. There are many campsites –sometimes a little crowded – but, all the other things you can do at the park make up for the congestion. There is the lake, fishing, boating, hiking, and all sorts of other activities that can be found at the park. Sibley also sits along the Glacial Lakes Scenic Byway and you can find rolling terrain and small little kettle lakes and prairie potholes all over the park acreage. With the ever increasing population in the area of New London and Spicer, this park and all it has to offer finds use during all the seasons of the year. As I said before, Sibley is a very large park and it took Julie and me quite sometime to just drive through the park and see the major sites. A person would have to devote a number of days in order to stay there long enough to experience all of the trails, potholes, the lake, and the other activities of the park. After staying at Sibley, it was time to head on back home. Our little cabin in the woods was calling us back. Now, we could have simply left the park, got on Hwy. 23 and headed straight up to St. Cloud to get home. But, as I stated before, I like to travel the back roads when I have the opportunity and this was one of those times. So, we headed north and meandered our way until we came to the city of Belgrade. There in the middle of town is a giant statue of a crow. We took pictures. I never knew that was there. Belgrade probably has some form of celebration with the crow being the focal point. Someday, we will have to go back there and see what all the hub-bub is about.

The next leg of the journey would once again get us heading in the direction of the Dakotas. When we reached the spot we were going to, we were within eye shot of the rolling fields of South Dakota. We left our home on Friday afternoon and headed southwest. It was the middle of the afternoon and with the miles we had to cover and the requisite stops that would be made along the way, it would be getting close to dark before we arrived at Big Stone Lake State Park. Leaving from home, we traveled the well used paths of Hwy. 18 to Brainerd, then Hwy. 371 south to Little Falls. At Little Falls, we tuned and headed west, crossed the Mississippi River and then continued past Long Prairie, southward further until we went through Sauk Center. There, we turned west again and drove through the long miles of corn and soy bean fields that can be found along the way towards Morris, Minnesota. We traveled through little towns like Cyrus, Alberta, and Chokio. Prime farm country out there in that area of the state. We noted that as we were driving, some of the wheat and grain fields that we were passing had been harvested or were in some intermediate stage of being harvested. Past Morris, west for a little while – then south to Ortonville.

Ortonville is a very nice city down in the valley along the shores of Big Stone Lake. The lake, which is partially created by a dam that is there next to the city, winds for some 26 miles to the north. We happened to show up in Ortonville on the same weekend that they were having an annual summer celebration – Cornfest. There were many activities going on in town and on the lake. It was reminiscent of that weekend when we drove down to Glacial Lakes State Park. When we drove through

Starbuck, there was some form of city wide celebration going on there, too.

The state park is about 8 miles north of Ortonville on Hwy. 7 which follows the shoreline of the lake and ultimately takes you deep into the little notch of Minnesota that pokes into South Dakota. Big Stone Lake State Park sits down along the shoreline of the lake and is below the terrace of land that the fields of corn, grain, and beans are planted. This is a lovely park. While we were there, the park was being used by many families and it is certainly set up to accommodate families. There is a playground, a nice toilet facility, boat landings, and trails to hike. The camp sites are nicely spaced and allowed us to set up easily and have an enjoyable evening there at the park.

Now, Big Stone Lake State Park isn't located just at that one spot where we were camped at. There are two other parts of the park that can be found further up Hwy. 7. The next morning, after a breakfast of cereal and fruit, we headed in that direction. The lower portion of the park is referred to as "the Meadowbrook" section. About 11 miles up the road, there is a small scenic over look to stop at. There are a couple of picnic tables and a vault toilet to use at that spot. The views of the lake to the north and south are fantastic. The final part of the park is just one mile further north of that over look. The north section is referred to as -"the Bonanza area". This area of the park has a boat landing and a group camp area available for use. There is a small interpretive center there, uphill a short distance from the boat landing. This center is used by students and classes from schools in the area that come to use the park.

After stopping in and checking out the rest of the state park there on the north end of the lake, we headed to the town of Beardsley. I can remember hearing about this town many times while growing up and I think it was because some friends of our family were from that area. Another reason to go visit Beardsley is a geographic feature that can be found just a couple of miles west of the town. Situated on the border between South Dakota and Minnesota, just west of Beardsley, is a large swampy area and it is within this swampy area that the continental divide lies. North of this swamp, water flows to Lake Traverse and then to the Red River and further north. South of the swampy area, it goes to Big Stone Lake, the Minnesota River, and then the Mississippi. Browns Valley is a little town that sits right on the border and very close to the edge of this large swampy area. Besides the continental divide being there, the area around Browns Valley has some significant history, too. Years ago, a skeleton of a man was found buried in that valley. It was evident at the time that this was not a settler's grave. The bones were collected and sent to the university to be dated. At first, the date they placed on the bones was about 3,000 years old. That surely made it a significant find for archeology in Minnesota. However, a number of years later, the bones were checked again with more precision and newer equipment and found that they were much older than originally thought. The bones, now, are thought to be around 9,000 years old. This new date places this man hunting in the area of Browns Valley just shortly after the glaciers had receded from the region. One can only imagine how differently the area looked at that time and how different the animals were that he was hunting. The Sam Brown State Monument is located next to a park area on the west side of Browns Valley.

When we had awoken that morning back at the campsite at Big Stone Lake, there was a fairly thick layer of fog that had descended on the area. We had driven through it for most of that morning so far and now that we were leaving the valley, we were headed right back into it. We stayed on the main road and the next town we came to was Wheaton, MN. We certainly didn't get to see much of the town because it was completely socked in by that same fog. After filling the truck with gas, we headed northeast to get to Fergus Falls. As we approached Fergus, the fog broke up and for the rest of the day we had beautiful, sunshine.

Our next stop on this leg of the trip was to go back up to the area of Pelican Rapids and to go see Maplewood State Park. This park is located about seven miles east of Pelican Rapids on Hwy. 108. When we were driving up toward Pelican Rapids on Hwy. 59, I remembered that the last time we were in the area there was some construction being done on the road leading over to the park. So, when we reached the little town of Erhard, I saw a sign for a detour for that road (Hwy. 108), I knew that I had better take it. Well, that wasn't the best idea I have ever had. We headed east and drove around on some roads that took us through some very beautiful country side. This area just east of Pelican Rapids is a continuation of the same rolling topography that we encountered when traveling around the Starbuck/Glenwood area. It is a lovely drive and I would recommend it to everyone. We were on curvy roads that snaked around the hills and small lakes and over the ridges. It was just a little while into the drive that I realized that we had completely turned around and we were heading back to the west, instead of east as when we first started. Shortly, we were back at Hwy. 59. Instead of getting back on the road and trying to find the park on our own, I made a call to the office at the park and they informed us that the road out to them was under construction but that it was still passable. So, we headed to Pelican Rapids and turned east on Hwy. 108 and in short order we were there. We turned off of the highway and onto the entrance road to the park. The office for the park was just a short way down the road from the entrance; but, the rest of the park was tucked way back in the woods and hills in the area. This park, as with all the other state parks, is beautiful. This is a large state park and it has over a dozen lakes and small ponds contained within. There are miles and miles of trails for hiking, biking, horse trails, and cross country skiing. With multiple campgrounds, picnic areas, boat launching spots, and remote campsites accessible by the hiking trails; this park has everything needed for a great camping experience. The one thing that struck me as we travelled through the park was the great variety of different tree species. There were oaks, aspen, birch, ash and maples. With the rolling hills and all of these different trees in the park, during the fall at the peak of the color change, driving through this park must be phenomenal. Julie and I both agreed that it would be well worth the drive out here during the fall to check out that event.

When we were done in Maplewood State Park, we moved on to the next park on our journey and that got us to the town of Battle Lake, Minnesota. Just north of the town sits a small state park with lots of history associated with it – Glendalough. This park sits on property that used to be privately owned and used as a corporate retreat. In fact, many high level dignitaries have been the guest at this location. Heads of foreign governments and a couple of president's have stayed here prior to it being established as a state park. Annie Battle Lake which sits entirely within the park is a lake that is carefully managed regarding fishing and there are strict limits and rules on what and how many fish can be kept. It is referred to as a 'Heritage Fishery'. Three other lakes are in the park and Lake Blanche sits along the north border. With all of this water and the marshes in the area, there is abundant opportunity to see all sorts of migratory bird species at the park. There are many trails to use but the only campsites at the park are for tent camping. Unfortunately, this doesn't fit in with the small trailer that we usually haul around. This didn't detract from the uniqueness of the park. If you are into cart in/hike in camping, this park has all sorts of entertainment for you. There is an interpretive center on the grounds and events and activities are held there all the time during the summer. Our next stop - Inspiration Peak.

Inspiration Peak State Wayside area is property that is managed by the state's Park Service. This peak is located on the back roads winding their way toward Alexandria. When I first was looking at the map and doing the planning for this adventure of ours, I saw the peak listed on the map and thought that it would be interesting to check it out. We turned off the road we were on, Otter Tail County Road 38, and turned up the road that led to the parking area. Right there at that corner, there was a restaurant that was named – The Peak. The road up to the parking area was quite steep. When we got to the top, it was then that we realized that bringing a trailer with us was not a great idea. The parking area sits at the base of where the hiking trail starts. It is not a large parking lot and it did take some maneuvering in order to get our rig turned around and ready for our departure. Next to the parking lot, there was a sign describing the peak. It seems that Inspiration Peak was a favorite location of one of Minnesota's premiere writers – Sinclair Lewis. According to the information at the park, he came to the peak many times. He is even quoted as saying – "any person who wanted to be the governor of the state should first have to climb to the top of Inspiration Peak in order to see so much of the state they wanted to govern."

The trail leading up to the top of this hill is steep, to say the least. This hill, and the surrounding area, was left here after the glaciers had retreated. There are several other hills in the area that are as large as this peak; but, they are further north and west and this particular one has such a commanding view the east, south, and west. From the top, you can see many lakes and other features in the region. It is well worth the climb to check out the view. But, in saying that, I do have to go back and talk about the trail leading to the peak. Again, I say, this is a very steep trail. There are several benches set up along the trail in order to take a break while hiking. In one area, there is a hand rail set up along the side of the trail to help get up that steep section. So, please take a care if you go to see this site. If you have any health conditions that would limit your ability to handle stressful physical activity, it would be wise to give this hike a second thought.

Now, anyone who knows me knows that I am not what you would refer to as a physical specimen. Those benches set up along the trail were at just the right locations to allow me to get a chance to sit and catch my breath. Then, we would continue to hike. I got up the hill and as I already said – it was worth the climb.

Lake Carlos was the next stop for us. We continued to travel along the back roads to get over to MN Hwy. 29, which would then take us right to the park. Lake Carlos State Park is located about ten miles north of Alexandria. It is a large park that has all the amenities needed to allow for a great camping experience. But, I was absolutely floored when we were driving through the camping area and started to drive by the beach. This park has a long sandy beach that runs along the north shore of Lake Carlos and it is located about 50 feet from the campsites in the Lower Campground. The lake is shallow at this end and this allows for good swimming. The campers bring their boats and simply beach them along the shore across from their campsites. When we drove by, there were boats, canoes, wave runners, and a sailboat all beached. There were hundreds of people lying along the beach soaking up the sun. The campsites in the Lower Campground are set close together and this is reminiscent of some of the other state park camp areas. However, the Upper Campground has sites that are spaced further apart and have brush and undergrowth among the trees and this allows for a more secluded feeling. Lake Carlos is a heavily used park because it is so closely located to a favorite vacation area in Minnesota – the Alexandria Lakes Region. After leaving this state park, we continued further east still following the back roads across Todd and Morrison County. We drove through the country side that brought us to Long Prairie and then on to Little Falls.

In Little Falls, we visited the site of the boyhood home of a great American – Charles A. Lindbergh, Jr. The state park is located on the west side of town along the west shore of the river. The land for the park was donated by the family to become a park in honor Charles A., Sr.

This park is small and there are only 38 sites to camp at; but, they are wonderful sites. They are nicely spaced apart and there is a lot of under growth between the big tall pine trees to allow for a lot of seclusion when camping. You might be able to hear your neighbors, but you would be hard pressed to see them. Personally, I wouldn't find camping at a park that is literally inside the city limits a very enjoyable experience; however, this park would be an exception to the rule. It has a large beautiful picnic area nestled under large pines and oaks. It is an enjoyable experience staying there because it allows you access to see all of the buildings contained on this historic site and to take time to walk through the museum that is on the park property. The museum helps to chronicle the early years and life of Charles Jr. and all of his accomplishments as an adult. Another item of note that very few people know of about the area of Little Falls is the unique mineral specimen that can be found near the city. About 8.5 miles away from town, there is an area referred to as Blanchard Dam. There is a trail that leads to a site where if a person were to dig into the ground, there are deposits of a mineral called staurolite found there. This mineral can sometimes be found as a pair, or twins, and it creates the form of a cross – a Maltese Cross or St. Andrew's Cross. The other name given to these little unique stones is 'the fairy stone' or 'fairy cross'. It can be easily found in the area and many are found for sale at rock shops and craft fairs held in the area around Little Falls. These crystals are not unique to Little Falls or Minnesota. These crystals can also be found in the state of Georgia and other areas of the country. However, it is cool that they can be found in a spot so centrally located here.

After we had finished with our visit to the state park in Little Falls, it was time to head back to our home and get ready for the upcoming work week.

The next leg of this epic journey would take us back to the southwest region and the south central region of the state. We left the little cabin in the woods and once again headed to Brainerd so we could pick up the good, major roads that would move us the fastest in the direction we wanted to go. After a short stop in St. Cloud to take care of some personal business, we were off and heading southwest. MN Hwy. 23 has become a very regular thoroughfare for us to use on these excursions. We were on our way to Montevideo, and then just a few miles west in order to get us to Lac Qui Parle State Park. We never did make it to Montevideo. Once we passed by Willmar, we realized we could take a county road straight across Chippewa County and get to the park a little faster. When we got to the town of Randall, we turned west. Driving into sun, as the afternoon progressed into early evening, we were driving by miles of beautiful corn and soybean fields. From time to time, we would also pass a wheat field. But, what was different now with the wheat fields than as compared to what we saw during an earlier leg of the journey? Well, now it was late August, now those fields were being harvested. All you saw left in the fields as we drove by them were the straw left after the harvester had passed. So, our journeying around the state that summer had taken us through the entire spectrum of the growing season in these areas of Minnesota. Early in the summer or late spring, we were able to view the farmers in their fields using the disc, plow, or harrow in order to prep the fields prior to planting. Then, a couple of weeks later, the planting were completed and now the corn and beans were just starting to poke their heads above the surface. Mid July, saw the corn as high as your thigh and the beans were starting to spread and flower. Now, at the end of August, we start to see the beginning of the very busy harvest season. As the shadows began to lengthen across the landscape, we traveled to the intersection of Chippewa County Road 13 and U.S. Hwy. 59. Down the gravel road ahead of us, just 3 miles away was the state park, to the south of the intersection – the small town of Watson. The park is located at the south end of the lake and is split with a portion of the park on the east side of the lake and a portion on the west. We quickly checked in and then drove to our campsite to set up. It was getting late and any exploring we would do would have to wait until morning.

The next morning when we woke, we started the preparations to break camp and then go exploring some of the sites in the area. At the top of the hill above the lake on the east side, there is a site where during the 1830's and 40's a small frontier fort existed. Fort Renville sat along the top of the hill and looked down over the river valley. Just a short distance down the hill from the fort, one of the first churches built in Minnesota had been established. It was built in order to try and bring Christianity to the natives. A church still stands on the spot where the original building was located. There is information posted on bulletin boards and on the walls inside of the building, telling the story of the history of the local tribes and the push of white settlers into the region.

It was inside this little church that I learned that the name given to the Plains Indians of Minnesota and the Dakotas was not –Sioux. The word Sioux was a derivation of a term that was used by the Chippewa Indians and the French that meant 'snake-like people' or 'enemy'. The term that the plains Indians used for themselves was – Santee. I didn't know that. According to the story that was being told on the walls of that small church, the tribe preferred to be called by that name – Santee. Or they preferred to be called the name given to them in their language – the Dakota (the people). Call me an old sentimental fool; but, I kind of prefer the name Santee. It has an old frontier, western flavor to it.

Up the hill just a short distance from the church along one of the established trails in the park is a tree. Well, there are thousands of trees around the park; but, this tree is special. This particular tree is the largest cottonwood in the state. So, we had to go see the tree. We walked the trail up to the crest of the hill and found that the trail was sloping back down the hill on the other side. But, over on that other side, the hill creates a small sheltered area and down near the bottom, sat this huge cottonwood. It was very evident right from the start why this tree grew as big as it did. It was sheltered down in this little hollow and what ever big storms blew through the area, the tree had some protection. I walked the trail down to the point where I could stand next to the tree. It was huge. It would have taken three or four guys my size just to reach around it. The main branches forking off the trunk of this tree would have made most big oaks look small. This tree is just a short walk from the road leading up the hill to the main office of the park. It would be well worth the stroll to see this giant.

After we got back to the truck, we drove down to the base of the hill close by the point on the river where the dam sits that creates Lac Qui Parle. Already in the early morning hours, many of the locals were gathering on the dam to dip their fishing lines in the water on the down stream side. It makes me wonder what they were trying to catch.

We turned east into the rising sun and headed to the next stop on our itinerary – Granite Falls. Just east of Granite Falls, and along the south bank of the Minnesota River is the Upper Sioux Agency State Park.

We took MN Hwy. 67 southeast out of Granite Falls. We drove

past the small Indian community of Upper Sioux Agency. Nice homes, beautiful clean streets and sidewalks, with a small school located right in the middle. Just down the road from there is the turn off to the state park. Once again, this is a park that if you weren't careful – you could just as easily drive right by and never know it. If you did drive by and not take the chance to stop in and visit this beautiful and very historic park, it would be your great loss. The name of this park refers back to the original intended use of this spot – it was an agency. It was the long arm of the Federal Government and was to monitor the activities of the Indians who were then living in a 20 mile wide reservation along the river. This was all established by a treaty that was signed in 1851. Unfortunately, the treaty and the conditions the Indians were forced to live under ultimately led to some mistreatment and near starvation, this culminated in the uprising in 1862. The park was established to carry on the tradition of keeping in touch with these important places in Minnesota's history.

The park is also located along the banks of the Yellow Medicine River, where it empties into the Minnesota. There is a steep drive down into the valley by the rivers. Much of the park is down there. But up above, on the terrace, there are open fields where there is an active effort to re-establish the natural prairie. At the end of one of the roads in the park that leads out to a scenic overlook site, there is a marker that tells the story of Mazomani (Iron Walker). He was a chief of the Upper Sioux and was involved in much of what lead up to and the uprising itself. Unfortunately, for Mazomani, he was severely wounded in one of the final skirmishes, near Wood Lake, a few miles south and west of the agency. Members of the tribe and survivors of the battle carried Mazomani all the way back to a spot very close to where this marker is located. It was there where he said his good byes and died. Mazomani's daughter, Isabelle Roberts, who was there at her father's bedside when he died, later became a very influential person for her people.

When I was young, I remember being told the tale about another very famous Sioux chief – Little Crow. Little Crow, too, met a very unfortunate end at the hands of the white settlers that had come in and taken over his homeland. I remember many times, as we drove around between my grandparent's homes in Litchfield and Hutchinson, seeing a lone tree standing out in a farm field not far from Hutchinson, where Little Crow had been shot and killed. A marker testifying to the history of that spot stood under that tree. I remember being told that story by my father and now here I learn of yet another story of an Indian chief of the Dakota.

Another little tid-bit of history with regards to the park, besides Mazomani's marker, there is another marker that is next to the road in the park that tells the story of a small village which was called – Yellow Medicine City. This was one on the first towns established out in this prairie region of Minnesota. The town was first settled by Mr. John Winter in 1866. It was platted and surveyed. Another resident in the area opened a law office. There was a stage coach stop and post office in the village. Someone else built a large two-story brick hotel. This little village became the county seat but with the changing of the times and the movement of even more settlers to the area, the county seat was moved to a newer and bigger area and then this little village was abandoned in 1878.

Needless to say, this area of the Minnesota River Valley and these communities along the valley has a long and storied history with regards to the settlement of the state.

If a person were to cross the river there at Upper Sioux Agency and then travel a little north and east, you would find the community of Sacred Heart, Minnesota. This small, ordinary, rural Minnesota town straddles U.S. Hwy 212 as it runs east and west through the state. If you didn't know better you might just sail through this town without giving it a second thought. But then, again, it would be to your loss. For this small town has its own connection with historical beginnings of the state. Just south of Sacred Heart there is a spot where the remnants of a building/home can be found. This was the home of a person who is very significant to the history of Minnesota. The man that I am referring to is Joseph Reshaw Brown.

Joe Brown was born in Maryland, on the east coast, in 1805. He was raised and lived for a short period of time in Pennsylvania. At the age of 13, he joined the U.S. Army and was a drummer boy. Ultimately, his service would bring him to the territory of Minnesota and Fort Snelling. He stayed at Ft. Snelling and when his enlistment was completed, he began to work at other careers and jobs. One significant job was working for the American Fur Trading Company and John Jacob Aster, one of the richest men ever to live in the United States. Joe Brown worked as a fur trader and spent time building and manning small fur trading posts across Minnesota. One of the more notable sites that he set up was a small post that was located near the present location of Henderson, Minnesota. The spot just west of Henderson has a large monument erected on the site and this is one of the many State Monuments that exist in Minnesota.

Another skill that Joe Brown developed besides his bargaining and trading savvy was surveying and platting. At one point, as a young man, he was asked to go into the Wisconsin territory, near a wide shallow spot of the St. Croix River, and to set a plat and survey the site for a new town. He did. He called the new town – 'Dakota'. Today, we know this town as – Stillwater, Minnesota. Later, he was asked to serve as a cabinet member for Henry Sibley, the governor of the newly formed State of Minnesota. He was the Indian Agent in the state government up until 1861. All the years that he had spent as a young man trading furs had taught him lessons on how to deal with the local natives and this knowledge and skill served him well in that government position. The Indian population spent many years dealing with Joe Brown. Many stories state that his being replaced as the Indian Agent was one of many factors that led to the Uprising in 1862. During his years as the Indian Agent at the upper agency, Brown had built a large three story stone home at a site on the north side of the Minnesota River. The home had to be large because he and his wife had twelve kids. The home was a veritable showplace and Brown used his home to entertain dignitaries frequently. During the conflict in 1862, Brown's home was pillaged and set on fire. Susan, his wife, and their children were safe but their home was destroyed by the fire. These remnants are what exist at the site near the Minnesota River south of Sacred Heart. This site is now recognized as one of Minnesota's State Waysides.

Joe Brown continued on his exploits in and around the state until his death in 1870.

He was a man among men. He was a soldier, a fur trader, businessman, engineer, inventor, statesman, husband and father. Brown County is named for him. It is sad that Minnesotans don't know more about this man from our collective pasts. His accomplishments and his connection to the state of Minnesota rank him up there with many other great men – Henry Sibley, Alexander Ramsey, Henry Rowe Schoolcraft, and others.

Joe Brown's story may have ended with his death in 1870. However, he fathered a son who also lives on in the history of Minnesota and the frontier. Samuel J. Brown was one of the children of Joseph and Susan Brown. Like his father, Samuel joined the Army when he came of age. He rose through the ranks as a Scout, no small consequence due to his heritage. (His father's long time association with the militia and his mother having mixed-Indian heritage.) Samuel was a member of the troop of soldiers stationed at Fort Wadsworth, near the present day location of Sisseton, South Dakota. In 1866, there were rumors flying that there was to be another uprising by the natives and the duty of warning the local settlers along the route from Fort Wadsworth east in to Minnesota fell to Sam. He was given a horse and rode 55 miles in a period of 5 hours warning the local populace. Once he returned to the fort, he learned that the reports of the uprising were false. For this escapade, Sam Brown became known as – the Paul Revere of the Northwest Frontier. There is a small city park and a monument dedicated to this son of Minnesota in Browns' Valley, Traverse County, Minnesota.

Now, let's get back to the original story line – our journey to the state parks. After Julie and I had finished with our visit to the park at Upper Sioux Agency, we headed back to the city of Granite Falls and pointed our rig southwest on Hwy. 23 once again. We were now headed to Marshall and the next stop which would be at Camden State Park. As we drove down Hwy. 23, we passed a sign at the side of the road that pointed out the small town of Wood Lake. This is the area where that final skirmish of the 1862 Uprising occurred.

We had driven past Marshall and were getting to the area where the state park is located. It was hard to discern from the state road maps we had of how or where to go to enter the park. Our mistake was in looking at the map and seeing a small road that went through the town of Lynd and appeared to parallel the railroad tracks all of the way to the park. So, we scooted off the highway and made our way through this little village and started driving down this small county highway that was snaking its way south out of the village. We passed all sorts of beautiful homes and farms as we traveled south to the point where all of a sudden the road dead ended. A small sign was there that informed us that this roadway was closed. Calling that trail that led further south a roadway was a bit of a stretch. It was all grown over with vegetation and if at one time it had been used as a way to get to the park – it was a long time ago. So, there we were – at the dead end, and needing to figure out how we were going to get turned around. Well, as I have said before in this story – thank god our trailer is just a little 15 foot long rig. If it had been any longer, we may not have been able to turn around in the tight spot we found ourselves. So, back up the snaky road to Lynd; then, back to Hwy. 23. We drove just a few miles down the highway and there to the right was the entrance to Camden State Park. The Redwood River runs through the state park. The valley created by this river and the freshwater springs that can be found along the valley walls were important sources of water and shelter to both the natives and the settlers back in the mid 1800's. Now, there is a beautiful park that showcases the rolling hills, draws, valleys, the river and all the surrounding area. Camden has very nice camping facilities and the campsites are shaded by large oaks, cottonwoods, and maples.

When we rolled into Camden and parked next to the office, we could never have known the funny thing that was to happen next. We entered the office and walked up to talk to the woman behind the desk – lo and behold, it was the same lady who had taken our reservation at Lac Qui Parle State Park the night before. As I walked to the desk, she looked up and said hello and asked did I recognize her. Well, we had a good laugh. It seems that she and her husband both work for the park service and that she splits her time between Lac Qui Parle and Camden. Her husband works at two other parks that we would shortly be visiting. We told her that we would be on the look out for him. It was a good visit and she filled us in on some of the wonderful details of the park and the area. She told us that we would not be disappointed if in the fall, we came back to the park to see the fall colors. I can imagine that with all of the tree cover, the oaks, cottonwoods, and maples; the fall color must be gorgeous. Camden State Park does have a small section of it that is located just a mile further down Hwy. 23 from the main entrance. This area is referred to as the Brawner Lake Area. There is a simple gravel road that is a one way road (we found that out the hard way) that leads around the lake to a small picnic area and boat landing. With the scarcity of lakes in the southern part of the state this little chunk of the park gets used heavily.

Our next stop would be to a state park down by Pipestone. It is called Split Rock Creek. Easily confused with Split Rock Lighthouse on the north shore of Superior, but a separate and lovely park all of its own. Split Rock Creek State Park is located south of Pipestone along the last few miles of MN Hwy. 23. We were familiar with this area already because of the trip we had made earlier in the summer down to Blue Mounds.

Once in Pipestone, we followed Hwy. 23 through town and then south until we got to the little village of Ihlen. We turned east and then south again right away at Ihlen, to take the back roads to the entrance of the park. The park is situated on the west shore of Split Rock Lake. This little lake is the only lake in Pipestone County. The lake was created when the dam on the creek was built in 1938. This park is a small park with just over 200 acres; but, within it, there is something very special. There is a parking area in the park that looks westward over a piece of park property that is virgin prairie.The soil in that spot has never seen a plow blade. You can look out across this patch of ground and look at the beautiful grasses and sedges that made up 'the ocean of grass' that was the Great Plains back in the early 1800's. This is a unique site and one of the only spots in Minnesota that can call itself – virgin prairie. The lake and the trees that grow up around it are a welcome site as compared to the miles and miles of prairie and field. With this being the only lake in the county, with Pipestone so close by, there are many visitors using the facilities. Julie and I agreed that this park, too, would be wonderful to come back to at some later date; but, we would need to make certain that we called for a reservation first.

When we left the park and the area of Ihlen, we found ourselves back tracking slightly on Hwy. 23. We were now headed a little way north and east. We were headed to Murray County, through Slayton, and on to the next park to visit – Lake Shetek State Park.

Lake Shetek is the largest lake in the southwestern region of Minnesota. The word 'shetek' is an Ojibwe word which is reported to mean "pelican." This is fitting; due to all the pelicans that can be found on and around the lake. This is a lovely state park that has a beautiful camping area that is shaded by oaks, elms, ash, and hackberry. This lake is a very popular fishing lake with all of the regular Minnesota fish species being found in the waters. Previously, the lake was stocked each year by the DNR because there were problems with 'freeze-out' during the winters. Now, an aeration system has been installed on the lake and that helps to keep the fish species from dying out in the winter. Lake Shetek was also one of the many areas in the state that were involved in the Uprising in 1862. On August 20th of that year, three different groups of warriors descended on the area and when they left there were 15 dead settlers and the rest had fled for their lives. On the grounds of the park is a small traffic loop that sits beside a very tall marble obelisk that marks the site of the mass grave for those settlers that were killed. Also in the park, there is a small settler's cabin that was moved there by the Murray County government in order to help preserve the cabin. This cabin was built by a married couple named – Koch. This little two room cabin is believed to be the oldest structure in Murray County.

When we were traveling up the road toward Lake Shetek, we passed through the little town of Currie. There on the north end of the town is a small park called – The End of the Line Railroad Park. There are a couple of steam engines, some rail cars, and cabooses that are set on tracks in the park. We were headed on our way to the state park and didn't have time to stop and take in the site of the railroad park. On our next trip down to the Slayton/Currie area – we will have to make the time.

Once we had finished with our visit to Lake Shetek, we were off to our next destination. We had been driving over a very large portion of the southern and southwestern regions of the state. As I have mentioned earlier, we have found through our travels this summer to have been witness to the growing season in action. From the early days of June when the fields had just been planted and you could barely see the plants starting to poke their cotyledons out of the ground to mid summer when the corn and beans were leafed-out and stretching to the sky. Now, we were passing by fields of corn that were so tall that I would have had a difficult time walking the fields. Soy beans were tall and bushy, heavy with the pods that were going to be harvested soon. We were driving the back roads of Minnesota passing through towns like: Heron Lake, Okabena, Windom, and Darfur. While we were in the area, we realized that there was another point of interest that we needed to see. Not far away from where we were driving was the town that became home to a woman whose writing captured the hearts and imaginations of hundreds of thousands of young girls. I remember when my sister Kathy received her first copies of the books about a young girl and her family living on the prairie. These were the books that inspired the development of several TV series and the careers of actors who became icons in family-oriented television. U.S. Hwy 14 as it travels through Minnesota and onto De Smet, South Dakota, is even dedicated to this woman: Laura Ingalls Wilder. So, we traveled to Walnut Grove and spent a short time seeing the sites there and possibly reliving just a little in our minds some of those times watching the shows on television.

After leaving Walnut Grove, we were on to the next destination. That next destination was to be a small state park in Jackson County, by the town of Lakefield - Kilen Woods State park.

Kilen Woods is often referred to as 'the oasis in the farm belt'. The park sits on the west banks of the Des Moines River. The land was purchased from a farmer by the name of Agil Kilen, hence the name of the park. Along with his farm, there were other settler properties that were purchased and all became part of the park. There can still be found the remnants of old cabins and ox-cart trails within the park and down by the river.

As is the case with small state parks, Julie and I found ourselves quite impressed by this one. Nice tree cover, great toilet and shower facilities and the quiet surroundings that can be found in a small park are those things that really hit home for me when I want to go camping. While we were there, we pulled into the picnic area and had ourselves a nice little lunch and enjoyed the smell of the wild blooming prairie flowers. There was an area that was set up to use as a ball field, horse shoe pits, and the picnic shelter there by where we parked. Trails ran throughout the park and you could hike all over the hillside and the banks along the Des Moines River. I really liked this little park and do agree that it is an oasis.

We left Kilen Woods that afternoon and had to make some tracks because the next place we wanted to get to that afternoon was up on the edge of Mankato. So, the truck was pointed north and we headed out. Once again, we found ourselves driving past huge fields of corn and soybeans. We passed by towns that I have heard about many times but had never been in the area to see. Mountain Lake was on the way, followed by St. James and Medelia, until finally we were on Hwy. 60 and the next stop would be Mankato.

U.S. Hwy. 169, after crossing the Minnesota River in Mankato, scoots out the southwest corner of the city. As you are driving south on Hwy. 169, you will see signs for the next park that we were going to visit. Minneopa State Park sits virtually on the edge of this metropolitan area. The park is really split into two different pieces: the first piece is that which sits down by the Minnesota River and this is where the campsites are located. Nice shade and secluded sites really help to disguise the fact that we were so close to a city. The second piece of the park is located over a steep hill and about 3 miles from the first part. This second part sits along the Minneopa Creek and it is here that you can find the tallest waterfall in southern Minnesota. In the language of the Dakota, 'minneopa' means – water falling twice. There is this bridge that crosses over the creek and from there you can look up stream about 50 feet and see this little ten foot high shelf that the creek runs over. Then down stream just a few yards is the big falls. As you walk around on the trail, you can look down into the basin created by the water and get a good feeling for how the water from this little creek has gouged out this little basin and pool and then the rest of the small gorge that leads down to the Minnesota River. There is a beautiful picnic area with huge oaks and cottonwoods giving some shade next to the waterfalls. When we were done walking along the trails and taking pictures of the falls, we got back in the truck and drove back up the steep hill we had gone over earlier. At the top of this rather steep hill is an historic cemetery. There were tombstones in this cemetery that were dated all the way back to the 1850's. One of the stones even had the inscription on it telling us that the young child buried there was the first person buried on that hilltop. As we walked among the stones and large Cedar trees, we read the names of the early settler families that had come to the Minnesota Valley to try and make a life. Some of the stones, even the very old ones, could still be read; but, others – there was nothing left to read. The passage of time had erased what ever it was that had been etched on to the faces of those blocks of granite and marble. Out on the edges of the cemetery there were markers that were on the edge of the brush and trees that at one time marked the outer most boundary of the space; but, with the subsidence of the ground around the hilltop, down the sloped sides of the hill, some of those burial sites were in danger of being lost completely – over the edge. As Julie and I were strolling among the stones, it struck me that mankind always attempts to leave an indelible mark on his world.

Whether that mark is in the offspring he sires, the buildings or crafts that he creates, or the poems he writes – mankind is always searching for a way to make certain he is not forgotten. But, we can never win this battle. The hands of time and Mother Nature will always prevail in this duel. The sites we saw in that cemetery are a testament to the fact that we can't win. Man will take a substance or a mineral that he feels is the hardest he can find – make his mark – and then set the piece to prove his existence. Yet in the blink of a geologic eye – the proof has weathered away to nothing. Ashes to ashes, dust to dust – as it always has been, and always will be.

Our next stop on this trip would be just a short way up Highway 68 from Mankato to New Ulm, Minnesota. In New Ulm, one will find Flandrau State Park. I don't want to take anything away from it. The park has miles and miles of great hiking, biking, and ski trails, a great picnic area and a swimming pond. There are big beautiful oaks, maples, hackberry, and cottonwoods. The park is a draw to dozens of species of migratory birds. The Cottonwood River runs along through the park on its way to empty into the Minnesota River. The campsites are split between two different areas in the park. This is wonderful park and the only draw back that I have with it is that it is right inside of the city of New Ulm. This is a personal preference of mine and should not influence of anyone else about going to this park. The city of New Ulm is rich in the history of the early settlement of the state and there numerous sites to be seen in the city and the surrounding region.

This park was named after a person who played an important role in Minnesota's history - Charles Eugene Flandrau. He was born in the east to a wealthy and influential family. He decided to move to the frontiers of Minnesota to practice law. When news of the troubles with the natives hit the wires, he was living in the area of Traverse Des Sioux (St. Peter). He gathered a troop of men together and led them to New Ulm. He was chosen to be the leader of those who had fled to New Ulm when the conflict started. For his effort, he has often been referred to as – 'The Defender of New Ulm'. He held the rank of colonel. He continued to be in charge of the troops responsible for the southwestern frontier of Minnesota. Flandrau is credited as giving the state its nickname – the Gopher State. He worked in the state government with Governor

Alexander Ramsey and sat on the Minnesota Supreme Court. He was a flamboyant man and was quick to lend his story telling prowess at many functions in the New Ulm area and the rest of the state. Charles Flandrau was another of the many famous sons of Minnesota.

Next stop – Fort Ridgley State Park. As we were traveling and had left the area of New Ulm, we traveled to the north and west and went through the nice town of Sleepy Eye. At Sleepy Eye, we took MN Hwy. 4 north. We were going to a state park that is located just across the Minnesota River on Hwy 4. This highway is the same highway that goes further north until it passes through towns like Cosmos, Grove City, Paynesville, and all the way up to Sauk Center. I am familiar with Hwy. 4 because it travels north up through Meeker County and further north into Stearns County; so I, having lived in Meeker and Stearns Counties, had driven on Hwy. 4 many times. I just hadn't traveled this far south on the road before.

So, about 8 or 9 miles north of Sleepy Eye, Hwy. 4 crosses the Minnesota River and starts the steep upward climb out of the valley. Just after starting up this hill, you will see the sign that points to the west directing you to Fort Ridgley State Park. This is a beautiful park that sits along and around the ridges and valleys created by a small creek that empties into the Minnesota River. This creek is called Fort Ridgley Creek. There is a very nice 9-hole golf course that sits on the park property and at the top of the hill is the location where Fort Ridgley was built. In 1853, the War Department had sent out a group of men to locate a spot along the Minnesota River where a fort could be built. The idea was that this installation would be there to give protection to all those settlers that were moving in to the region after the treaty – Traverse des Sioux - was signed in 1851. The natives had been moved to two different areas along the Minnesota River and these were the reservations – the Upper Sioux Agency and the Lower Sioux Agency.

Now, the site that the men had picked was a wonderful spot that gave great, commanding views of the Minnesota River Valley both to the east and the west. It was up on top of the escarpment above the river and from there you could see miles and miles to the north across the open prairie. The problem with the spot was that it was miles away from either of the two parts of the reservation and this didn't allow the soldiers to be able to monitor what the natives were doing. The Dakota Conflict started on August 17th, 1862. On August 20th, a large band of Indians attacked the fort and were pushed back by the men manning their positions. Fort Ridgley didn't have a wall, it didn't even have a stockade. It was just a collection of two story and one story buildings. The soldiers at the fort fought from shallow trenches that they were able to hastily dig into the ground. The buildings and their second story windows became spots to sharp shoot from and gave a slight advantage in being able to see over a larger area. The natives were attacking up from the river through the small gullies and draws. Artillerymen, who stood their ground and manned their guns, were instrumental in pushing the marauders back with the fire from their canons. After the first attack proved fruitless, the Indians gathered themselves and decided to go down river and attack New Ulm. However, when they got there they were met by Major Charles Flandrau (who we have talked about earlier) and the troop of soldiers he was leading. The second attack on the fort occurred on August 22, 1862, and that attack was squelched, also.

At the top of the hill is a lovely, restored stone building that was one of the buildings that housed officers and their families. Now, that building acts as the interpretive center. The foundations of many of the other buildings that made up the fort can be seen and the story of the battles and the men who fought there are told on the story boards that sit among the ruins. Having served in the U.S. Army, and being Infantry and Cavalry when I served, caused a near chill to run down my spine while I was walking around the site. To see the area where those men fought and died. I was struck with the realization that some of these men, especially the officers, had their families at the fort with them. They were literally fighting to save their families. The level of devotion and heroism which was displayed on that site nearly 150 years ago is almost incomprehensible.

I will go back to Fort Ridgley again, soon, for nothing more than to enjoy the nice park, maybe do some golfing, to spend more time reading about the battle at the interpretive center, and to walk the grounds in order to get an even more personal idea of the scope of those harrowing days in August of 1862. Another thing that I have begun to realize with all the traveling we have been doing in order to write the story of our journey, is that the Uprising of 1862 was huge in its scope. The last major battles between the white settlers and the natives to happen in the state of Minnesota occurred during the Uprising. Go to Grove City, Minnesota, and you can read the marble monument that marks the spot in Acton Township where the first settlers were killed. Go to the spot three miles east of Wood Lake, Minnesota, and drive around the fields and see the sites of the last major battle during the Uprising. But these are just two sites out of the dozens in the southwest part of the state that were involved in the conflict. Places like: New Ulm, Sunburg, Redwood Ferry Crossing, Birch Coulee, Hutchinson, Forest City, Lake Shetek were all involved in the fighting. Another thing that I am beginning to realize with all of this traveling is how much I didn't know about this state that I was born in and live in. During my school days, I had my classes in social studies, geography and history. But, the curriculum taught in almost all of those classes had to do with the United States, the 'larger' history of the country itself and its place among other nations in the world. I wasn't learning anything about the actual spot on the planet that I was standing on. Maybe this is one of the downfalls of our educational system and the fast paced life that we lead these days. We forget to slow down and learn the important lessons that are all around us. Thus far, during our journey to visit all of the state parks in Minnesota, I have learned many lessons. I have a much greater appreciation for those that settled into this area and made it the beautiful state that it is today.

When we had finished taking in the sites and visiting the camp and park at Fort Ridgley, we drove back to Hwy. 4 and headed north. We only went just a few miles north when we came to the intersection of Hwy. 4 with Hwy. 19. We turned right and headed east. We passed through the towns like Gibbon, Winthrop, and Henderson. Henderson is a lovely little town that sits down in the Minnesota River Valley southwest Belle Plaine. As we were traveling down the hill into the town and then got close to the river, we could see that this town has also had an ongoing problem with the flooding that occurs on the Minnesota River. They have very large levees that protect the town along the river bank and sections where walls can be erected to close off the roadways.

Once we were across the river, we rolled up to Belle Plaine and then headed to the next state park – Minnesota Valley State Recreation Area. This park is located next to the Minnesota River between Belle Plaine and Jordan. The park is situated along the river in that area, stretching all the way to Chaska and Shakopee. The park is made up of several Forest Service areas and a couple of areas managed by the DNR. There are miles and miles of trails to use for hiking, skiing, horse back, or snowmobiling. There are several boat launches along the river to access the water. The campground is located in the park area near Belle Plaine. It is a nice camp with nice tree cover, shade, and the sites are nicely spaced to allow for seclusion. Yet, all of this is just a short drive from the city area and a major U.S. highway. This recreation area gets a lot of use for the simple fact that it is so close to the Metro Area.

Once we had finished snooping around the valley there in the recreation area, we pointed the nose of the pickup north and started the drive home to the cabin in the woods. We moved up through Chaska and continued to head north on the west side of the Cities figuring that we could cut some time off our trip rather than going all the way into the metro area and driving on the interstate highways. Boy, we were wrong. We got caught in traffic and road construction. The construction was such that it nearly moved us all the way west again until we were south of Buffalo. We got through Buffalo, Monticello and ultimately back to Hwy. 169 going north from Elk River. About two hours later we pulled back into our driveway and completed another leg of the journey.

The next part of the journey would take us on a small looping trip to visit 4 state parks that aren't necessarily hundreds of miles away from where we live. We decided to drive down to a small town that is very near the border of Wisconsin, near the bottom of the nose on the Indianhead. We drove south from our home and turned east onto Hwy. 18 and drove around the north and east side of Mille Lacs until we got down to Isle. There we turned east again and headed to the interstate. Once we got onto I-94, we were making good time and drove down to the intersection of I-94 and MN. Hwy 95. We turned east on Hwy. 95 and headed to the small town of Almelund. This little town holds a yearly festival celebrating its heritage. The celebration is near the end of August and seeing that it was the first part of September, we had just missed all of the fun. We turned north and traveled on a small well-used county highway for about 3 miles and got to the park just as it was starting to get seriously dark – Wild River State Park. One of the other distressing things that we realized as we have been traveling – this business of the sun going down sooner and sooner in the evening is really biting into our ability to reach some of the places we want to get to. Another distressing thing to realize is that you have arrived at the state park actually one day early. Here we are at the park wanting to get to the camp site that was reserved for us on Saturday; however, it was Friday evening. Well, I must say, the staff at the park was very accommodating and seeing that the site that we had reserved was also open that night and they changed our reservation. We headed out from the park office and drove to the camping area. On the way out there, we were happy to see many deer standing around on the sides of the road as we drove. We got to the campsite and backed into the spot just about the time it was nearly too dark to see. Hopefully my ability to back the truck up and park that little trailer was fast enough that we didn't disturb our neighbors across the road too much. We slept that night and then as is the case when we are out camping – we were up before the dawn and had eaten breakfast and were already looking forward to what Saturday had in store for us. We toured around the park to see the sites and were very impressed at the facility they have there for campers who want to bring their horses and do some riding. One of my co-workers had mentioned to me that we should check out the 'Horse Camp' area. It was beautiful, with very tall pines and nice parking and 'back in' sites for campers to use. There were tethers set up at each site for the horses and there was even a wheel barrow and a couple of shovels to help with cleaning up. It was a very nice facility for those people to use.

Wild River State Park is also located very near the small town of Sunrise. This small town was one of the first towns to be established in the state. This town was one of the towns instrumental in the logging that was going on in the mid 1800's. The town also has claims to fame for being the birth place to an Illinois governor and a Hollywood actor. One of the historic sites inside of Wild River State Park is the site of the Nevers Dam. This dam helped to raise the river level and allowed for easier floating of the logs down the channel and to the mills when logging was at its peak.

After we left Wild River, it was just a short drive to the next stop which was at Taylors Falls – Interstate State Park. This park is the second or third oldest park in the state and was started in 1895. It was established in a coordinated venture with the state of Wisconsin which at the time was opening a state park just across the river. It was the first time anything like this had occurred between two states.

Interstate was created to help protect the very unique geologic formations that can be found there. First, and foremost, this area of the river had been very popular for many years prior to the park being established. The Dalles – or that region of the river which stretched to the north of Taylors Falls – was a very popular tourist attraction. People came to visit the area by steamboat and train. The area around Taylors Falls and St. Croix Falls was first inhabited around 1825 when a fur trading post, operated by the Columbia Fur Trading Company, and Fort Barbour were first built. Then, there was the rush of lumbermen that came in the 1840's to exploit the great white pine resource that was in the region. The lumber industry continued to dominate in the area for decades. The Dalles area of the St. Croix River is an area where the basalt bedrock forms high cliffs on either side of the river. These cliffs channel the water quite nicely and also allowed those lumberjacks a perfect highway to transport the logs to the mill. However, there were some problems. The worst was when floating the logs in the river caused a log jam to occur. The Dalles area is best known for a huge log jam that occurred in 1886. The jam stretched for 7 miles up the river.

Another geologic oddity that can be found in the park is 'the pot holes'. Glacial pot holes were formed when abrasive sand and other sediments rubbed and eroded away at the bedrock. The cause of this rubbing and erosion were the torrents of water that were flowing over the falls and through the river valley during the time that the ancient glaciers were melting. The pot holes come in a variety of differing sizes and depths. All of the pot holes can be found in the part of the park that is to the east of the stop light in Taylors Falls. There are small ones and large ones, shallow and deep. Some of the pot holes have even been given unique names, like: the Cauldron, the Lily Pond, the Squeeze, and the Bake Oven. One of the best know of the holes is – the Bottomless Pit. Now, it isn't bottomless; but, it is over 60 feet deep and is recognized as the deepest 'Pot Hole' in the world.

The basalt bedrock that is at the surface of the ground in and around the area of Taylors Falls allows for unique formations and scenery. There is also a very active industry in the area to mine the basalt and crush it; then, send it off to market all over the country and the world to be used in many different applications. With the beautiful St. Croix Valley, the rolling hills, the deeply cut topography of the region from the creeks and streams that empty into the St. Croix, and all of the sites to be seen and experienced – it is little wonder that this is a popular place to come and visit.

Once we had finished with our visit to Taylors Falls, we scooted down the road just a short distance to the next state park. Minnesota Hwy. 95 has been given another name, it is called – the St. Croix Trail. It follows the river as it goes south along the border between the two states. Driving along this trail will allow you to experience the lovely valley and the beautiful vistas which can be seen when cresting over the tops of some of the hills. The St. Croix Trail starts all the way up at the point where Hwy. 95 breaks left and travels to the south away from MN Hwy. 8, which continues to travel west toward Lindstrom, Chisago City, and Forest Lake. At the start of the trail there is a small village called – Franconia. There is a unique exhibit that can be found at Franconia. On the west side of the road you will pass by The Franconia Metal Art Museum. This is a collection of unique sculptures made out of all manner of metals and metal scraps. Many different sculptures can be viewed and this would be a wonderful spot to stop and check out the ingenuity of some of the pieces there. Further south along the trail, you will pass through the towns of Copas, Marine-on-St. Croix, Stillwater, Bayport, Lakeland, Afton, and Basswood Grove. Finally, the trail comes to an end when the roadway intersects with U.S. Hwy. 10, just outside of Prescott, Wisconsin.

Our destination was a State Park just a couple of miles north of Marine-on-St. Croix – the William O'Brian State Park. This is another lovely park that sits along the west bank of the St. Croix River. It has two lovely campgrounds for visitors, an interpretive center, many miles of trails, boat landings and picnic areas. It is a park that is open year round for use by the public. Marine-on-St. Croix has the distinction of being the oldest logging settlement in the state of Minnesota. One of the big businessmen that moved into the area to oversee the logging was Mr. William O'Brian. The land that the park sits on was donated to the state by Alice O'Brian in honor of her father, William. When entering the park and driving up to the main office, there is a large granite boulder that is sitting on a small patch of grass and this boulder is a monument to Alice. On the boulder, a plaque is attached telling the story of Alice and her father.

Another part of the park that is accessible only by canoe is Greenberg Island out in the channel of the river. This island was donated in 1958 by Mr. David Greenberg, in memory of his parents. The island has no camping sites or easy access. This limits any visitors and has allowed this island to become a haven to wildlife. This park is a wonderful place to camp at and to visit to use its many different recreational resources. If you were living in the Twin Cities area, this park would be easy to reach – not too far from home, but far enough to allow you to get away from the city.

After finishing in William O'Brian, we headed further south to the next destination. We continued our trek down the St. Croix Trail until we came to the town of Afton. Just 3 miles south of Afton, on the trail, is a large recreational area that would meet the needs of anyone during almost any time of the year. This area that I refer to encompasses the Afton Alps Golf Course, the Afton Alps Ski Area, and Afton State Park.

Afton is another of the special state parks which is set up specifically to be used by those people who are looking to do remote, rustic, tent camping. This park is very similar to Lake Maria State Park in its intended use. In order to use almost any of the facilities in this park, you had better be prepared to hike. The Visitors center is just a short distance from the parking area and one of the picnic areas is right there next to the lot; however, that is all that can be easily accessed. The park has many miles of trails and they wind around and over all of the scenic hillsides and terraces contained in the park. The camping area in the park is ¾ of a mile away from the parking lot on a trail that is of moderate difficulty for hiking. Afton has also gone one step further in its effort to keep the park a very remote and rustic experience. They have instituted a new rule as of 2009 that the camping area is a "pack-in, pack-out" zone. Anything brought into the camping area for use must be brought out by the campers when they are finished. At one time, there were garbage cans all around the camping area. Now, it is up to the campers themselves to keep the area looking beautiful. There has been very limited improvement to anything in the park, the trails are challenging in many spots as they run up and down the hills and ravines. Sandstone outcroppings in the park along the trails and some of the scenic vistas that can be found create a great experience here at Afton.

While visiting Afton State Park, we decided to have a picnic. We have our trailer and that plus not desiring to sleep in a remote site in a tent, limits the amount of use we would get from this park. We had a very good time while picnicking and once we were done with our meal it was time to head out and get to the last destination on this short leg of our journey. We were headed into the heart of the Twin Cities Metro Area to visit Fort Snelling.

This unique piece of Minnesota history is wonderful to visit. The Visitors Center, which sits on top of the bluffs over looking the spot where the Minnesota and Mississippi Rivers come together, is a commanding locale and it is no wonder that it was chosen as the site for the fortification. However, it was not always known as Fort Snelling. It was originally called Fort St. Anthony, in reference to the waterfalls just a short distance up the Mississippi River. It was built between the years 1820 and 1824. After its completion, it was re-named Fort Snelling after the young commander, Col. Josiah Snelling, who was in charge during the construction.

Fort Snelling has a long and storied history of service to Minnesota and to the nation. It has been used for housing and training troops since its creation, during the Civil War, during the Indian Wars, the Spanish-American War, and the two World Wars. The state park is located below the Visitors Center and at the base of the bluffs where the two rivers meet. Numerous islands and back waters, plus Snelling Lake, create the state park and the miles of trails, picnic areas, and recreational fields that can be found there. One of the islands that make up the park down at the confluence of the two rivers is called Pike Island. It was named after Zebulon Pike, a great American explorer, who spent some time exploring the Upper Mississippi. Pike Island is also important historically with regards to the 1862 Sioux Uprising. After the hostilities had been brought under control by the troops led by Henry Sibley, the various tribes were moved from their reservations and were forced to live on Pike Island under the watchful guard of the soldiers at the fort. After a time, the various tribes were moved to other reservations and Pike Island was used for various other purposes. Fort Snelling State Park is a 'day-use' park. Activities can and are held at different times throughout the year and the park is open to visitors all year long.

One other tid-bit of fact about Fort Snelling is that in 1820, the installation's doctor, began to take weather measurements. These measurements became part of the national weather information gathered each and every day of the year. These measurements continued unbroken until 1995 when the National Weather service moved their office from the International Airport to Chanhassen, Minnesota. This gathered data ranging all the way back to 1820, gives Minnesota the distinction of having one of the longest records of weather related information in the entire country. One other item of interest that visitor's to the park may consider looking into is the grave site of a horse. There is a grave site inside the walls of the old fort and it is marked showing the spot where a horse named Whiskey is buried. I strongly urge anyone who has a soft spot in their hearts for horses to look up this horse in Minnesota history. He was the last horse to be stationed at Fort Snelling. He had a very unique role at Fort Snelling and the story of the people who knew him, worked with him, and loved him is a tale that will bring a tear to your eye.

After our self-tour of the fort and the park was done, it was time to head home once again and prepare for the upcoming week.

The next part of our journey was going to take us to the north shore of Lake Superior. Earlier, in the month of August, I had made reservations for a site up in Cascade River State Park. The reservation had been made for September 19th; but, here we were heading north on the 18th. So, we made a little change in our route and decided to head north to one state park that had eluded us so far in all of our travels. Making this minor change to our itinerary happened to work out to our benefit because it allowed us to skip some major congestion that was going to be occurring on the drive between Duluth and Two Harbors. This particular weekend in September was the weekend that an in-line skating marathon was being held on the highway between the two cities. As I said, this only promised to be a major headache to us if we were to get caught in the traffic jam that the event would obviously create. So, change our direction the first night and then sneak back over to the north shore on MN. Hwy. 1 and drive through the little town of Finland would help us to skip all the hassle.

As we drove north, we passed through many towns that have huge historical significance to this state and the iron ore industry that used to be king in the region. Cities and towns like Coleraine, Taconite, Nashwauk, Hibbing and all the rest have had to try and re-create themselves after the down turn in the iron ore business on The Range. Calumet, Minnesota, has the state park now. However, even with the park there, Calumet has not bounced back to the city it once was.

We had driven up to Hibbing and there we had to make a short side trip to a spot that I have had my picture taken at numerous times in my life all the way back to when I was 10 or 11 years old. We went to the Hull-Mahoning Mine over look site. As I said, I have been at this mine many times in my life and boy how things have changed. At one time, the scenic over look was just a gravel road leading up to a dusty site where an old Euclid dump truck and a couple of old steam-shovel buckets were set. There was a chain link fence put up at the edge of the pit to stop anyone from doing anything kind of stupid. If you really wanted to show off the lack of brain power, you could try climbing the fence. That was then. Now, there is fence up all over and a paved parking lot. There is a small store set up on the site and they sell souvenirs to any of the visitors that come to see the mine. There is a paved trail that leads down to the big dump truck and there have been a few more, old steam shovel buckets added to the collection. Who ever decided to make this change – they did a good job. The area looks nice and well kept and it was actually very pleasant strolling around taking in the sites and looking at all the goodies in the store.

This pit mine is the largest iron ore pit in the world. It had originally started out as four separate operations; but, as the industry grew and more of the ore was removed, these four smaller mines became a monster. Some refer to the mine as the Mini Grand Canyon of the North. It is over 600 feet deep. It is 1.5 miles across and 3.5 miles long.

Now, with the small souvenir shop located at the gate leading down to where the dump truck and buckets are sitting, this helps to control and monitor access to the site. The city of Hibbing has created a small city park and camping area just a few blocks down the road from the over look site. One more block down the road from the city park area is a museum dedicated to Greyhound buses.

While we were visiting, we could hear some activity in the pit off to the southwest. This may have been trucks and loaders continuing to work and remove the valuable ore that is found here. But, the activity going on today is nothing when compared to the heyday of the iron ore business.

After finishing taking pictures at the over look, we continued heading north, turned on County Road 5 just before getting to Chisholm and headed to the town of Side Lake, Minnesota, to spend a night at McCarthy Beach State Park.

We arrived at the park to find that the main office was all closed up. No one was at home. Now that it was after Labor Day and the peak of the camping season was done, there was a severe reduction in the manpower for the park and the office itself would only be open on Saturdays and Sundays for limited hours. So, we drove around the park, which was still surprisingly busy, found a spot we liked and started to set up. Later, we went and paid our fee at the drop box next to the office and then spent some time exploring this nice little park. There are nice facilities, a swimming beach, trails, canoe/kayak rental, and fishing available within the park. This would be a nice park for a family to visit. We enjoyed our stay.

The region around Side Lake and the state park have always been areas used for timber production. The trees in the area were first logged by a couple of men who started a saw mill near the present location of the city of Hibbing. These two men's names were Hibbing and Trimble. In 1895, a railroad spur was laid into the region by the Swan River Logging Company from Saginaw, Michigan, and then the logging of the big stands of red and white pine started in earnest.

When we had finished with our touring of the park, we went back to where the camper was and fixed a little meal and then settled down to enjoy the evening. The next morning, after breakfast and getting everything packed back up and ready to roll, we headed to the north shore.

We drove back through Side Lake and proceeded to head east on some of the back roads in the area trying make our way over to MN Hwy. 1. It was my intent to use this opportunity to take Hwy. 1 all the way to

Finland, a small town near the North Shore about 8 miles from Silver Bay. Now, I did have other reasons too. There were a couple of places that we would be driving past that we wanted to get more pictures of - the Soudan Mine and Bear Head Lake State Park.

Driving through the deep part of the woods, passing areas of clear cut timber land, marshes, swamps and small isolated lakes really instilled into us the fact as to how far out in the boonies we were. Secretly, I was saying little prayers concerning the safety and well being of my pick up and its engine and drive train; because, if we would have had a break down out in that area – well, we could have just started living in our little trailer. We were way beyond anything remotely resembling cell phone reception and many of the roads that we were driving on had not seen a vehicle on them in some number of days. Ultimately, we made it through without any problems and saw some wildlife and a whole lot of trees along the way. Once we were on Hwy. 1, this took us right to Tower and Soudan. After a short stay getting the pictures I wanted to take and then finding a wayside along the road in order to take a bathroom break, we headed toward Ely. The short detour south on the road back to Bear Head Lake only delayed us a few minutes. We had left McCarthy Beach State Park so early in the morning that day that by the time we got to Ely the stores and shops there were just starting to open up. I asked Julie if she wanted to stop and do any shopping because there are many very unique places to see and visit in the town. She answered no and so – we continued through town until we got to the point where the road took a serious turn to the southeast and lead the way to our destination – Finland.

It had been many years since I had been on the section of Hwy. 1 that runs between Ely and Finland. The human mind is a wonderful thing in regards to its ability to block out negative or bad experiences from a person's memory. I think this is what must have happened to me because I am pretty sure I would have remembered this little section of highway if it had been any thing like a normal road. But no, this highway has to be one of the curviest roads in existence. According to the map, the two towns are only about 56 miles apart - say, about one hour driving time. Not on this road. There are portions of the road that I believe are just built up road beds that travel right through the swamps and marshes. In other areas, there are walls of bedrock on either side of you attesting to the fact that they used some explosives to fashion that section of the highway. If the road wasn't curving to the left or right, it was ascending or descending up and down the many ridges, hills, and hummocks that can be found in the area. Suffice it to say, it was a tough drive.

Now that I have all of that bad stuff out of the way, I can now tell you that this section of Hwy. 1 is one of the prettiest roads to travel on. The terrain, the trees, the lakes, swamps, marshes and all of the other sites to see along the way afford a wonderful experience when driving this part of the highway. Keep your head about you and your eyes on the road because there is no telling what you may encounter while driving this part of Hwy. 1. There is the odd semi truck hauling logs or other supplies, other vacationers heading to their next destinations in their campers and RV's, or any number of different forms or wildlife – all of these can be encountered on this drive. With the curves and hills that are found along the way – you just never know what might be standing out on the highway. The state highway department has started to place moose crossing signs along the road now – so watch out, you hit a moose with your car or truck, its going to hurt.

Just before we arrived at Finland, we saw a sign on the side of the road directing us to turn here if we wanted to go to the George H. Crosby Manitou State Park. Well, what a coincidence, we did want to go to that park – so we turned there. We only drove about ½ mile when the pavement suddenly stopped and now we were driving on a dirt road. Now, this was not one of your normal well established dirt roads that say had been there for the last 100 years. No, this dirt road had the look of it as having just been chiseled out of the earth. I should have picked up on the fact that this was a portent of events to come. But, I didn't. The town of Finland is located on the north side of a very tall ridge of hills and old mountains still referred to as the Sawtooth Mountains. This range of high country stretches all the way along the north shore of Lake Superior, to the Canadian border and beyond. As we had been driving down Hwy. 1 towards Finland, every once in a while you would catch a glimpse of this ridge. The gravel road that we had turned on to was paralleling this ridge as we drove northward. We were driving past low lying marshes and swamps and there was a river that meandered its way through this pretty valley. There were points along our drive that we saw that the roadbed was barely above the level of the water in the marshes and the river. We drove by pieces of machinery that were parked along the side of the road as if their one and only job was to be there for when the road needed to be repaired. And by the looks of this dirt road, that would be fairly often.

It wasn't all bad. There was wonderful scenery to see as we drove along. I told Julie to keep her eyes peeled on the swamps and marshes that we were passing; because, if we were going to see a moose on this trip – this was the area where it would happen. Alas, no moose was sighted. After traveling about 7 miles on this road, we got to an intersection and there at the corner was a small wooden sign indicating with an arrow that the state park was off to the right and straight up this hill. I took a long and hard look at the path they were indicating was a road. The thing that we had been driving on for the last seven miles was a road – marginal, but still a road. That goat path up the side of the hill shouldn't have been called a road. I looked at my lovely wife and let loose with a silly chuckle trying to indicate the absurdity I was feeling for their suggestion to drive up that goat path. I looked at that small wooden sign and decided the arrow on the sign must have meant that we had to travel further ahead on the dirt road to get to the park, not the goat path. So, off we went continuing on the meandering path of the road as it paralleled the river and we drove even further into the back country. Happily, the dirt road didn't get any worse and we drove past lots of beautiful scenery. After another seven miles we got to another intersection – no state park. Hmmm, there seemed to have been a small error in judgment. Other state parks that we had been to during the summer had had long drives back through the country to finally get to the Ranger's office. But, out here at this next intersection, there wasn't even a hint of a state park nearby. I checked the maps that were with us in the truck and then decided we had better head back to the goat trail.

When we got back to the spot where the sign post was, we turned in the direction indicated by the arrow and started to slowly drive up this hill and into the thick woods crowding the sides of the path. After about one mile, we were a couple of hundred feet higher in elevation and there at the side of the path were two covered bulletin boards with information as to how to get to all of the remote campsites that could be found in the valley and along the hiking trails leading up into the hills. Here we were – the George H. Crosby Manitou State Park. This park is completely devoted to those vacationers and campers who desire the remote back woods experience. We were idling in the truck next to the Information Center of the park. This was the spot were hikers would indicate what campsite they would be staying at. Then, they would drive their vehicles to the small parking area still further ahead. This was not the place to be if you are hauling a trailer; even if it was a small one like ours. I looked up the goat path ahead of us and I didn't really like the thought of having to continue further up the path to see what the parking area was going to look like. But, when I looked in the rear view mirrors, the thought of having to try and back our truck and trailer down the goat path all the way back to the intersection with the dirt road was even less appealing. So, we went further up the hill. As we started to move, I jokingly said to Julie that I hoped we wouldn't meet another vehicle because there was hardly room on the goat path for our truck and trailer let alone another vehicle going in the opposite direction. So, what happens about 30 seconds later – here comes a Subaru wagon with two hikers in it heading down the hillside to go into town. GREAT !!!

I found the widest spot I could crowd over on and as the smaller vehicle passed us, it was only by a mere inch or two.

We got to the parking lot and by the grace of God there was just enough area clear cut of trees and brush to allow me to turn us around. Happily, we headed our way down the hill, past the Information Center, and finally back to the intersection with the dirt road. We took the picture we needed of the sign for the park and then headed back to Finland and to continue onward with the journey and to our next destination, on the other side of the tall ridge of hills – the North Shore.

When we got to the intersection of Hwy. 1 and Hwy. 61, we turned left and headed up the highway towards Grand Marais. We had only been on Hwy. 61 for a couple of miles when we crossed a river that was listed as the Manitou River. This was the river that we had been driving along side of during that little excursion to the G.S. Crosby Manitou State Park. Later, we would learn that we had also been driving past and around the Baptism River that also meanders around in the hills north of Finland. The Baptism River ultimately dumps into Lake Superior at Tettegouche State Park.

We continued on our drive up Hwy. 61 until we got to the next stop and that was at one of the state's Waysides. We were driving up the highway and had just crossed over a bridge and saw a sign that pointed to the left and said – Caribou Falls Wayside. So, I turned there and pulled into the very small parking lot. I want to emphasize that this is a small parking lot. It is very likely that the parking area was designed to allow parking for those individuals who were going to leave their cars in the parking area and then hike the trails up into the hills and along the river. It was not designed to handle some idiot driving a long pick up truck and towing a small trailer.

Just a few miles down the road from this parking lot was the town of Little Marais. We had passed through this little town and were heading up towards Temperance River State Park; so, it was kind of a surprise to see all of a sudden one of the state waysides that we wanted to stop at. There were 4 or 5 other cars and vans parked there and we were the only one with a trailer. For good reason, this parking lot wasn't meant to have a trailer in it. The Caribou Falls State Wayside is a trail head location for trails that lead up into the hills and down to the shore of the lake. There is a rather nice large waterfall that can be seen when hiking on the trails leading up in to the woods. There was a large sign board near the back of the parking lot that had a map painted onto it showing the locations of the trails and all the sites to see along the way. My biggest concern at the moment was trying to figure out how I was going to get my truck and trailer turned around in the this extremely tight spot that already had cars in it. Well, after about 10 minutes of 4 feet forward, turn the steering wheel slightly, then 4 feet back, then turn the wheel slightly again and go through the whole process about another 25 times and you will figure out how much it took to get turned back in the correct direction. This was the second time in less than 2 hours that we had found ourselves in an almost impassable spot. We had other places to get to yet during that day and we didn't have the time to stop and go hiking up in to the hills to see the waterfall. We will return at some later date, stay at Tettegouche or Temperance River, and then come back here with just our hiking gear and the pick up, sans the trailer, and then go get pictures of that waterfall.

After leaving the Caribou State Wayside, we continued northeast. We passed through the small town of Taconite Harbor and passed by the huge plant that stills sits along the shore of the lake. We drove on until we were just about to get to the town of Schroeder, Minnesota, when we came across another of the waysides. This one is the Cross River State Wayside and there is a wonderful little story that is the reason that this wayside exists. In 1846, there was a missionary in this area whose name was Father Frederick Baraga. He and an Indian guide were in a canoe out on Lake Superior in October of 1846. A sudden storm blew up out on the lake and the two men in the canoe were swept across the water until they were blown on to the shore near the spot where this river, the Cross River, empties into the lake. Father Baraga felt fortunate to have survived the ordeal and he felt that there had been some divine intervention which had lead to their survival; so, he erected a large wooden cross at the shore of the lake near the spot where they landed. The cross was there for many years and it became a local spot of interest. The river was even given the name Cross River in honor of that marker. However, the sands of time, weather and rot took their toll on the good friar's marker. The State went to the site and removed the remnants of the first cross and erected a large granite cross on the site. That new cross still stands at the mouth of the river as testament to the event.

Up on the highway, there is a bridge that spans the river and there is a very nice parking lot to pull into in order to go see a beautiful waterfall that sits very close to the highway. In fact, you can just stand on the pedestrian walk way portion of the bridge and take pictures of the waterfall which is right there on the uphill side of the road. I can only imagine that at the height of the spring runoff of water from the snowmelt, this little waterfall must be a spectacular site to see. Across the road from the wayside parking area, there is a small gift shop for visitors to browse through.

After taking some pictures, we headed on through Schroeder and just a ½ mile up the highway is the Temperance River State Park. Julie and I were both very impressed with this state park nestled along the shore of the lake. There are great camping sites in both of the two camping areas in the park. Nice views of the lake from the camping area on the north side of the bridge and there are sites on the south side camping area that are so close to the lake that you could throw a stone and hit the water. We both agreed that we would come back to this park in the future to stay and to enjoy the beautiful scenery, trails, river, and the lake. The Temperance River coming down the steep hillside to the north and west cuts a rough, rugged, and narrow gorge through the bedrock there in the park near the highway and under the highway bridge. Even at this time late in the season, the water moving and tumbling through the gorge and over the stair steps of falls was impressive. We were easily able to crawl on down to the edge of the rocks and get under the bridge to take some great pictures of the river. I doubt that this could be done during the spring time when the river levels are higher.

The series of falls that are found there near the bridge are just the tip of the ice berg, so-to-speak, with regards to other sites along the Temperance. There is another waterfall, the Hidden Falls, just 0.2 miles up the river from the bridge and another falls about 0.6 miles up the river from the bridge. With Schroeder being so close by and all the sites to see at this park, we will definitely have this state park on our short list.

There is an interesting story that accompanies Temperance State Park and the history of this area. The native tribes have lived along the North Shore of Superior for thousands of years and this is verified by many of the artifacts that have been found in locations all along the shore from Grand Portage to Duluth. Europeans first arrived in the region with the coming of the French in the 1660's and into the 1700's. Two of the first white men to ever see the chiseled bluffs and hills of the north shore were Pierre Esprit Radisson and Medard Chouart, Sieur de Groselliers, as these two men explored the shore line and the lake in the 1660's. The local Ojibwe tribe had a name for the Cross River that roughly meant – Wood of the Soul River. Earlier, I told you how the river got its present name from Father Baraga. Now, the river that is just ¾ of a mile up the shore from the Cross River was originally called 'kawimbash' or Deep Hallow River by the native tribe. In 1864, a man exploring the north shore of the lake, Thomas Clark is reported to have called it the Temperance River because it didn't have a bar close to its mouth.

The highway between Schroeder and Lutsen along the north shore in 2009 was being worked on by the state highway department. They have the entire road tore up and are re-building it from the base up. Once it is complete, this should be a very nice drive up to Lutsen. On our way up this section of Hwy. 61, we passed by the area where the Ray Berglund State Wayside is located. That whole State Wayside is not available for visitors because of the construction. The Onion River is the stream that can be accessed from the Berglund Wayside. There is about a ½ mile walk along the edge of the bluff looking down on the river. When the construction on the highway is done, it would be interesting to come back up here and take a stroll on the trail.

After passing through Lutsen and getting away from the construction, it was smooth sailing all the way up to Cascade River State Park. That was the park that we were going to spend the night at. We got there, checked in at the main office and then headed to our campsite. This park like all the others is another example of the lovely country or woods that can be found here in the state. The camping area was nicely spaced apart and the sites were nice and level. We were able to easily set up our camper and prepare for the night's rest. However, it was only the early part of the afternoon and we had a lot of exploring yet to do.

We took off from Cascade River and continued to head north on the highway after we had finished getting the trailer all set up for the night. The next spot along the way that we came to was the lovely city of Grand Marais. I have been to and through this town many times. The feature of the area that takes my breath away every time is that drive down the slope toward the middle of town. There you are driving into town from the south on Hwy. 61. You are heading to the spot in the town where the highway takes a rather sharp bend to the northeast. As you drive down the highway you are going deeper into town and spread out beyond the town is Lake Superior. What I think is so cool is the expansive way the lake opens up into the distance beyond the town to the east. There is another place on the north shore that gives me that same kind of feeling each and every time I see it and that is the sight of the cities of Duluth and Superior, Wisconsin, all sprawled out below as you crest over the hill on I-35, near the Spirit Mountain exit at night. The lights of the cities that trace the streets and boulevards and the avenues of man set against the stark blankness of the dark over the lake and harbor create a wondrous site to see. It's a cool site.

Here, in the city of Grand Marais is the beginning of the famous Gunflint Trail. When Grand Marais was just a small Indian village on the lake shore, the natives had already developed the trail to allow access to the many inland lakes and to the Boundary Waters Canoe Area. When the French came to the North Shore in the 1700's, they were exploring the area and they found a rock that was abundant in the region that would make a spark when struck the right way with a piece of steel. This rock was not flint, it was chert; but, the French named the lake they were located by "Gunflint Lake", and hence the name of the trail. This paved road, which is also called Cook County Highway 12, winds through the back country until it ends close to Lake Saganaga on the border with Canada. The Gunflint Trail is a popular access road to the BWCA and there are many outfitters and resorts that can be found along its winding path. One particular trail, which can be found heading east through the woods from the Gunflint, is the trail that leads to Devils Track State Wayside. This is a wayside area located north and east of Grand Marais and is accessed by a trail head that is on the Gunflint Trail. The Devil's Track is a remote area and has many of the north shore trails running through it. There are many nice spots to view the gorge that is created by that small river. When we left Grand Marais to continue our journey up the shore, we came along the bridge that crossed the Devil's Track River. There wasn't much water flowing down through the jumble of rocks and boulders when we passed; but, then again, it is probably a completely different story in the early part of the spring. As I have said before, Julie and I are definitely going to have to come back to the north shore some time this next spring just so we can revisit all of these sites we have been seeing – but, to see them when they are in their glory and to see the tons of water rushing and crashing its way to the big lake.

So, there we were continuing up Hwy. 61. The next spot we stopped at was the Kadunce River State Wayside. This little wayside is very similar to the other waysides on the north shore because it has access to the trail systems and there are trails to follow along this river and others that lead down to the lake. The difference is that this wayside has picnic tables to use and a nice parking area to rest in. The trails that lead down to the lake and the mouth of the river will allow visitors to wonder around on the beach, enjoy the beauty of the site, and an opportunity to see if you can find any agate-type treasures among the rocks and sand.

After visiting the wayside, we hit the road again and in just a few miles we were at the Judge C.R. Magney State Park. This park is located on both sides of the lower section of the Brule River. This state park is another one of the 'jewels' of Minnesota. Much like Old Mill State Park, this park has a small campground with no electric sites. There are only 27 campsites; but, oh, are they beautiful sites. This state park is full of tall standing White Pines and there is sufficient brush, undergrowth, and spacing between the sites to allow for nice seclusion while camping.

We are definitely coming back to this park in the future. The Brule River basically heads straight north and uphill from the camping area and there are two very picturesque waterfalls – the Upper Falls and Devil's Kettle – that can be found along the river trail about 0.7 miles from the parking area. If you are people like us, people who like to camp and get away from all the hub-bub and congestion and not be camping with neighbors only 15 feet away, yet still be afforded the breath-taking views of the north shore – this is the campground for you. As the name implies, this park was named after a man who was a judge. But, then, he was so much more. Judge Magney was a lawyer from Duluth, he was also mayor of Duluth for a period of time, he sat on the Minnesota Supreme Court, and he was a strong advocate for the state parks; especially those along the North Shore. While he was alive, he was involved in getting 11 new areas designated as state parks and waysides along the shores of Lake Superior. Prior to Judge Magney's influential support, this area was a spot where workers from the CCC (Civilian Conservation Corps) had a camp set up. They lived here while they helped to create the infrastructure of the north shore that is still in use today. Many of the bridges, roads, and facilities that are available to visitors of the north shore were created by these men.

After finishing the wonderful visit to the Judge C.R. Magney State Park, we again headed north to the last two spots we wanted to go to on this end of the North Shore – Grand Portage National Monument and Grand Portage State Park. As you drive along the highway heading northeast, it is very evident that the hills and peaks in the area are becoming much taller and prominent. One of the tall peaks along the highway is Mount Josephine. It is over this tall peak that Hwy. 61 travels in order to get to Grand Portage. Up near the very top, the highway department was gracious enough to place a wayside/scenic overlook. If you are on this road, passing by this spot, you must stop. The views of the big lake from this spot are incredible. We took pictures.

When we got down to the bottom on the other side of Mount Josephine, there we were at Grand Portage. Grand Portage is also the home to the reservation for the Grand Portage Band of the Ojibwe. They have a nice community there and a casino to visit. Along with these things there is also the Grand Portage National Monument. There is an interpretive center built on the site of where the Northwest Fur

Trading Company had established a trading post in the early years of the exploration of this region. It was from this stockade and post that the likes of Daniel Greysolon, Sieur duLhut, Alexander Ramsey, and many other explorers of the interior of Canada and the U.S. got their start. But, the local Indians had been quite familiar with this locale for hundreds of years before the French and British arrived. The Ojibwe phrase for the area was – Git-che-O-ni-ga-ming – the great carrying place. For many generations, they had known about the need to portage around the lower end of the Pigeon River. The waterfalls and the rapids along its course were too hard to navigate and to ford around. So, they had established the trail that basically climbs straight up the hills and onto the more navigable waters 4.5 miles inland.

About a half dozen of the buildings that were located at the trading post and the stockade wall have been rebuilt and are now manned by workers who re-enact the daily activities of how life was like on this frontier in the late1700's. This fur trading post was instrumental in moving the huge bounty of furs and trade from the inland, down to the lake, and then off to the east to Montreal and ultimately Europe. After the end of the French and Indian War in the 1763, this area and the rest of Canada came under the rule of the British Empire. The trading post that was located here then became the headquarters for the Northwest Fur Company in 1784 and continued its mission of trade with the Indians and the trappers. This was the central location for trade in the area until 1803, when the company moved its main operations to Fort William, which is located further northeast along the shore and is near the current site of Thunder Bay, Ontario.

There are many artifacts that are on display at the interpretive center and in the buildings inside the stockade. Julie and I had a very enjoyable time wondering around on the grounds and learning about the history of the area. One more site to take in near the National Historic Site is a small wonder of nature that lives on the shore of the lake. There is an ancient, gnarled cedar tree that literally grows up and out of a rock along the shore of the lake. It is thought that this tree may be 300 years old. It is a sacred site to the Ojibwe tribe and in the past gifts of tobacco and other harvests has been left at the foot of the tree to bring good fortune if a person were to be traveling on the big lake. In the language of the tribe, the tree is called – 'Manido-Gree-Shi-Gance.' This gets translated to

– 'spirit-little-cedar.' In 1987, the tribe at Grand Portage was finally able to purchase the land on which the tree is located. Access to the spot is controlled now by the tribe so as to preserve the tree for years to come.

After we finished at the National Historic Site, it was just a short drive along Hwy. 61 until we got to the border. There, about two hundred yards from the customs station is the entrance to Grand Portage State Park. This state park is another of the 'day-use' parks managed by the Department of Natural Resources and the Parks Department. When we were there, the park was in the midst of getting a complete facelift. The office was gone and the parking area was all ripped up. The state was rebuilding everything in the park to make it an even more enjoyable place to visit in the future. When completed, which should be in the summer of 2010, there will be a new office, an interpretive center, new parking lot and toilet facilities.

The trails leading to the river and the two different waterfalls had not changed and they were still open for our use when we got there. We walked down the trail along the river and as we got closer and closer to the High Falls, you could hear the rumble in the distance getting louder and louder. There is a very nice elevated boardwalk that has been built along the trail to make it an even nicer hike up to the High Falls. This is an outstanding waterfall and even late in the year the cascade of water coming over it was impressive. The trail along the river continues on for about another 1.7 miles until it reaches the site of the Middle Falls. The trails wind through the woods along the side of the river and the gorge created by it. It is a lovely hike and not too strenuous and you get the reward of seeing two wonderful waterfalls.

So, there we were. Julie and I had now made it to the third of the four corners of the state. When we were hiking along side the river and down among the rocks, we could have thrown a chunk of wood and hit Canada. You can't get much closer than that.

When we got back to the truck, we climbed aboard and headed back down the highway that had taken us all the way to this spot in the northeast corner. We passed by all of those other sites that we had seen earlier and got back to Cascade River and to our little camper. We parked the truck, had a little meal and as the night closed in around us we settled down to sleep. The next day would find us heading southwest. We would be stopping by a lighthouse, another two waterfalls, and a rocky beach.

So, that next morning when we woke, it was early and there seemed to have developed a mist over the lake and it was trying its best to work its way up the shore and hillside toward the camp. Hardly a soul was moving around besides us that early in the morning, so we took that opportunity to go hiking along the trails that lead out from the camping area. The trail system that is contained within Cascade River State Park is an extensive one. Nearly all the trails in and around this park are here due to the hard work of the men of the CCC and the dedicated staff of the Park's department. There was a camp for the workers near the Cascade River in the 1930's. There are trails for all levels of experience to enjoy. Plus the remote camping sites that can be found along the trails, two tall peaks to traverse for the really experienced hikers, and then the simpler trails near the lake and campgrounds. We hiked around on the trails near the campground so we could see the different waterfalls along the Cascade as it heads to the shore of the lake. It was a nice hike and the waterfalls were beautiful. We took pictures.

Once our little stroll on the trails was completed, we loaded the last of our gear up and headed south down Hwy. 61. We made good time down the highway because it was still early enough in the morning that there was little traffic to have to deal with. But, as we traveled along and got further and further down the shore, the traffic started to build. We got all the way back to the junction of MN Hwy. 1 and just after passing it, we saw the signs for Tettegouche State park. Tettegouche is another large state park along the shore and offers miles and miles of multi-use trails for hiking, skiing, and snowmobiling. There are two different camping areas in the park with one of them being a cart-in camp with remote sites down by the lake and the second being a camp for tents, trailers, and RV's up the hill close to the river. The camp area up on the hill is also closer to the three different sets of waterfalls along the Baptism River. The history behind this chunk of the North Shore is a diverse and long one. Just down the highway is the city of Silver Bay. This city has a rich history in and of itself with regards to the role it played in the iron ore business. Prior to the age of iron and taconite on the north shore, the industry that was king was logging. A logging company from New Brunswick was the first to move into this area and to start to harvest the huge stands of white and Norway pine that used to populate the hills. The names of the lakes around the state park are related to that company's origins out on the east coast and the Algonquin language. After the logging in the region was slowing in the early twentieth century, the land that the park sits on was sold to a couple of different private organizations and was used as a semi-private hunting and fishing reserve up until it was finally legislated in 1979 that the property would become a state park.

There are two points of interest at the spot along Hwy. 61 where the entrance to the park is located. You will also find a large wayside rest area. There are some hiking trails that wind around along the top of the bluff above the shore and other trails that lead all the way down to the shore near the wayside. There are two or three scenic over look spots on these trails that will allow visitors to get a fantastic view of Palisade Head. We took pictures.

After we had had our fill of the beautiful sites and trails around Tettegouche, we once again headed south on the highway. We passed through the city of Silver Bay, then Beaver Bay, and shortly there after we were at one of the most famous spots on the North Shore – Split Rock Lighthouse. The area around Split Rock Lighthouse has a long history too. In the late 1890's and into the 1900's, there was a saw mill set up at the mouth of the Split Rock Creek and it was there to help harvest the red and white pines. There was some commercial fishing that occurred on the lake in this area and the fishermen involved in the activity were living in and around an area that was called – Little Two Harbors. This site was just down the shore about a ½ mile from the lighthouse in the small sheltered cove that exists there. The fishermen were predominantly of Norwegian heritage and their fishing industry lasted well into the 1920's. The lighthouse itself wasn't built until 1909 in response to a terrible storm that occurred in 1905 where six different ships wrecked on the rocks in the area. The lighthouse and its large fog horn building were in operation until 1969 when improvements in navigation equipment on boats and ships made the lighthouse obsolete. The Minnesota Historical Society took over the care and operation of the site in 1976. The state park here at the location of the lighthouse is a park devoted to those campers who want to do their camping in remote 'tent' campsites. Those are the only facilities available for staying at Split Rock. There are large parking areas to accommodate all the visitors that come to see the lighthouse and all of the other restored buildings on the site. There is also a large interpretive center and gift shop set up near the parking lots. The Lake Superior Hiking Trail runs through the state park property up the hill from the lighthouse and the camping area. This state trail can be accessed by the other trails in the park. Another important trail that can be found at Split Rock Lighthouse is the new Gitchi-Gami State Trail. This trail is paved and follows along side of Hwy.61 and is still in the process of being created. The section that runs through Split Rock heads up the shore toward Beaver Bay and all the way down to Gooseberry Falls and beyond. Julie and I have been to Split Rock Lighthouse before and it wasn't necessary for us to stay and take the tour of the grounds and buildings again. So, when we were done taking some pictures, we got back on the road again and headed down the shore to Gooseberry Falls. Prior to getting to Gooseberry, there is a small wayside/scenic overlook site on the shore side of the highway. It is about one mile down the road from the entrance to Split Rock and will give you a chance to take pictures of the lighthouse from a distance.

When we reached Gooseberry Falls, it was a shock to see how much had changed since the last time that Julie and I had been there. I remember visiting this area 25 years ago with friends from college and you parked your car in a small parking area right next to the highway. The bridge was barely able to accommodate the flow of the vehicular traffic let alone the hundreds of visitors that would be on foot wondering around. There was a camping area but most of the time it was full. This is a popular place to visit. Just a few years ago the State decided to do some improvements to the park, the bridge and the area around the falls. If one were to say that Itasca State Park is the 'Grand-daddy' of all the state parks; then, Gooseberry Falls is the 'Showplace.' There is a large interpretive center and gift shop in the park now. Inside this building you can find exhibits telling of the area, wildlife exhibits which include a timber wolf, all manner of birds and smaller mammals, and a large display of mounted fish – trout, bass, walleye, northern, etc. The gift shop is there in the building along with bathrooms for visitors to use. This facility is great and there have been many improvements made to the camping area, too. An amphitheater, picnic areas, trails and beautiful viewing of the lake all add to the uniqueness of this state park. The new bridge that was built can now easily handle all the traffic, both vehicle and human. The new bridge has a catwalk that spans the river. This catwalk hangs underneath the bridge, below the roadway, and allows a great view up the river toward the Upper Falls and down the river toward the Middle and Lower Falls. Up near the highway, the area that used to be a parking lot has now been converted into Gateway Plaza. This plaza is dedicated to children visiting the falls and there are several interpretive sign boards up along the walk area. There is a Memorial Statue in the plaza and scenic overlook sites.

Gooseberry Falls State Park isn't just about those sites near the campgrounds and all the buildings. There are eighteen miles of multi-use trails in the park that can be used during all the seasons. A couple of those trails lead up the hill following the river for about one mile to where they reach the site of Fifth Falls; yet another waterfall that is in this park.

The history of the Gooseberry area closely resembles all the other parks along the North Shore. The area was home to many of the tribes of Indians that have lived along the shore of Superior – the Cree, Dakota, and the Ojibwe. Then, in the 1660's with the arrival of the French began the era of white settlement into the region. The Gooseberry River has been found named on French maps of the north shore as far back as 1670. The Ojibwe had a name for the river – Shab-on-im-i-kan-i-sibi, which translates to a reference to gooseberries. In the late 1800's, the timber industry moved in and a saw mill was also located at the mouth of this river. By the 1920's the trees that were being harvested were gone and then the tourism industry started on the North Shore. Legislation was passed in 1933 in order to preserve the region and especially the area around Gooseberry Falls. In 1934, the CCC came to the river and helped to create the park. There is a long stone wall in the park called 'Castle in the Park.' This 300 foot long retaining wall, the original highway bridge, trails and the campgrounds were built by those men of the CCC. In 1937, Gooseberry Falls was officially named a state park.

After we had finished our visit to Gooseberry, it was time to head home. Once again, it was Sunday afternoon and the new work week was ahead of us. We took the opportunity to drive along the North Shore Scenic Drive, which is the old Highway 61. But, before we got there, we did have to stop and visit the last of the State Waysides that are located along the north shore. Flood Bay State Wayside is just 1 mile northeast of Two Harbors on Hwy. 61. There is a very nice parking area that also has access to a single vault toilet. Flood Bay and the surrounding wetlands in the area offer sanctuary to many different species of bird and mammal. The lake shore is just a few feet away from the parking lot and it is a pebble strewn spot offering ample opportunity to search and possibly find agates.

When we finished with our visit to Flood Bay, we passed through the city of Two Harbors, through two small communities of Knife River and French River, then into the northeast corner of Lester Park – which meant we were back to Duluth. This was a very enjoyable leg to our 'epic journey' and now we are planning where to go next. The next area of the state that needs to be investigated is the southeast corner. Because we took our trip to the North Shore so late in the season, the southeast corner of the state would have to wait for spring and summer of 2010.

In the summer of 2010, we did return to the North Shore. We went with the purpose of checking out all those sites that were being worked on in the summer of 2009. We hooked up our small camper and headed up the highway. We stay at Tettegouche and used that as a base in order to drop the trailer and continue our drive up the shoreline. The improvements to the parking area and the roadside trail at the Ray Berglund Wayside are phenomenal. It allows visitors to see the sites and access the trails in much safer fashion. We continued northeast on the highway and took the opportunity to take many more pictures of the sites along the way. Finally, we crested over Mount Josephine again and made our way back to Grand Portage State park. The improvements to the park have been completed and they are wonderful. The parking areas for visitors are nice and large. There are paved walkways all around leading to the picnic area, the river, and the new visitor/interpretive center. The improvements to the park have made this destination in the northeast corner of the state much nicer.

The next leg of the epic journey was going to take us to the southeast corner of the state. When we started out heading down the road, we left our little cabin in the woods at about 1pm and made our way to the Twin Cities. Being that we live just south of Aitkin, we are about 100 miles north of Minneapolis and we were able to take Hwy 169 straight down to I-94 and that would then get us to I-35 which we would follow south to Albert Lea, Minnesota. It was shortly after traveling through Maple Grove and heading past Plymouth that we realized that we had lived too long in a wooded, rural area. We had actually left our home just at the right time in order to get us to the Cities just as the heaviest of the Friday afternoon traffic hit the highways. We had to deal with a little bit of a slow down around Hwy 100 and France Ave.; but, once we got past there, it was smooth sailing the rest of the way through the metro area. We passed through Burnsville and were on our way south.

It was still just a little after mid afternoon, when we were driving down I-35 and found that we were approaching Faribault. We had plenty of time to still make it to Albert Lea and make a small side trip at the same time. So, while we were passing by Faribault, we took the exit for MN Hwy. 60 to the west and drove about 14 miles and came to the location of Sakatah State Park. This state park is located along the Cannon River, between the towns of Morristown and Waterville.

This area of the state and along the Cannon River is the ancestral home of the Wahpekute band of the Dakota tribe. The wide spot in the Cannon River that was named Sakatah by the white settlers has always been a lake. Historically, the lake was larger. On the east end of Upper Sakatah, there is a spit of land that juts out from the north bank and another chunk of land that juts out from the south creating a narrow passage for the channel of the river to flow through. A bridge and a road way were created to cross at that spot. This is a natural 'choke point' and it has helped to keep higher water levels in what became Upper Sakatah to the west and separated Lower Sakatah to the east there along the Cannon River.

In the 1820's, Alexander Faribault explored through this area of the state and set up a fur trading post on the river near the city that bears his name. Faribault established many other trading posts and one of them may have been along the shores of this lake.

Besides all of the beautiful scenery, the rolling hills and farmland and the lakes and river, one of the special attractions in the area of the park is the Sakatah Singing Hills State Bicycle Trail. The trail is built on the old railroad beds that were built back in the 1870's and 1880's. The state trail is a multi-use trail for hiking, biking, and snowmobiling. The state trail is 39 miles long and runs on the railroad bed between Faribault and Mankato.

The park itself has plenty to draw people to it to use for recreation. There is a boat landing for the public to use. There is also a fishing pier out into the lake for campers to use. There is approximately ten kilometers of other trails to use for hiking in the park to see the rolling terrain that the park sits on. The park has an excellent campground with very nice sites. It is easy to get to this park and with the good fishing that can be found on the lakes and river – this park must get a lot of use.

We got down to Albert Lea and found our way to the east side of the city and the state park we were going to spend the night at. Myre – Big Island State Park sits on an old glacial end-moraine. With the assistance of archaeologists, it has been found the humans have been living in the area of the lake for thousands of years. Albert Lea Lake is a lake of over 2500 acres and it has a large (116 acre) island on the northeast side of it. The island was made a park in 1947 due to the efforts of one of the residents of Albert lea and since then, the state has continued to add to it size and created the park that exists today. Myre – Big Island is a lovely park with the surrounding rolling fields, the lake, and the woodlands. It allows a very enjoyable camping experience. Julie especially liked the great shower facilities that were there to use. I spent some time driving around on the island and some of the other roads in the park. Julie walked along on some of the trails. We both saw a lot of the different wildlife that can be found in the park and out on the lake. I was very impressed with some of the campsites that were out on the island. When the sun was setting in the west, I was given a lovely view of the sunlight reflecting off of the water. For that simple reason alone, I can imagine that those campsites on the island, where I saw that view, are reserved quickly by people coming to visit this state park.

The next morning, we packed up our gear, hooked up the little trailer, and made our way east toward our next destination – Lake Louise Sate Park.

We left Albert Lea and headed east on I-90. We drove through the city of Austin about 15 minutes later. Just after we got past Austin, we took a left turn and headed southeast on MN Hwy 56, which would take us straight to a town by the name of LeRoy.

I would like to ask the readers to please think back to earlier in the story when I was describing the fields that we drove by up in the Red

River area in northwestern Minnesota. Also, recall the fields that I told you about when we were driving around over by Lakefield and Windom. As we drove toward LeRoy, we were driving past huge cornfields. We were driving past huge farms. The homestead would be up a long gravel driveway that had to be at least a half mile long or more. The place where the buildings were was easy to identify because it was the place where all the trees were found; the rest of the area was devoted to fields and these fields were covered in corn and soybeans.

After about 20 miles driving on MN Hwy. 56, we arrived at LeRoy. This small quiet town is located about as close to the southern border of the state as you can get. When we were driving up to the town, in the distance we could see that there were wind generators south of town. So, while we drove through town, we got to an intersection of a county road that headed south and turned there. I don't think we drove a mile before we crossed the state line. This was an interesting road because right there at the state line the road took a sudden 90 degree turn to the east and continued for about 100 yards and then took another 90 degree turn to the south. This tiny little section of roadway was given the name – State Line road. The road even had a street sign indicating that name. So, there we were. We had driven into Iowa. Kind of like a mirror image of the mistaken little trip we took into Canada for about 100ft. back in July of 2009 in Noyes.

As we were driving back to town, there was an interesting display set up on the west side of the road. It looked like some kind of historic marker or some kind of important site. There was a large concrete sidewalk leading out into a grassy lawn and at the end of the concrete there was a bench and some display boards. We pulled over to check it out. This display was a representation of the wind generators that could be seen south of town. The sidewalk that was laid out across this lawn was the same dimensions as the towers that the wind generators sat on top of. A shorter, second side walk off to the side and connecting to the end of the first walkway was the same dimensions as the wind vanes on the tower. The display boards explained the entire site and tried in simple detail to explain how the towers generated electricity. These towers are amazing pieces of engineering and these tall towers – the ones that have a tower 265 ft tall – generate enough electrical power that one tower can supply the needs of up to 200 homes. The wind farm is being built in stages and when it is complete, there will be 182 wind turbines up and generating electrical power.

After finishing reading about the wind generator project, we got back into the truck, passed back through town and as we neared the west end of town there was County Road 14 heading north and we turned there. One and a half miles later, we were at the entrance of Lake Louise State Park. This is a small park but it is nestled next to the lake and the two small branches of the Iowa River that come together in the park to help create the lake. Lake Louise holds the distinction of being the oldest continuous use park that we have here in the state. The area around Leroy was surveyed and platted in 1853 and soon after the town got its start. Originally the town was located right up near the river because soon after the town got its start, a grist mill was built next to the river and the people dammed the river in order to give the mill power. This set up with the mill and the town near the lake lasted only a couple of years. When the railroad came into the area, they built the tracks a mile and a half south of the mill and the dam. After a time, the town migrated down to where the rails were and the grist mill ultimately closed. The family that owned the mill and the land by the lake donated some of the property to the town to use as a recreational area. The lake was named after one of the members of the family that donated the property and the town named the area - Wildwood. In 1962, the town of Leroy, donated the park to the sate and for a number of years the state acquired more and more property around the lake and the rivers to a total of 1,168 acres. The park offers much to be seen and experienced. There are species of wild flower that are on the endangered list in Minnesota, plus the dozens of other wildflowers that can be seen blooming in the park during the spring and summer. This beautiful little park in southern Minnesota would be a good place to go if you would like to find a nice, quiet, out-of-the-way place to spend some time.

After we finished with our visit to Lake Louise, we headed north on County Road 14 for about 6 miles and then cut cross country on some of the gravel roads heading to our next destination – Forestville/Mystery Cave State Park.

This next state park exists in two parts about four miles apart and both parts are about 7 miles southeast of the town of Spring Valley. We stuck to the back roads and came up to the park from the west. Just after we passed over the county line separating Mower County from Fillmore County, we came upon the small town of Ostrander. This small town is just west of U.S. Highway 63 about 7 miles north of the Iowa border. As we passed the town and crossed over the highway, it was apparent that we were also crossing into a different part of the state. The south, southwest, and the western part of the state are dominated by the rolling, open fields of the farmland. These areas of the state were where the prairies started and continued to the west and south. In the southeast corner of the state you can find a region that is dominated by the steeply cut river valleys and sandstone bluffs. This is the start of a region that encompasses most of this part of the state and continues down into Iowa and Wisconsin. It is referred to as – the driftless area. During the last period of glacial advance, the glaciers stopped north and west of here and as they melted, the melt water ran across the landscape and began to cut the deep ravines and valleys that can be seen throughout the region. As the waters rushed south, they cut down and through layers of soil and rock that had been laid down hundreds of millions of years earlier. The sandstone and limestone bluffs are a testament to a time when this region was a shallow sea.

The limestone that can be found in the area is very prone to erosion and is easily dissolved by water. Limestone and other types of sedimentary rock make up areas that are sometimes referred to as 'karst' topography. Natural cracks and fractures in the rock allow water to flow through into subterranean areas. After the passage of millions of years this water can open these small cracks and fractures into huge caverns and cave systems. On the surface, one may not even have a clue that hundreds of feet below them there would be a huge cave or a flowing underground river. Sedimentary rocks like limestone and dolostone are very common types of rocks which can be found all over the world. They create the same type of 'karst' topography in those other areas of the world. From time to time, you might see an item in the news that reports that a 'sinkhole' had suddenly opened up and was responsible for swallowing up a car or a house. Sinkholes are some of the prime indicators of karst topography. These sinkholes, as they develop, are just one of many surface features that can be seen that would indicate an even more expansive system of caves, grottos, and waterways – under the surface. This is what exists in the southeast corner of our state. Forestville-Mystery Cave State Park is a spot that you will be able to see first-hand this special type of land feature.

Forestville was once a small town that was nestled near the banks of the South Branch of the Root River. Today, some of the buildings from the town have been restored and volunteers come during the summer months to act out the parts of residents of the town from 1899. Visitors to the park can stroll through the town area and down by the river. There are over seventeen miles of hiking trails to hike along with several scenic over look spots to take in the surrounding scenery. A person should be warned however that the trails are not for people who are novice hikers or for people that may have medical conditions that would cause them to have trouble with strenuous activity. Some of the trails climb right up along the contours of the bluffs and these trails get quite steep. Forestville is one of the most popular state parks for people who want to bring their horses along and do some trail riding. There is a large campground set up across the river for those campers who bring horses. There over are 60 sites at the campground and over 20 have electric hookups. From that camp, there is easy access to the fifteen miles of riding trails in the park.

There are many activities that draw people to the park. A person might visit the park in order to try fishing the Root River and the two smaller creeks that empty into the Root River in the park. Like many of the rivers and creeks in this corner of the state, these waterways offer good opportunity to catch Brown and Brook trout. Many people visit the park to do some bird watching. If you visit the park to hike the trails, one of the many sites to definitely see is the Big Spring. This spring is the source of Canfield Creek. There is a trail named for the spring and it follows the creek for about two miles south of the main campgrounds. It is well worth the hike along the trail to see the spring and the crystal clear water.

Most people would be quite satisfied with going to a state park that had all of these activities to choose from; but, this state park goes one better and also offers the wonders of Mystery Cave. Jump in your car and drive the 4 miles west to the site of the other part of this state park. At the site of Mystery Cave, there is a large interpretive center with a wonderful educational display inside, a large picnic area outside and then there are tours of the cave that occur throughout the day during the summer and on weekends in the spring and fall. Taking the tour of the cave is highly recommended.

Julie and I really enjoyed our stay at Forestville-Mystery Cave State Park taking in all the sights and activities; but, we had to move on down the road and head to the next park – Beaver Creek Valley State Park. We had stopped by the Ranger's office on our way out of the park and they informed us that the easiest way to get over to the area of Caledonia area was to go south until we got to MN Hwy. 44 and take that east. We did exactly what they said. I was not aware that there was such a large population of Amish in this area of the state. As we traveled east on Hwy. 44, we saw several carriages along the road side selling quilts and other crafts. We drove past many farms that were owned by these quiet people. We traveled through the towns of Harmony, Mabel, and Spring Grove on our way to finally arriving at Caledonia. We travelled past beautiful farm fields and through the bluffs and valleys of the region. We stopped at one of the popular dining establishments in Caledonia to eat lunch before we headed over to the state park.

We left Caledonia and headed west for about five miles and found ourselves entering a lovely small state park that is nestled at the bases of some of the bluffs in the area. Beaver Creek and the state park is representative of the same land features that we talked about over by Forestville. The bluffs and the valleys in the area are all part of the 'karst' topography and within the borders of this park the water that creates Beaver Creek literally bubbles up out of the ground. Possibly, the number one reason for visitors coming to this park is to fish the brown trout that are found in the river. Now, don't get me wrong, this park has trails to hike, birds and wildlife to see, and great campsites to use and would be a lovely spot to come spend some vacation time enjoying. But, Beaver Creek is an 'A' rated trout stream. It is very easy to get to the spot where the creek begins. We were driving along one of the roads in the park, passed by a small picnic area and literally drove across the creek to get to the other side where the campsites are located. We headed down this small road past the camping sites and got to a turn-around spot. We were able to park the truck there and took a short walk down a trail to the spot where out of the ground in three different spots – you could see the water bubbling up from under the rocks. The water was as crystal clear as you can imagine and that spot on the ground was a naturally shaped bowl, so a small pool of water was there and then it trickled off to the north creating the stream. As we looked further down the creek, you could see more and more of these small water sources bubbling out of the rocks along side of the creek and up on the small hillside to the east. This was the beginning spot for Beaver Creek. The creek continues to pick up more and more sources for water as it snakes its way further through the park. Some years ago, a study of the creek was done and there were trout found living in the stream only 600 feet from the start of the creek. As I have already said before, it is redundant to say this is a beautiful state park because all of the state parks are beautiful. However, this park is very unique because of this trout stream and that makes it very special. We had a great time visiting that small park by Caledonia and we will return in the future to spend more time there camping and possibly trying to catch some of those elusive brown trout. We left the park and made our way back to town and then headed northeast toward our next destination – Great River Bluffs State Park. When we arrived at Caledonia and made our way over to visit the park we had finally made it to the fourth corner of the state.

We drove northeast and crossed the Root River valley and then found ourselves traveling along U.S. Hwy. 61 south of Winona, Minnesota. Great River Bluffs State Park sits on top of a couple of the bluffs overlooking the Mississippi River valley. We were on Hwy. 61 and there is a road that leads up to the top of the bluff from the highway. What we didn't realize was that the road leading up the bluff was still under construction, it was all gravel and evidence of recent work being done on the road. Oh yes – it was also very steep. This road we had turned onto just went up, up, and up. Finally, we made it to the top where the road finally crested the top of the bluff and I was very thankful that we were only hauling our little 12 foot camper. If, we would have had a bigger rig or a large camper in tow, the drive up that steep grade would have been much more interesting. There is nothing wrong with accessing the park from Hwy. 61, but if you are driving a larger rig – I would suggest using the I-90 entrance. This entranced is much easier and simple to get to.

When we arrived at the entrance to the park, it was easy to see that the state was in the midst of making many improvements. There was a building that was under construction just a short distanced from the small Ranger's shack. There was another public facility being constructed in front of us along the side of the road as we were getting ourselves checked in for the night. We made our way down the road toward the camping area and that was about two miles away. We were able to see some good views of the river valley as we were driving down the road; but, about 2/10's of a mile from the camping area is a scenic overlook of the valley that will just about take your breath away. We drove past without stopping, but we knew we would be coming back in order to stop by and enjoy the view from the overlook spot.

We got to the campgrounds and found our site. All most all of the sites were nice and level with good shade and overhead cover. There was abundant undergrowth between the sites; so, we felt nicely isolated from our neighbors. We got the camper unhooked and set up for our nights stay at the park and then headed back out of the park to do some exploring of the river valley.

We were driving out on the same road we drove in on and after just a short distance we came to the scenic overlook spot. The park service has widened the road a little bit right at this spot but it will only accommodate one or two cars at a time. When we drove up to the site, there was already a car there and a young couple was standing near the bench trying to take a picture. Well, with a small digital camera and trying to get a picture of the two of them and the scene in the background was causing them some difficulty. As I stepped out of the pickup, I volunteered to take the picture for them, which I did. But, the picture didn't turn out so good and I was kind of disappointed. This young couple had relayed the story of the significance of this scenic overlook to Julie and me. You see, approximately a year earlier this young man had proposed marriage to this young woman at this very spot. What they wanted to do was to get a picture of themselves at the spot – one year later. As I said, I was disappointed with how the picture had turned out on their camera when it suddenly struck me – I had in my hands a top of the line Nikon and I suspected it would take a great picture. I had them smile really big and the picture – well, it turned out great. Julie suggested that the couple give us their email address so that we could email the picture directly to them right from our camera. Later that night, when I had the laptop computer all set up and I had downloaded all the pictures we had taken that day, I simply emailed the file with their picture directly to them. Later, we received a return email stating they got the picture and they liked it.

The happy incident of meeting this young couple is just one example of many of the little things that has happened to Julie and I as we have traveled all over this state visiting the state parks. It is the special occasions like this one, or seeing the albino deer at Mille Lacs Kathio State Park, or meeting the same Park Ranger at Lac Qui Parle and then seeing her again the next day at Camden that have helped to keep our travels fun and exciting.

We headed out from the park that afternoon to do some exploring of the river valley and exploring the city of Winona. I had never been to Winona before and we enjoyed driving around and seeing what the city had to offer. We also realized that we were very close to another place we needed to visit. Just a little way north of Winona on Hwy. 61 is the John A. Latsch State Park. Getting to this small state park took us on an adventure that allowed us to see areas of the state that I don't think anyone was meant to see.

Earlier in the year, Julie and I had decided to update our cell phones. We changed the company that we had previously and we went with a service that I had been told by a co-workers had pretty good reception up in our neck of the woods by Aitkin. With the upgrade to a new cell phone company, we were able to buy fancy new phones that come with all sorts of bells, whistles, and gadgets. On the phones, we have the capability of getting on the internet and we are able to use a map program that is available. It is pretty cool to be able to have the device just talk you all the way to your destination. We had used it several times and it had taken us exactly to the location desired. So, while I was driving, Julie had plugged in the name 'John A. Latsch State Park' and we followed the directions the program gave us.

We were about seven miles north of Winona and Minnesota City when the program on the cell phone told us to turn left and up a gravel road. The name of the road was 'Whitman-Doerring Road'. According to the program, it was saying that the entrance to the state park was four and a half miles further ahead. We continued to drive and started heading up the hill. We had not gone more than a mile when I started to get concerned that there was something wrong with the directions we were following. When we had turned off of Hwy. 61, we had turned onto a gravel road. Now, after just one mile, it was no longer a road we were on – more like a driveway. At one point as we continued on, we passed by a home on the left and I swear we drove through their front yard. This was strange; but, we didn't question it. We just continued along the path we were following. It wouldn't be long before we got to a point where the road had deteriorated into little more than a path. As we continued up the valley, we did pass by a very nice alpaca farm that was located there. We saw all sorts of different colored alpacas in the farm yard and grazing on the grass on the fields in the valley. The farm was off to the left on the north side of the valley and the driveway/road we were on was on the south side of the valley. We hadn't gone more than a quarter mile further up the road when it took a sharp turn and began to hug the hill on my side of the truck. Julie, trying to sound casual, told me that if by chance a deer would run out onto the trail in front of us, I was supposed to turn into the hill. I, wondering why she would make such a statement, asked her why and then looked out her passenger side window. Immediately, I knew the reason why. On her side of the road, the hill fell directly away and it was a very steep drop – all the way to the bottom of the valley. There was absolutely no shoulder on that side and the only thing there to slow you down if you did accidently go over the side and fall were the trees and shrubs growing up out of the side of the bluff.

Now, I finally accepted the fact that the directions we had been following were horribly wrong. The farther we crawled up the trail on the side of the bluff, the more that the trail we were on continued to deteriorate. There was lots of tree cover and shade over the trail and that was probably one of the important facts why there weren't more 'wash-out' problems on the trail. As we continued to follow the trail up the hill, I knew I just had to tough it out and make it to the top, where ever that was going to bring us; because, there was no way I was going to try and back down the trail we were on. This trail in a way reminded me of driving out of Yellowstone National Park on the East Entrance Road. There are points along that drive where the road has virtually been carved out of the side of the mountain, with sheer rises on one side and sheer drop offs on the other. Just as the knuckles on my hands were turning a brilliant shade of white (from grasping the steering wheel so tight) we crested over the top edge of the bluff. We turned a slight corner and there we were on the top of the bluff with a soy bean field on one side and an alfalfa field on the other. Off in the distance, I could see a farm – the main house, barn, machine shed, and two silos. I asked Julie how much farther did the program say we had to go and she said 'One Mile'. I told her that if it was one mile, it would put us right into the front yard of that farm. Well, that was exactly where we ended up – in the driveway of the farm. There we sat staring at the farm around us and absolutely nothing around or near that remotely looked like a state park. We had a good laugh. If there was anyone home at that farm and they saw us sitting there, they were probably scratching their head and asking "Why?" when we turned the truck around and headed back down the hill on the same trail. We picked our way back down the hillside and past all the sites we saw just minutes earlier and got back to Hwy. 61. We sat there trying to decide what had gone wrong with the directions. We knew we were near the park and decided to turn north and drive just a little further on the highway. We hadn't driven more than about one mile further when we drove right by the entrance to the park – big sign, vault toilets and all.

We made a quick turn-around at the next intersection and drove into John A. Latsch State Park. John Latsch was a successful businessman from Winona and it is said that he loved all things about the outdoors; but, most of all, he loved to fish on the Mississippi River. The park is dedicated to him. The entrance to the park is most easily accessed from the south bound lanes of Hwy. 61. There is a small picnic area and a vault toilet. There are some remote campsites to use at the park and a trail that leads up the small valley to some overlook spots. If you are in for a hike up hill that will reward you with a great view of the river valley, this is a good spot to stop and visit. This park is only a little over 400 acres in size; but, it is a beautiful spot or wayside to stop at and take a break from driving.

The next park that we went to visit after our adventure trying to find the John A. Latsch State Park was to drive west and go to a wonderful state park just north of the city of St. Charles, Minnesota. This park is Whitewater. Whitewater State Park is located on Hwy. 74 between the towns of St. Charles and Elba. This park is another one of the great state parks that can be found in this region of sandstone bluffs and winding river valleys. The park and the surrounding area of the state are fantastic examples of the geologic forces that occurred in order to create what we see today. The dolomite and limestone that sit on top of the sandstone were first laid down millions of years ago. The forces of nature worked and worked since then and carved the landscape that we see today. Humans first moved into these sheltered valleys as far back as the last ice age. These tribes of people found subsistence on the animals that lived near the glaciers like the giant buffalo, the North American camel, reindeer, and mammoths. They found shelter in these deep valleys that the melt water from the glaciers helped to carve. Humans have continued to live in this region since. The Mdewakanton band of the Sioux named the river that flows through this valley 'Minneiska'. This term means 'whiter water', hence the name of the park. The Indians gave this place that name because of some clay deposits that can be found here in the river valley. When this clay is eroded during heavy rains and snow melt, the particles enter the water and give the stream a pale color.

Today, the forces of nature are still in control in the valley, as they always have been. When white settlers moved into the region in the early parts of the 19th century they brought with them the farming techniques that helped to transform this land. However, these practices only helped to increase the effects of erosion and soil loss due to natural forces. In 2007, a large storm system moved into the southeast corner of Minnesota and the valleys in and around the state park received over eleven inches of rainfall. The flooding and landslides that occurred devastated large parts of the park and the valleys. One of the mudslides even changed the course of the Whitewater River. The state of Minnesota had to spend a great deal of money in order to repair the damage that was done. They did a very good job and today the park is a wonderful place to visit and enjoy. There are miles and miles of hiking trails, an interpretive center on the grounds of the park where you can learn more about the 2007 flood, and fishing for trout on another one of the many excellent fishing streams in this area of the state. The park is totally family oriented. There are trails accessible to all members of the family, playgrounds, the nature center, and much more for people to enjoy when they come to camp.

Whitewater State Park is a park that fits in the same category as that of Itasca, St. Croix, and Gooseberry Falls. Everyone in the family would find an enjoyable time here. It is easy to get to and has all the amenities needed for a great outdoor experience.

After spending some very enjoyable time at Whitewater, we moved on to the next park to visit and were surprised to find out that it is only about 11 miles away to the northwest. Upstream on one of the branches of the Whitewater River you will come across a small section of land that was donated to the state by one the states senators – James A. Carley. The intent of the Senator and one other family, who also donated land to the state, was to preserve a native stand of white pines that grow on the north side of the river. The stand of white pines had survived through all of the years during the settlement of the state and on through the years when forestry and logging were the number one industries. However, even with all the efforts of man to preserve the trees, the forces of nature stepped in and dealt a devastating blow to the pine grove. In 1957, a large hailstorm caused much damage to the trees. Some had to be selectively harvested due to the damage done. Most of the trees survived and with careful management by the Park Service, the grove of pines still survives and can be viewed from the picnic area or enjoyed by walking along the trail that leads through the grove. This is a great little park that is in an 'out-of-the-way' location. The park has the basic amenities available like vault toilets and fresh water; but, everything else would need to be brought in by the campers. The trails in the park are designed to be multi-use and are used a lot during the winter months for cross country skiing. Because of the topography of the area these trails have a wide variety of difficulty ranging from easy to most difficult. Many of the trails have overlook spots to stop at and enjoy the scenery. The park is nestled inside of a large loop in the North Branch of the Whitewater River and so it is also very popular for people who are looking to do some trout fishing. This is a small, quiet park where you would definitely get away from it all.

The next park on our itinerary took us north on I-35 toward Owatonna. We took the opportunity to drive U.S. Hwy. 14 west and passed through more of the beautiful farmland of southeastern Minnesota. We passed through the city of Rochester, passed by Kasson and Dodge Center, and finally made it to Owatonna. Unfortunately, we weren't paying attention to the map like we should have because when we were on U.S. Hwy. 14;

we passed by several roads that would have taken us to the park. Well, we know better now.

Rice Lake State Park is located about 7 miles east of Owatonna on Cty. Hwy. 19. The lake and the surrounding area was part of the oak savanna that existed here and across southeastern Minnesota and eastern Iowa. The savanna was an area where the border between the forested areas of the east met with the prairies to the west. This area was scattered with small groves of oaks when white settlers first moved into the region. The Indians had been using the resources of Rice Lake for many generations. The name of the lake gives hint to one of the primary items that was sought here. Rice Lake is also one of the sources of the Zumbro River. The Zumbro and its branches snake their way across the landscape of southeastern Minnesota through Rochester and continue north and east until it empties into the Mississippi River near the small town of Kellogg.

At the park, there are over 7 miles of multi-use trails to be used by visitors to enjoy nature, bird watching, and cross country skiing. The lake and its wild rice are a huge draw for migratory waterfowl and the wooded areas surrounding the lake allow good shelter for deer and many other animal species. The park has a very nice campground with nicely shaded sites. There are over a dozen remote campsites that can be accessed by the trails or by crossing the lake in a boat or canoe. There is a nice picnic area, a playground for kids, and with the city of Owatonna just a short drive away helps to create the family atmosphere that makes this park a popular place to visit.

After we had finished our visit to Rice Lake State Park, we made our way back to I-35 and headed north. Our next stop would take us up the highway and then through the city of Faribault. We traveled out of the northeast corner of the city on Hwy. 20 and followed that road for about 4 miles. At the small town of Canon City, Hwy. 20 intersects with Hwy. 27 and we took Hwy. 27 east. After driving about 5 miles east, I started to look to the north and there I could see a very large expanse of woods. After driving through so many miles of the southern part of the state and becoming accustomed to seeing woods only where there was a water source like lakes and rivers, or near homesteads, farms, or towns; it was a surprise to see such a large tract of woodland.

About one mile south of the southeast corner of the park, Hwy. 27

turned north and took us one mile north to the intersection with the road that leads into the state park. At that intersection, the small town of Nerstrand, Minnesota, is just three quarters of a mile to the east. We turned west and headed into the woods.

The story behind this large section of diverse woods is a part of the larger story of this part of the continent and the ecosystems that can be found in the region. As I have already written about in this story, Minnesota is the meeting place for several different bioregions. There are the boreal pine forests to the north. There is the rolling prairie to the west and southwest. There is 'the big woods' that moved into Minnesota from Wisconsin in the east and started near Red Wing and Stillwater moving west and northwest to Fergus Falls, Pelican Rapids, and Detroit Lakes. Finally, the oak savanna (which we were just discussing on the previous pages) helped to create the border between 'the big woods' and the prairie. These make up the major bioregions that can be found here. The 'big woods' was a variety of forest that was made up of specific varieties of tree species. They included: sugar maples, butternuts, bitternut hickory, ironwood, and white ash. These were the trees that made up the huge forested areas of southern Wisconsin and had moved into Minnesota and had created the large band of deciduous forests between the boreal pines of the north and the prairies of the south and west.

One of the rangers at the park was nice enough to explain to me how the forest that was being protected by the state park came to be. He pointed out that the oak savanna was instrumental in getting this patch of 'big woods' this far south and separated from the rest. When oaks begin to spread out and as a grove grows larger and larger, the trees naturally set themselves up in rows. There will be a row of trees that will grow to maturity and when they drop their acorns - these will help to form the next row of trees, which coincide with the outer edges of the branches on the previous row. As this continues, the savanna expands and then this allows the 'big woods' species to expand further and establish themselves into new areas. Over the course of hundreds and thousands of years, the savanna helped the big woods steadily move south until it reached this area of the state.

So, here, forty five miles south of where the rest of the big woods existed was a patch of over 5,000 acres of hardwood forest. When the first white settlers moved into the state this was a singular vibrant forest all on its own. Speculation has it that the natural forces that help to control the prairie may have been responsible for separating this piece of the big woods from the rest. Grass fires, which help to keep a prairie healthy and stable, may have moved in and burned the areas between this section of 'big woods' near Nerstrand and the larger portion of the 'big woods' to the north. When the white settlers moved into Minnesota in the early 1800's and farming became the predominant industry in this area, many of the acres of big woods were harvested by those settlers. The harvesting of the hardwoods in this area continued until the mid 1940's when the park was finally established. Today, the 1280 acres of 'big woods' in this park would be special if only for the reason that it is still here and represents the forests that used to exist. But, there is another reason why this forest stand is special – it still retains the oak species.

So, in the north and east, the 'big woods' was made up of sugar maples, butternuts, bitternut hickory, iron wood, and white ash. Here, the park boasts all of those species plus white, red, and scrub oaks.

The state park has a very nice camping area, a large picnic area with a play-ground, and there are miles of hiking trails that can be used year round. Prairie Creek runs through the park on both the north and south sides. Along one of the trails on the north side of the park, you can see a small waterfall named Hidden Falls. West of the main entrance into the park on Hwy. 29, you can pull in to a small parking area and hike in to four remote campsites set up along the trails.

It would be an understatement to say that there is a lot of tree cover on the sites in the campground. All of the sites are easily accessible and there are many sites that can be used by visitors bringing RV's and large trailers.

We only spent a short period of time at Nerstrand Big Woods State Park. We had to get back on the road and head north to get home. In a state that has over 14,000 lakes and ponds inside of its borders, with more rivers and streams then you can shake a stick at, it is difficult to find a state park that doesn't have a water resource as part of its central theme. This state park is unique in that respect. The Prairie Creek runs through the park but the park is here because of the trees.

One of the last parks that we went to visit is one of the most remote of the state parks. Julie and I left our house early in the morning on a

Friday after I had finished one of my night shifts at the hospital. We were heading north.

Like many families in the state, we own a boat. We have a 16 foot Lund with a 20 horse Johnson outboard motor on the back and this rig works very well for any fishing and recreating we want to do on the smaller lakes around our house. On bigger lakes, like Mille Lacs, it would all depend on how hard the wind was blowing and what the size of the waves were on the lake as to whether we would take our boat out. We were heading to Lake of the Woods, our little Lund wouldn't nearly be sufficient to handle that lake. My sister and her husband, Kathy and Mike, own a larger boat and it has a nice large outboard motor on the back and would give us the power and size we would need in order to cross twenty miles of Lake of the Woods and reach our destination – Garden Island State Recreation Area.

The history of this region is long and has been influenced by many different groups of people. At least three different native tribes lived in the region and used the lake as a resource for food. The Cree tribe lived here at one time and they were displaced by the Dakota as they were pushed further west out the region surrounding Lake Superior. The Dakota were eventually replaced by the Ojibwe. The Ojibwe were feeling the pressure of the ever increasing population of white settlers as they moved further and further into the interior of the continent in the 1700's and 1800's.

During the late decades of the 1600's, the French Voyagers made their way into the central part of the continent setting up trading posts to move valuable furs back to Europe. The first French explorer to make it into the area was Jacques Du Noyon. He set up a trading post on the Rainy River not far from the big lake in 1688 and is said to have been the first European to see Lake of the Woods. Many more explorers and traders traveled into the area and in 1732, Pierre Gaultier, with a flotilla of fifty canoes with men and equipment, paddled into Lake of the Woods and established Fort St. Charles about 12 miles northwest of Garden Island.

For many centuries and into the European Colonial Period, England and France had always been competitors; if not, outright combatants. It was no different in the mid 1700's. In 1763, the French and English had just finished fighting the Seven Years War. In colonial North America, and in our American history, we know the Seven Years War by a different name – The French and Indian War. With the ending of that conflict, much of what was once part of France in North America then became part of England. Oh, except that rather large chunk that France sold to the United States in 1803, the Louisiana Purchase. The forts and many of the fur trading posts that had been established by the French were abandoned and England sent in more of its own explorers. The control of these areas in the upper Mississippi River Valley by foreign powers was soon to end. In September of 1783, the Treaty of Paris was signed by the British government and the United States bringing an end to the Revolutionary War. In this document, it was agreed that the northern boundary of the United States would be set at the 49th Parallel. This then became the border that separated the newly emancipated colonies from the British holdings further north.

If you were to look at a map of the United States, it is very easy to recognize the 49th Parallel, it is that nice straight line that makes the northern border of the states of Washington, Idaho, Montana, North Dakota, and into Minnesota. But, that nice straight line gets all screwed up when it reaches Lake of the Woods. The explanation for this involves mistakes made in mapping the Upper Mississippi River Valley and the actual wording in the Paris Treaty. When the treaty was signed and ratified, it was thought that the Mississippi River continued to run further north. They never knew that the river actually turned south at Lake Bemidji. In the language of the Treaty, it stated that the starting place for 49th Parallel border would be in line with the northwest corner of Lake of the Woods. So, a survey team was sent out to the lake and the team was led a very famous surveyor, mapmaker, and explorer – David Thompson. This man was instrumental in the exploration of the United States Northwest and most of Canada, west of Lake Superior. He identified the northwest corner of Lake of the Woods and then surveyed a line straight south until he reached the 49th Parallel. It was his actions in identifying the border on that side of the lake that created the Northwest Angle – that small chunk of Minnesota that isn't directly connected to Minnesota. In truth, the Northwest Angle isn't unique in this matter; there are three other spots along the northern border that are 'cut off' in similar fashion by the border agreement.

Today, most of the Northwest Angle is part of one of the Red River

Indian Reservations. Garden Island, 762 acres in size, is located southeast of the Angle. The island is a sand and gravel mass that is tree covered and offers good habitat for many of the bird species that spend the summer at the lake. There are six different Bald Eagle nests that have been identified on the island. While we were on the lake we saw dozens of different bird species. We saw nesting ducks, gulls, terns, and other species along the shore lines. While crossing the water, we saw many pelicans, loons, and cormorants.

We had arrived at Zippel Bay State Park and used the boat landing there to launch the boat. The bay is created by what appears to be a natural breakwater that nearly covers the entire opening where the various branches of Zippel Creek empty into the lake. We motored our way slowly out of the bay and then into the larger portion of the lake. Thank God we had the larger boat and a big outboard on the back. The winds were blowing from the northwest at between ten and fifteen miles per hour and that was creating some nice wave action. The instant we hit left the bay, we were buffeted by the waves and it continued this way for about the first ten miles as we headed straight north toward the island. Garden Island is just over 20 miles straight north of Zippel Bay. We used our GPS system to help keep us on the right bearing and just under one half hour later we reached some smoother water. This allowed us to go a little faster and we made it to the island in just about one hour. On the eastern tip of the island, on the north shore there are several docks that are placed out into the water. There are five or six picnic tables and fire rings available for visitors to use to prepare a shore lunch while visiting the island. After a short visit taking pictures and looking at the scenery, we got back in the boat and headed south, back to Zippel Bay. The return trip was easier because the wind had quieted somewhat and the waves were much easier to handle. We had beautiful sunshine with scattered clouds while we were out on the lake and it was a great way to spend the day.

Lake of the Woods is a monstrous piece of water. It is 90 miles from north to south and 55 miles wide. There is over 1400 square miles of water with 14,000 islands. The lake may be a huge piece of water; but, it is relatively shallow with regard to its size. Because of this, when winds are strong or storms are brewing, boating on the lake can be particularly hazardous. Years ago, prior to the dam that was built near Kenora,

Ontario, the water level of the lake was much lower. It was the low water level prior to the white settlers moving into the region that helped give the island its name.

Many of the earliest reports from the French and English explorers told of the gardens that were being tended to on the island by the natives. When the water levels were low, the families would leave the area around Warroad and walk along the shoreline and cross the shallows to the island to tend their fields. In 1859, the British sent Simon J. Dawson, a surveyor and explorer to the lake and he sent back an account of stopping at the island to visit with the natives there. He saw them tending to a field of corn that was at least five acres in size and a three acre field of squash and pumpkins.

After finishing his visit with the Indians on the island, Dawson continued on his trek and forged the trail that led from the west side of Lake of the Woods to another large lake further northwest – Lake Winnipeg.

Julie and I really enjoyed our trip up to Garden Island. We had a great time boating across the lake enjoying the sun and the spray of the water in our faces. If you want to visit the island and don't want to brave the open water in your own boat, there are launch services out of Rocky Point, Wheeler's Point, and Angle Inlet that will get you out to the island. During the winter months, after the freeze up, you can drive a car or snowmobile out to the island.

We had hauled the boat out of the water, cleaned it off and emptied the bilge and live well like all good boaters should do; then, we headed south and back to our little cabin in the woods.

Throughout all of our travels criss-crossing the state and going to all of these different state parks, we had actually missed one park and that one was going to be the last one for us to visit. We had gone through all sorts of meticulous planning in trying to determine what would be the fastest routes we could take and what order we might want to visit the different parks. Early in this story, I had told you about how we started our journey by coordinating our visits to the parks with Julie visiting lots of different quilt shops around the state. Now, after two full summers of travel, we found ourselves checking the inventory and cataloging all the parks we visited and came to realize we still needed to visit Frontenac State Park.

It was the very last park to visit out of all of them in the state. Well, this was going to mean that we had one more leg in our epic journey to plan and then complete.

The summer of 2010 has been a real scorcher for those of us who live here in Minnesota. Day time temps in the 90's and humidity levels into the 70's was making for one long and sticky season. Rain was coming down in buckets all over the state. A fair amount of dangerous weather had also shown up in the state and the poor people of Wadena, Kiester, and many other towns could attest to that fact. Julie and I, however, were very fortunate in planning our trips to coincide with those weekends that saw slight breaks in the heat and humidity and only slight problems with rain. This, too, was different than last summer. In 2009, it seemed that every time that we hooked up the camper and pointed the truck toward the Dakotas, it was time for a rainy weather system to develop. As I told you previously, other than a little wind and some white caps on the lake, our trip up to Garden Island couldn't have been a more perfect weekend.

The weekend that we headed southeast to make our visit to Frontenac coincided with two other events that I was very interested in. In St. Paul, a man who volunteers his time, was offering anyone who wanted to come to the Oakland Cemetery and listen to him talk about some of the people buried in the cemetery. Well, Oakland Cemetery is the oldest 'continually used' cemetery in Minnesota and there are thousands of people buried there, many of which have significant ties with the history of this state. On this particular weekend, he was going to be giving us a tour on those former residents of the state that had been involved with the Dakota Uprising in 1862. Anyone who knows me knows that the Uprising is a subject that I am very interested in.

The second event that we were coordinating with out trip to the state park was also related to the Uprising in 1862. It was going to be an open house, of sorts, at one of the locations where a stockade had been built to protect the citizens during the harrowing night the Indians came to attack. We planned on heading up to the small town of Forest City, in Meeker County, on the second day of our trip. So, we headed down to St. Paul to go on the tour of the cemetery first; and then, continued on to the river valley down by Lake Pepin. Unfortunately we were unable to spend the night at Frontenac because all of the camping sites had all ready been spoken for. (At least, the ones you could reserve in advance.) This caused us to make reservations at one of the other state parks there in the southeast region – Nerstrand Big Woods.

After a tiring morning walking all over a very large cemetery, we finally headed to our destination at Frontenac State Park. We made our way through the rest of St. Paul, got onto U.S. Hwy 61 and were heading our way to the park; or, so I thought. Once again, we were using the mapping feature on our cell phones to help guide us around all the twists and turns in St. Paul. Hey the directions it had been giving us earlier in the morning had taken us exactly to the front gate of the cemetery. Well, here we are traveling through Cottage Grove and down Hwy. 61 when suddenly the little voice on the phone tells us to turn onto U.S. Hwy 10 and head into Prescott, Wisconsin. For about five minutes we took a short jaunt through Prescott and then turned south again, but now we were traveling on Wisconsin Hwy. 35, we thought that the phone and its map feature was playing the same kind of trick on us as it did when we tried to find the John A. Latsch State Park. But no, as it turned out, the map system the phone was using to give us directions was trying to get us to our destination by the shortest and fastest route. Who would have thought that it was easier to get to this Minnesota state park by driving there through Wisconsin?

We 'stayed the course' and continued on southward traveling through the small town of Diamond Bluff before turning west again and re-crossing the river near Hager City and into Red Wing, Minnesota. That short drive along the Wisconsin side of the river allowed me to get reacquainted with the sandstone bluffs of Pierce County. It is a huge understatement to say that there is some pretty country and amazing sights along that stretch of highway.

Just a couple of miles down the river from Red Wing, along Hwy. 61, you come across the little town of Frontenac. Now, the locals call this collection of houses 'new' Frontenac. It seems that when Hwy. 61 was built, it drew people and businesses out to the intersection of County Road 2 and Hwy. 61. For all practical purposes, this was Frontenac; but, the original town that was established along the river bank still exists and it is just a short one half mile drive beyond the entrance to the state park on Cty. Rd. 2.

We arrived at the park, and like we had done so many times before, the first thing I did was pull to the side of the road at the entrance and grabbed the camera. I went around and got the picture I needed of the big, beautiful sign announcing the entrance to the park. After visiting the Ranger's Station at the entrance, we drove into the park and up the rise onto the top of the bluff and began checking out this very delightful spot.

Following the tarred road around on the top of the bluff brought us to a picnic area that had several fabulous overlook spots for looking down into the river valley and across into Wisconsin. Much the same as when we visited Great River Bluffs State Park, the view from the top of this bluff was amazing. Lake Pepin lay out below us and you could see the busy traffic of boats heading up and down the lake. The picnic area had nice paved walkways and tables all over with fire rings to use. There is a mix of tree species (oaks, maples, ash and birch) that supply lots of shade. There is a small monument on the south end of the picnic area that is dedicated to John Hauschildt. As a youth, he grew up in this area and in fact had a two hundred acre farm on the bluff before it was a state park. His generosity of donating this land to the state allows us to enjoy the beautiful views from the top of the bluff.

But there are many other reasons why the bluffs along this portion of the west bank of Lake Pepin are important. Archeologists have studied several sites at the park and have unearthed evidence that this area was an important place among the cultures of Native Americans stretching back in time as far back as hundreds of years before the birth of Jesus. Within the park is a ridge of high ground covered with woods and meadows that is sacred ground for the Fox and Dakota Indians. Just a short walk down a trail in the camping area of the park you will come across a large boulder sitting on top of the bluff overlooking Lake Pepin, this rock is called In-Yan-Teopa. It is another sacred site for those who lived here prior to the coming of the white settlers.

For a period of time during the mid to late 1800's, there was a quarry that existed at the base of the bluff and the limestone was mined for use in other areas of the country. Most notable of these locations is in New York City, the Cathedral of St. John the Devine was built using limestone from the Frontenac quarry. Also, in the late 1800's, Frontenac had a period where it was a very fashionable place to come and visit. People from all over the country – New Orleans, New York, St. Louis, and St. Paul – used to come here to relax along the shores of the lake.

After finishing gazing out across Lake Pepin from the vantage point of high on the bluff, we walked back to the truck and went to check on the campground and other amenities of the park. There is one campground that sits on top of the bluff with beautiful mature trees all over that give nice shading to the campsites. There is a fine shower and toilet facility located near the end of the second loop of campsites. Many trails intersect and cross the road leading through the campground. As we were driving around, we stopped a man that was walking along the road and asked him what his opinion of the park was. He told us that he and his wife have been visiting this park for many, many years. He described it as "well managed and quiet." He also told us that just four years ago, he and his wife started to volunteer to serve as 'the campground hosts' during the month of August. He said that they always enjoy the time they spend at the park and look forward to many more years of camping here. What better testament could a park have?

We finished our short tour of Frontenac State Park, and then started to make our way over to where we would be camping for the night. Along the way to Nerstrand Big Woods State Park, we drove through the city of Lakeville and then took the long westerly drive up the valley, around and sometimes over the bluffs, until we finally got out of the river valley area and returned to the wide expanses of the farm fields of Minnesota. We passed through some towns that I have been familiar with by hearing about them on the news or reading about them in the paper – Zumbro Falls, Zumbrota, Wanamingo, and Kenyon. All the time that we were driving along MN Hwy. 60, we passed through beautiful rolling landscapes dotted by farmsteads which were surround by tall standing corn or lush green soybeans. Once again, I found myself amazed and in awe of this wonderful state that I live in.

At Nerstrand Big Woods, we set up our little camper under the shade of some tall oak and ash trees. The heat of the day had passed; but, it was still plenty warm enough to break a sweat while we got the camper ready for the nights sleep. Thankfully, we have a small fan that we can use to help move the air around and it makes sleeping in our little rig quite enjoyable. We spent the night there at the park and were able to help keep ourselves cool with the fan and in the morning after a small breakfast we hit the road once again. We were off to see what the next interesting spot would be that we could find in Minnesota.

Well, it didn't takes us long to find that next interesting spot. In fact, we drove to it as we were making our way west and north towards our next destination in Meeker County. We had kept to the road ways south of the Metro area in order to try and avoid any undue traffic. This ultimately brought us to Hutchinson and then we started driving north to get to Meeker County on Highway 15. You go about five and a half miles north of Hutchinson and you will come to the intersection of Meeker County Road 18 going to the west. We turned onto that road and drove to what is going to become the next state park in Minnesota. We were at Greenleaf. The little hamlet of Greenleaf is made up of a small collection of homes and buildings and it is at the intersection of Minnesota Highway 22 and County Road 18. My mother grew up in this area. My grandfather's farm was in McLeod County on Highway 15 just a few miles away. My father grew up in the area just south of Dassel; so, both of them are very familiar with the region. They told me that years ago Greenleaf was quite the little community. Greenleaf is about seven miles south of Litchfield on MN Hwy. 22.

This new area that the state is starting to develop will actually be a State Recreation Area, much like what can be found at Cuyuna Country and the Red River at East Grand Forks. The road leading to Greenleaf Lake is about one mile east of the intersection of Hwy. 22 and Cty. Rd. 18. Take that road north about one half mile and you will now be driving past Greenleaf Lake. There is a small road that leads into the south end of the lake where the public access is and there is a nice fishing pier set up at that site. The state of Minnesota is still in the developmental stages with the park and there are plans for trails, developing the lake and its neighbor lakes, and camping facilities. It will be interesting to watch as this area continues to grow into the beautiful park it will be in the future.

One other item of note that I would like to mention here is related to the interest I have in the Dakota Conflict. As I have spoken about earlier in the story, I have a deep interest in the conflict that occurred here in Minnesota in 1862. About four miles east of the road leading to

Greenleaf Lake, on County Rd. 18, you will find a solitary granite stone placed on the south side of the road. This marker is set near the spot where the Dakota Chief, Little Crow, was shot and killed. In my opinion, it is well worth the short moment necessary to stop and recognize this tiny spot in our state that represents such an important event in the history of our state.

When we were finished with the visit to the area of Greenleaf Lake, we headed north on Highway 22 to Litchfield and then Forest City. Forest City, in Meeker County, was one of the important spots during the Dakota Conflict and there is a small stockade and some buildings located just south of the town. The fortification represents the one that was built by the settlers in the area when the Dakota Conflict threatened them. We had an enjoyable afternoon visiting there and seeing the attractions. When we were done, we pointed the truck north again and headed once again back to our little cabin in the woods.

Here ends the story of our journey all over this great state, visiting all of the state parks and other points of interest. We drove many, many miles. We zigzagged our way east and west and rolled north and south and never once was I disappointed in any part of the journey. Julie and I look forward to many more adventures and enjoyable nights spent in relaxation at these wonderful jewels of our state – The Minnesota State Parks.

The State Parks,
State Recreation Areas,
State Waysides,
and other Points of Interest.

Afton

6959 Peller Avenue South
Hastings, Minnesota 55033
651-436-5391

- Park is located next to the Afton Alps Ski Area. To get to the Park/ Ski area go south on MN Hwy. 95 for seven miles until you reach the intersection of County Road 20. Go east on County Road 20 for three miles.

- Afton State Park is devoted exclusively to those that desire a remote and nature- oriented setting. The development in the park has been kept to a minimum and nearly all the areas in the park open for use have to be reached by hiking the trails.

- The camp ground is accessible only by trail and it is ¾ of a mile away from the parking area. There are 28 rustic sites. There are vault toilets, firewood and fresh water spigots available at the campground.

- There are twenty miles of hiking trails, 18 miles of cross country ski trails, 5 miles of horse back trail, 4 miles of mountain bike trail, and 4 miles of snowshoe trail. Numerous shelters along all the trails, scenic observation sites on the trails, swimming area, and a fishing pier on the river bank.

- Two rustic group camps are also available for use.

- This park offers very beautiful scenic views of the river valley, the rock outcrops, and many different species of animal and plants in the park.

- As of 2009, Afton's remote camping area has become a 'Pack-in, Pack-out' area. This means everything you bring in with you, must come out with you – even your garbage. No garbage cans will be in the camp area. You have to carry it out with you and dispose of it at the containers near the parking areas.

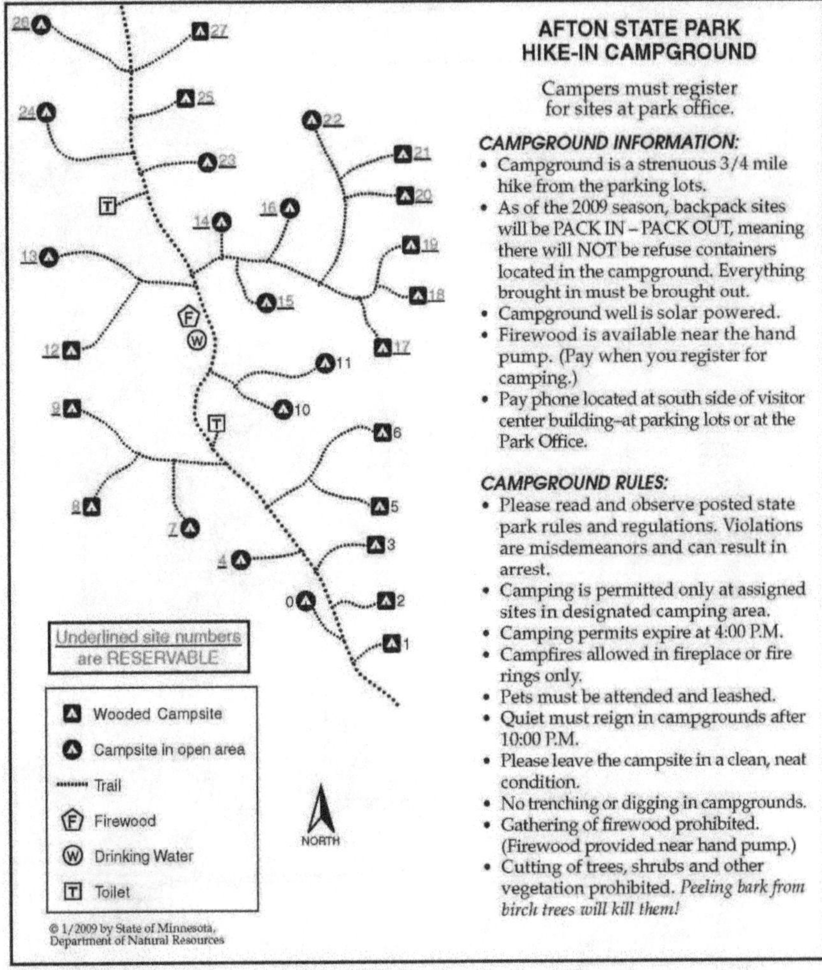

AFTON STATE PARK HIKE-IN CAMPGROUND

Campers must register for sites at park office.

CAMPGROUND INFORMATION:

- Campground is a strenuous 3/4 mile hike from the parking lots.
- As of the 2009 season, backpack sites will be PACK IN – PACK OUT, meaning there will NOT be refuse containers located in the campground. Everything brought in must be brought out.
- Campground well is solar powered.
- Firewood is available near the hand pump. (Pay when you register for camping.)
- Pay phone located at south side of visitor center building–at parking lots or at the Park Office.

CAMPGROUND RULES:

- Please read and observe posted state park rules and regulations. Violations are misdemeanors and can result in arrest.
- Camping is permitted only at assigned sites in designated camping area.
- Camping permits expire at 4:00 P.M.
- Campfires allowed in fireplace or fire rings only.
- Pets must be attended and leashed.
- Quiet must reign in campgrounds after 10:00 P.M.
- Please leave the campsite in a clean, neat condition.
- No trenching or digging in campgrounds.
- Gathering of firewood prohibited. (Firewood provided near hand pump.)
- Cutting of trees, shrubs and other vegetation prohibited. *Peeling bark from birch trees will kill them!*

Note: This park ***may*** have RESERVABLE sites other than in the main campground. See the main park map for the locations of any additional camping or lodging sites.

AFTON STATE PARK

FACILITIES AND FEATURES

- 28 backpacking campsites
- 2 picnic grounds with a total of 50 tables
- 20 miles of hiking trail
- 18 miles of cross-country ski trail
- 5 miles of horseback riding trail
- 4 miles of bike trail
- 4 miles of snowshoe trail
- Visitor center with interpretive displays, information, and a pay telephone
- 2 rustic group camps
- 1 canoe campsite

LOOKING FOR MORE INFORMATION?

The DNR has mapped the state showing federal, state and county lands with their recreational facilities.

Public Recreation Information Maps (PRIM) are available for purchase from the DNR gift shop, DNR regional offices, Minnesota state parks and major sporting and map stores.

Check it out - you'll be glad you did.

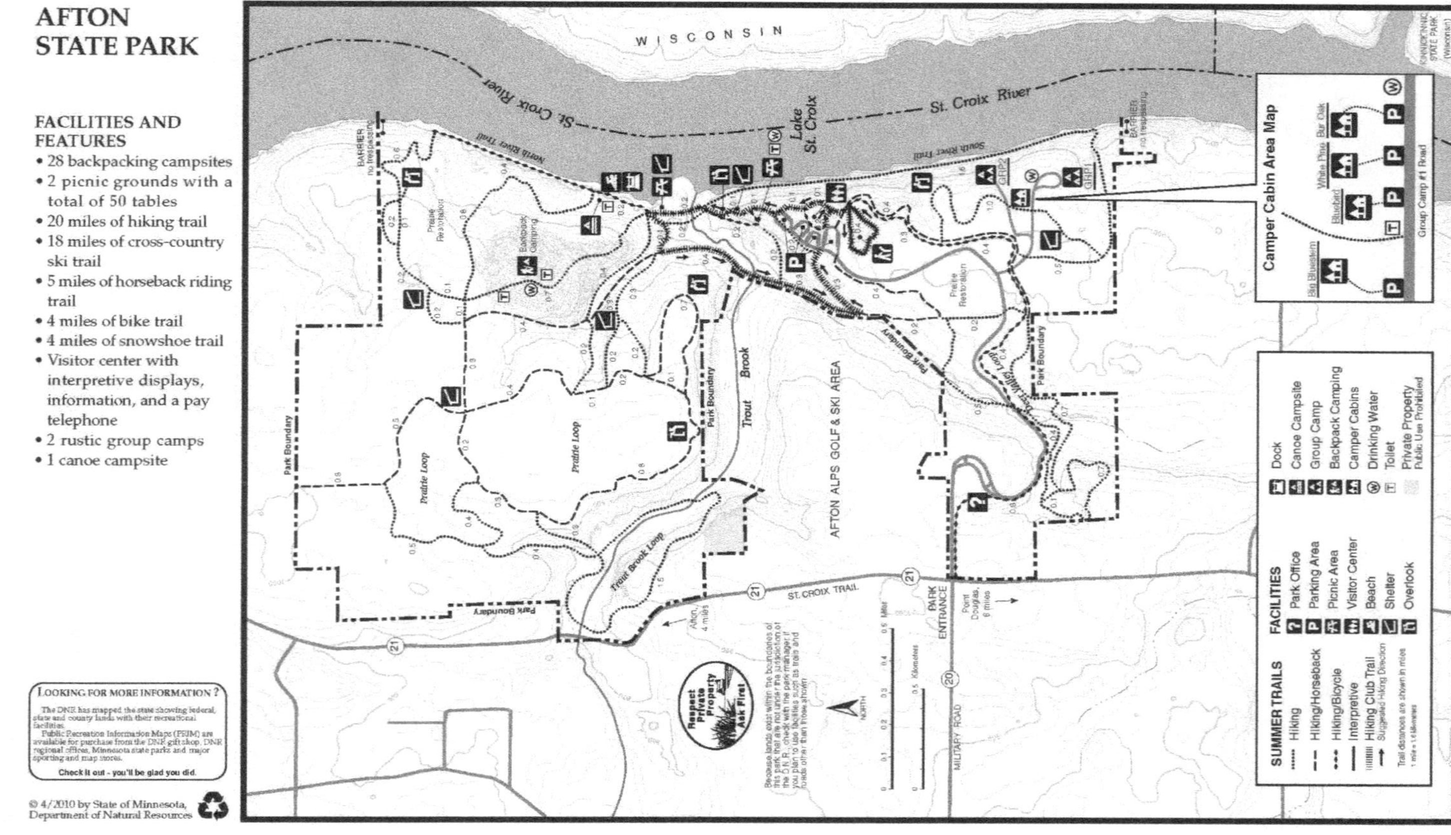

Banning

P. O. Box 643
Sandstone, Minnesota 55072
320-245-2668

- This small state park is located just north of the town of Sandstone, MN. This park is situated in stands of Birch and Aspen and fairly thick undergrowth. Small Red pines are starting to grow around the park and are establishing themselves in the undergrowth.

- The campground has 34 camp sites and there are 12 sites that have electrical hook-up capabilities. There is a toilet/shower building in the campground and there are vault toilets and water spigots set throughout the campground.

- Other amenities that are offered at Banning are boat launch sites, picnic areas, 14 miles of hiking trails, 11 miles of skiing trails and 5 miles of snowmobile trail. There are scenic overlook sites set up along the trails. There are 4 remote campsites along the river that can be reached by canoe.

- The park is a very popular destination for cross country skiing during the winter. During the spring and summer, the park is a huge destination for canoeists and kayakers because of the rapids and waterfalls that can be found along the Kettle River and the small tributaries that flow into the Kettle.

- Also of note, the old sandstone quarry next to the river and some of the buildings associated with the quarry. The old Village of Banning site and the "Bat Cave" are also located in the area.

- The area of Banning State park and the town of Sandstone were all involved in the huge Hinckley Fire of 1894. Evidence of the fire can still be found in the park. The Hinckley Fire museum is located in Hinckley, seven miles south on I-35.

- The sites in the campground have lots of undergrowth and allow for very secluded camping. The sites that we felt were very nice were - # 1, 2, 18 and 25.

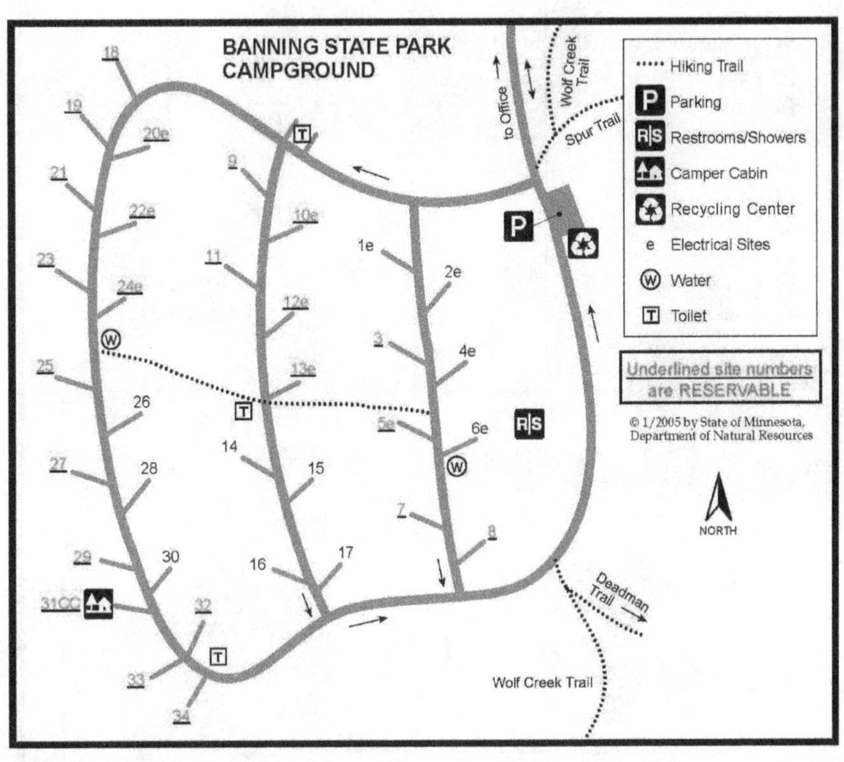
BANNING STATE PARK
CAMPGROUND
to Office
Wolf Creek Trail
Spur Trail
Hiking Trail
Parking
Restrooms/Showers
Camper Cabin
Recycling Center
e Electrical Sites
Water
Toilet
Underlined site numbers are RESERVABLE
© 1/2005 by State of Minnesota, Department of Natural Resources
NORTH
Deadman Trail
Wolf Creek Trail
18
19
20e
21
22e
23
24e
25
26
27
28
29
30
31CC
32
33
34
9
10e
11
12e
13e
14
15
16
17
1e
2e
3
4e
5e
6e
7
8

BANNING STATE PARK

VISITOR FAVORITES

- Canoeing and kayaking
- Hiking along the Kettle River
- Wolf Creek Falls
- The sandstone quarry
- Kettle River fishing
- The "Kettles"
- Log Creek arches
- Spring flowers and Fall colors
- The Bat Cave— for information and location of bat cave (Robinson Ice Cave) please contact park staff.

FACILITIES

- 33 semi-modern campsites
- 1 Camper Cabin
- 4 canoe campsites
- 7 picnic sites with a total of 15 tables
- 3 small boat landings
- 14 miles of hiking trail
- 11 miles of skiing trail
- 5 miles of snowmobile trail

LOOKING FOR MORE INFORMATION?

The DNR has mapped the state showing federal, state and county lands with their recreational facilities.

Public Recreation Information Maps (PRIM) are available for purchase from the DNR gift shop, DNR regional offices, Minnesota state parks and major sporting and map stores.

Check it out - you'll be glad you did.

Bear Head Lake

9301 Bear Head Lake State Park Road
Ely, Minnesota 55731
218-365-7229

- The park is located 18 miles east of Tower, MN. Take Hwy 169 east as if going to Ely; then, at the intersection of Hwy 128 - go south for six miles. Everything about this park speaks to the remoteness of its location.

- If you and the family were looking for a nice place to stay and be near the Boundary Waters - this is your place.

- 73 camp sites divided between three loops in the one campground.

The 1st loop contains sites 1 through 24. These are non-electric sites and do allow for more seclusion because the loop is set away from the other two loops.

- Loop 2 has sites 25 to 50. This loop also contains all of the electric hook-up sites.

- Loop 3 has all of the remaining campsites and this loop is the closest to the lake.

- There are vault toilets, fresh water spigots, a flush toilet/shower facility located centrally in the camping area. There are numerous fishing piers and a boat landing, swimming beach, and a picnic area on Bear Head Lake. Boat and canoe rental is available. There is also a boat landing on Eagles Nest Lake. There are 4 remote campsites accessible by hiking in to them.

- There is over 6 miles of hiking trail in the park and those trails access into the Taconite State Trail system.

- There are 5 camper cabins and one guest house available for reservation.

- The park is full of tall beautiful pines and there are camp sites available that would allow for nice seclusion. We liked sites 9 to 18, because of the seclusion. We also liked Sites # 46, 48, and 55.

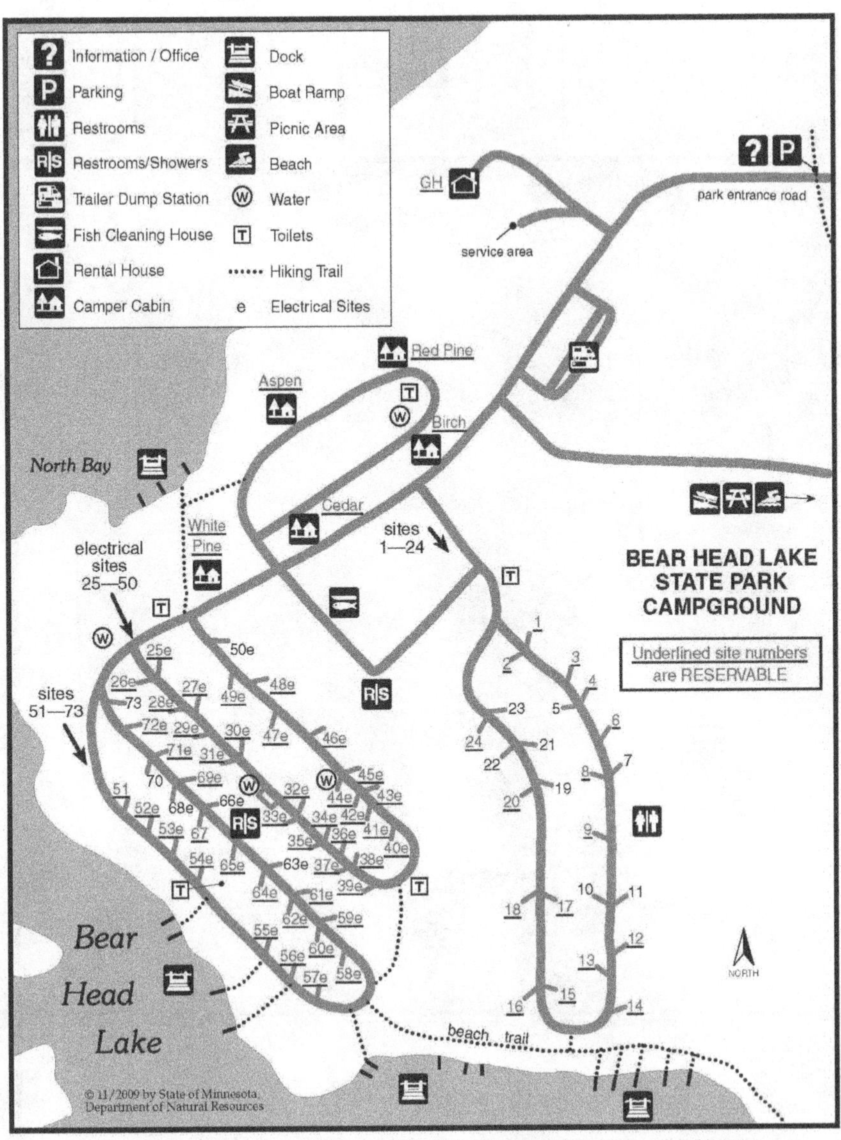

Note: This park *may* have RESERVABLE sites other than in the main campground. See the main park map for the locations of any additional camping or lodging sites.

BEAR HEAD LAKE STATE PARK

FACILITIES AND FEATURES

- 73 semi-modern campsites (45 with electricity) with a modern sanitation building
- 4 backpack sites
- One boat-accessible campsite
- Boat access on Bear Head Lake
- Boat access on Eagles Nest Lake #3
- Rustic group camp with a hand-pump and pit-type sanitation units
- Large picnic area with a sandy swimming beach
- Boat, kayak and canoe rentals
- Dump station
- Picnic shelter
- Guest house
- 5 camper cabins
- Snowshoe rental
- Fishing pier and boat docks

VISITOR FAVORITES

- Fishing and boating on Bear Head Lake
- Beautiful sand swimming beach
- Snowmobile trails that link with the Taconite State Trail
- Miles of good hiking and skiing trails

LOOKING FOR MORE INFORMATION ?

The DNR has mapped separate areas of the state showing federal, state and county lands with their recreational facilities.

Public Recreation Information Maps (PRIM) are available for purchase from the DNR gift shop, DNR regional offices, Minnesota state parks and major sporting and map stores.

Check it out - you'll be glad you did.

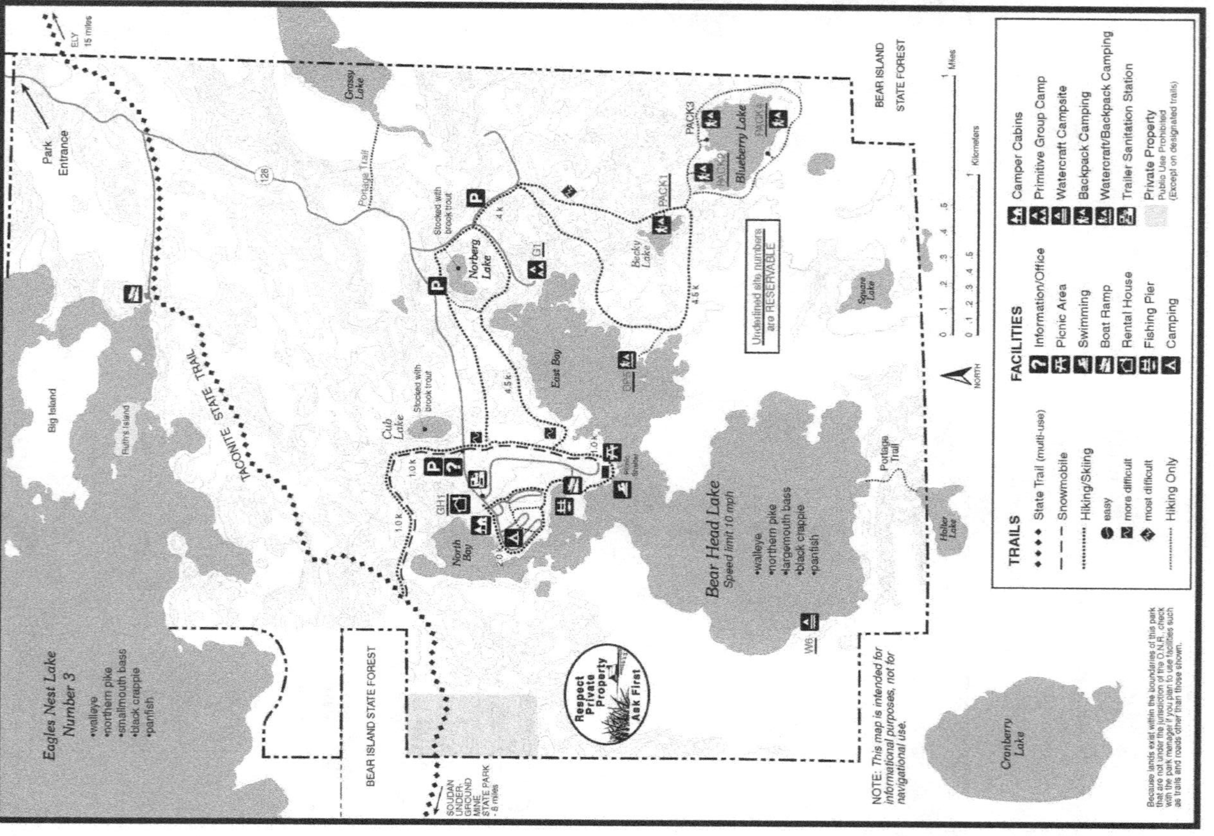

Beaver Creek Valley

15954 County Road 1
Caledonia, Minnesota 55921
507-724-2107

- This park is located 5 miles west of Caledonia, Minnesota, at the end of Houston County Road 1. This park is the most south-easterly of all the state parks.

- This state park may be small but it is loaded with things to do; not the least of which is one on the best trout fishing streams in the state. In the park, you can actually walk to the spots where the water comes gurgling up out of the ground that creates this trout stream..

- There is over 6 miles of trails in the park with several scenic overlook spots. Three remote group camps, a large picnic area with shelter, a camper cabin to reserve for use, a flush toilet and shower building along with water spigots and vaults toilets.

- All of the traditional campsites sit along on both sides of the road that follows along beside the creek. Many of the sites on the side by the creek are very close to the water. There are 26 semi-modern sites, sixteen rustic sites and a half dozen cart in sites for those people who really want to get away from it all.

- Spacing between the sites in the park at times gets a little tight; but, with all the beauty and the uniqueness of this little part of Minnesota – you barely notice.

- There are trees and cover all along the road and beside the river and this gives good overhead cover and shade to the camp sites. Large oaks, cottonwoods, and aspens can be found all over. There is very little under growth between the sites. All of the campsites are nice and level and easy to back into with a trailer.

- The camp sites we liked best were: 4, 14, 16, 24 and 26.

- One unique note at this park, when you drive out past the picnic area and head to where the campsites are – you have to drive through the water of the Beaver Creek to get to the road on the other side. This is the only state park we have been at where you can do that.

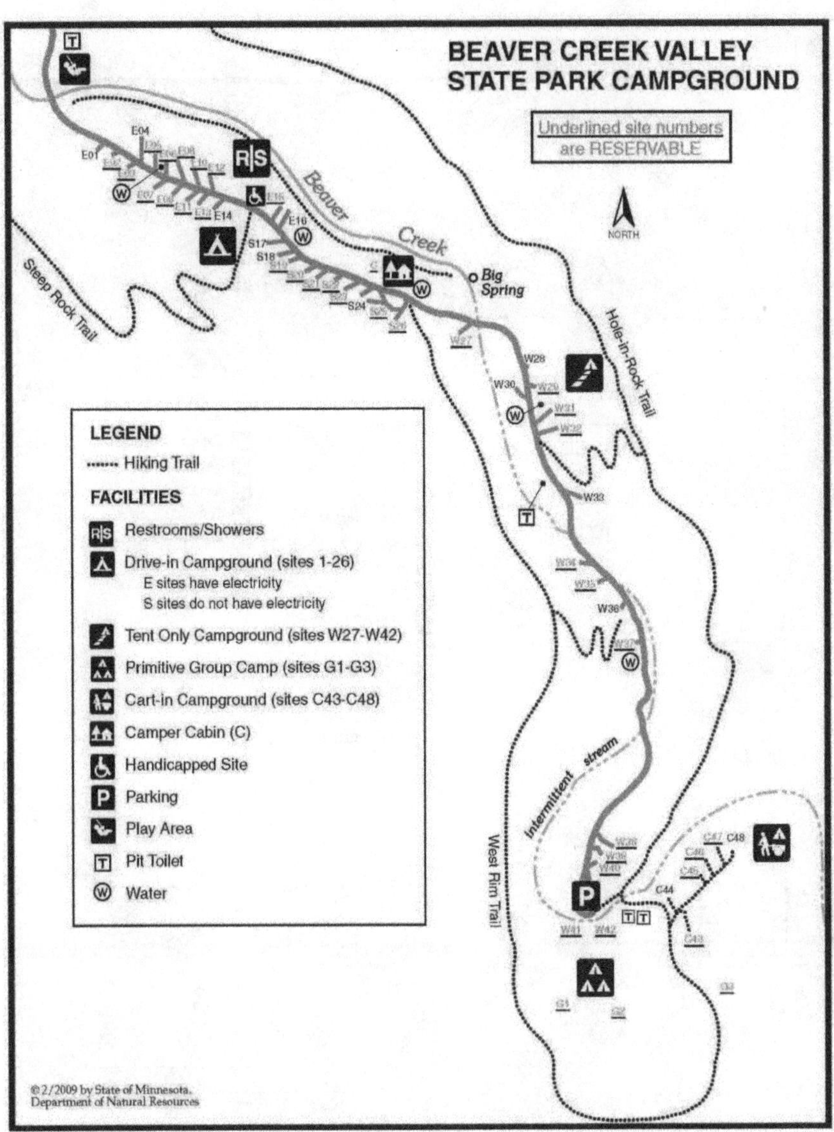
BEAVER CREEK VALLEY
STATE PARK CAMPGROUND
Underlined site numbers
are RESERVABLE
NORTH
Beaver
Creek
Big
Spring
Steep Rock Trail
Hole-in-Rock Trail
West Rim Trail
intermittent stream
LEGEND
Hiking Trail
FACILITIES
Restrooms/Showers
Drive-in Campground (sites 1-26)
E sites have electricity
S sites do not have electricity
Tent Only Campground (sites W27-W42)
Primitive Group Camp (sites G1-G3)
Cart-in Campground (sites C43-C48)
Camper Cabin (C)
Handicapped Site
Parking
Play Area
Pit Toilet
Water
© 2/2009 by State of Minnesota,
Department of Natural Resources

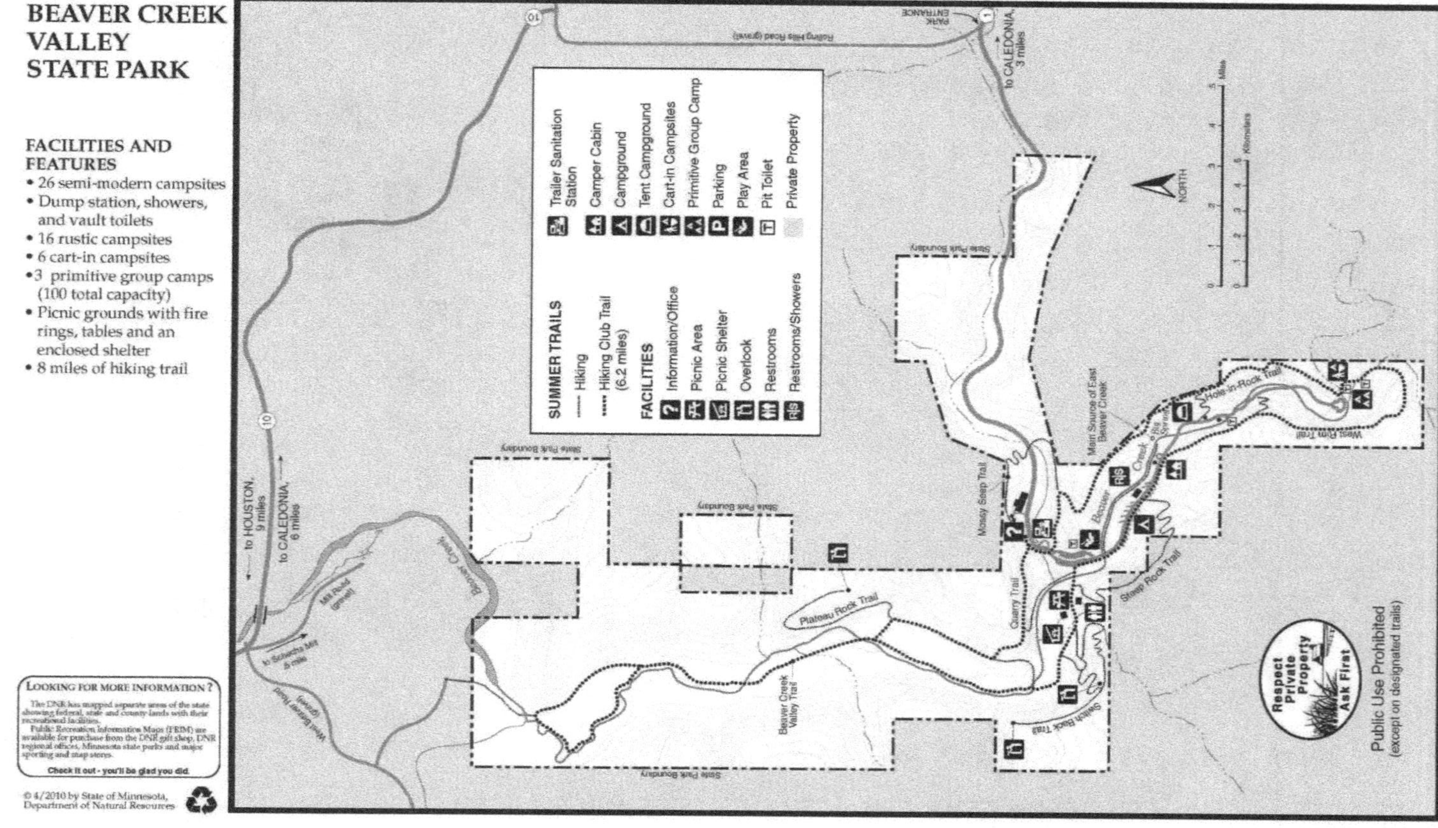
BEAVER CREEK
VALLEY
STATE PARK
FACILITIES AND
FEATURES
• 26 semi-modern campsites
• Dump station, showers, and vault toilets
• 16 rustic campsites
• 6 cart-in campsites
•3 primitive group camps (100 total capacity)
• Picnic grounds with fire rings, tables and an enclosed shelter
• 8 miles of hiking trail
LOOKING FOR MORE INFORMATION?
The DNR has mapped separate areas of the state showing federal, state and county lands with their recreational facilities.
Public Recreation Information Maps (PRIM) are available for purchase from the DNR gift shop, DNR regional offices, Minnesota state parks and major sporting and map stores.
Check it out - you'll be glad you did.
© 4/2010 by State of Minnesota, Department of Natural Resources
to HOUSTON, 9 miles
to CALEDONIA, 6 miles
10
West Beaver Road (gravel)
to Schechs Mill .5 mile
Mill Road (gravel)
Beaver Creek
State Park Boundary
SUMMER TRAILS
Hiking
Hiking Club Trail (6.2 miles)
FACILITIES
Information/Office
Picnic Area
Picnic Shelter
Overlook
Restrooms
Restrooms/Showers
Trailer Sanitation Station
Camper Cabin
Campground
Tent Campground
Cart-in Campsites
Primitive Group Camp
Parking
Play Area
Pit Toilet
Private Property
Rolling Hills Road (gravel)
PARK ENTRANCE
1
to CALEDONIA, 3 miles
Beaver Creek Valley Trail
Plateau Rock Trail
Mossy Seep Trail
Quarry Trail
Switch Back Trail
Steep Rock Trail
Main Source of East Beaver Creek
Big Spring
Hole-in-Rock Trail
West Rim Trail
NORTH
Miles
Kilometers
Respect Private Property
Ask First
Public Use Prohibited
(except on designated trails)

Big Bog

P. O. Box 428
Waskish, Minnesota 56685
218-647-8592

- This park is located a couple of miles north of Waskish, MN on State Hwy 72.

- A small campground area with a mix of electric and non-electric sites. There are nice tall trees around the campground and little to no undergrowth between the sites. This State Park is very amenable to family camping. Absolutely fabulous toilet and shower facility.

- There is an inlet of water that comes up beside the campground from Upper Red Lake and this allows easy access to fisherman. There is a boat landing and docks on the east side of the campground. There is also a fish cleaning shack near the bathrooms.

- Swimming beach, hiking trails, picnic areas, and 5 camper cabins allow for numerous enjoyable experiences at this park.
- The big bog that the park name refers to is at a site nine miles further north on State Hwy. 72. It is referred to as the Ludlow Island Area. There is a picnic area with shelter, some hiking trails, and a very modern boardwalk that is 1 mile long.
- All the sites in this park are very level and would easily access tents and trailers.

(Small pond near the boardwalk at Big Bog SRA)

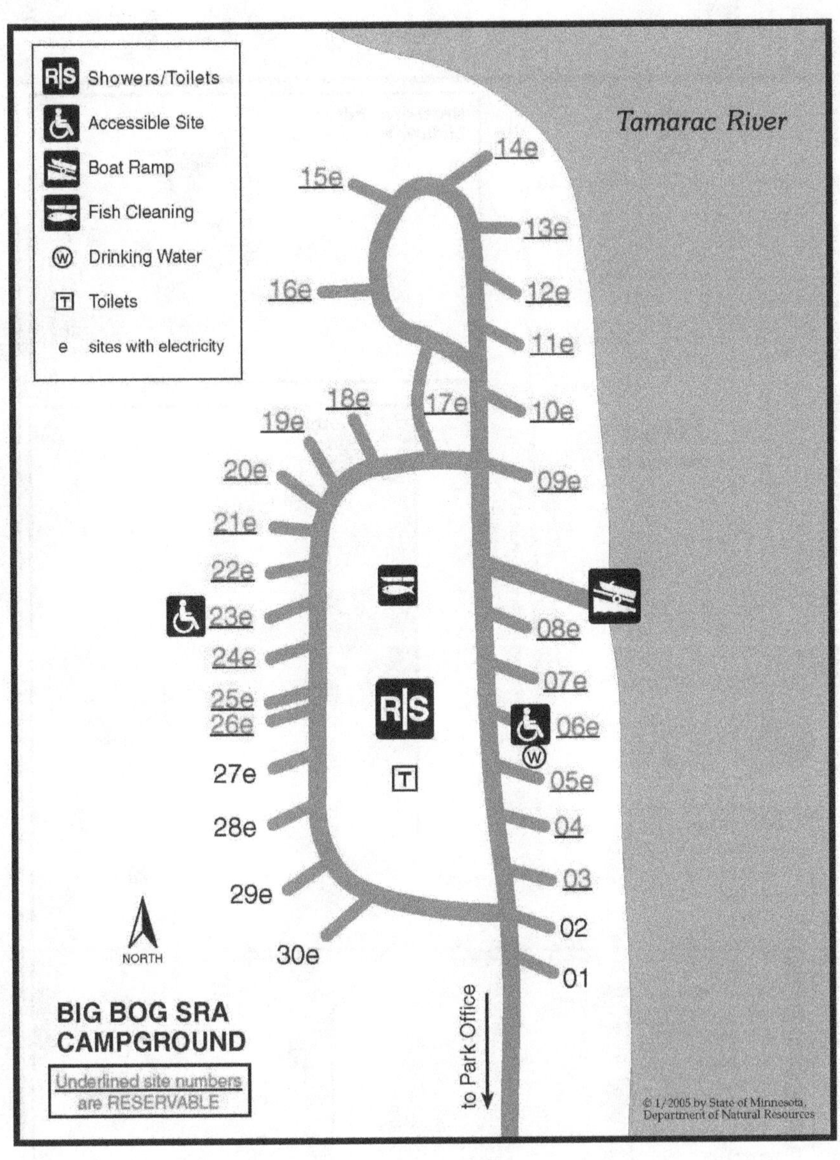
Showers/Toilets
Accessible Site
Boat Ramp
Fish Cleaning
Drinking Water
Toilets
e sites with electricity
Tamarac River
14e
15e
13e
16e
12e
11e
18e
17e
10e
19e
20e
09e
21e
22e
23e
08e
24e
07e
25e
26e
06e
27e
05e
28e
04
03
29e
02
30e
01
NORTH
BIG BOG SRA
CAMPGROUND
Underlined site numbers
are RESERVABLE
to Park Office
© 1/2005 by State of Minnesota,
Department of Natural Resources

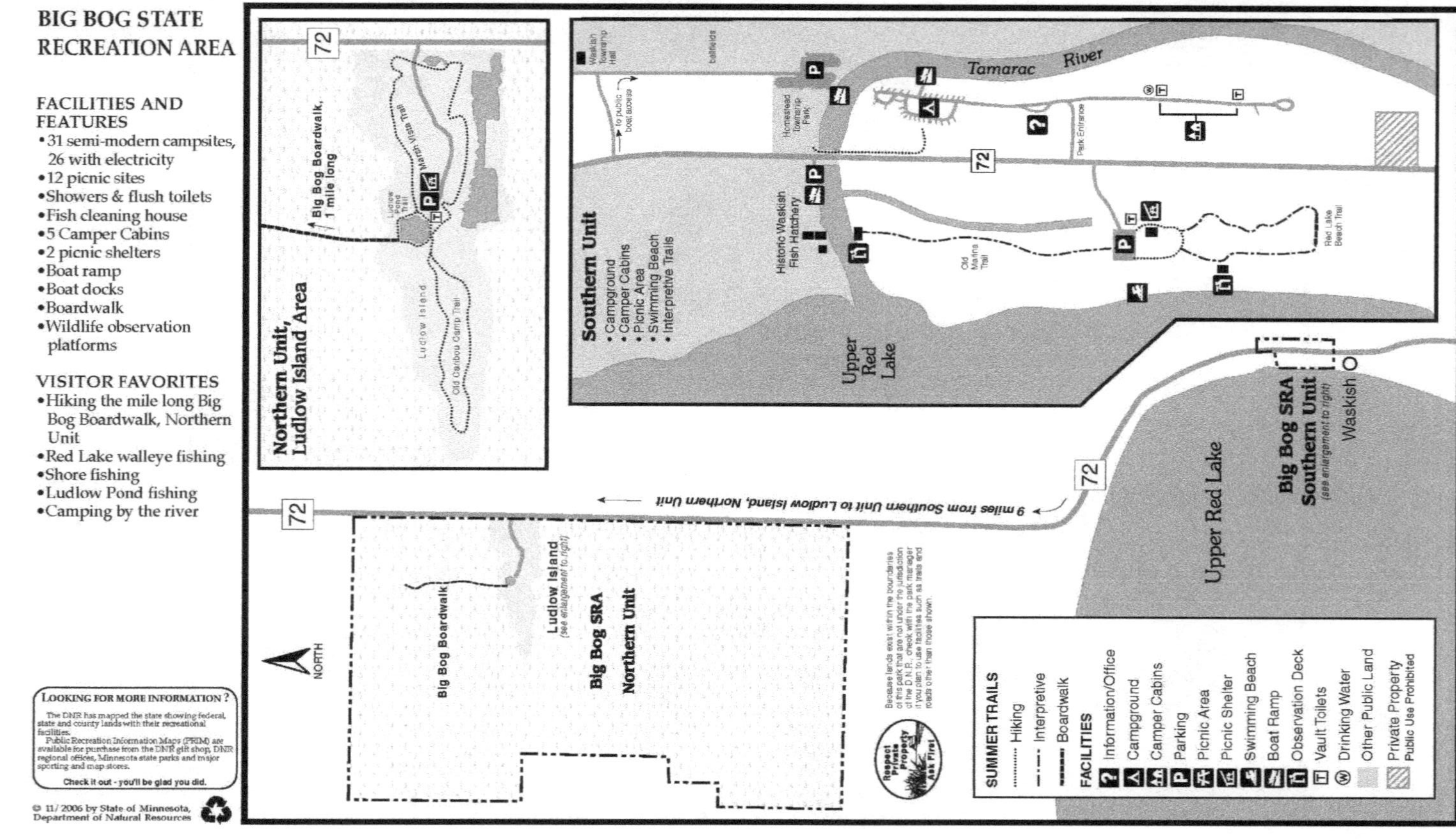
BIG BOG STATE RECREATION AREA
FACILITIES AND FEATURES
•31 semi-modern campsites, 26 with electricity
•12 picnic sites
•Showers & flush toilets
•Fish cleaning house
•5 Camper Cabins
•2 picnic shelters
•Boat ramp
•Boat docks
•Boardwalk
•Wildlife observation platforms
VISITOR FAVORITES
•Hiking the mile long Big Bog Boardwalk, Northern Unit
•Red Lake walleye fishing
•Shore fishing
•Ludlow Pond fishing
•Camping by the river
Northern Unit, Ludlow Island Area
Big Bog Boardwalk, 1 mile long
72
Ludlow Pond Trail
Marsh Vista Trail
Ludlow Island
Old Caribou Camp Trail
Southern Unit
• Campground
• Camper Cabins
• Picnic Area
• Swimming Beach
• Interpretive Trails
Waskish Township Hall
to public boat access
ballfields
Historic Waskish Fish Hatchery
Homestead Township Park
Tamarac River
Upper Red Lake
Old Marina Trail
Park Entrance
Red Lake Beach Trail
NORTH
Big Bog Boardwalk
Ludlow Island
(see enlargement to right)
Big Bog SRA
Northern Unit
9 miles from Southern Unit to Ludlow Island, Northern Unit
Upper Red Lake
Big Bog SRA
Southern Unit
(see enlargement to right)
Waskish
Respect Private Property Ask First
Because lands exist within the boundaries of this park that are not under the jurisdiction of the D.N.R., check with the park manager if you plan to use facilities such as trails and roads other than those shown.
SUMMER TRAILS
Hiking
Interpretive
Boardwalk
FACILITIES
Information/Office
Campground
Camper Cabins
Parking
Picnic Area
Picnic Shelter
Swimming Beach
Boat Ramp
Observation Deck
Vault Toilets
Drinking Water
Other Public Land
Private Property
Public Use Prohibited
LOOKING FOR MORE INFORMATION?
The DNR has mapped the state showing federal, state and county lands with their recreational facilities.
Public Recreation Information Maps (PRIM) are available for purchase from the DNR gift shop, DNR regional offices, Minnesota state parks and major sporting and map stores.
Check it out - you'll be glad you did.
© 11/2006 by State of Minnesota, Department of Natural Resources

Big Stone Lake

35889 Meadowbrook State Park Road
Ortonville, Minnesota 56278
320-839-3663

- This park is located 7 to 8 miles north along the shores of Big Stone Lake, north of the city of Ortonville.

- This very pretty state park is nestled on the shores of the lake. The campsite areas are open; but, there is a lot of distance between each of the sites, this allows for some seclusion from your neighbors. The sites are fairly level and there are a number of them that are very close to the shore.

- There are vault toilets and a toilet/shower facility. There are water spigots for fresh water, a picnic area, boat ramp, a playground area for children, and a swimming beach. There are some trails available above the camping area for hiking. There are big beautiful cottonwood trees and oak trees all around the camp grounds.

- There are 37 campsites and they are divided into two loops. The 1st loop has sites #1 to 20 and all of the 10 electric sites are in that loop. The 2nd loop has the remaining sites.

- Big Stone Lake State Park has two other locations set up along the east shore of the lake. Approximately 10 miles up Hwy 7 from the Meadowbrook site (the main and southern most part of the park) is a scenic overlook that gives excellent views of the lake and surrounding territory. There is one picnic table there and a vault toilet.

- Another mile north on Hwy 7 is the Bonanza Area. This area has an educational center, group camp, picnic area, vault toilets, and a boat landing. There is approximately two miles of hiking trail available at the Bonanza area.

- Big Stone Lake Park is popular due to the fishing and boating available on the lake.

- We liked sites # 14, 17, 32, 34, and 36.

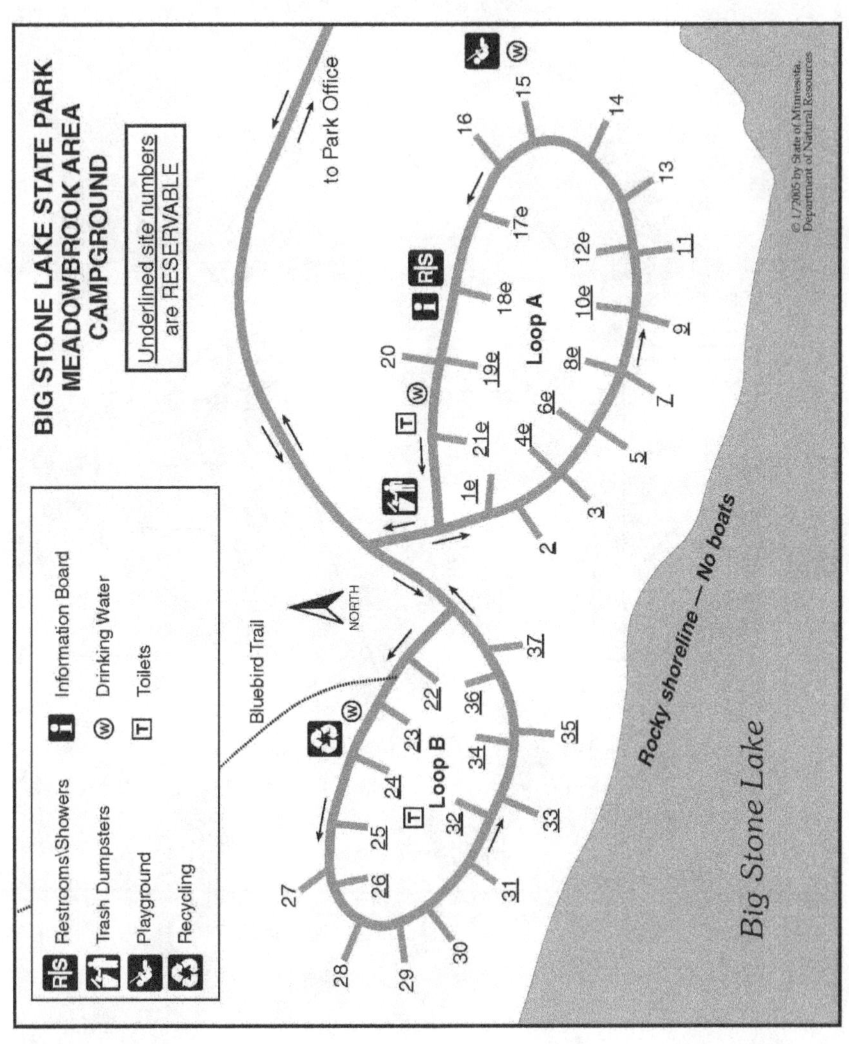
BIG STONE LAKE STATE PARK
MEADOWBROOK AREA
CAMPGROUND
Underlined site numbers are RESERVABLE
Restrooms\Showers
Trash Dumpsters
Playground
Recycling
Information Board
Drinking Water
Toilets
Bluebird Trail
NORTH
to Park Office
Loop A
Loop B
Rocky shoreline — No boats
Big Stone Lake
© 1/2005 by State of Minnesota, Department of Natural Resources

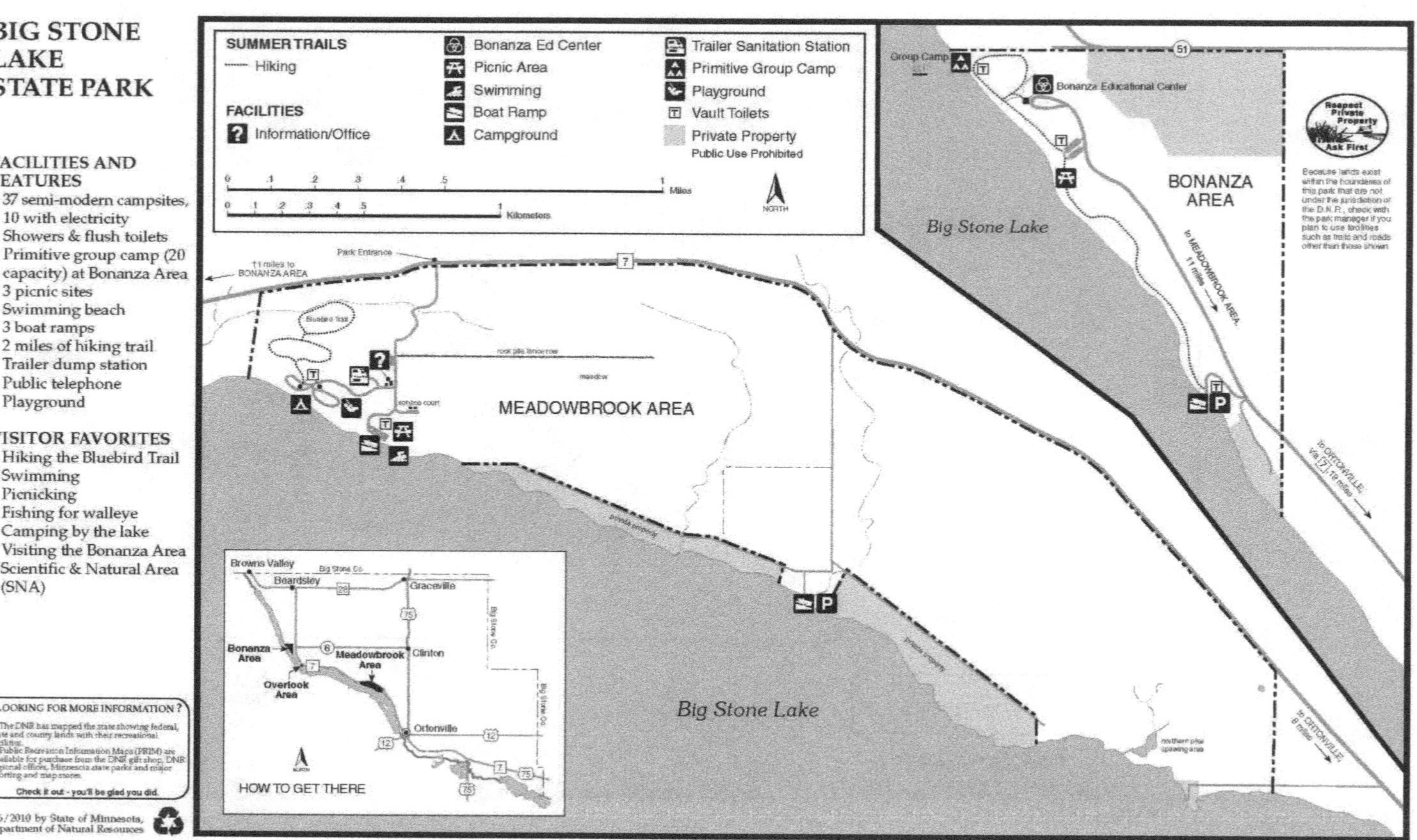
BIG STONE LAKE STATE PARK
FACILITIES AND FEATURES
• 37 semi-modern campsites, 10 with electricity
• Showers & flush toilets
• Primitive group camp (20 capacity) at Bonanza Area
• 3 picnic sites
• Swimming beach
• 3 boat ramps
• 2 miles of hiking trail
• Trailer dump station
• Public telephone
• Playground
VISITOR FAVORITES
• Hiking the Bluebird Trail
• Swimming
• Picnicking
• Fishing for walleye
• Camping by the lake
• Visiting the Bonanza Area Scientific & Natural Area (SNA)
SUMMER TRAILS
Hiking
FACILITIES
Information/Office
Bonanza Ed Center
Picnic Area
Swimming
Boat Ramp
Campground
Trailer Sanitation Station
Primitive Group Camp
Playground
Vault Toilets
Private Property
Public Use Prohibited
Miles
Kilometers
NORTH
Park Entrance
11 miles to BONANZA AREA
7
MEADOWBROOK AREA
Big Stone Lake
Big Stone Lake
Group Camp
Bonanza Educational Center
BONANZA AREA
51
to MEADOWBROOK AREA 11 miles
to ORTONVILLE via 7 19 miles
to ORTONVILLE 8 miles
Browns Valley
Beardsley
Graceville
Bonanza Area
Meadowbrook Area
Clinton
Overlook Area
Ortonville
Big Stone Co.
HOW TO GET THERE
© 6/2010 by State of Minnesota, Department of Natural Resources

Blue Mounds

1410 161st Street
Luverne, Minnesota 56156
507-283-1307

- This lovely state park is located about 2 miles north of Luverne, MN, on U.S. Highway 75. The park is named for the fantastic 'up-thrust' of bedrock cliffs that face to the east.

- There are 73 camp sites located in the main camp area. 40 of the sites have electric hook-up. There is also a more remote camp are with 14 cart-in sites.

- There are two very nice restroom/shower facilities in the main camp area. There are freshwater spigots, vault toilets, an amphitheater, playground, swim beach, 15 miles of hiking trails, along with trails for biking, snowmobiling and the trail that leads to the cliffs.

- There are two small lakes that are formed by dams and they are good lakes on which to try and catch fish or to enjoy boating and canoeing.

- The camping areas have nice tree cover that give good shading; however, there is little to no undergrowth between the sites. The sites have good spacing, but you will still be close to your camping neighbors.

- Several farms in the area raise buffalo and you can see them from the park grounds.

- We liked sites # 11, 29, 48, 55, 59, and 60.

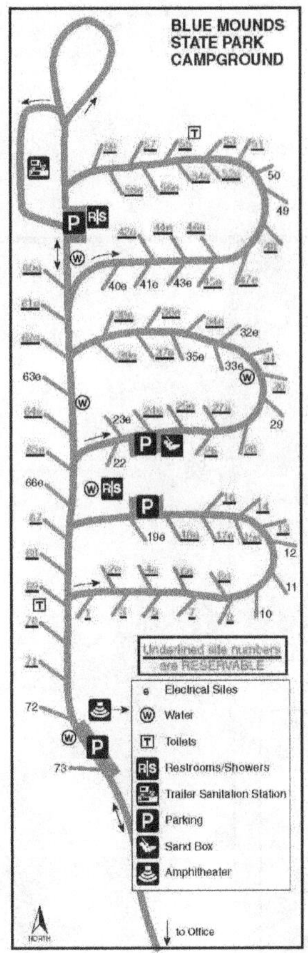
BLUE MOUNDS
STATE PARK
CAMPGROUND
50
49
40e
41e
43e
32e
35e
33e
63e
23e
22
29
66e
19e
12
11
10
72
73
Underlined site numbers are RESERVABLE
e Electrical Sites
Water
Toilets
Restrooms/Showers
Trailer Sanitation Station
Parking
Sand Box
Amphitheater
NORTH
to Office

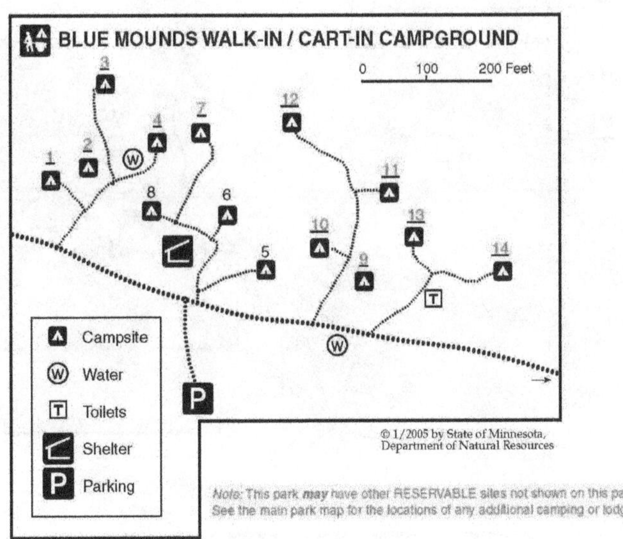
BLUE MOUNDS WALK-IN / CART-IN CAMPGROUND
0 100 200 Feet
1
2
3
4
5
6
7
8
9
10
11
12
13
14
Campsite
Water
Toilets
Shelter
Parking
© 1/2005 by State of Minnesota, Department of Natural Resources
Note: This park may have other RESERVABLE sites not shown on this page.
See the main park map for the locations of any additional camping or lodging sites.

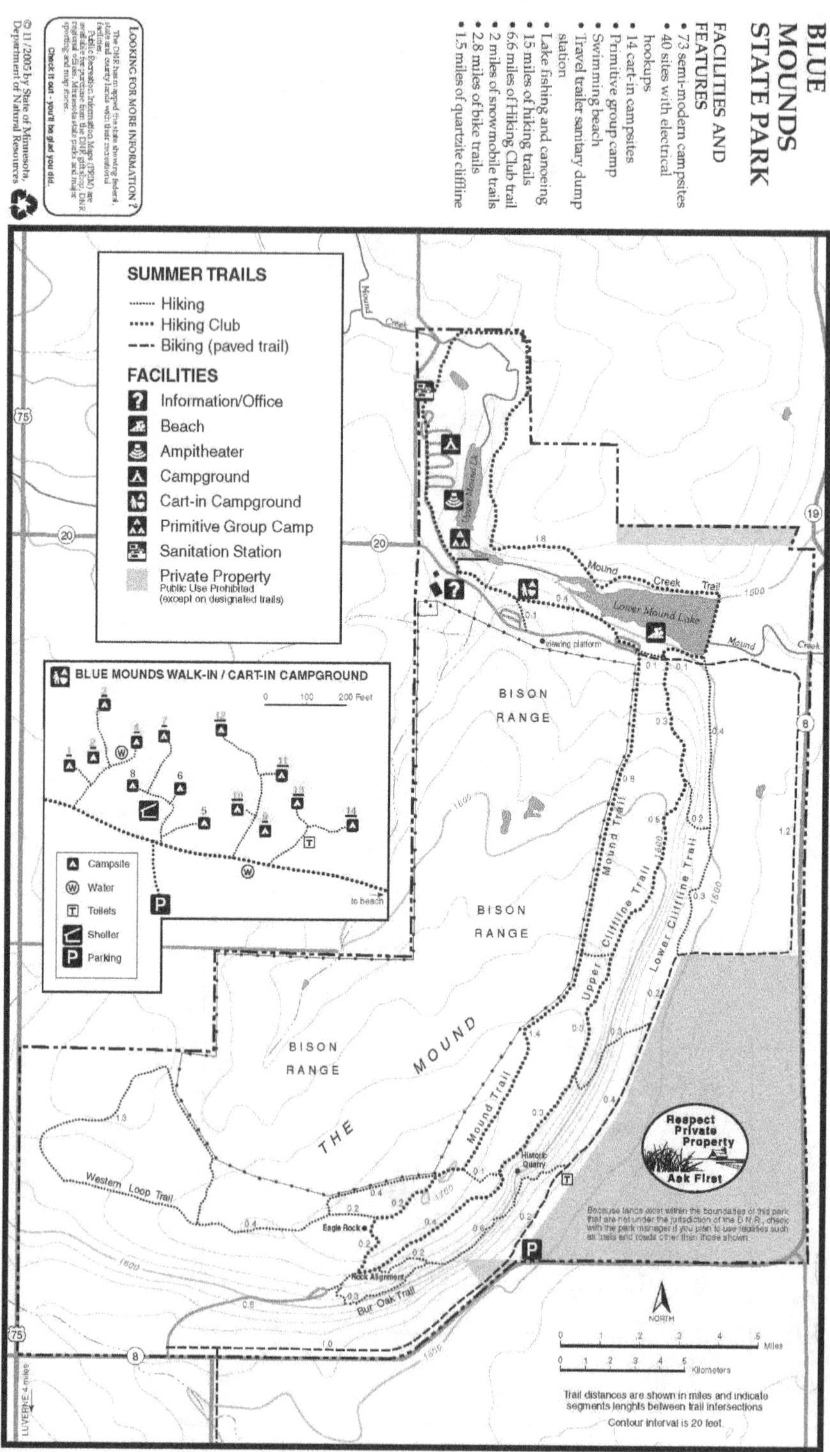
BLUE MOUNDS STATE PARK
FACILITIES AND FEATURES
• 73 semi-modern campsites
• 40 sites with electrical hookups
• 14 cart-in campsites
• Primitive group camp
• Swimming beach
• Travel trailer sanitary dump station
• Lake fishing and canoeing
• 15 miles of hiking trails
• 6.6 miles of Hiking Club trail
• 2 miles of snowmobile trails
• 2.8 miles of bike trails
• 1.5 miles of quartzite cliffline
LOOKING FOR MORE INFORMATION?
© 11/2005 by State of Minnesota, Department of Natural Resources
SUMMER TRAILS
Hiking
Hiking Club
Biking (paved trail)
FACILITIES
Information/Office
Beach
Ampitheater
Campground
Cart-in Campground
Primitive Group Camp
Sanitation Station
Private Property
Public Use Prohibited (except on designated trails)
BLUE MOUNDS WALK-IN / CART-IN CAMPGROUND
Campsite
Water
Toilets
Shelter
Parking
to beach
Mound Creek
Upper Mound Lake
Mound Creek Trail
Lower Mound Lake
viewing platform
BISON RANGE
BISON RANGE
BISON RANGE
THE MOUND
Mound Trail
Upper Cliffline Trail
Lower Cliffline Trail
Western Loop Trail
Eagle Rock
Rock Alignment
Bur Oak Trail
Historic Quarry
Respect Private Property
Ask First
NORTH
Miles
Kilometers
Trail distances are shown in miles and indicate segments lenghts between trail intersections
Contour interval is 20 feet.

Buffalo River

565 – 155th Street South
Glyndon, Minnesota 56547
218-498-2124

- Park is located 4.5 miles east of the town of Glyndon, MN. It is 14 miles east of Moorhead.
- This is a small Park with 41 campsites. Most of these sites have electric hook-ups available. Sites are relatively close together and there is little underbrush; so, there won't be much seclusion from your camping neighbors.
- There are toilets and showers on site, picnic area, there is a small

pond with swimming beach, and a storm shelter very near the campgrounds.

- There are about seven miles of hiking trails and these trails have observation points set up along the paths.

- The Minnesota State University at Moorhead has set up a Science Center very near the park. There is a field near the park entrance where prairie restoration is occurring.

- The camp sites we liked in the park were: 16, 18, 35, 39, and 41.

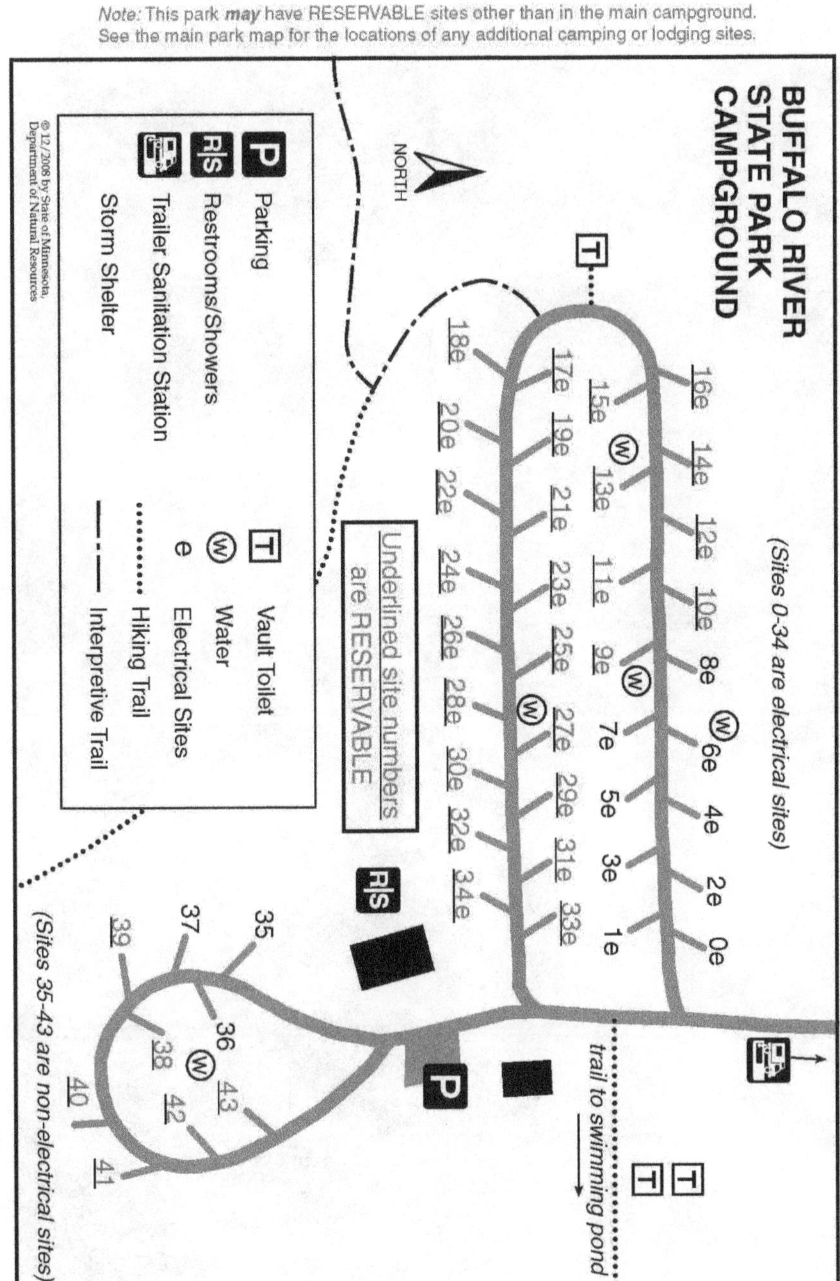
Note: This park may have RESERVABLE sites other than in the main campground.
See the main park map for the locations of any additional camping or lodging sites.
BUFFALO RIVER STATE PARK CAMPGROUND
(Sites 0-34 are electrical sites)
NORTH
16e 14e 12e 10e 8e 6e 4e 2e 0e
15e 13e 11e 9e 7e 5e 3e 1e
17e 19e 21e 23e 25e 27e 29e 31e 33e
18e 20e 22e 24e 26e 28e 30e 32e 34e
Underlined site numbers are RESERVABLE
trail to swimming pond
35 36 37 38 39 40 41 42 43
(Sites 35-43 are non-electrical sites)
Parking
Restrooms/Showers
Trailer Sanitation Station
Storm Shelter
Vault Toilet
Water
e Electrical Sites
Hiking Trail
Interpretive Trail
© 12/2008 by State of Minnesota, Department of Natural Resources

(Golden Rod in bloom)

BUFFALO RIVER STATE PARK

FACILITIES AND FEATURES

- Semi-modern campsites
- Showers
- Picnic area
- Swimming beach
- Trailer dump station
- Pioneer group camp
- Cross-country ski trails
- Nature trails
- Picnic shelter

VISITOR FAVORITES

- Camping
- Swimming
- Hiking
- Nature observation
- Skiing
- Picnicking

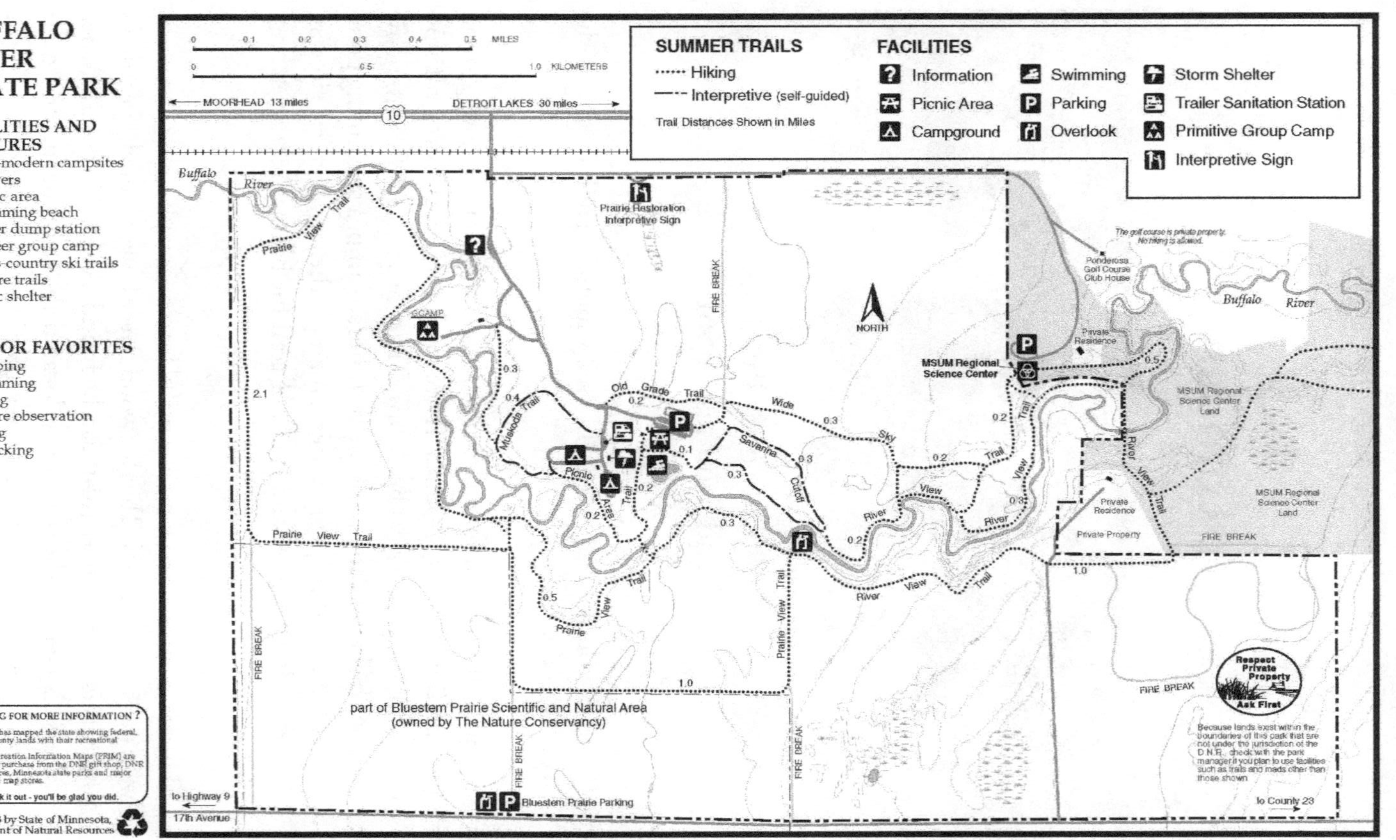

LOOKING FOR MORE INFORMATION?

The DNR has mapped the state showing federal, state and county lands with their recreational facilities.

Public Recreation Information Maps (PRIM) are available for purchase from the DNR gift shop, DNR regional offices, Minnesota state parks and major sporting and map stores.

Check it out - you'll be glad you did.

Camden

1897 County Road 68
Lynd, Minnesota 56157
507-865-4530

- This park is located off of MN Hwy. 23 about ten miles south of the city of Marshall.

- The park has two different camp areas – the Upper Campground and the Lower Campground. There are a total of 80 sites with 34 of them having electrical hook-ups. There are three different picnic areas with shelters at two of them. A horse camp, a swimming pond that is fed by fresh spring water, an amphitheater, historic sites on the grounds and miles and miles of trail for hiking, biking, skiing, Horse back riding, and snowmobiling.

- The park is made up of a very beautiful forest of maples and basswoods with oaks interspersed. The Redwood River flows through the valleys and this is a river where trout can be found. A small lake – Brawner Lake is also part of the park and is located about 1 mile further south on Hwy. 23. There is a fishing pier, picnic area, and boat landing at the lake.

- One of the prize sites to see at Camden is in the fall with the changing colors of the leaves on the trees. With the variety of tress species at this park, the colors will be fantastic.

- Lower Camp has nice tree cover, good shading. The area underneath the trees is open and does not allow much for seclusion. Large Maple and Cottonwood trees can be found throughout the Lower Camp. Both Campgrounds have fresh water spigots and vault toilets. The flush toilet/shower buildings are very nice.

- The Upper Camp has many sites that are more open to the sun with a little shade. This Camp area has nice level sites just like the Lower Camp. The Upper Camp has 7 sites that allow for the vehicles to completely pull through for setting up.

- We liked Sites # 22, 23, 30, 34, 42, 44, 75, 81, and 82.

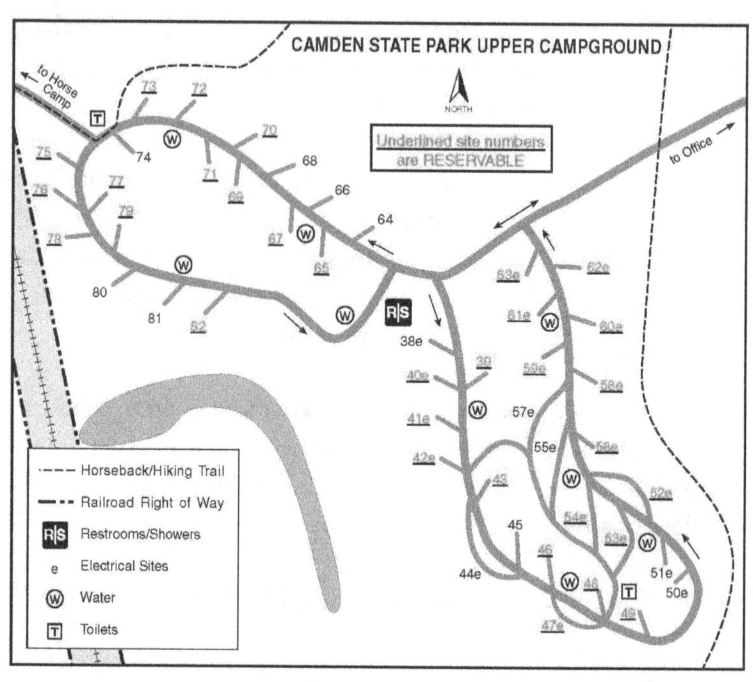
CAMDEN STATE PARK UPPER CAMPGROUND
NORTH
Underlined site numbers are RESERVABLE
to Horse Camp
to Office
73 72 70 68 66 64
74 71 69 67 65
75 76 77 79 78
80 81 82
38e 39 40e 41e 42e 43
62e 63e 61e 60e 59e 58e 57e 55e 56e
52e 54e 53e 51e 50e
45 44e 46 48 49 47e
Horseback/Hiking Trail
Railroad Right of Way
R|S Restrooms/Showers
e Electrical Sites
W Water
T Toilets

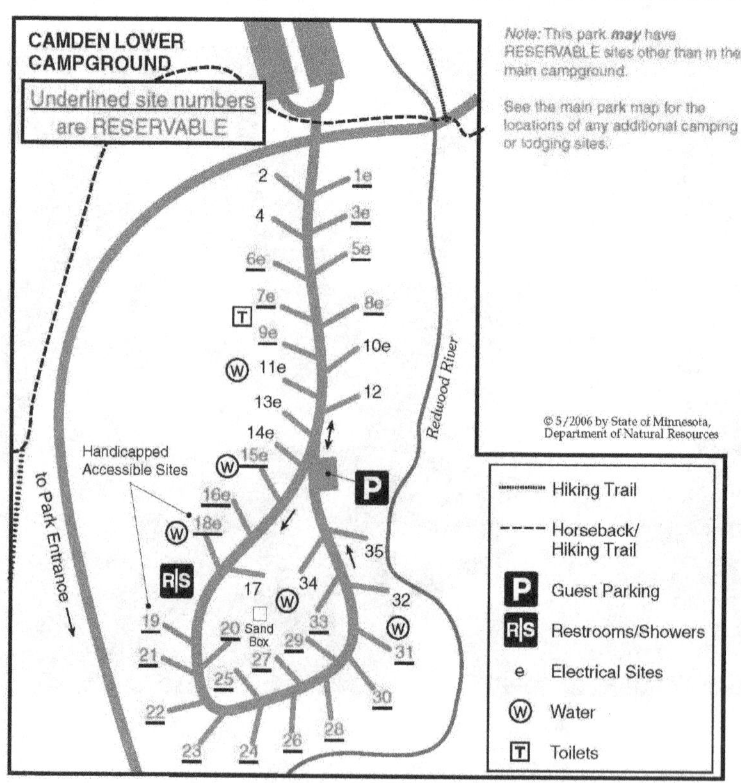
CAMDEN LOWER CAMPGROUND
Underlined site numbers are RESERVABLE
Note: This park may have RESERVABLE sites other than in the main campground.
See the main park map for the locations of any additional camping or lodging sites.
2 1e 4 3e 6e 5e 7e 8e 9e 10e 11e 12 13e 14e 15e
16e 18e 17 34 35 32 33 31 29 30
19 20 21 27 25 22 23 24 26 28
Sand Box
Handicapped Accessible Sites
to Park Entrance
Redwood River
© 5/2006 by State of Minnesota, Department of Natural Resources
Hiking Trail
Horseback/ Hiking Trail
P Guest Parking
R|S Restrooms/Showers
e Electrical Sites
W Water
T Toilets

CAMDEN STATE PARK

FACILITIES AND FEATURES

- 80 semi-modern campsites (34 with electric hook-up)
- Dump station, flush toilets and showers
- Primitive group camp (50 capacity)
- 3 picnic grounds, two with a shelter
- Spring-filled swimming pond
- 14.8 miles of hiking trails
- 10.2 miles of horseback trail
- 4.2 miles of bike riding trail
- 5.0 miles of ski trails
- 1.4 miles of skate ski trails
- 7.6 miles of snowmobile trails
- Horse riders' campground

VISITOR FAVORITES

- Dakota Valley Trail
- Maple-basswood forest
- Bubbling clear springs
- Swimming beach
- Trout fishing
- Brawner Lake
- Winter warming house
- Bluebirds
- Souvenir items

LOOKING FOR MORE INFORMATION?

The DNR has mapped the state showing federal, state and county lands with their recreational facilities.

Public Recreation Information Maps (PRIM) are available for purchase from the DNR gift shop, DNR regional offices, Minnesota state parks and major sporting and map stores.

Check it out - you'll be glad you did.

SUMMER TRAILS
Hiking
Horseback/Hiking
Mountain Bike/Horseback/Hiking
Hiking/Biking
0.5 Trail distances shown in miles.

FACILITIES
Information/Office
Picnic Area
Overlook
Historic Site
Parking
Campground
Primitive Group Camp
Equestrian Camping
Swimming
Amphitheater
Boat Ramp
Fishing Pier
Trailer Dump Station
Private Property
Public Use Prohibited (except on designated trails)

NOTE: SEASONAL FOOTBRIDGES
Some footbridges on trails crossing the Redwood River may not be in place due to seasonal periods of high water. Check at the Park Office for current conditions.

CAMDEN LOWER CAMPGROUND
Underlined site numbers are RESERVABLE

Respect Private Property Ask First

Because lands exist within the boundaries of this park that are not under the jurisdiction of the D.N.R., check with the park manager if you plan to use facilities such as trails and roads other than those shown.

Carley

Carley State Park c/o Whitewater State Park
Route 1, P.O. Box 256
Altura, Minnesota 55910
507-932-3007

- This state park is located four miles south of Plainview, Minnesota, on Wabasha County Highway 4. This small state park is located about ten miles northwest of Whitewater State Park. Carley State Park is located on the inside of a large loop in the north branch of the Whitewater River.

- The Whitewater River is a registered trout stream and there are several places within the park to access the good fishing that can be found here.

- The park was originally donated to the state by a former state senator- James Carley and a local resident in the area as a means to try and preserve a native stand of white pine that still existed along the hillsides near the river. That stand of white pines still exists and can be viewed from the picnic area.

- There is a small monument and plaque with a tall flagpole nearby that is a monument to Senator Carley. There is a remote group camp area and several remote camp sites in the park. There are 20 sites in the main campground. Two vault toilets and a water spigot. The picnic area also has a small picnic shelter available for use.

- There are several miles of multi-use trails in the park. Winter camping is allowed in the park and the trail system allows for excellent cross-country skiing.

- There are abundant trees in the park to give shade on the camp sites. There is a lot of undergrowth to help separate the sites. There only 20 sites; but, these sites are diverse and could be used by tent or trailer. The parking pads are relatively flat and it would be easy to level a small RV in any of the sites.

- Camp sites in the park that we liked were: 1, 6, 10, and 14.

- Carley State Park is a small park and doesn't have all of the amenities that can be found at Whitewater State Park; however, if you are looking for a nice quiet park to spend some time 'away from it all' – this would be a good choice.

(Carley Monument at Carley State Park.)

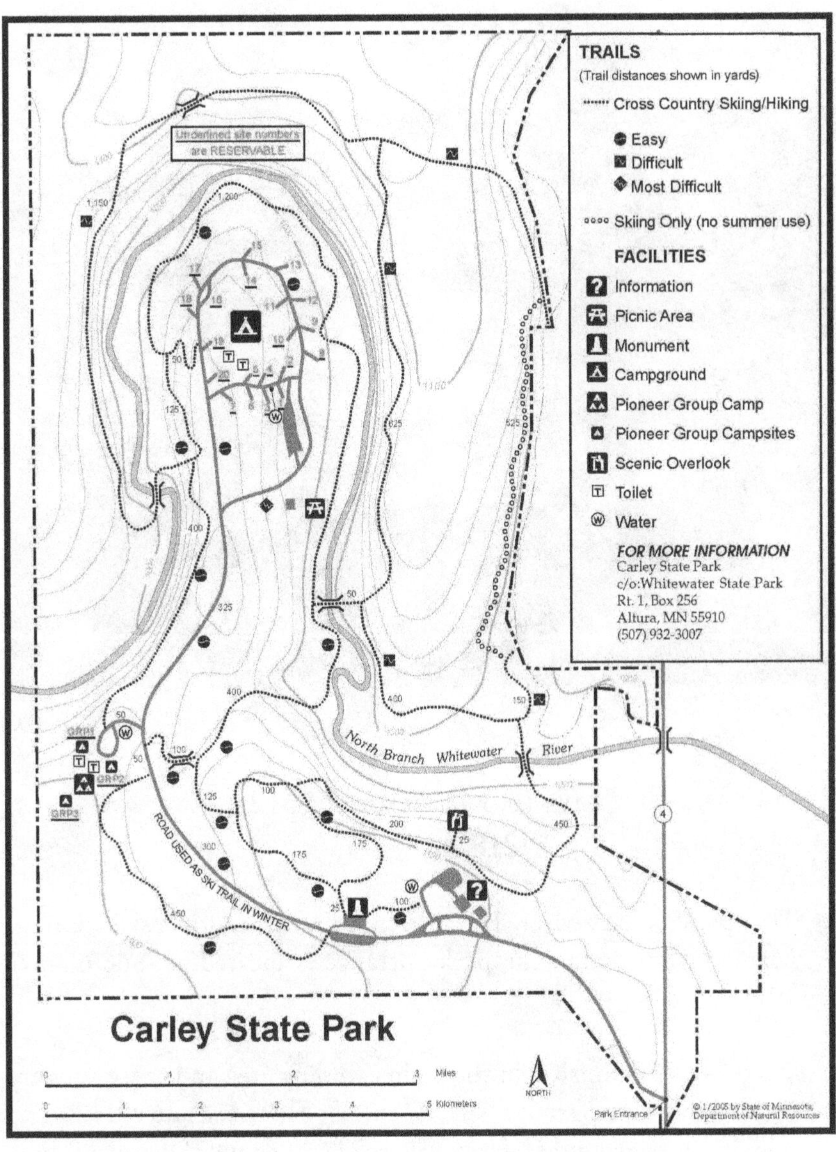
TRAILS
(Trail distances shown in yards)
Cross Country Skiing/Hiking
Easy
Difficult
Most Difficult
Skiing Only (no summer use)
FACILITIES
Information
Picnic Area
Monument
Campground
Pioneer Group Camp
Pioneer Group Campsites
Scenic Overlook
Toilet
Water
FOR MORE INFORMATION
Carley State Park
c/o:Whitewater State Park
Rt. 1, Box 256
Altura, MN 55910
(507) 932-3007
Underlined site numbers are RESERVABLE
North Branch Whitewater River
ROAD USED AS SKI TRAIL IN WINTER
GRP1
GRP2
GRP3
Carley State Park
Miles
Kilometers
NORTH
Park Entrance
© 1/2005 by State of Minnesota, Department of Natural Resources

Cascade River

3481 West Highway 61
Lutsen, Minnesota 55612
218-387-3053

- This park is located on Hwy. 61 nine miles southwest of Grand Marais, Minnesota. The park entrance is located at mile marker 101.

- There are 40 campsites in the main camping area and these sites are divided into three groups – A, B, and C. There are lots of trees and undergrowth around each site. There is a toilet and shower building. There are vault toilets and water spigots throughout the park. There are five camping sites that are accessible along the hiking trails. There are two Group Camp areas, too.

- There is a trail center building located in the park that is open year round. It has a wood stove, picnic tables, electric outlets and pop-machines.

- There are 18 miles of hiking trails, 17 miles of cross country ski trail, snowmobile trails and there is access to the North Shore State Trail and the Lake Superior Hiking Trail.

- There is a nice picnic area near the lake on the other side of the highway. The entrance to the picnic area is located about ½ mile down from the park's main entrance. There are seven picnic sites.

- Two high peaks along the north shore can be reached on the trails inside the park - Moose Mountain and Lookout Mountain.

- The trails in the park are of varying difficulty; however, it is strongly recommended to take a walk along the trails close to the camping area – these trails will take you to the beautiful waterfalls in the park.

- Sites that we liked were # A2, A14, B9, C2, C8, and C21.

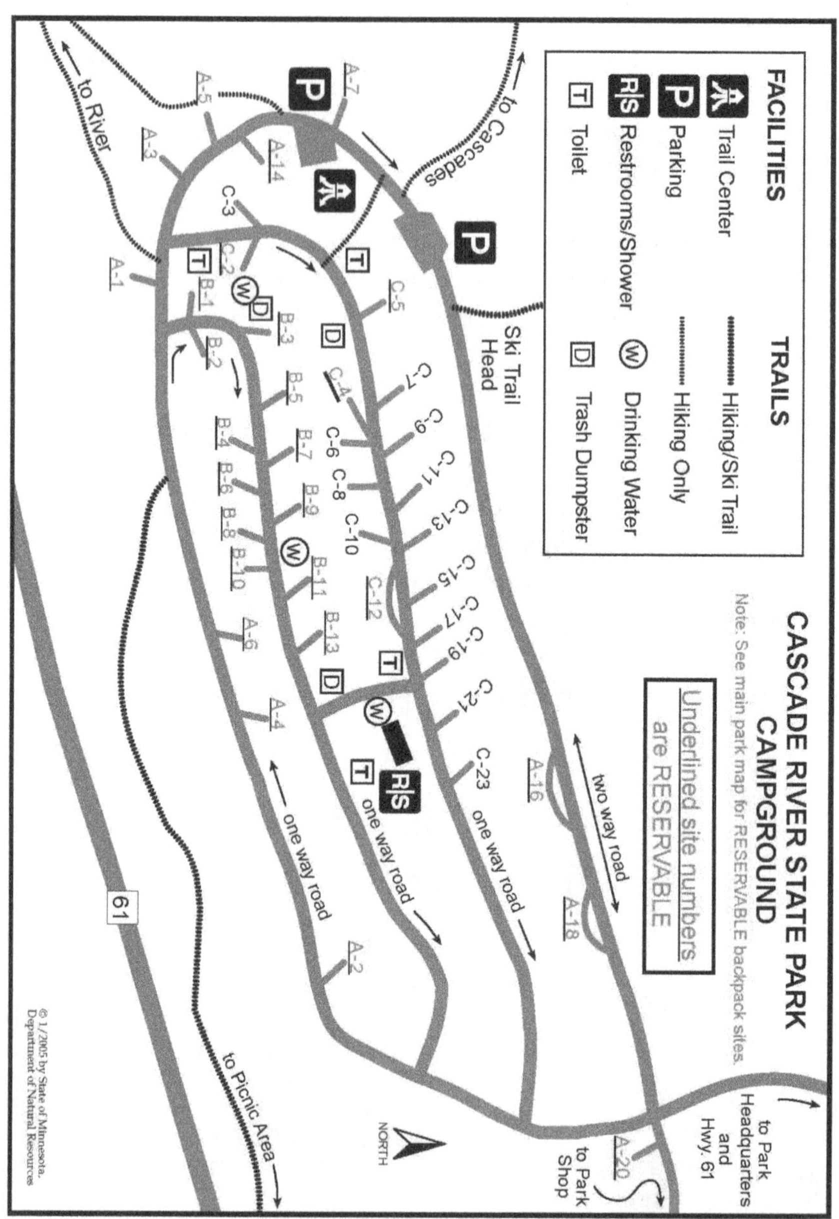

Note: This park ***may*** have RESERVABLE sites other than in the main campground. See the main park map for the locations of any additional camping or lodging sites.

CASCADE RIVER STATE PARK

FACILITIES AND FEATURES

- 40 semi-modern campsites with showers, flush toilets, and trailer sanitation station.
- A year-round trail center building with picnic tables, a wood stove, electrical outlets and a pop machine.
- Group camp with two campsites
- Five backpack campsites
- Access to Superior Hiking Trail
- 18 miles of hiking trails
- 17 miles of cross country ski trails
- Two miles of snowmobile trail with access to area trails and the North Shore State Trail
- Seven picnic sites along Lake Superior
- Lake and trout stream fishing

VISITOR FAVORITES

- Waterfalls of the Cascade River (0.5 mile/0.8 kilometer loop hike)
- Hiking to Lookout Mountain, 600 feet above Lake Superior (3.5 miles/5.6 kilometers, round trip)
- One and a half miles of rugged Lake Superior shore
- Hiking along the Cascade River

LOOKING FOR MORE INFORMATION?

The DNR has mapped the state showing federal, state and county lands with their recreational facilities.

Public Recreation Information Maps (PRIM) are available for purchase from the DNR gift shop, DNR regional offices, Minnesota state parks and major sporting and map stores.

Check it out - you'll be glad you did.

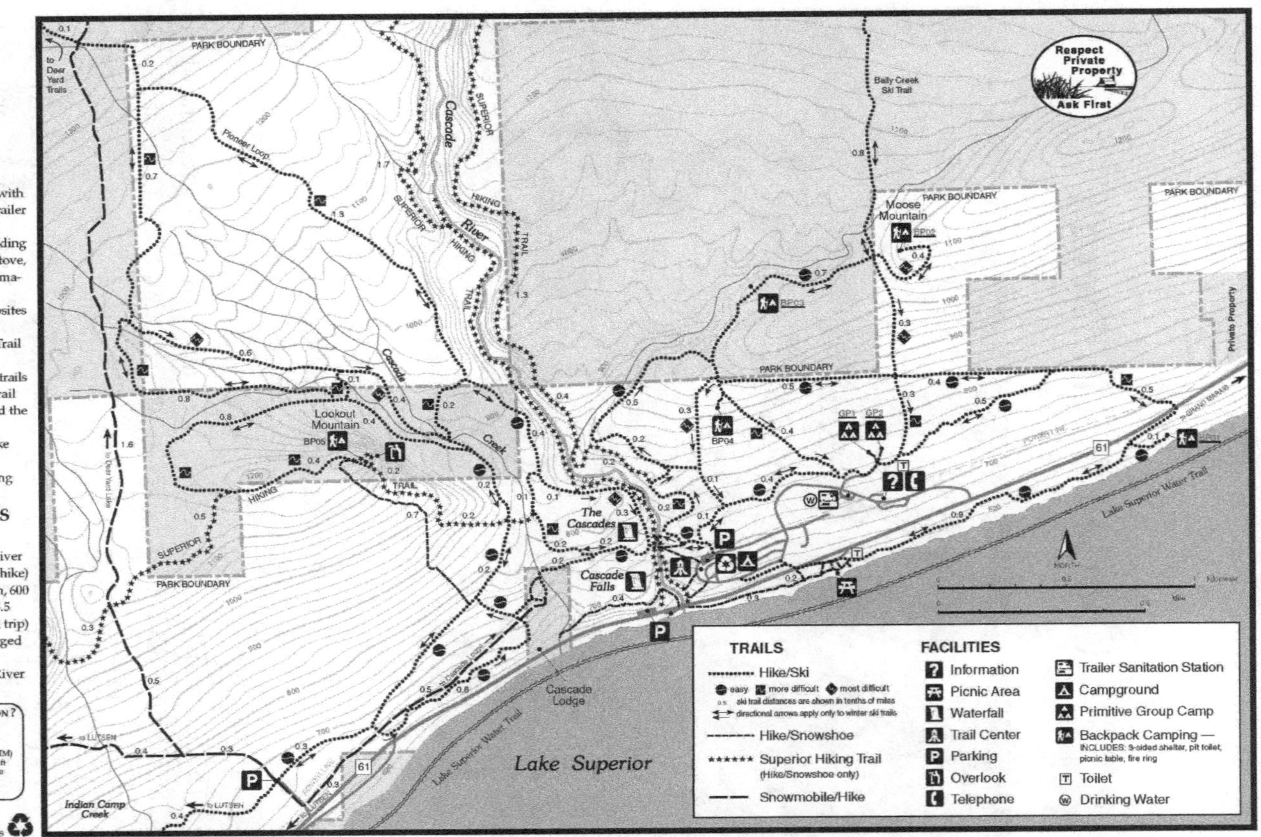

Charles A. Lindbergh

P.O. Box 364
Little Falls, Minnesota 56345
320-616-2525

- This lovely 570 acre park is located along the west shoreline of the Mississippi River as it makes its way through the southwest section of Little Falls, MN.

- The park is populated by large oaks and pines throughout. There is plenty of shade and the camping area is small with only 38 campsites. 15 of the sites have electrical hook-ups. There is a lot of undergrowth in between the camping sites and will allow for a nice secluded feeling, even though you are inside the city limits.

- There is a beautiful picnic area, 8 miles of hiking trails, and 5 miles of cross country ski trails. There are boat access ramps on to the river, remote campsites on some of the trails, water spigots, vault toilets, and a nice flush toilet/shower facility.

- There is the Lindbergh House which is an historic site. There are tours and other activities that occur in the park. There is also a museum on site chronicling the life and history of Charles Jr., who flew the Spirit of St. Louis across the Atlantic.

- We liked sites # 12, 13, 19, 25, 26, 27, and 35. We were impressed by all the sites. There is lots of seclusion and shading between the camp sites.

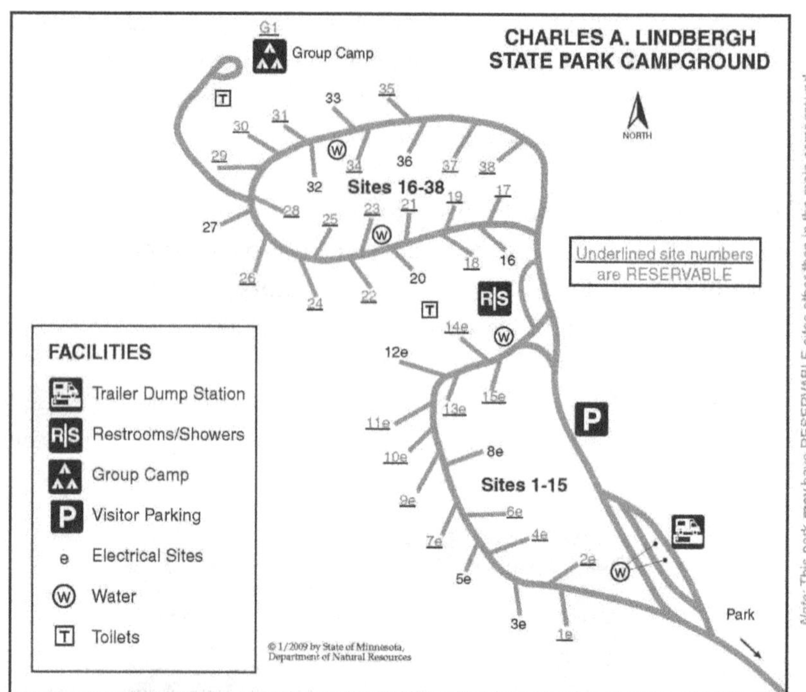

(Morning Mist)

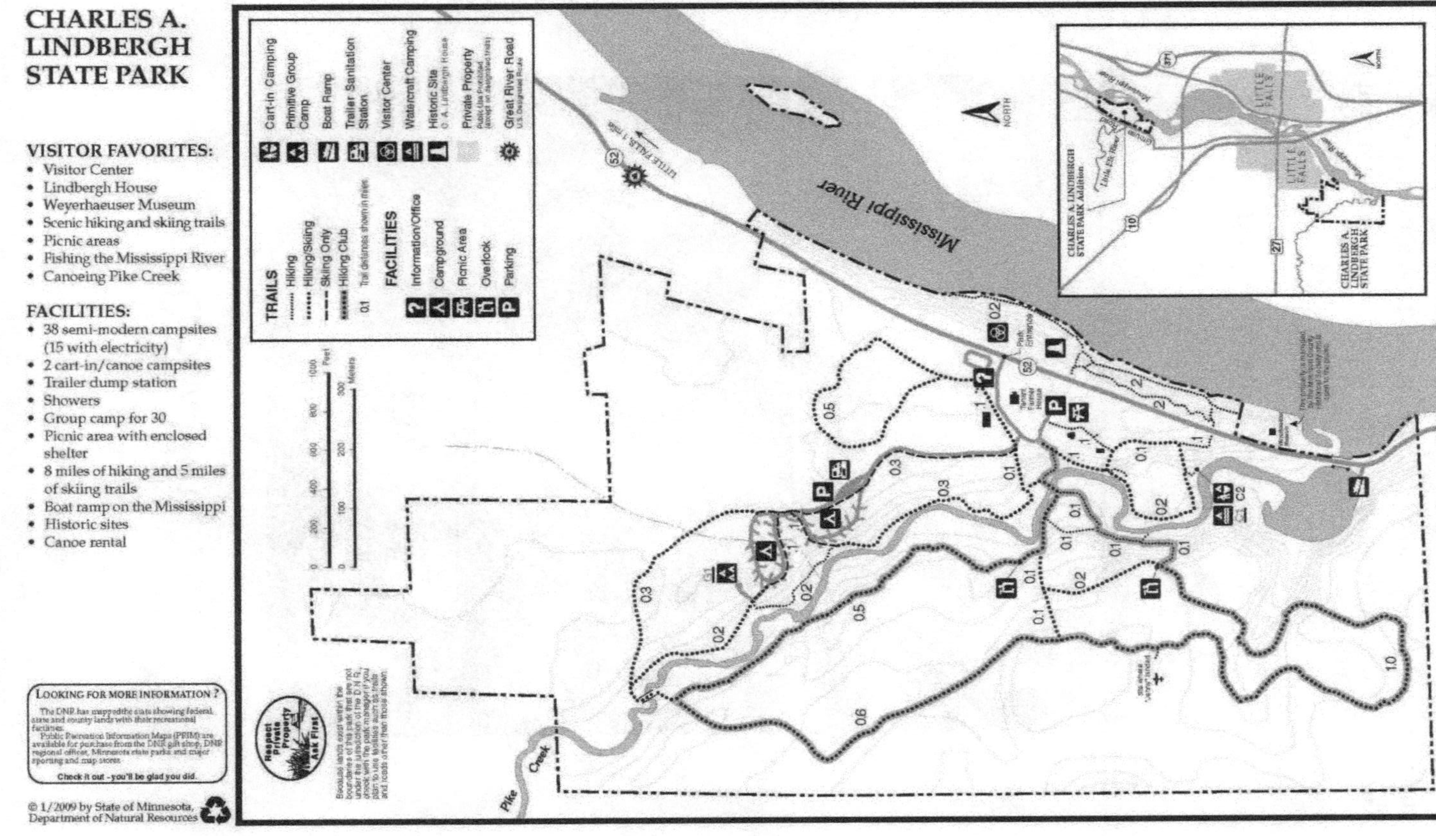

CHARLES A. LINDBERGH STATE PARK
VISITOR FAVORITES:
• Visitor Center
• Lindbergh House
• Weyerhaeuser Museum
• Scenic hiking and skiing trails
• Picnic areas
• Fishing the Mississippi River
• Canoeing Pike Creek
FACILITIES:
• 38 semi-modern campsites (15 with electricity)
• 2 cart-in/canoe campsites
• Trailer dump station
• Showers
• Group camp for 30
• Picnic area with enclosed shelter
• 8 miles of hiking and 5 miles of skiing trails
• Boat ramp on the Mississippi
• Historic sites
• Canoe rental
LOOKING FOR MORE INFORMATION?
Check it out - you'll be glad you did.
© 1/2009 by State of Minnesota, Department of Natural Resources
TRAILS
Hiking
Hiking/Skiing
Skiing Only
Hiking Club
0.1 Trail distances shown in miles
FACILITIES
Information/Office
Campground
Picnic Area
Overlook
Parking
Cart-in Camping
Primitive Group Camp
Boat Ramp
Trailer Sanitation Station
Visitor Center
Watercraft Camping
Historic Site
C. A. Lindbergh House
Private Property
Great River Road
Respect Private Property
Ask First
Pike Creek
Mississippi River
LITTLE FALLS, 1 mile
Tenant Farmer House
Park Entrance
NORTH
CHARLES A. LINDBERGH STATE PARK Addition
LITTLE FALLS
CHARLES A. LINDBERGH STATE PARK

Crow Wing

3124 State Park Road
Brainerd, Minnesota 56401
218-825-3075

- The park is located nine miles south of Brainerd, MN, on U.S. Hwy 371. This was the site of the former village of Crow Wing and a fur trading post.

- A wonderful park with lots of history with regards to this area's use by the native tribes and then followed by the white trappers and settlers later. The park was the site of a great Indian battle between the Dakota and the Ojibwe in 1768. There is also a white-settlement historical site within the park with an interpretive trail that is easily followed.

- There is an amphitheater, boat launch, picnic areas, primitive camp sites accessible by hike or boat, canoe and boat rental and 14 miles of hiking trail.

- The park has 61 sites for camping. 12 sites are electric. Camping area has a lot of mixed tree species - pine and hardwoods. There is a little underbrush between sites - so, the sites have minimal seclusion. There are a lot of Raspberry bushes in amongst the underbrush - paradise - when the berries are ripe.

- A very nice set of flush toilets and showers. Also, vault toilets are all around.

- Sites that we liked were - # 4, 20, 21, 30, 31, 34, 35, and 36.

- There is nice close access to the Mississippi River from the campground. This is a very nice family oriented park.

(Mississippi River at Crow Wing State Park)

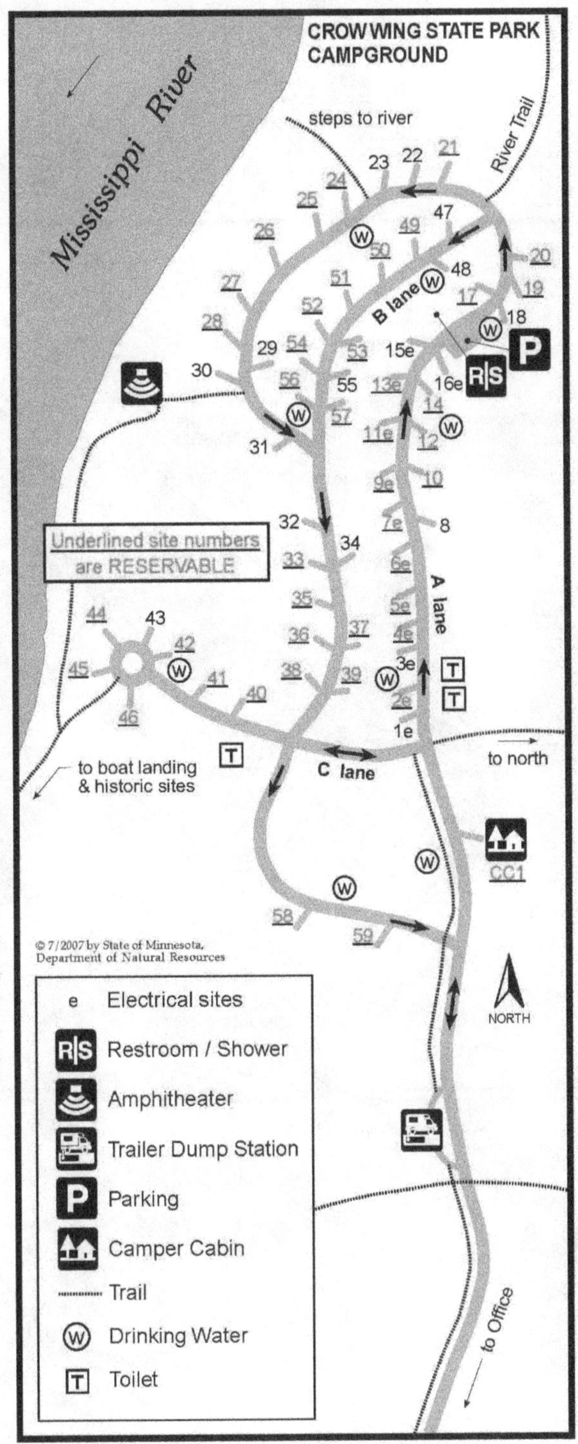

Note: This park may have RESERVABLE sites other than in the main campground. See the main park map for the locations of any additional camping or lodging sites.

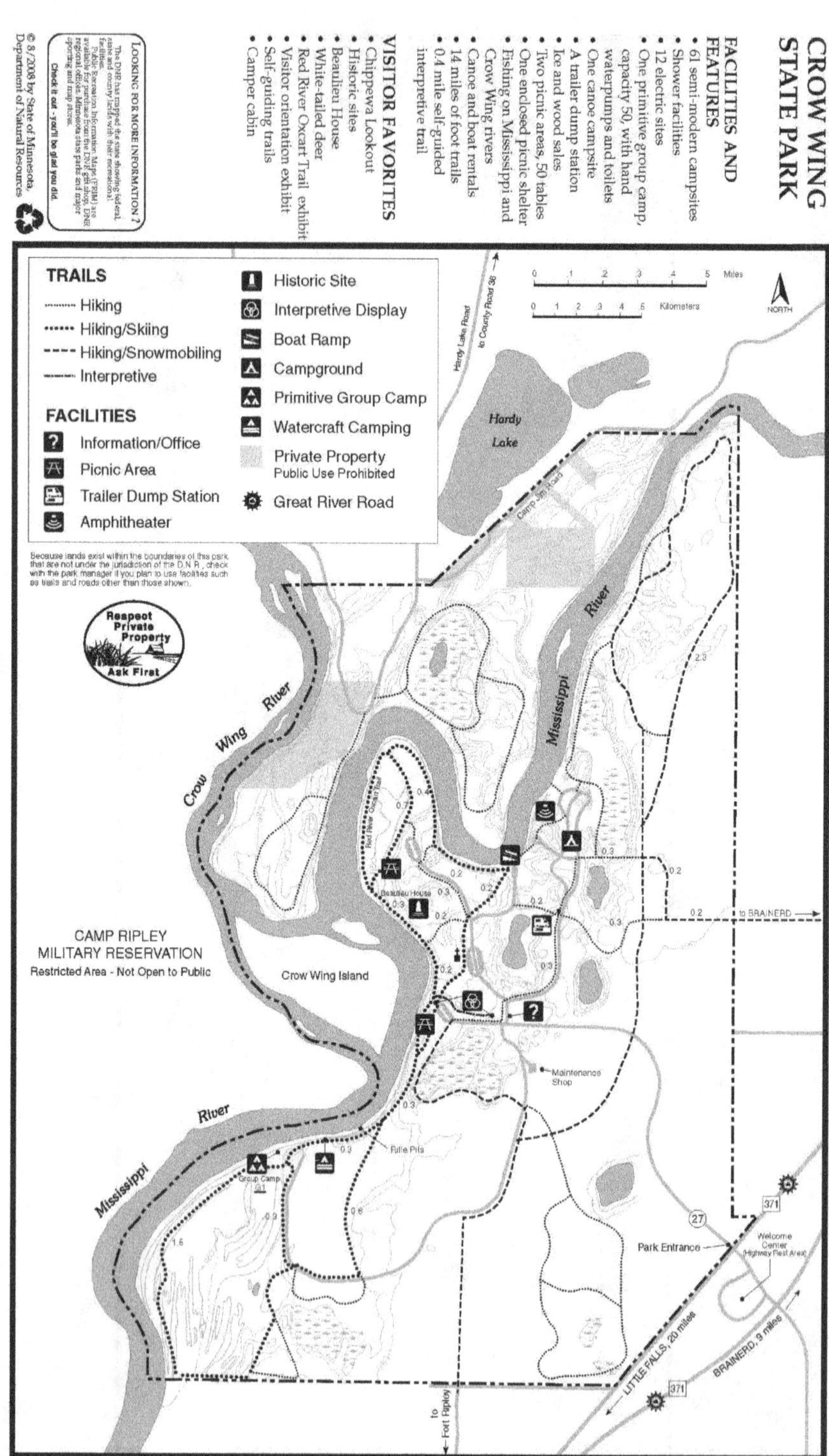

CROW WING STATE PARK
FACILITIES AND FEATURES
• 61 semi-modern campsites
• Shower facilities
• 12 electric sites
• One primitive group camp, capacity 50, with hand waterpumps and toilets
• One canoe campsite
• A trailer dump station
• Ice and wood sales
• Two picnic areas, 50 tables
• One enclosed picnic shelter
• Fishing on Mississippi and Crow Wing rivers
• Canoe and boat rentals
• 14 miles of foot trails
• 0.4 mile self-guided interpretive trail
VISITOR FAVORITES
• Chippewa Lookout
• Historic sites
• Beaulieu House
• White-tailed deer
• Red River Oxcart Trail exhibit
• Visitor orientation exhibit
• Self-guiding trails
• Camper cabin
LOOKING FOR MORE INFORMATION?
Check it out - you'll be glad you did.
© 8/2008 by State of Minnesota, Department of Natural Resources
TRAILS
Hiking
Hiking/Skiing
Hiking/Snowmobiling
Interpretive
FACILITIES
Information/Office
Picnic Area
Trailer Dump Station
Amphitheater
Historic Site
Interpretive Display
Boat Ramp
Campground
Primitive Group Camp
Watercraft Camping
Private Property
Public Use Prohibited
Great River Road
Because lands exist within the boundaries of this park that are not under the jurisdiction of the D.N.R., check with the park manager if you plan to use facilities such as trails and roads other than those shown.
Respect Private Property
Ask First
Miles
Kilometers
NORTH
Hardy Lake Road
to County Road 36
Hardy Lake
Camp Jim Road
Mississippi River
Crow Wing River
CAMP RIPLEY
MILITARY RESERVATION
Restricted Area - Not Open to Public
Crow Wing Island
Beaulieu House
Maintenance Shop
Rifle Pits
Group Camp
to BRAINERD
Park Entrance
Welcome Center (Highway Rest Area)
LITTLE FALLS, 20 miles
BRAINERD, 9 miles
to Fort Ripley
27
371

Cuyuna Country

P.O. Box 404, 307 3rd Street
Ironton, Minnesota 56455
218-546-5926

- This is a new addition to the state park system. It is located north of Highway 210, just outside of the towns of Crosby/Ironton.

- The park has a single campground with seventeen nice level sites. There are water spigots available throughout the camping area and now there are electrical hookups available on about half of the campsites.

- There is access to the multi-use Cuyuna Lakes State Trail and several other hiking trails in the park. There is a group camp site in the park and picnic areas that are so close to the water that you could almost fish from the seat of the picnic table.

- Many of the lakes inside of the park are reclaimed mine pits. The waters are clean, deep, and cool. Many of these lakes have been stocked with rainbow, brown and brook trout.

- The Depot Museum and the Croft Mine Historical site are close by in Crosby.

- Numerous other boat landing sites at other lakes in the park with good parking, paved roads, and vault toilets at the landings.

- There is a single set of vault toilets in the camping area. No shower facilities available. The sites on the east side have shading from the trees, sites # 6 to 12 are mostly in the open at this time. There are many small saplings that have been planted to try and gain more shade.

- We liked sites - # 2, 5, 15, and 16.

- The Ranger Station for this recreational area is located in Ironton on 3rd Street, about one mile from the camping area.

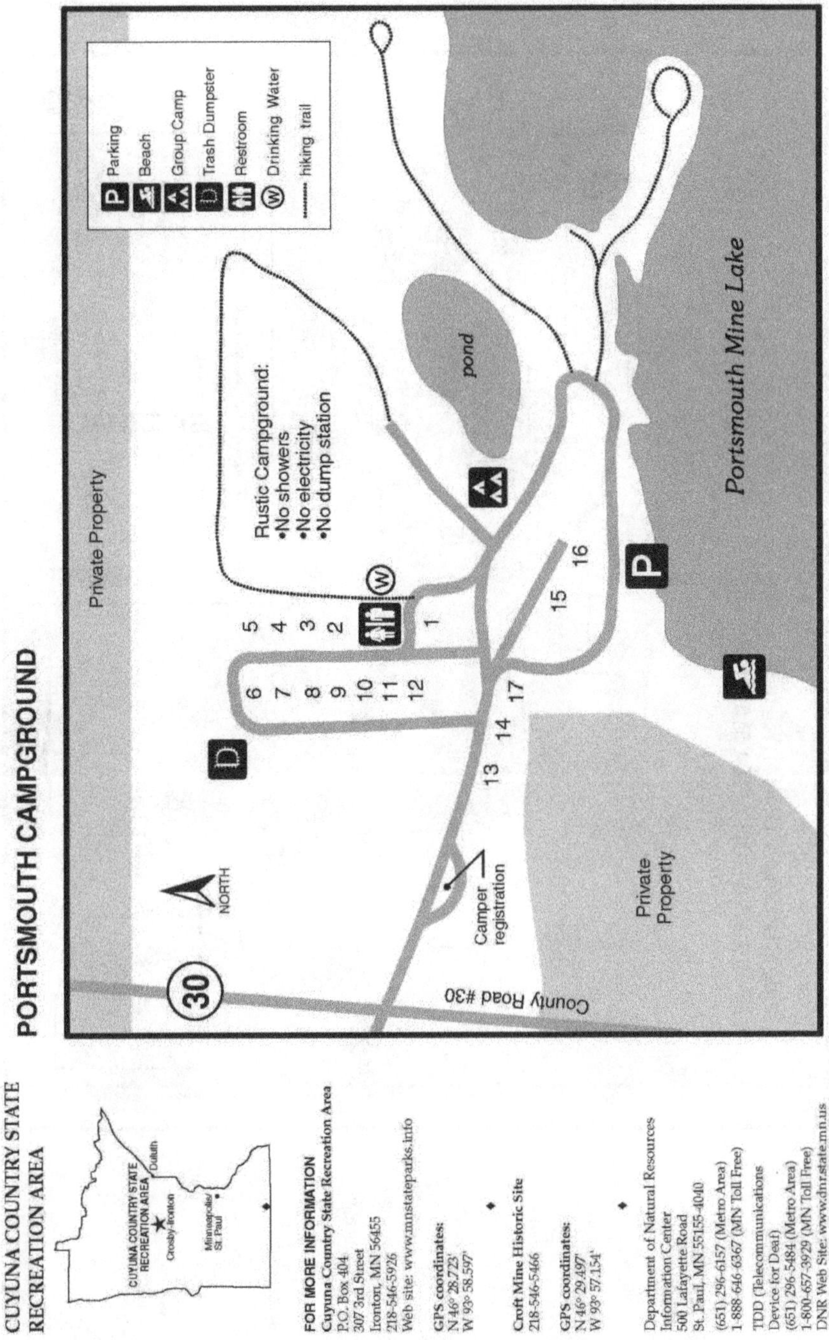

PORTSMOUTH CAMPGROUND

Private Property

P Parking
Beach
Group Camp
Trash Dumpster
Restroom
W Drinking Water
hiking trail

30
NORTH
D
Rustic Campground:
•No showers
•No electricity
•No dump station

6 7 8 9 10 11 12
5 4 3 2 1
W
County Road #30
Camper registration
13 14 17 15 16
pond
P
Private Property
Portsmouth Mine Lake

CUYUNA COUNTRY STATE RECREATION AREA

FOR MORE INFORMATION
Cuyuna Country State Recreation Area
P.O. Box 404
307 3rd Street
Ironton, MN 56455
218-546-5926
Web site: www.mnstateparks.info

GPS coordinates:
N 46° 28.723'
W 93° 58.597'

♦

Croft Mine Historic Site
218-546-5466

GPS coordinates:
N 46° 29.497'
W 93° 57.154'

♦

Department of Natural Resources
Information Center
500 Lafayette Road
St. Paul, MN 55155-4040
(651) 296-6157 (Metro Area)
1-888-646-6367 (MN Toll Free)
TDD (Telecommunications
Device for Deaf)
(651) 296-5484 (Metro Area)
1-800-657-3929 (MN Toll Free)
DNR Web Site: www.dnr.state.mn.us

CUYUNA COUNTRY STATE RECREATION AREA

- New state recreation area with limited services & facilities
- Open 8:00 AM to 10:00 PM daily

FACILITIES AND FEATURES

- 17 rustic campsites
- Group camp
- Designated trout lakes*
- Scuba diving opportunities
- Cuyuna Overlook
- Cuyuna Lakes State Trail
- Croft Mine Historical Site

♦

PROHIBITED USES

- Off-highway vehicles
- Target & trap shooting
- Remote camping
- Building or maintaining a fire except in a fire ring at Portsmouth Campground
- Consuming or displaying intoxicating liquors

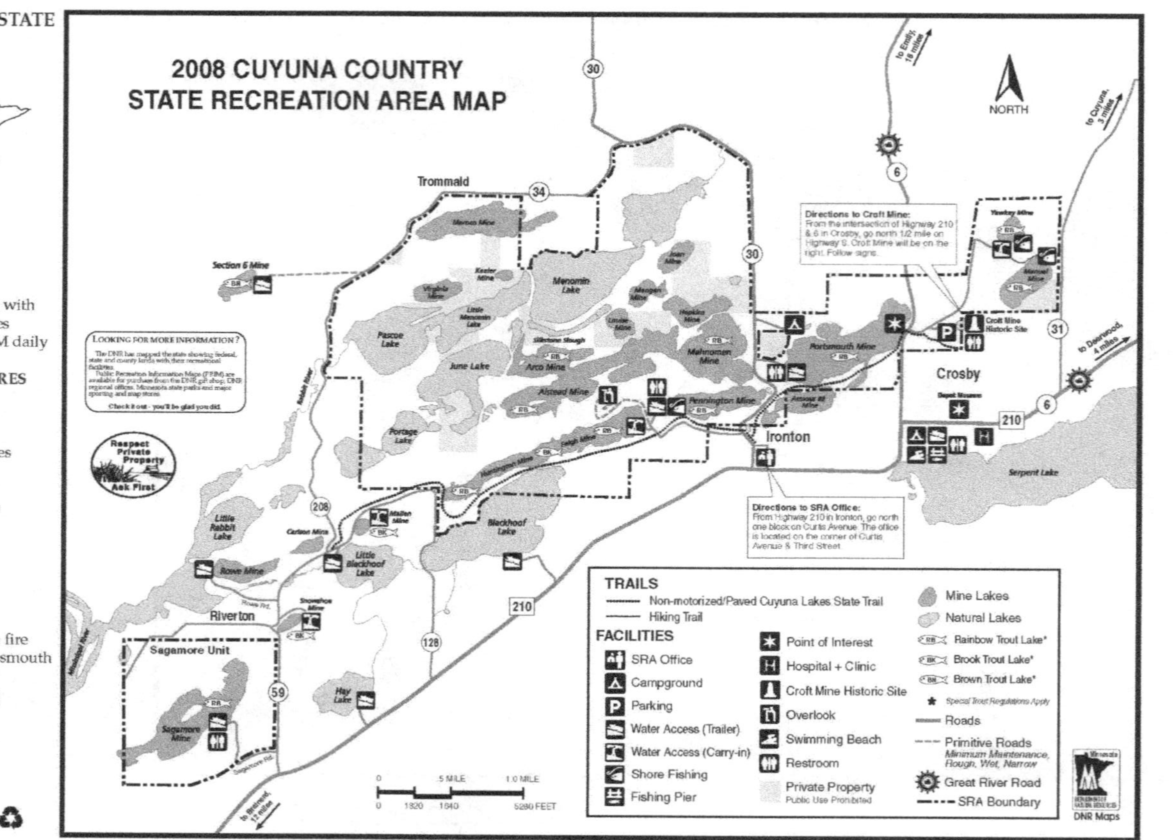

Father Hennepin

P.O. Box 397
Isle, Minnesota 56342
320-676-8763

- The entrance to this park is just outside the city limits of the town of Isle, Minnesota. The park sits on the southeast shore of Mille Lacs Lake. The park can be reached by taking MN Hwy. 47 north to Isle and then turning west on MN Hwy 27. If you are traveling on Hwy 169, you drive north past Onamia and turn east on Hwy. 27. Continue on Hwy. 27 driving east through the small towns of Cove and Wahkon until you reach the park entrance

- The park is named for Father Louis Hennepin who is believed to be the first white explorer to reach this area in the 1670's and 1680's.

While on his mission to the area, he was taken prisoner with two of his companions by Indians in the region and brought to this area of Mille Lacs to be watched over by the band of Indians that lived here at the time. It is reported that Hennepin and his two companions spent much of their time as captives staying on the small island just to the east of the park in Isle Bay.

- This park is very family oriented. There are two different camping areas and two fishing piers for use along the lake shore. There is a playground for children, two boat landing areas, over 7 miles of interpretive hiking and cross country skiing trails, remote camp sites, and a large picnic area with tables and fire rings.

- The camping areas are equipped with water spigots, vault toilets, and each camp area has its own shower facility with flush toilets.

- Lakeview Campground is closest to the lake. It has one of the two boat landings for the lake near it. All of the camping sites with electrical hookups are located in this campground. Seven of the campsites for Lakeview are located at the base of the hill down by the lake shore. There is good tree cover in this camp and should provide plenty of shading. However, there is not a lot of under growth between the campsites and the bulk of the sites in this campground are close together.

- The other camping area in the state park is Maple Grove Campground. This camping area is set back from the lake and there is more undergrowth between the campsites. The sites are also spaced a little farther apart here.

- Sites that we liked were: 3, 4, 7, 13, 27, 33, 55, 65, 71, 75, 90, 92, 97, 100, and 102.

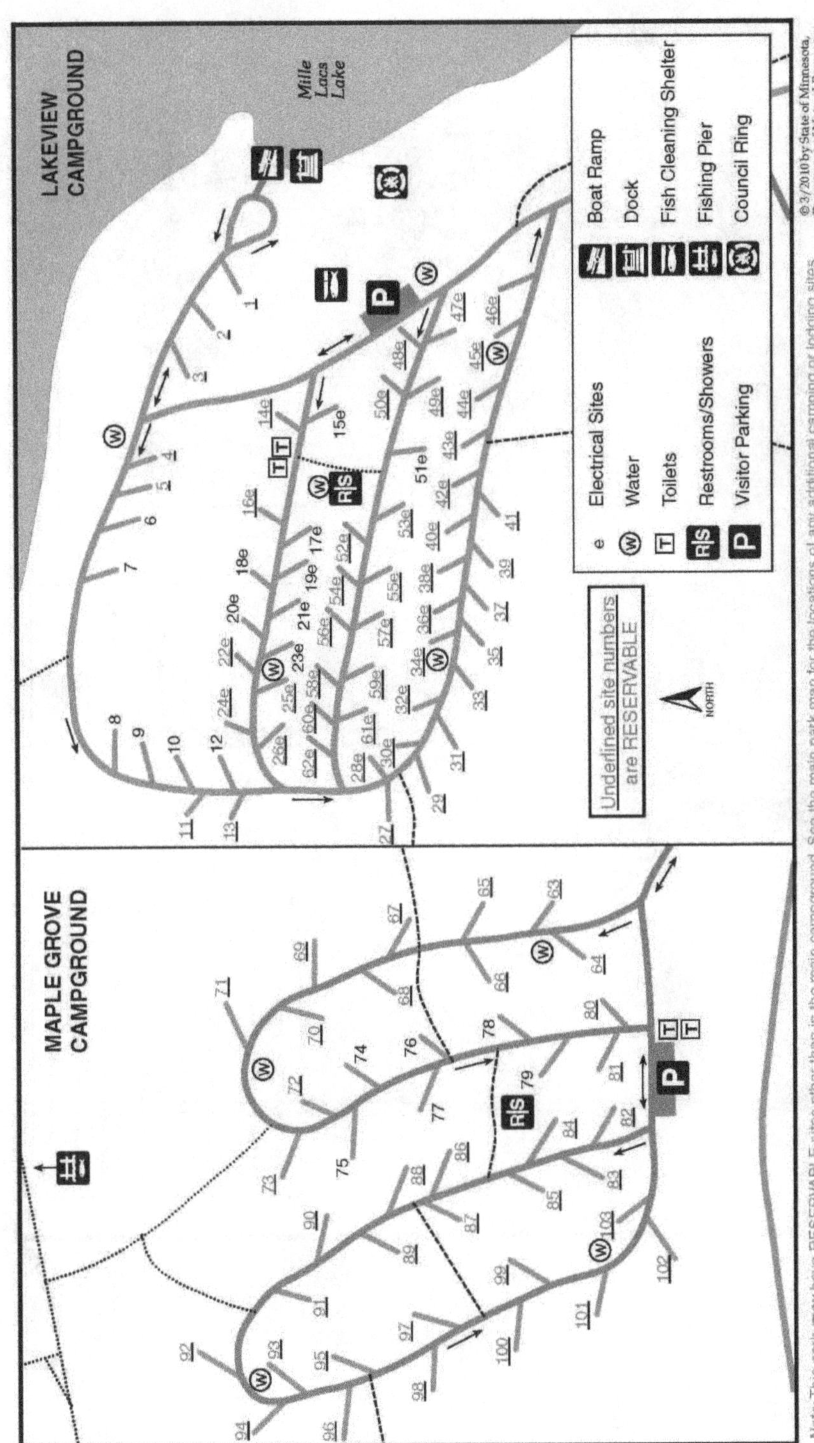
MAPLE GROVE CAMPGROUND
LAKEVIEW CAMPGROUND
Mille Lacs Lake
Underlined site numbers are RESERVABLE
NORTH
e Electrical Sites
W Water
T Toilets
R|S Restrooms/Showers
P Visitor Parking
Boat Ramp
Dock
Fish Cleaning Shelter
Fishing Pier
Council Ring
Note: This park may have RESERVABLE sites other than in the main campground. See the main park map for the locations of any additional camping or lodging sites.
© 3/2010 by State of Minnesota, Department of Natural Resources

FATHER HENNEPIN STATE PARK

FACILITIES AND FEATURES

- 103 semi-modern camp-sites
- 41 electrical sites
- Primative group camp
- Water, toilet and shower facilities
- Trailer dump station
- Picnicking, parking areas and two picnic shelters
- 4.5 miles of hiking trails
- 2.5 miles of cross-country ski trails
- 2 drive-in boat ramps
- 2 fishing piers
- Sandy swimming beach
- Fishing on Mille Lacs Lake

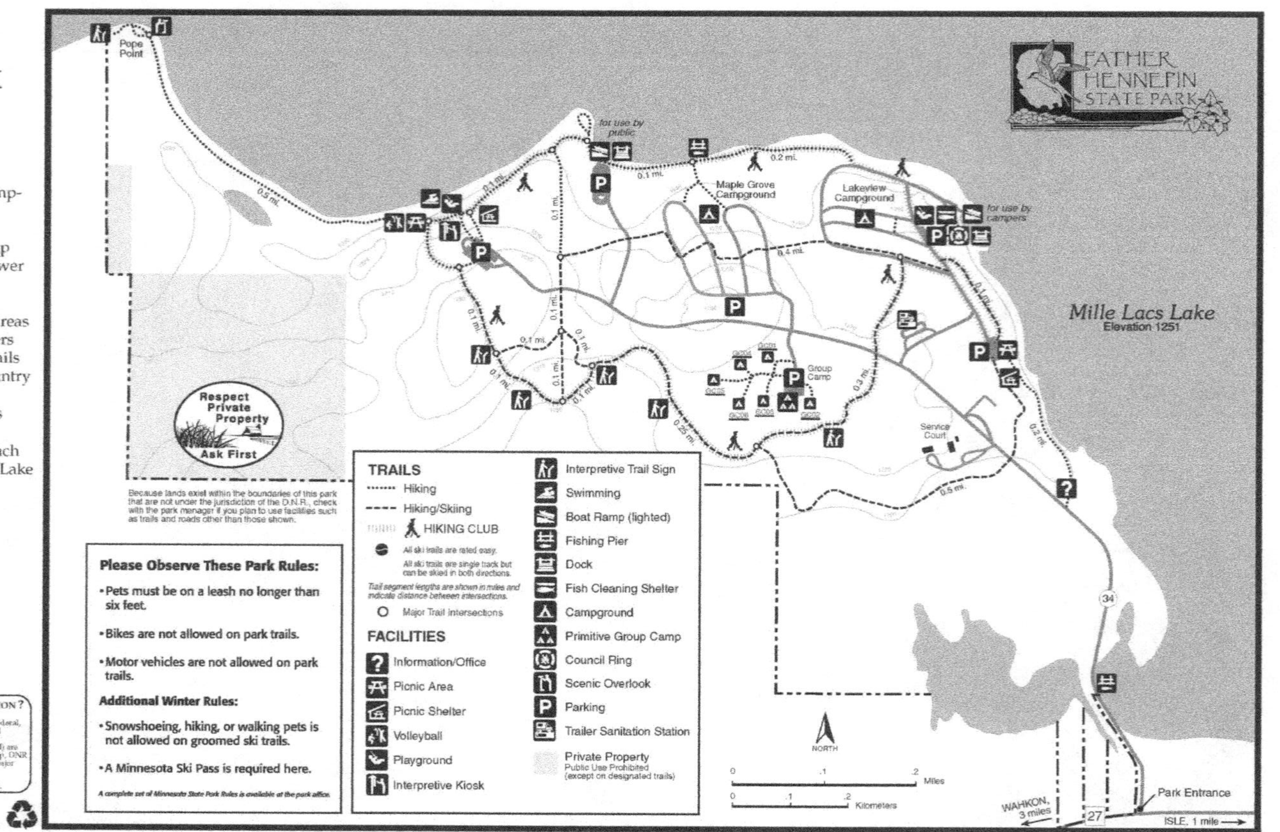

LOOKING FOR MORE INFORMATION?

The DNR has mapped the state showing federal, state and county lands with their recreational facilities. Public Recreation Information Maps (PRIM) are available for purchase from the DNR gift shop, DNR regional offices, Minnesota state parks and major sporting and map stores.

Check it out - you'll be glad you did.

Flandrau

1300 Summit Avenue
New Ulm, Minnesota 56073
507-233-9800

- This state park is located partially within the southern city limits of the city of New Ulm. The park sits in a valley created by the Cottonwood River. The Cottonwood flows into the Minnesota River about ½ mile further down stream from the park.

- There are over 90 campsites throughout the park. 34 sites have electric hook-ups, 22 sites that are non-electric, and 33 drive in rustic sites. There are also 3 remote walk-in sites. All the sites are easily accessed and are level.

- There is a beautiful swimming area created at the park, a short walk from the river. There is a modern group camp area that can handle up to 110 people. There are 8.5 miles of hiking trail and 7.5 miles of cross country ski trail. There is a large picnic area with shelters available.

- There is a very nice toilet/shower facility in the camp area. Vault toilets, water spigots, play grounds, volley ball, horse shoe pits, and scenic overlook spots along the trails.

- Flandrau State park is named after Charles Eugene Flandrau, a famous Minnesotan and a man of great importance in the history of New Ulm. The stories of Flandrau and the city of new Ulm are very interesting and there is more detail about the story in the narrative.

- The campsites are spaced fairly close together in the camping area. The sites inside the loops are especially close together. The sites on the outsides of the loops do offer some distance from the neighbors and some undergrowth of grass and brush between the sties.

- We liked sites # 11, 13, 17, 28, 34, 64, 67, and 87.

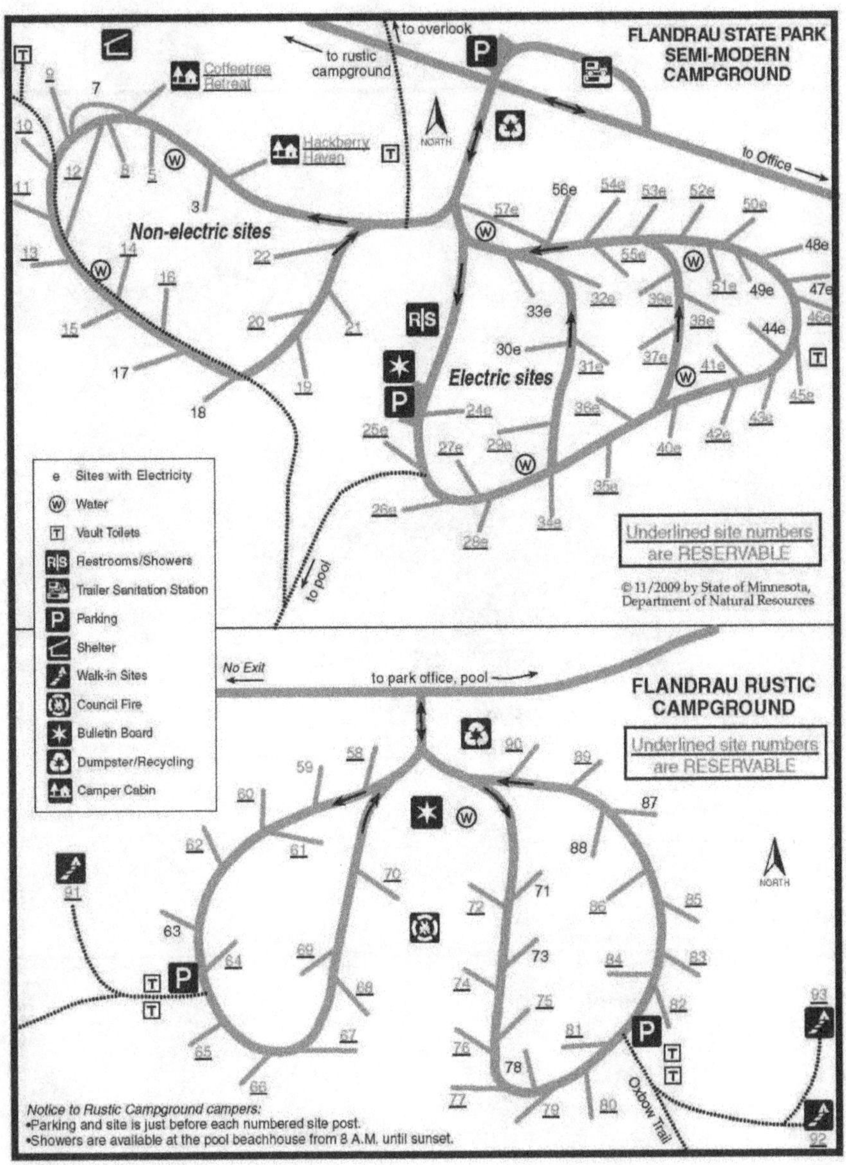
FLANDRAU STATE PARK
SEMI-MODERN
CAMPGROUND
to overlook
to rustic campground
Coffeetree Retreat
Hackberry Haven
NORTH
to Office
Non-electric sites
Electric sites
e Sites with Electricity
Water
Vault Toilets
Restrooms/Showers
Trailer Sanitation Station
Parking
Shelter
Walk-in Sites
Council Fire
Bulletin Board
Dumpster/Recycling
Camper Cabin
to pool
Underlined site numbers are RESERVABLE
© 11/2009 by State of Minnesota, Department of Natural Resources
No Exit
to park office, pool
FLANDRAU RUSTIC
CAMPGROUND
Underlined site numbers are RESERVABLE
NORTH
Oxbow Trail
Notice to Rustic Campground campers:
•Parking and site is just before each numbered site post.
•Showers are available at the pool beachhouse from 8 A.M. until sunset.

FLANDRAU STATE PARK

FACILITIES AND FEATURES

- 34 electric semi-modern campsites
- 2 Camper Cabins
- 18 non-electric semi-modern campsites
- 33 rustic drive-in campsites
- 3 rustic walk-in sites
- Dumping station, showers, and flush toilets
- Camping reservations accepted: 1-866-857-2757
- Volleyball
- Horseshoes
- Log play structure
- Modern group center (110 lodging capacity)
- 60 picnic sites with an enclosed beach house shelter
- Swimming pool with sand bottom
- 8 miles of hiking trails
- 8 miles of ski trails

POINTS OF INTEREST

- Trail overlooks: Indian Point, Grassland, Cottonwood and River Loop
- Swimming pool and beach house
- Historic WPA-era buildings
- Group center

Forestville/Mystery Cave

21071 County Road 118
Preston, Minnesota 55965
507-352-5111 (Main Park)
507-937-3251 (Mystery Cave)

- This state park is located mid way between the towns of Spring Valley and Preston. It lies about 3.5 miles south of MN Hwy. 16 on County Road 5.

- There is almost too much one can say about this park. The variety of things to do in this park would require a person to stay for days on end in order to see and experienced it all. There is a restored town site to visit, trout streams to fish, archeological dig sites, a separate horse camp, remote group camps, miles and miles of trail, wildlife to see and beautiful landscapes of the surrounding bluffs.

- The park is a wonderful place to go to visit for anyone who is interested in geology. The rock formations that are visible with the naked eye are wonderful. The 'karst' formations in the area are easily seen and can be studied in great detail. But, let's not forget that just 4 miles west of Forestville is the other half of the park – Mystery Cave. This is the largest single cave system in Minnesota.

- The horse camp and the riding trails at Forestville are the most heavily used of all the state parks. There dozens of sites for large horse trailers, many with electrical hookups, and 15 miles of riding trail.

- The traditional campground has over 70 sites with 23 sites having electrical hookups. There are showers and flush toilets available at each of the camps. There are vault toilets and spigots throughout the different camps and at the picnic areas. Access to three very highly rated trout fishing streams. Many campsites are within easy walking distance of the streams.

- The traditional campground is divided into three 'loops'. Loop C is the only loop that has electric hookups. There is lots of trees and cover around all the sites for shading and seclusion.

- The sites we liked are as follows: A7, A10, A15, A21, B27, B34, B38, B40, B46, C56, C58, C61, C62, C65, and C70.

- The Mystery Cave section of the park has a wonderful interpretive center with an amphitheater, large parking area, a big beautiful picnic area and tours of the cave system that run throughout the summer and on weekends in the spring and fall. You can choose either the one hour tour or the two hour tour of the cave.

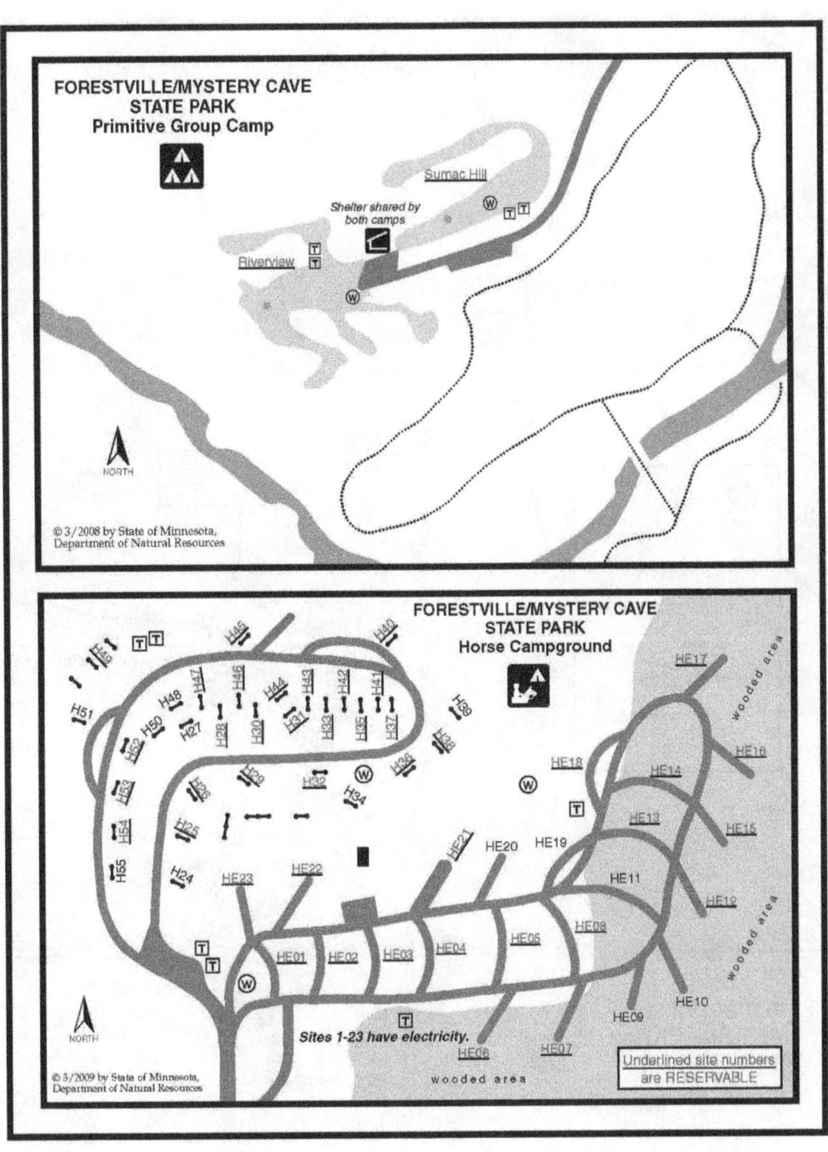
FORESTVILLE/MYSTERY CAVE
STATE PARK
Primitive Group Camp
Sumac Hill
Shelter shared by both camps
Riverview
NORTH
© 3/2008 by State of Minnesota, Department of Natural Resources
FORESTVILLE/MYSTERY CAVE
STATE PARK
Horse Campground
wooded area
Sites 1-23 have electricity.
Underlined site numbers are RESERVABLE
NORTH
© 3/2009 by State of Minnesota, Department of Natural Resources

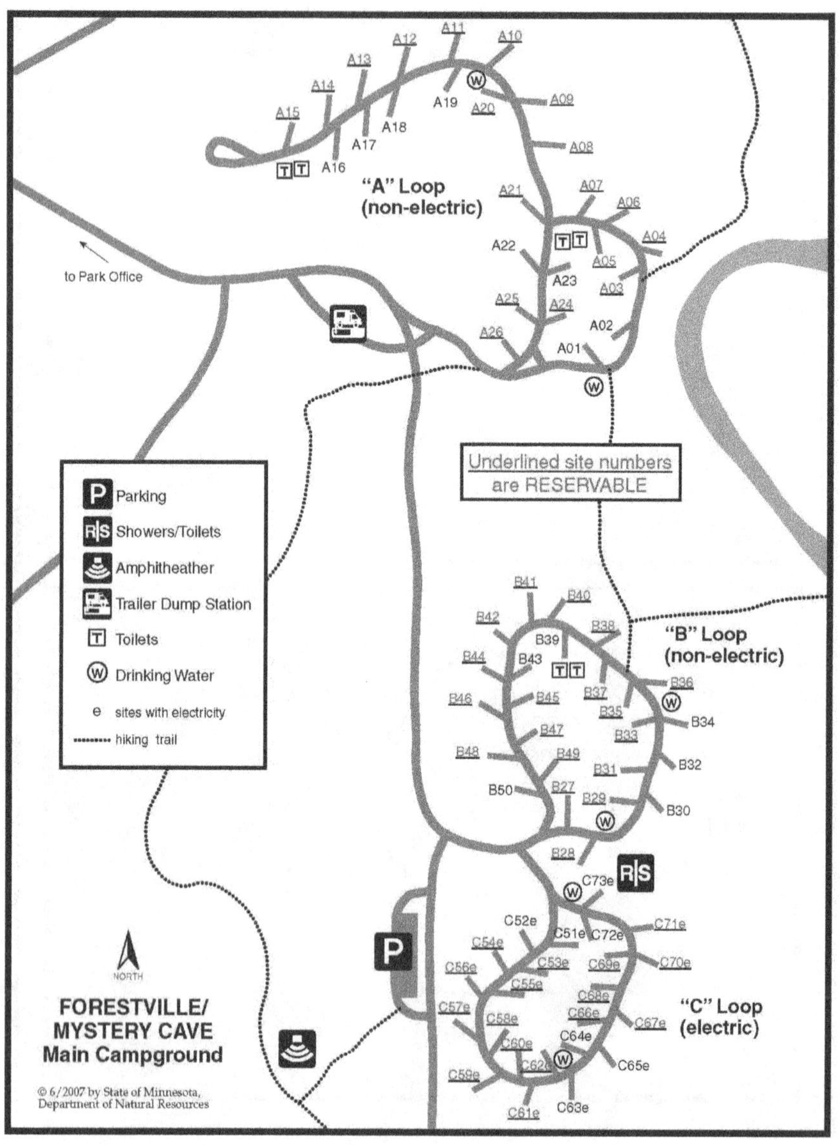
"A" Loop
(non-electric)
to Park Office
Underlined site numbers
are RESERVABLE
"B" Loop
(non-electric)
"C" Loop
(electric)
Parking
Showers/Toilets
Amphitheather
Trailer Dump Station
Toilets
Drinking Water
e sites with electricity
hiking trail
NORTH
FORESTVILLE/
MYSTERY CAVE
Main Campground
© 6/2007 by State of Minnesota,
Department of Natural Resources

FORESTVILLE/ MYSTERY CAVE STATE PARK

FACILITIES:

- 73 semi-modern campsites (23 with electrical hookups)
- Showers, flush toilets and dumping station.
- Horseback riders campground (57 unit capacity, 23 sites with electricity)
- Main picnic area with an enclosed shelter and 60 tables
- Mystery Cave picnic area with an additional 20 tables
- 17 miles of hiking trail
- 15 miles of horseback riding trail
- 11 miles of skiing trails
- 5.5 miles of snowmobile trails
- Summer season interpretive amphitheater
- Winter warming shelter

VISITOR FAVORITES:

- Mystery Cave tours
- Historic Forestville
  - Forestville Store & Post Office
  - Thomas & Mary Meighen Residence
  - Meighen Farm Buildings
  - 1899 Gillette-Hertzog Bridge
- Trout fishing
  - Canfield Creek
  - Forestville Creek
  - South Branch Root River
- Spring wildflowers and birding
- Big Spring (source of Canfield Creek)
- Historic markers throughout park

LOOKING FOR MORE INFORMATION?

The DNR has mapped the state showing federal, state and county lands with their recreational facilities.

Public Recreation Information Maps (PRIM) are available for purchase from the DNR gift shop, DNR regional offices, Minnesota state parks and major sporting and map stores.

Check it out - you'll be glad you did.

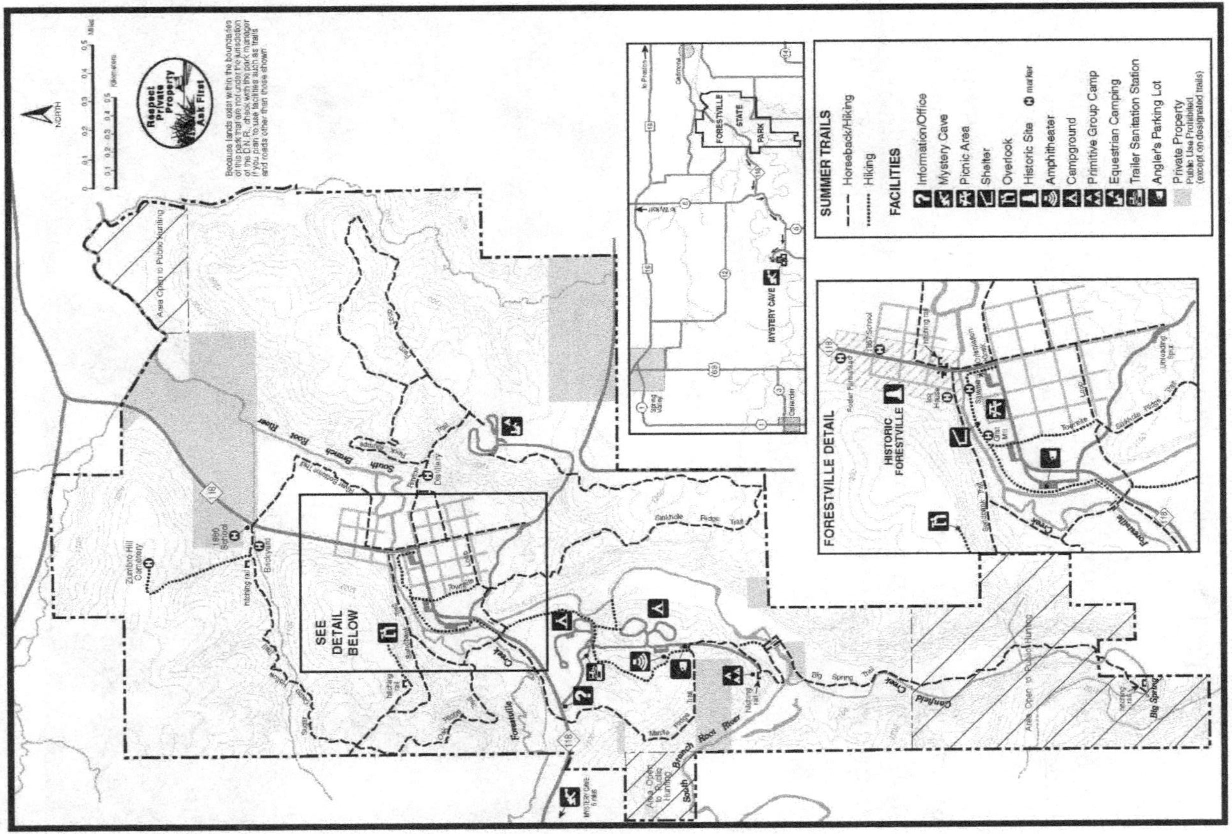

Fort Ridgley

72158 County Road 30
Fairfax, Minnesota 55332
507-426-7840

- This park is located about six miles south of the town of Fairfax, Minnesota, on MN. Hwy 4. This is a wonderful park not only for its scenery and the views of the Minnesota River Valley; but, because of the history of the site.

- This small park is located up the slope and on top of the escarpment over looking the Minnesota River Valley. There is lovely little 9-hole golf course on the property.

- There are 22 campsites in the main camping area. 15 of the sites have electric hook-ups. 12 camp sites are listed as rustic or walk-in sites. There are miles of hiking trails, biking trails and horseback trails. There is a separate horse camp area that is on the north side of the park and separate from the golf course and other camping areas. There is a picnic area on top of the escarpment by the interpretive center and a non-denominational cemetery.

- There are vault toilets, water spigots, a flush toilet/shower facility, a nice picnic area along the banks of the Fort Ridgley Creek, amphitheater, play ground areas, and a large interpretive center at the top of the escarpment that tells the history of Fort Ridgley and the Sioux Uprising in 1862.

- The campground has nicely secluded sites with decent spacing, and there are lots of huge cottonwoods in the camping area. We liked sites # 5, 11, 13, 15, 20, 22, 38 and 39.

- We both agreed that this little state park will be on our list of places to come back to in order to spend more time camping.

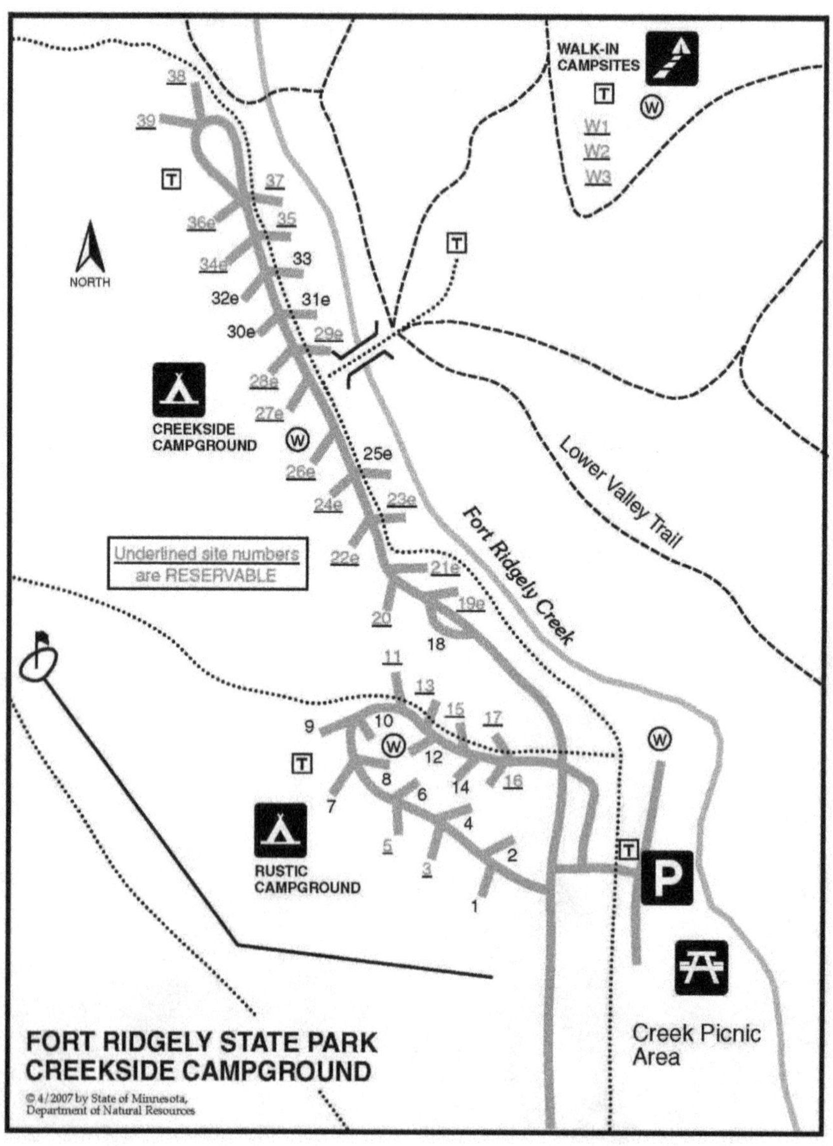
WALK-IN CAMPSITES
W1
W2
W3
NORTH
CREEKSIDE CAMPGROUND
Underlined site numbers are RESERVABLE
Lower Valley Trail
Fort Ridgely Creek
RUSTIC CAMPGROUND
Creek Picnic Area
FORT RIDGELY STATE PARK
CREEKSIDE CAMPGROUND
© 4/2007 by State of Minnesota, Department of Natural Resources

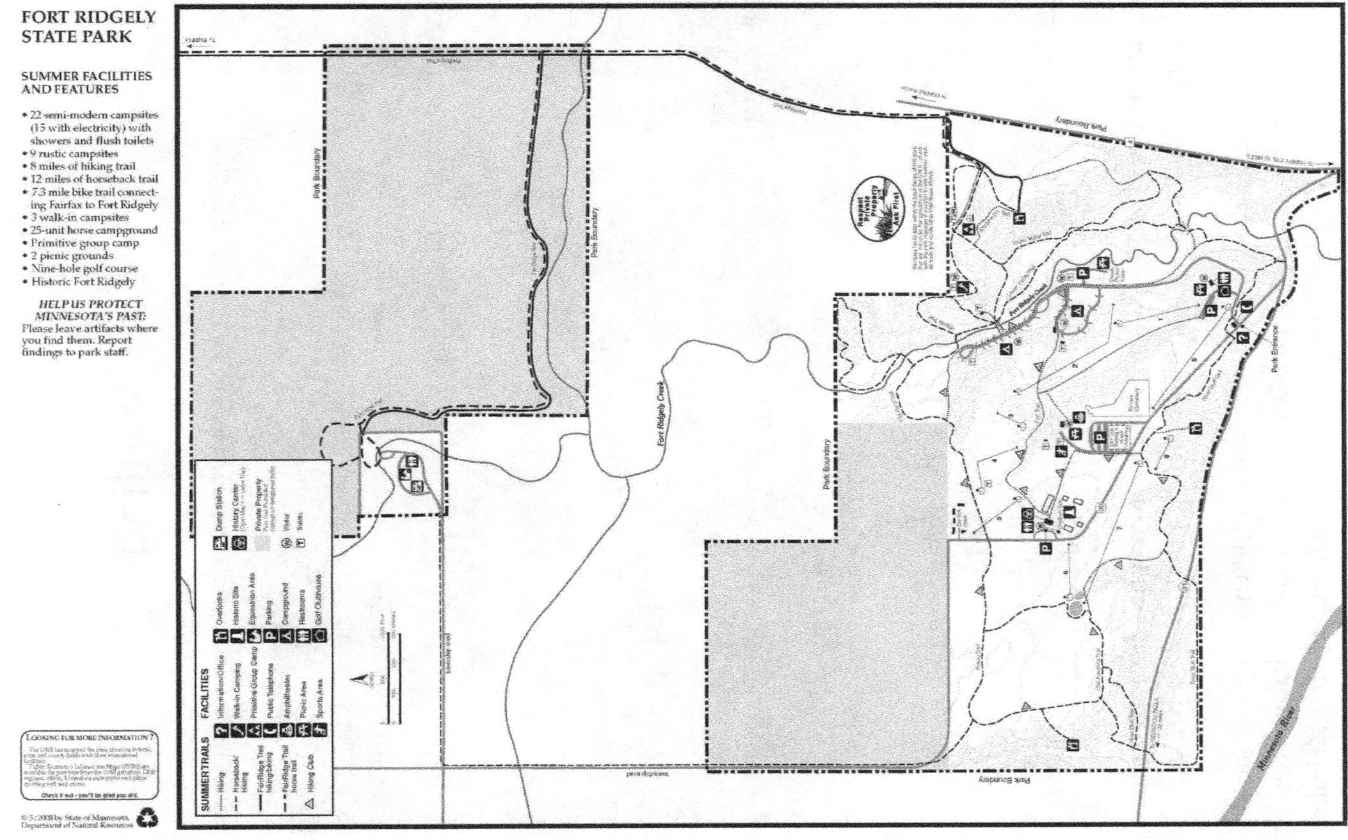
FORT RIDGELY
STATE PARK
SUMMER FACILITIES
AND FEATURES
• 22 semi-modern campsites (15 with electricity) with showers and flush toilets
• 9 rustic campsites
• 8 miles of hiking trail
• 12 miles of horseback trail
• 7.3 mile bike trail connecting Fairfax to Fort Ridgely
• 3 walk-in campsites
• 25-unit horse campground
• Primitive group camp
• 2 picnic grounds
• Nine-hole golf course
• Historic Fort Ridgely
HELP US PROTECT
MINNESOTA'S PAST:
Please leave artifacts where you find them. Report findings to park staff.
LOOKING FOR MORE INFORMATION?
Check it out - you'll be glad you did.
© 5/2008 by State of Minnesota, Department of Natural Resources
SUMMER TRAILS
Hiking
Horseback/Hiking
FairRidge Trail hiking/biking
FairRidge Trail horse trail
Hiking Club
FACILITIES
Information/Office
Walk-in Camping
Primitive Group Camp
Public Telephone
Amphitheater
Picnic Area
Sports Area
Overlooks
Historic Site
Equestrian Area
Parking
Campground
Restrooms
Golf Clubhouse
Dump Station
History Center
Private Property
Water
Toilets
Park Boundary
Fort Ridgely Creek
Respect Private Property Ask First
Park Entrance
Minnesota River

Fort Snelling

101 Snelling Lake Road
St. Paul, Minnesota 55111
612-725-2389 (Main Park)
612-725-2724 (Visitor Center)

- Located off of MN Hwy. 5 in Minneapolis, very near the International Airport and some of the park sits beneath the Mendota Bridge.
- Ft. Snelling is day-use park. It sits at the confluence of the Minnesota River with the Mississippi. Many of the islands and back waters of the rivers are parts of the park. Pike Island, named after Zebulon Pike, has many hiking trails on it. Picnic Island is just what it says – many different picnic areas with more than adequate parking.

- There are boat launch sites, canoe access points, Snelling Lake which is spring fed and empties into the Minnesota River. There is a fishing pier and swimming beach on Snelling Lake.

- There are 18 miles of hiking trails and 5 miles of paved biking trail. The Historic Sibley house is within the park. There is a golf course and recreation fields for playing football, rugby, or soccer.

- The Visitors Center which sits on top of the bluff overlooking the rivers and valley is open all year round. It offers wonderful scenic views of the surrounding area and the center itself offers a little history of the area and the fort.

Duluth
Minneapolis/St. Paul
FORT SNELLING STATE PARK

FORT SNELLING STATE PARK

FOR MORE INFORMATION
Fort Snelling State Park
101 Snelling Lake Road
St. Paul, MN 55111
Main Office: (612) 725-2389
Visitor Center: (612) 725-2724
Reservations: (612) 725-2390
(visitor center, chapel, picnic shelters)

♦

Department of Natural Resources
Information Center
500 Lafayette Road
St. Paul, MN 55155-4040

(651) 296-6157 (Metro Area)
1-888-646-6367 (MN Toll Free)

TDD (Telecommunications
Device for Deaf)
(651) 296-5484 (Metro Area)
1-800-657-3929 (MN Toll Free)

DNR Web Site: www.dnr.state.mn.us
State Parks Page: www.mnstateparks.info

FORT SNELLING STATE PARK is located in the heart of the Minneapolis/St. Paul metropolitan area. The park entrance is off State Highway 5 at Post Road near the Minneapolis/St. Paul International Airport. Highway map index: J-17.

WILDLIFE: The forested river bottoms consisting of cottonwood, green ash, elm, silver maple, and willow along with marshes and wet meadows support a variety of wildlife. The park harbors an abundance of white-tailed deer as well as fox, woodchucks, badgers, and skunks. Snapping, soft-shelled, and wood turtles can often be seen on a log or a rock along the rivers or in the lakes.

INTERPRETIVE PROGRAM: Naturalists conduct a variety of interpretive programs year-round in the visitor center and the park. Programs focus on the geology, wildlife, vegetation, and water resources of the park. Contact the visitor center or the park office for details on the programs.

SO EVERYONE CAN ENJOY THE PARK...

- Please treat it with respect and help us protect it by following the rules.
- Permits are required for all motor vehicles entering a state park. They may be purchased at the park office or the Information Center in St. Paul (see "FOR MORE INFORMATION" to left)
- The park is open 8:00 A.M. to 10:00 P.M.
- The use of firearms, explosives, slingshots, traps, seines, nets, bows and arrows and all other weapons is prohibited.
- Pets must be leashed at all times. Pets are not allowed in park buildings.
- Parking is permitted in designated areas only.
- Motor bikes and all other motorized licensed vehicles are allowed only on park roads, not on trails.
- Enjoy park wildlife and plants but do not disturb them.
- Do not scavenge dead wood.
- Build fires only in fire rings or fireplaces. Camp stoves and portable grills may also be used.

♦

This information is available in alternative format upon request.

"Equal opportunity to participate in and benefit from programs of the Minnesota Department of Natural Resources is available to all individuals regardless of race, color, creed or religion, national origin, sex, marital status, status with regard to public assistance, sexual orientation, age or disability. Discrimination inquires should be sent to the Minnesota Department of Natural Resources, 500 Lafayette Road, St. Paul, MN 55155-4031; or the Equal Opportunity Office, Department of the Interior, Washington, D.C. 20240."

DNR Maps

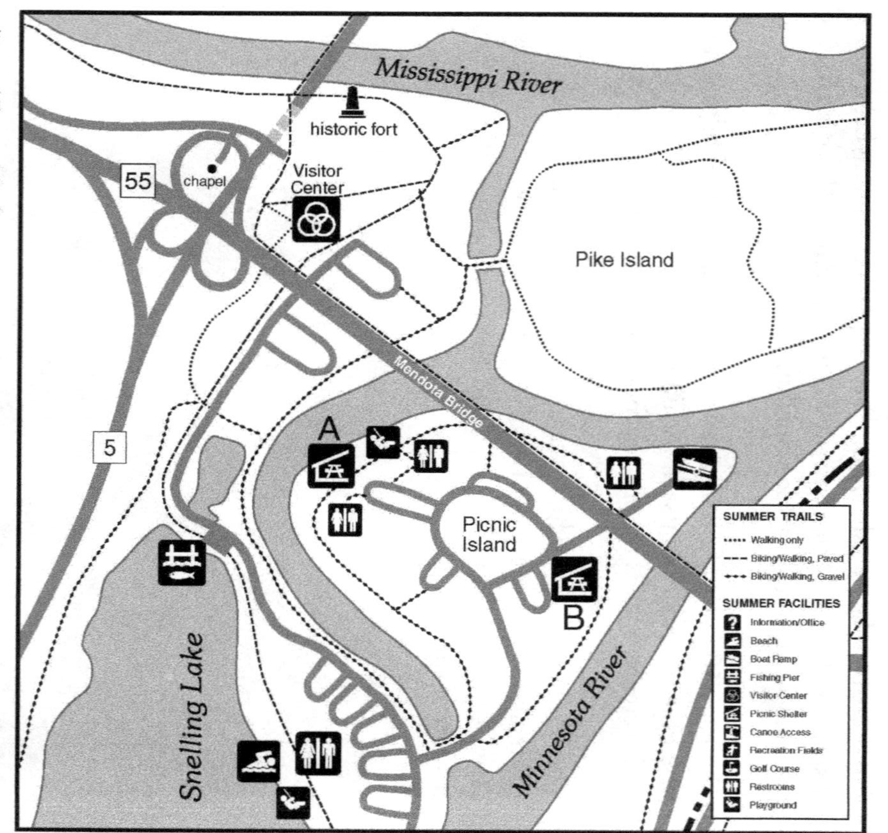

FORT SNELLING STATE PARK

SUMMER FACILITIES AND FEATURES

- 150 picnic sites
- Swimming beach and changing facilities
- River and lake fishing
- 2 drive-in boat ramps
- Canoe access to Snelling Lake and to the Minnesota River
- 18 miles of walking trails
- 5 miles of paved biking trails
- Year-round visitor center
- Golf course
- Recreation fields for soccer, rugby and softball
- Historic site within walking distance
- Picnic shelters for large picnics and events

Visit Our Nature Store

Located in the park's visitor center, the store has a variety of merchandise for sale including clothing for kids and adults, books, food items, toys, ornaments and nature-related gift items.

Proceeds from the sale help fund resource management and education programs for the DNR Division of Parks and Recreation.

LOOKING FOR MORE INFORMATION?

The DNR has mapped the state showing federal, state and county lands with their recreational facilities.

Public Recreation Information Maps (PRIM) are available for purchase from the DNR gift shop, DNR regional offices, Minnesota state parks and major sporting and map stores.

Check it out - you'll be glad you did.

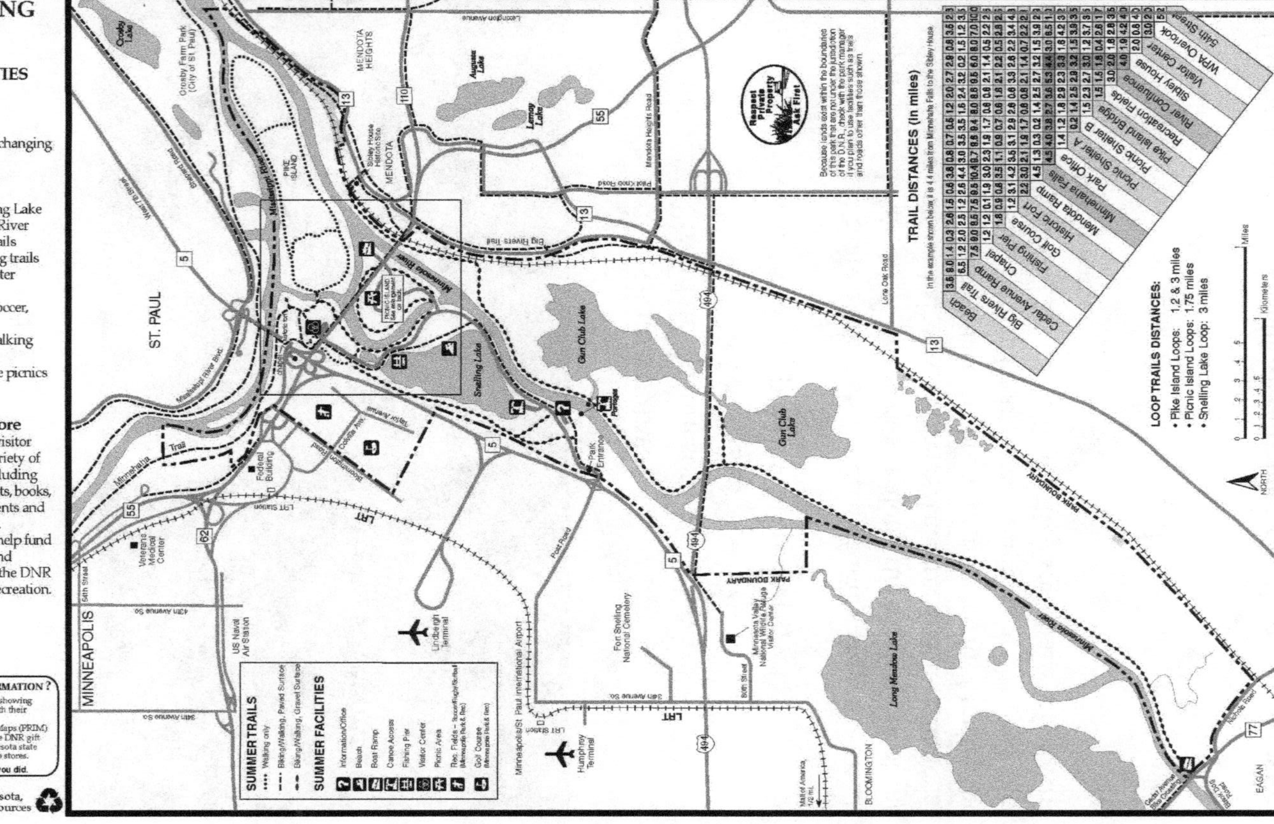

TRAIL DISTANCES (in miles)

In the example shown below, it is 4.4 miles from Minnehaha Falls to the Sibley House

	Big Rivers Trail	Cedar Avenue Ramp	Chapel	Fishing Pier	Golf Course	Historic Fort	Mendota Ramp	Minnehaha Falls	Park Office	Picnic Shelter A	Picnic Shelter B	Pike Island Bridge	Recreation Fields	River Confluence	Sibley House	Visitor Center	WPA Overlook	54th Street
Beach	3.6	8.0	1.4	0.3	2.6	1.5	0.6	3.8	0.8	0.7	0.6	1.2	2.0	2.7	2.8	0.8	3.6	2.3
Big Rivers Trail		6.5	1.2	2.0	2.5	1.2	2.6	4.4	3.0	3.5	3.5	1.6	2.4	3.2	0.2	1.5	1.2	3.5
Cedar Avenue Ramp			7.5	9.0	8.5	7.5	9.5	10.4	8.7	8.8	9.4	8.0	8.6	9.5	6.0	8.0	7.0	10.0
Chapel				1.2	1.2	0.1	1.9	3.0	2.3	1.9	1.7	0.8	0.8	2.1	1.4	0.5	2.2	2.5
Fishing Pier					1.8	0.9	0.8	3.5	1.1	0.9	0.7	0.6	1.8	2.1	2.2	0.5	2.8	2.5
Golf Course						1.2	3.1	4.2	3.6	3.1	2.9	2.8	0.6	3.3	2.8	2.2	3.4	4.3
Historic Fort							2.2	3.0	2.1	1.9	1.7	0.8	0.8	2.1	1.4	0.7	2.2	2.1
Mendota Ramp								4.5	1.3	0.3	0.2	1.4	2.5	2.7	3.2	1.5	3.9	2.3
Minnehaha Falls									4.5	4.0	3.8	2.7	3.6	5.3	4.4	3.0	6.5	1.3
Park Office										1.4	1.2	1.8	2.9	2.3	3.3	1.8	4.2	3.2
Picnic Shelter A											0.2	1.4	2.5	2.9	3.2	1.5	3.9	3.5
Picnic Shelter B												1.5	2.3	2.7	3.0	1.2	3.7	3.5
Pike Island Bridge													1.5	1.5	1.8	0.4	2.6	1.7
Recreation Fields														3.0	2.0	1.8	2.8	3.5
River Confluence															4.0	1.9	4.2	4.0
Sibley House																2.0	0.8	4.0
Visitor Center																	3.0	2.0
WPA Overlook																		5.2

Franz Jevne

State Highway 11
Birchdale, Minnesota 56629
218-783-6252
(contact c/o Zippel Bay State Park)

- This is a small State Park just a couple of miles from the small town of Birchdale, MN. The park sits along the south shore of the Rainy River - about half way between Baudette and International Falls. This park doesn't have an office to register in. During the summer months there may be an Intern camping at the park who helps maintain the sites and facilities. Registration is left to the honesty of the campers.

- There are only 18 campsites and of those- only three have electricity.

- This park represents primitive camping well. There are two water spigots down by the main entrance and in that area are four campsites three of those being the three electric sites.

- The second camping area is further along the road in the Park and there is some steep hills leading to that campground. All of the sites in this second camping area are primitive with lots of trees and undergrowth between sites. There is a large rock outcrop that is just southwest of the camping area about 100 yards.

- There are three camp sites that sit right along the banks of the river. These are walk in camp sites. They are very primitive camping but they would allow the camper to literally fish right from the shore.

- None of the sites in this park are meant to accommodate large campers. Small pop-up campers or small pull behinds would be all that could fit in these small sites.

- There is a boat launch just outside the front entrance of the park that allows access to the Rainy River.

- There is about 5 miles of hiking trails - some run right along the banks of the river.

- From my viewpoint, the greatest recreational opportunity at this park is the ability to fish in the river which is known for its walleye population.

- Sites #5 and 6 would be good for trailers. Regarding the sites up on top of the small hill, these are sites mainly for tents; however, sites #10 and 11 could accommodate small pop-ups.

- This is a small park that allows remote secluded camping and few neighbors.

(Looking northeast toward Canada, across the Rainy River.)

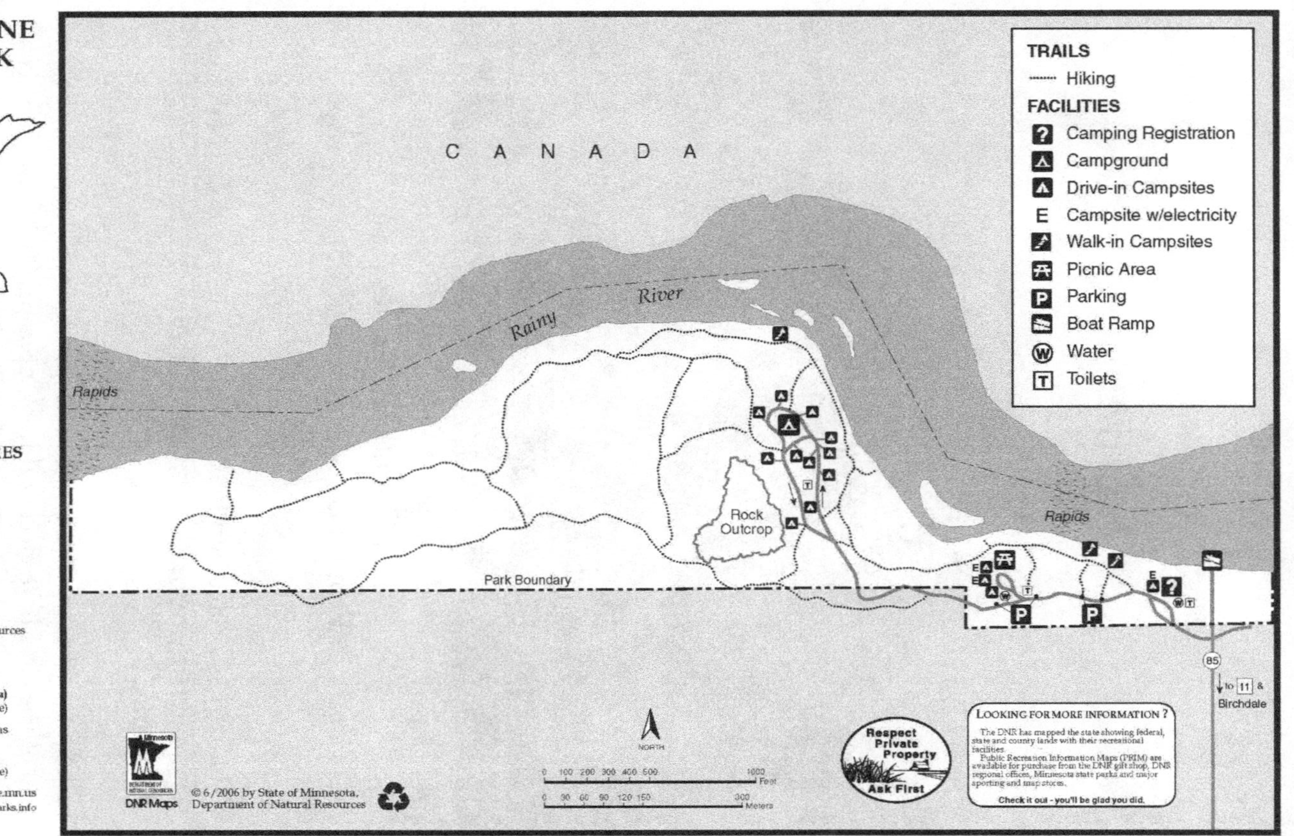

FRANZ JEVNE STATE PARK

FACILITIES AND FEATURES

- 18 campsites
- Picnic area
- Hiking trail
- River fishing

SPECIAL FEATURES

- Rock outcrop

♦

FOR MORE INFORMATION
Franz Jevne State Park
c/o Zippel Bay State Park
3684 – 54th Avenue NW
Williams, MN 56686
(218)-783-6252

♦

Department of Natural Resources
Information Center
500 Lafayette Road
St. Paul, MN 55155-4040

(651) 296-6157 (Metro Area)
1-888-646-6367 (MN Toll Free)

TDD (Telecommunications Device for Deaf)
(651) 296-5484 (Metro Area)
1-800-657-3929 (MN Toll Free)

DNR Web Site: www.dnr.state.mn.us
State Parks page: www.mnstateparks.info

Frontenac

29223 County 28 Boulevard
Frontenac, Minnesota 55026
651-345-3401

- This park is located over looking Lake Pepin on top of a bluff that is approximately ten miles southeast of Redwing, Minnesota, on U.S. Hwy. 61.

- There are 58 campsites in the main campground on top of the bluff, 19 of the sites have electrical hook up capability. There are six all-season cart-in camp sites located along the trails in the park.

- There is a shower/flush toilet facility at the main campground. There are also vault toilets and water spigots throughout the park for use.

- Many of the trails in the park can be accessed from the camping area and the picnic area. The picnic area is about three quarters of a mile way from the campground to the east. The picnic area has several scenic overlook spots that will give visitors fantastic views overlooking Lake Pepin and Wisconsin in the east.

- There is a group camp available for use that will handle up to 35 campers. There is also an amphitheater located across the road from the main campground. There are over 25 total miles of trails for use in the park. There is 13 miles of trail for hiking, over six miles for cross country skiing and the rest for snowmobiling in the winter. These trails have several scenic over look sites to stop at.

- One historical item of note – In Yan Teopa Rock. This rock sits on top and near the edge of the bluff over looking the lake below. It was of importance to the tribes that lived in this area before the arrival of white settlers. It can be reached easily by the trails in the park.

(Overlooking Lake Pepin from Frontenac State Park picnic area.)

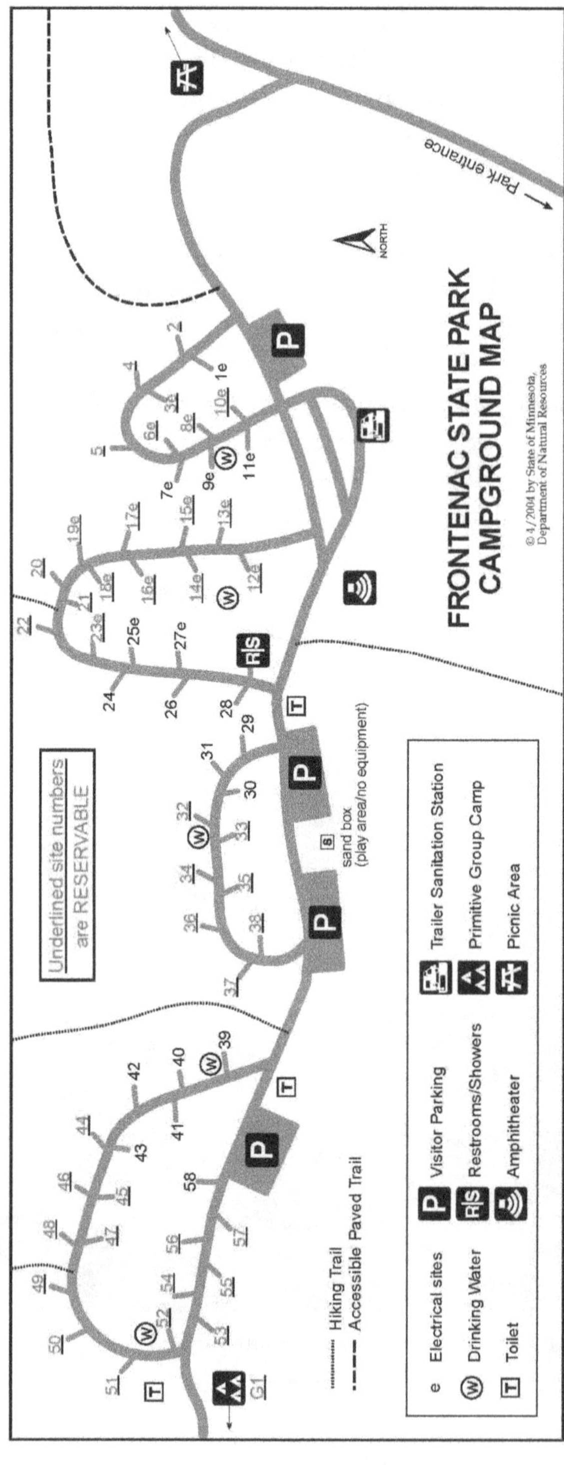
FRONTENAC STATE PARK
CAMPGROUND MAP
© 4/2004 by State of Minnesota, Department of Natural Resources
NORTH
Park entrance
Underlined site numbers are RESERVABLE
sand box (play area/no equipment)
Hiking Trail
Accessible Paved Trail
e Electrical sites
Drinking Water
Toilet
Visitor Parking
Restrooms/Showers
Amphitheater
Trailer Sanitation Station
Primitive Group Camp
Picnic Area
Note: This park may have RESERVABLE sites other than in the main campground.
See the main park map for the locations of any additional camping or lodging sites.

FRONTENAC STATE PARK

SUMMER FACILITIES AND FEATURES

- 58 site semi-modern campground/19 with electricity
- 6 rustic, all-season cart-in campsites
- Dump station, showers, and flush toilets (seasonal)
- Primitive group camp with running water. Capacity 35 (seasonal)
- 40 site picnic ground & Trail Center with electrical service. Seasonal modern restrooms. Vault toilets in winter.
- 13.5 miles of hiking trail
- 6.2 miles of skiing trail
- 5.5 miles of snowmobiling trail
- Sledding hill with warming shelter.

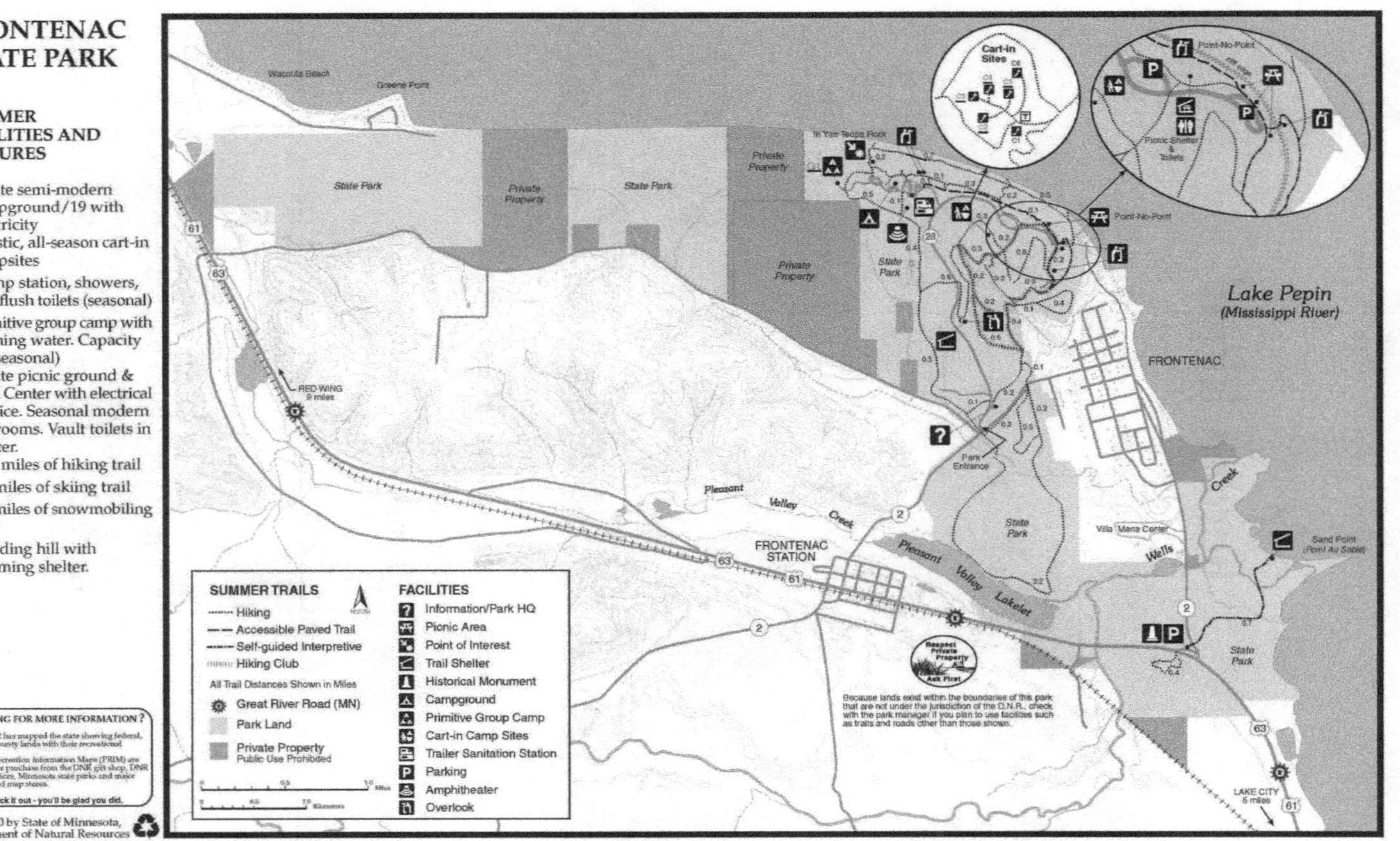

LOOKING FOR MORE INFORMATION?

The DNR has mapped the state showing federal, state and county lands with their recreational facilities.

Public Recreation Information Maps (PRIM) are available for purchase from the DNR gift shop, DNR regional offices, Minnesota state parks and major sporting and map stores.

Check it out - you'll be glad you did.

Garden Island

Garden Island State Recreational Area
3684 54th Avenue NW
Williams, Minnesota 56686
218-783-6252
(contact c/o Zippel Bay State Park)

- This recreational area is located out in the open waters southeast of the Northwest Angle in Lake of the Woods. The island is located twenty miles straight north of Zippel Bay State Park. This island is set up with several picnic tables and fire rings, two docks out into the water to moor a boat to, and a single vault toilet. There is no camping allowed on the island.

- The island was given its name because local Indians who lived around

Lake of the Woods had gardens of corn, pumpkins, and squash planted there when the area was first explored by the French and English.

- The island is a wonderful spot to stop at in order to have a shore lunch while out on the water enjoying the fishing of Lake of the Woods. But, it is also very enjoyable to motor out to the island to see the many different bird species that use it for nesting. There are at least six separate bald eagle's nests identified on the island. Eagles, pelicans, ducks, geese, gulls, and cormorants are just some of the birds that can be observed all over Lake of the Woods.

- There are several ways to access the island. There are three different private launch services on the lake that will take visitors out to the island. One is located at Wheeler Point, near the mouth of the Rainy River, and another at Rocky Point. Both of these are on the south shore of Lake of the Woods. The third launch service is located up on 'the Angle' and to get there you would have to cross into Canada to drive there. Last, a visitor can bring their own boat and launch it from the facilities at Zippel Bay.

(Looking east on the north shore of Garden Island, Lake of the Woods.)

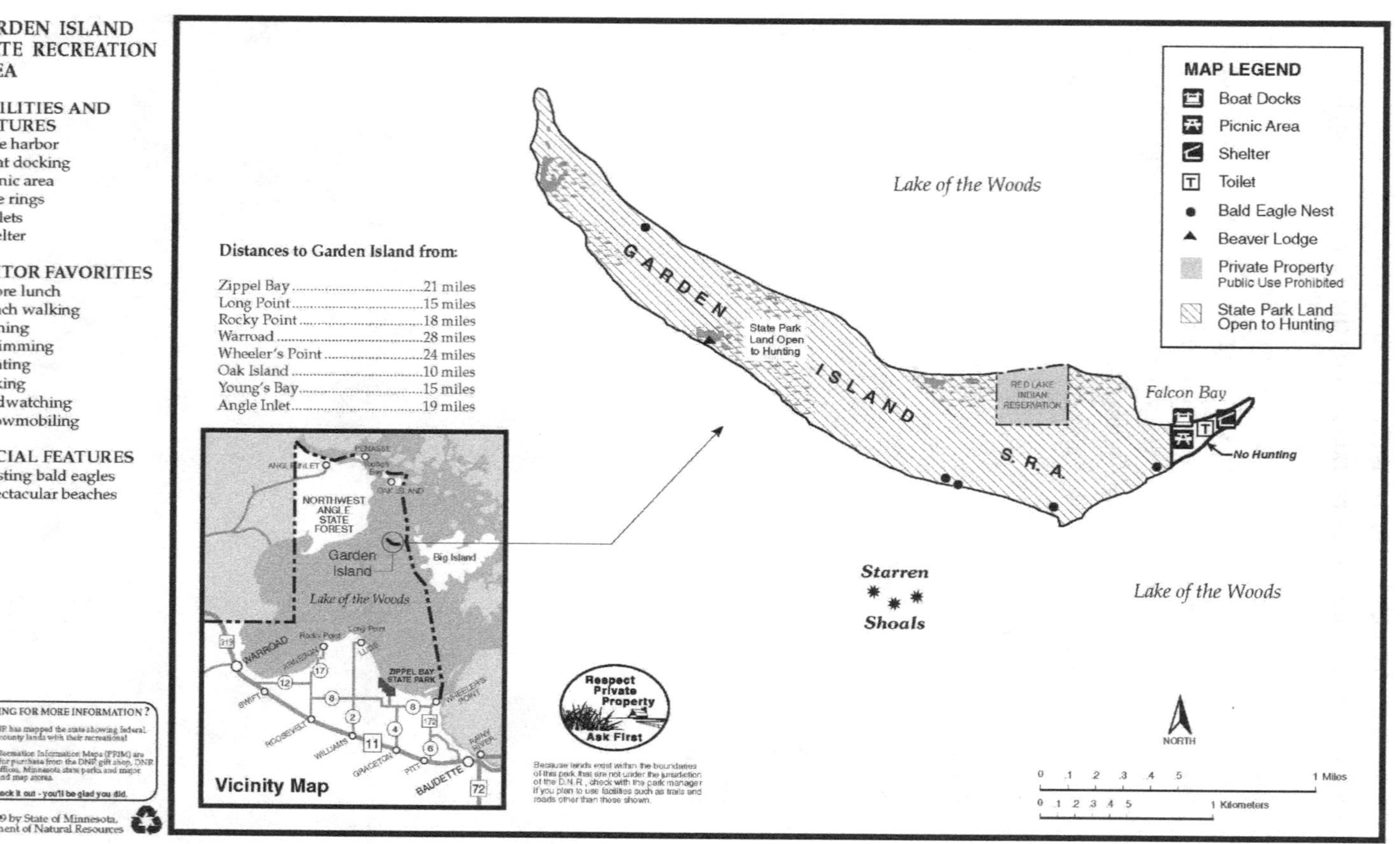
GARDEN ISLAND STATE RECREATION AREA
FACILITIES AND FEATURES
• Safe harbor
• Boat docking
• Picnic area
• Fire rings
• Toilets
• Shelter
VISITOR FAVORITIES
• Shore lunch
• Beach walking
• Fishing
• Swimming
• Boating
• Hiking
• Birdwatching
• Snowmobiling
SPECIAL FEATURES
• Nesting bald eagles
• Spectacular beaches
LOOKING FOR MORE INFORMATION?
Check it out - you'll be glad you did.
© 9/2009 by State of Minnesota, Department of Natural Resources
Distances to Garden Island from:
Zippel Bay ....21 miles
Long Point ....15 miles
Rocky Point ....18 miles
Warroad ....28 miles
Wheeler's Point ....24 miles
Oak Island ....10 miles
Young's Bay ....15 miles
Angle Inlet ....19 miles
Vicinity Map
NORTHWEST ANGLE STATE FOREST
Garden Island
Lake of the Woods
Big Island
ZIPPEL BAY STATE PARK
WARROAD
BAUDETTE
MAP LEGEND
Boat Docks
Picnic Area
Shelter
Toilet
Bald Eagle Nest
Beaver Lodge
Private Property Public Use Prohibited
State Park Land Open to Hunting
Lake of the Woods
GARDEN ISLAND S. R. A.
State Park Land Open to Hunting
RED LAKE INDIAN RESERVATION
Falcon Bay
No Hunting
Starren Shoals
Lake of the Woods
Respect Private Property Ask First
Because lands exist within the boundaries of this park that are not under the jurisdiction of the D.N.R., check with the park manager if you plan to use facilities such as trails and roads other than those shown.
NORTH
0 .1 .2 .3 .4 .5 1 Miles
0 1 2 3 4 5 1 Kilometers

George H. Crosby Manitou

George H. Crosby Manitou State Park
5702 Highway 61
Silver Bay, Minnesota 55614
218-226-6365
(contact c/o Tettegouche State Park)

- This park is located about 8 miles north of Finland, Minnesota. There is a tar county road that turns to gravel road that takes you to the entrance road. Turn right and about one mile up the hill is the park.

- This little park is for remote, rustic camping. The sites can only be reached by backpack and hiking into the park. Do not take a trailer or a big RV up to this park because there is very limited space on the road. The parking area at the trail head in the park is also very limited in size.

- There are eight loop hiking trails in the park, one of the trails leads down along the Manitou River and there is access to the Superior Hiking Trail system from the park.

- The scenery leading out to this park is fantastic and I can only imagine that camping along the trails in the park would be quite an experience.

GEORGE H. CROSBY - MANITOU STATE PARK

VISITOR FAVORITES

- The cascades on the Manitou River
- View of Lake Superior from the hills
- Hiking trails along the river

FACILITIES

- 21 backpack campsites along the Manitou River and Bensen Lake
- A walk-in picnic area on the west side of Bensen Lake with pit toilets, but no water
- 23 miles of backpacking and snowshoeing trails
- Lake and stream trout fishing

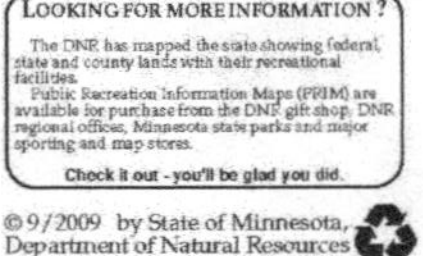

TRAILS

- Hiking/Snowshoeing
- Superior Hiking Trail
- North Shore State Trail
- Private Property Public Use Prohibited (except on designated Trails)
- State Park Land Open to Hunting

1.0 Trail distances are shown in miles and indicate distance between major trail intersections.

FACILITIES

- Information/Office
- Picnic Area
- Overlook
- Shelter
- Campsite

Underlined site numbers are RESERVABLE

Because lands exist within the boundaries of this park that are not under the jurisdiction of the D.N.R., check with the park manager if you plan to use facilities such as trails and roads other than those shown.

Glacial Lakes

25022 County Road 41
Starbuck, Minnesota 56381
320-239-2860

- This park is south of Starbuck, MN, south of Lake Minnewaska. The park is located along the Glacial Ridges Scenic Drive that runs east and west in this area of the state. The drive along the scenic byway allows for spectacular vistas and landscapes seen from the tops of the many ridges and hillcrests.

- There are 38 camping sites, electric and non- electric. The electric sites are basically the first 14 sites in the Lower campground. The campgrounds were created on hilly terrain but the park still offers nice level sites for campers and RV's.

- There are 13 miles of trails for horse, hiking, and bikes. There are a few remote campsites for those people who want to hike back and get a more primitive experience.

- The park is covered in big, beautiful white oaks and ash trees. There are also some iron woods.

- Campsites that we liked were # 28, 31, and 33.

- This is a nice open park, well suited for families and family activity. There is not a lot of under brush - so, you will be very aware of all your neighbors.

- There is a swim beach, boat ramp and a dock for fishing. There are canoe and boat rentals available.

(A picture perfect wildflower)

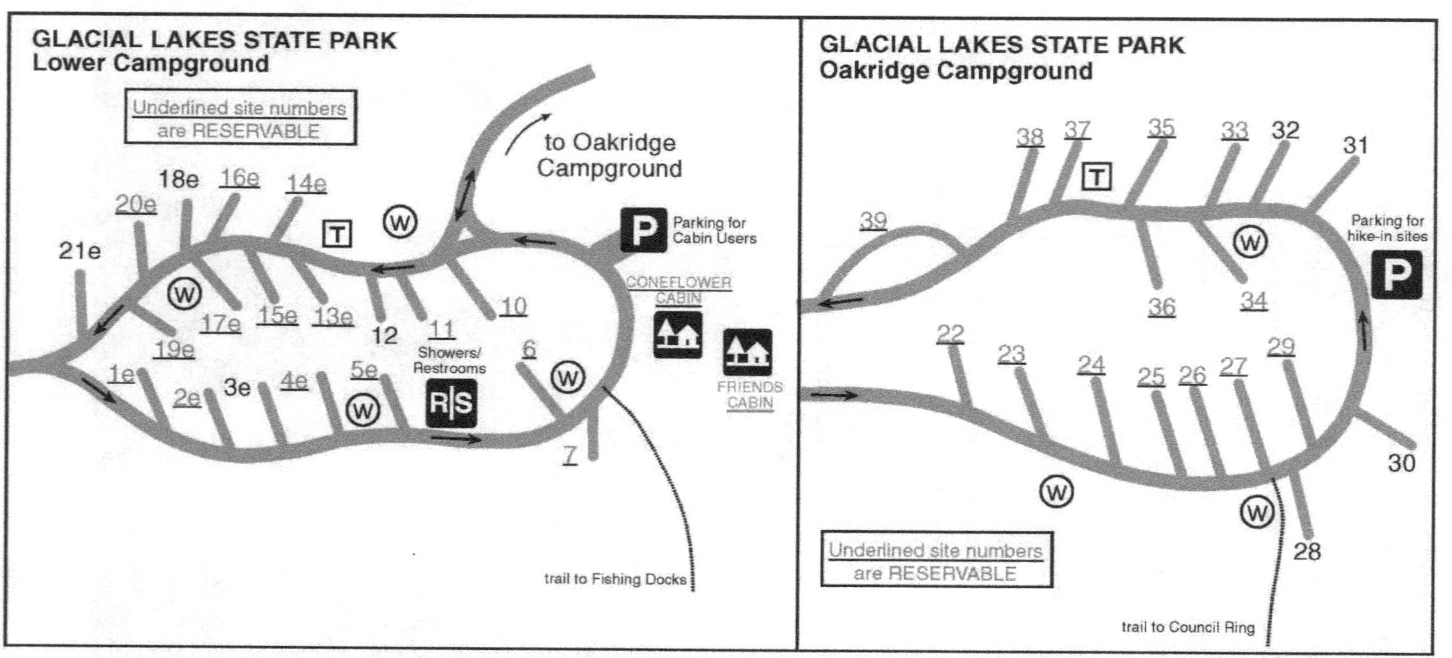
GLACIAL LAKES STATE PARK
Lower Campground
Underlined site numbers are RESERVABLE
to Oakridge Campground
Parking for Cabin Users
CONEFLOWER CABIN
FRIENDS CABIN
Showers/ Restrooms
trail to Fishing Docks
GLACIAL LAKES STATE PARK
Oakridge Campground
Parking for hike-in sites
Underlined site numbers are RESERVABLE
trail to Council Ring
Note: This park may have RESERVABLE sites other than in the main campground.
See the main park map for the locations of any additional camping or lodging sites.
© 5/2009 by State of Minnesota, Department of Natural Resources

GLACIAL LAKES STATE PARK

FACILITIES AND FEATURES

- 38 campsites in the shade of oak woods, 14 electric sites
- 6 Camper Cabins
- Hot showers and modern toilet facilities
- Swimming in a crystal clear lake
- Handicapped accessible campground and beach
- Nature trails
- 4 backpack campsites
- 1 group camping area
- Camping reservations
- Horseback-riders trailer parking/staging area/camping
- Picnic area below oak covered hills
- Scenic overlook with picnic deck
- Fishing for largemouth bass, panfish and northern pike
- Canoe and rowboat rentals
- Boat launching ramp and parking
- 9 miles of snowmobile trails
- 6 miles of cross-country ski trails
- 9 miles of horseback riding trails

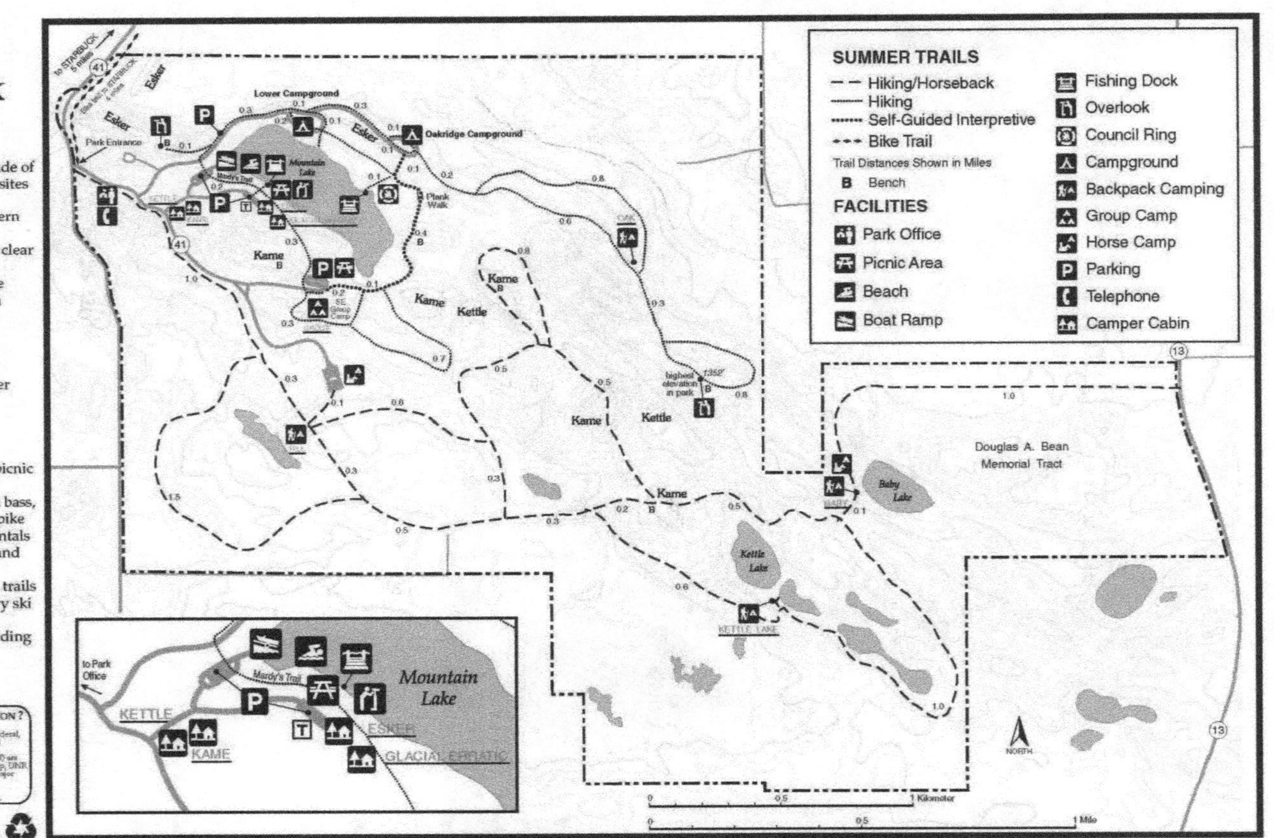

LOOKING FOR MORE INFORMATION?

The DNR has mapped the state showing federal, state and county lands with their recreational facilities.

Public Recreation Information Maps (PRIM) are available for purchase from the DNR gift shop, DNR regional offices, Minnesota state parks and major sporting and map stores.

Check it out - you'll be glad you did.

Glendalough

25287 Whitetail Lane
Battle Lake, Minnesota 56515
218-864-0110

- This park is located about three miles north and east of Battle Lake, MN

- This beautiful small park has about 1900 acres and access to 6 different lakes from the park. There are no campsites available at this park for trailers. In fact, all the camp sites are cart in, remote access sites, and then there are five campsites that are accessed by boat or canoe.

- Canoes and kayaks are available for rent at the main park office.

There are several group camp areas, a nice picnic area, boat launch sites, fishing piers, and flush toilets/showers at the main camping area and vault toilets throughout the park.

- There are two different interpretive trails and a couple of miles of hiking trails and cross country ski trails. There are numerous wildlife observation sites along the trails.

- One special feature of the park is on the east side of the park is a wildlife protection area that completely surrounds Lake Emma. This area will especially offer good viewing of bird and wildlife species.

- Annie Battle Lake in the park is a 'Heritage Fishery". This means there are restrictions concerning the use of motors and electronic equipment on that lake and the fish that can be taken.

- The park has many species of hardwoods all over and provides shade in the camping areas and along the many trails. There are still sections of native prairie that exist within the park.

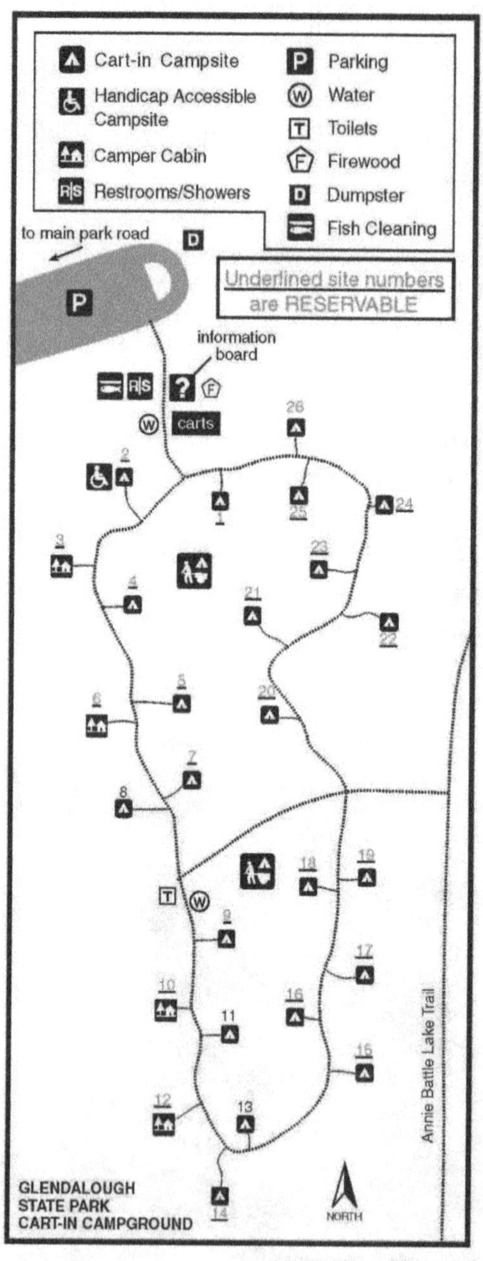

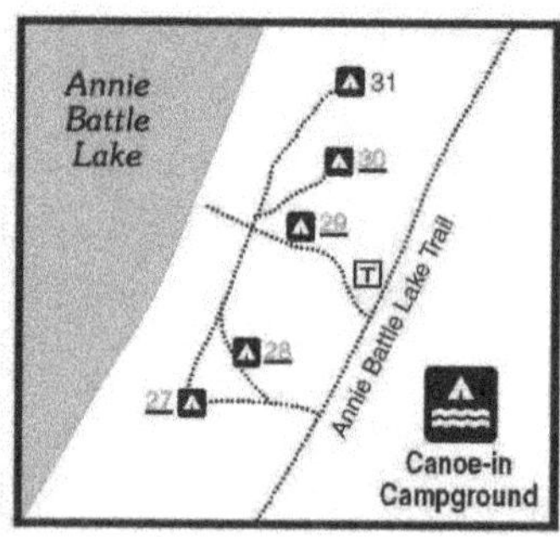

Note: This park ***may*** have RESERVABLE sites other than in the main campground.

See the main park map for the locations of any additional camping or lodging sites.

GLENDALOUGH STATE PARK

FACILITIES AND FEATURES

- Cart-in campground, providing 22 tent sites and 4 camper cabins (2 seasonal, 2 year-round), along with modern restroom and shower facilities, in a wooded setting near Annie Battle Lake.
- 5 canoe-in/hike-in/bike-in campsites and a canoe-in group camp on Annie Battle Lake.
- Traditional group camp on Battle Creek with a view of two lakes.
- Hiking and groomed ski trails through rich hardwood forests; across native prairie; to wildlife viewing wetlands; and around park lakes.
- Wildlife observation throughout Glendalough. Binoculars and field guides are available to observe large populations of resident deer, waterfowl, and songbirds.
- "Heritage Fishing" from shore or boat. Annie Battle Lake offers a primitive fishing experience in a quiet, non-motorized setting.
- Canoeing and kayaking on Annie Battle Lake and connecting waterways. Rentals are available at the park.
- Fishing pier and boat launch on Molly Stark Lake, providing access for modern fishing and water recreation.
- Picnicking and swimming on two lakes. Both lakes have natural sand beaches and crystal clear water. Shelter rentals available.
- Park hours: 8 a.m. to 10 p.m.

LOOKING FOR MORE INFORMATION?

The DNR has mapped the state showing federal, state and county lands with their recreational facilities.

Public Recreation Information Maps (PRIM) are available for purchase from the DNR gift shop, DNR regional offices, Minnesota state parks and major sporting and map stores.

Check it out - you'll be glad you did.

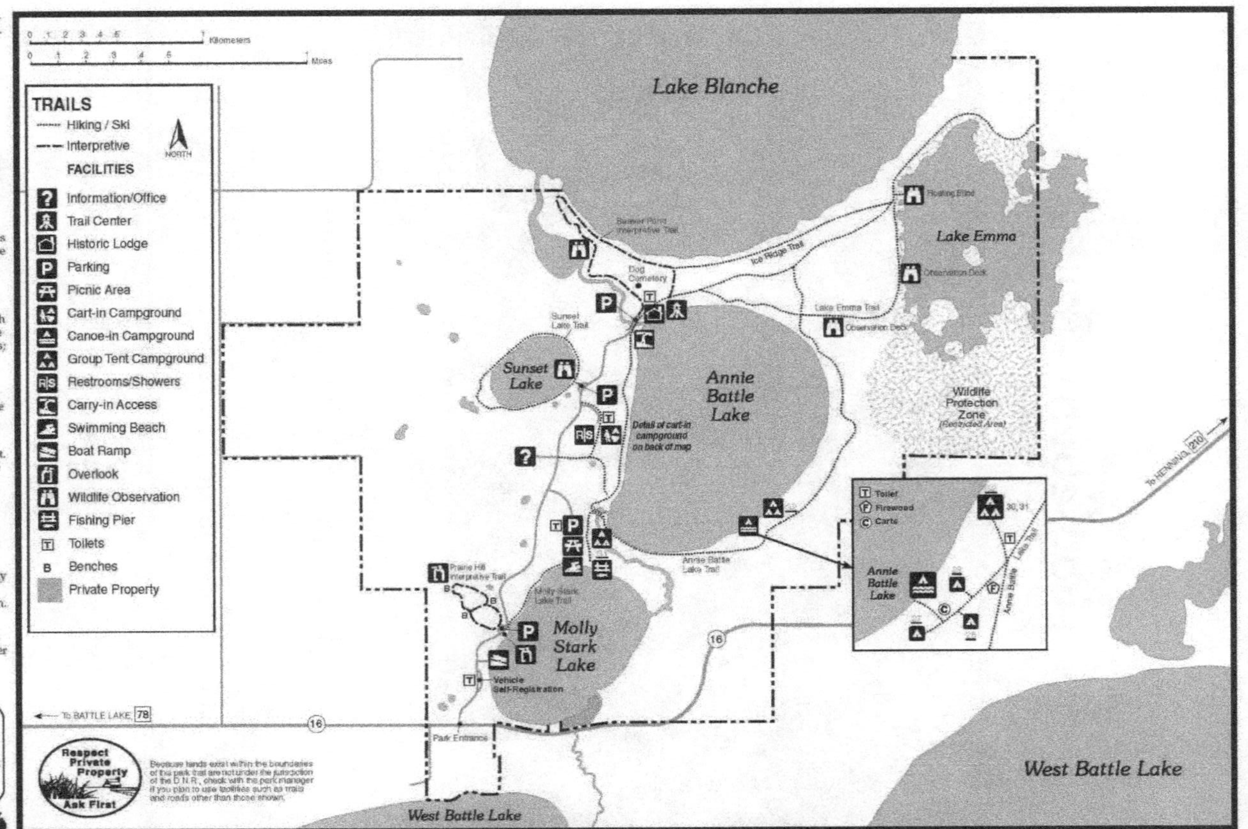

Gooseberry Falls

3206 Highway 61 East
Two Harbors, Minnesota 55616
218-834-3855

- This park is located about 13 miles northeast of Two Harbors, Minnesota on Hwy. 61.

- Many improvements have been made to this state park over the years. If Itasca is 'The Grand Daddy' of the state parks; then, Gooseberry is - the 'Showplace'. There is a Visitor's Center with gift shop and wildlife displays. The area around the Gooseberry River and this section of the Superior shoreline has been inhabited for many hundreds of years. In the 1930's, the CCC helped to create the park that exists today. Some of this history can be read about in the Interpretive Center.

- The new highway bridge over the river also has a catwalk to allow hikers to follow the trails to the other side of the river. Gateway Plaza now sits where the old parking area used to be.

- There is a beautiful camping area with 69 campsites available for use. There are three group camping areas near the lake and three picnic areas. There are over 18 miles of trails in the park and they have shelters and observation sites along the way. There are five different sets of waterfalls along the lower end of the Gooseberry River. The Middle Falls is the most famous and the most visited falls in the park. However, the other waterfalls are just a short hike from the visitor's center and the camping area.

- There are three different foot bridges that cross the Gooseberry River and several other small foot bridges that cross the other streams to allow easier access to the different parts of the park on the various trails. The Gitchi-Gami State Trail runs through the park and follows along the side of Hwy. 61 all the way to Split Rock Lighthouse. The Lake Superior State Trail can be accessed from the park.

- There are toilet/shower facilities in the camping area, vault toilets, water spigots, and covered picnic shelters. There are nice sites in the camping area with trees and under growth to allow for seclusion from the neighbors.

- The sites in the campground we liked were - # 6, 10, 13, 19, 36, 40, 41, 42, 47, 58, 60, 64, and 70. Most of the sites are nice and level with good gravel pads to park trailers on.

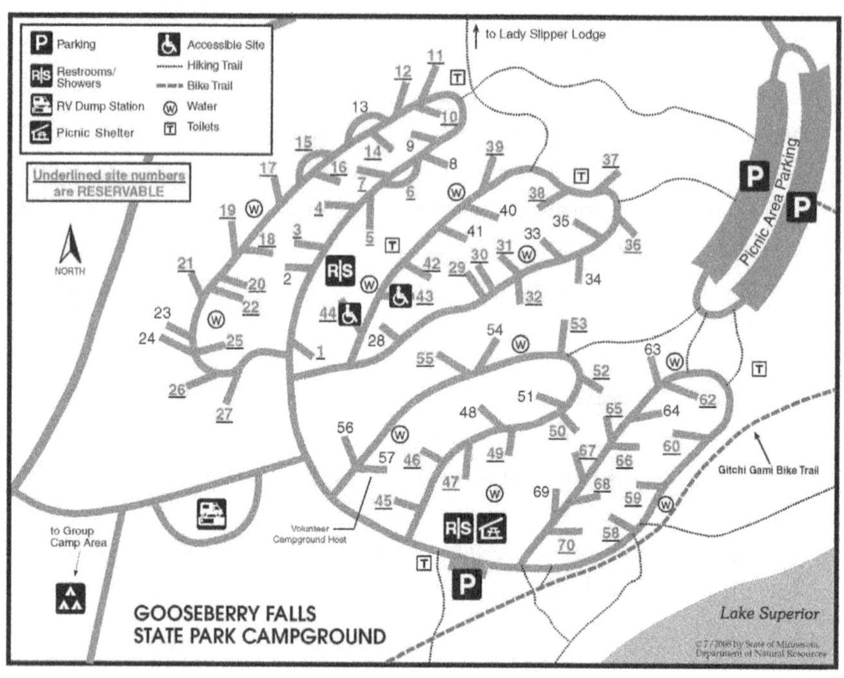
Parking
Accessible Site
Restrooms/ Showers
Hiking Trail
Bike Trail
RV Dump Station
Water
Picnic Shelter
Toilets
Underlined site numbers are RESERVABLE
NORTH
to Lady Slipper Lodge
Picnic Area Parking
Gitchi Gami Bike Trail
to Group Camp Area
Volunteer Campground Host
GOOSEBERRY FALLS
STATE PARK CAMPGROUND
Lake Superior

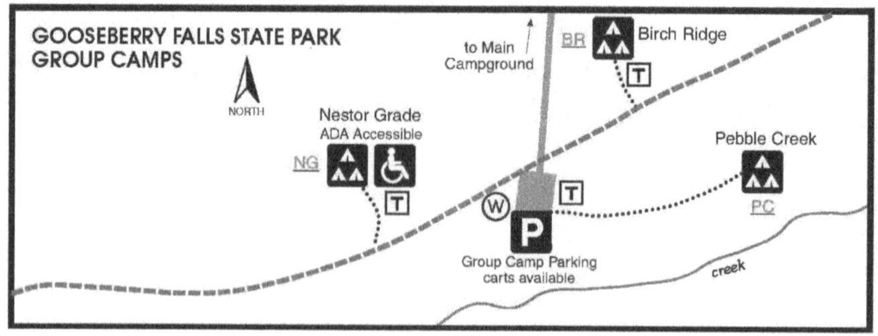
GOOSEBERRY FALLS STATE PARK
GROUP CAMPS
NORTH
to Main Campground
BR
Birch Ridge
Nestor Grade
ADA Accessible
NG
Pebble Creek
PC
Group Camp Parking
carts available
creek

GOOSEBERRY FALLS STATE PARK

FOR MORE INFORMATION:
Gooseberry Falls State Park
3206 Highway 61
Two Harbors, MN 55616
(218) 834-3855

http://www.dnr.state.mn.us

VISITOR FAVORITES

- Scenic rocky gorge where water plunges over a series of 30-foot waterfalls
- Lake Superior shoreline with well-exposed ancient lava flow
- "Castle in the Park" stone wall & other historic CCC buildings
- Gateway Plaza overlooks and outdoor signs for kids by kids
- River View, Gitchi Gummi & Fifth Falls trails
- Superior Hiking Trail access
- Connection to paved Gitchi Gami bike trail

FACILITIES AND FEATURES

- 1687 total park acreage
- Visitor Center with Nature Store & Trail Center
- 69 semi-modern & 3 group campsites near Lake Superior
- 18 miles of year-round trails
- 3 picnic areas
- Seasonal naturalist program
- Trout fishing

LOOKING FOR MORE INFORMATION?
The DNR has mapped the state showing federal, state and county lands with their recreational facilities.
Public Recreation Information Maps (PRIM) are available for purchase from the DNR gift shop, DNR regional offices, Minnesota state parks and major sporting and map stores.
Check it out - you'll be glad you did.

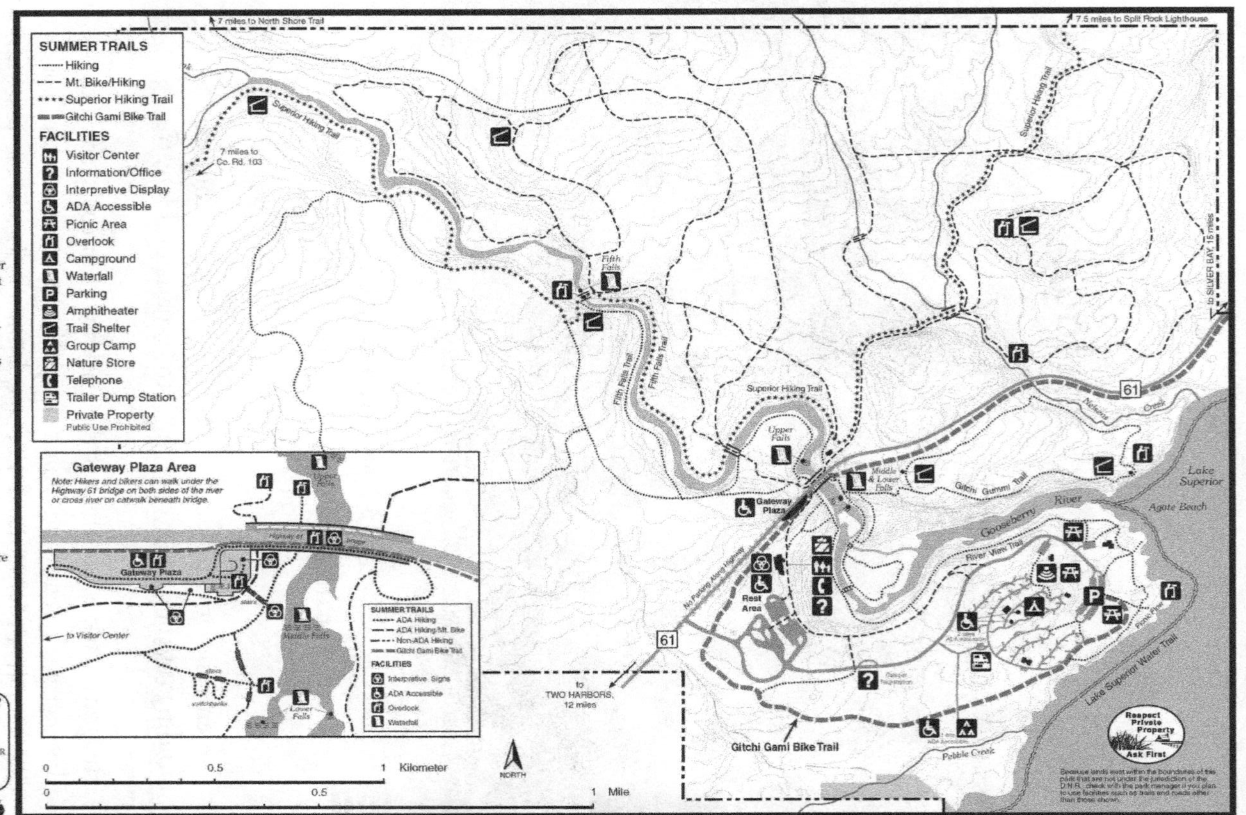

Grand Portage

9393 East Highway 61
Grand Portage, Minnesota 55605
218-475-2360

- The entrance to the park is about 200 yards from the customs buildings at the border crossing into Canada on Hwy. 61.

- The state park is another of the parks within the system that is a 'day-use' park. The land which the park sits on is actually leased to the state from the Grand Portage Indian tribe. Their reservation encompasses this entire area near the northeast tip of the state and along the border with Canada.

- There is a picnic area at the park and about 5 miles of trail to hike on. The Pigeon River forms the border between the U.S. and Canada.

The river as it approaches the lake is so rugged and has so many falls and rapids – it can't be navigated. So, the portage was created to reach the calmer waters of the inland many hundreds of years ago by the Indians.

- The High Falls which is about 0.6 miles away from the parking area and can be easily reached on the trails and boardwalks that have been built. This waterfall is among the in Minnesota and is a site to see regardless of the season of the year.

- While this book was researched and written, the park was under going major renovation and will have a new Visitor's Center/Office, an Interpretive Center, new parking and picnic areas, and new water and bathroom facilities.

GRAND PORTAGE STATE PARK

FACILITIES AND FEATURES

- Day use activities only
- Picnic area on the Pigeon River
- 5 miles of hiking trails
- Nature Store
- Interpretive programs

VISITOR FAVORITES

- Two waterfalls including High Falls, the highest falls in Minnesota
- Native American culture

NEARBY

- Hiking trails to Lake Superior and nearby peaks.
- Camping at Grand Portage Marina. Scenic views of Lake Superior. 29 RV sites w/full hookups (water, sewer, electricity). Restrooms & showers. Tent camping available.

LOOKING FOR MORE INFORMATION?

The DNR has mapped the state showing federal, state and county lands with their recreational facilities.

Public Recreation Information Maps (PRIM) are available for purchase from the DNR gift shop, DNR regional offices, Minnesota state parks and major sporting and map stores.

Check it out - you'll be glad you did.

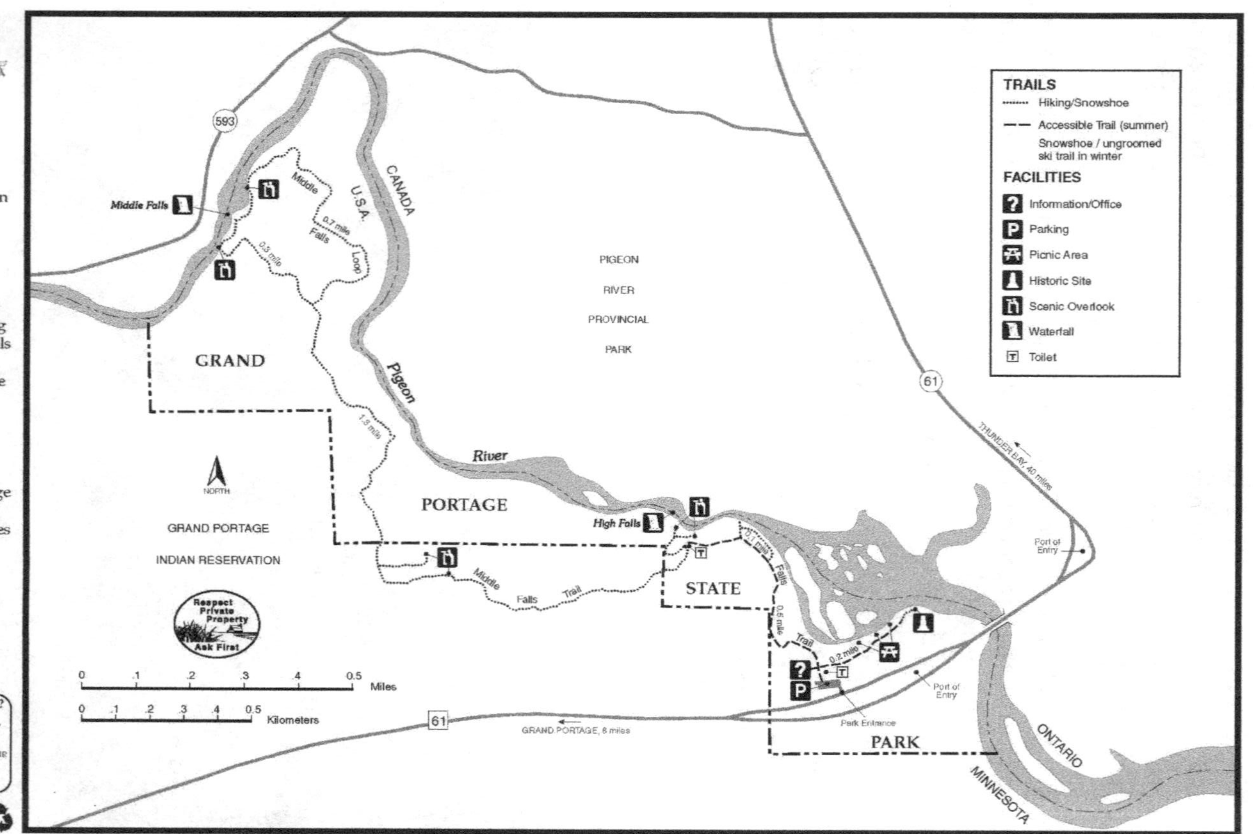

Great River Bluffs

43605 Kipp Drive
Winona, Minnesota 55987
507-643-6849

- This park is located on the bluffs over looking the Mississippi River Valley. The park has two accesses – one is from U.S. Highway 61 about 13 miles south of Winona. Turning west on County Hwy. 3 and traveling up a steep incline to the top of the bluff. The second entrance is from Interstate 90 at Exit #266. Turning north onto County Hwy. 3 to the park entrance.

- The park has one main campground. There is a group camp and several remote camp sites available to use on the hiking trails. There are at least eight scenic over look spots along the trails in the park.

One of the best sights is on the roadway leading to the campground. There is a small area to pull vehicles to the side at the overlook site.

- There is a nice picnic area on top of the bluff with 20 tables, fire rings, and char coal grills.
- The campground consists of 31 camp sites. The camp sites are set up around a single loop, with sites on the outside and the inside of the loop. There is a very nice flush toilet/shower facility in the middle of the loop. There are water spigots and vault toilets also available.
- The sites are well covered by trees for shade. On the outside of the loop, under growth between the sites is sufficient to allow good seclusion. There are picnic tables and fire pits available at each site. Electric sites are also available for reservation.
- A mixed selection of white pines and red pines are intermixed with hardwood species all over on the top of the bluff. There are over eight miles of trails running all over the top of the bluff and leading to all the overlook opportunities.
- The sites that we liked at the campground were: 7, 8, 15, 19, 23, and 29.

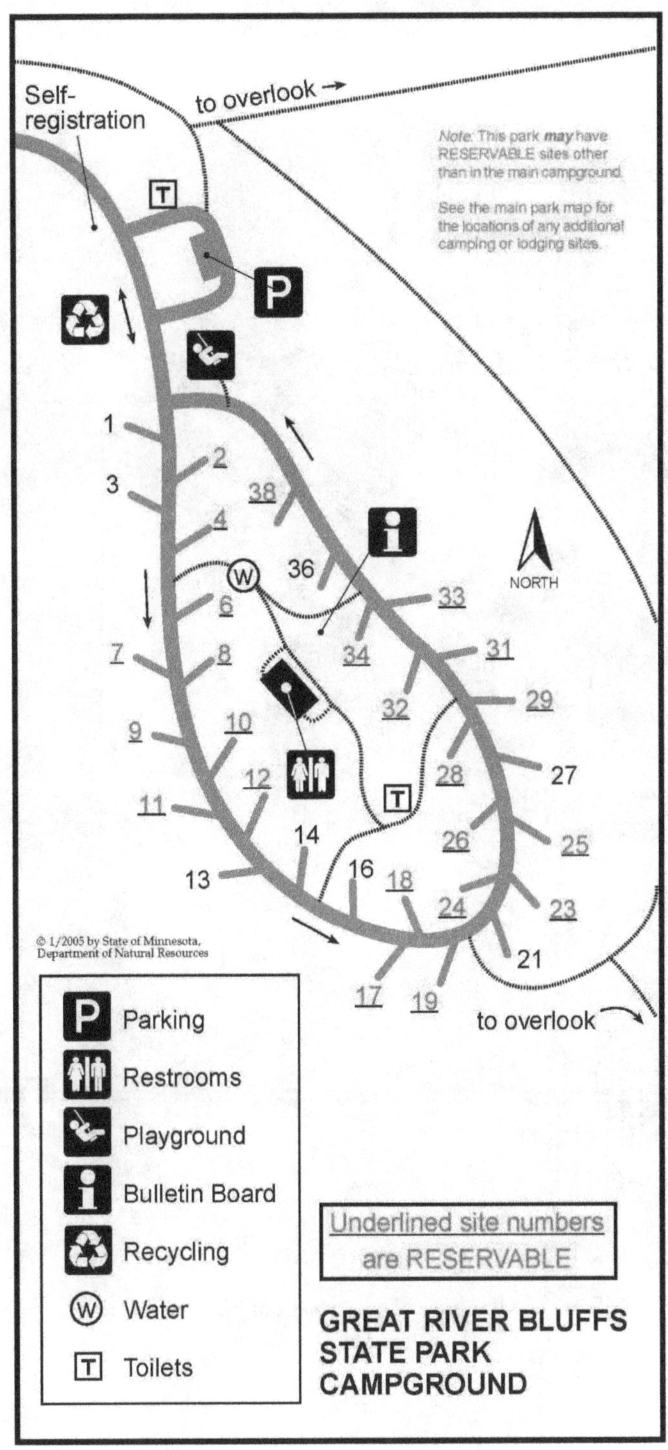
Self-registration
to overlook
Note: This park may have RESERVABLE sites other than in the main campground.
See the main park map for the locations of any additional camping or lodging sites.
T
P
1
2
3
38
4
36
W
33
NORTH
6
7
8
34
31
32
29
9
10
12
28
27
11
T
26
14
25
16
18
13
24
23
21
© 1/2005 by State of Minnesota, Department of Natural Resources
17
19
to overlook
Parking
Restrooms
Playground
Bulletin Board
Recycling
Water
Toilets
Underlined site numbers are RESERVABLE
GREAT RIVER BLUFFS STATE PARK CAMPGROUND

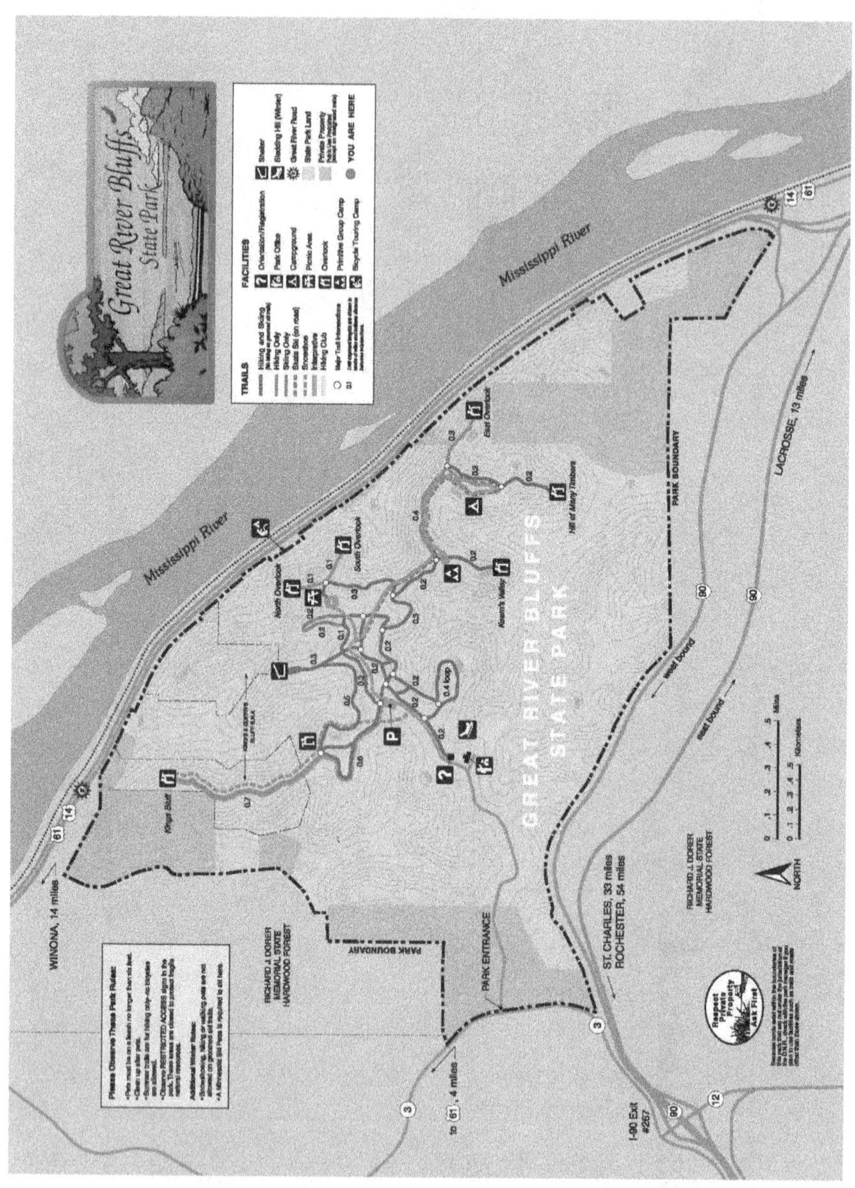
Great River Bluffs State Park
Mississippi River
Mississippi River
GREAT RIVER BLUFFS STATE PARK
PARK ENTRANCE
PARK BOUNDARY
PARK BOUNDARY
WINONA, 14 miles
LACROSSE, 13 miles
ST. CHARLES, 33 miles
ROCHESTER, 54 miles
RICHARD J. DORER MEMORIAL STATE HARDWOOD FOREST
RICHARD J. DORER MEMORIAL STATE HARDWOOD FOREST
I-90 Exit #267
West bound
East bound
North Overlook
South Overlook
East Overlook
NORTH
TRAILS
FACILITIES
YOU ARE HERE
0.4 loop

Greenleaf Lake
State Recreational Area

Minnesota Highway 22
Litchfield, Minnesota 55355

- On the previous page are pictures of what will be developed into one of the newest additions to the State Park and Recreational Area system. Greenleaf Lake is nestled in rolling hills and marshland. As you can see in the pictures, a boat landing was already in existence when the state made the decision to include this area into the Parks and Recreation system. The fishing pier is also already established and the lake offers very good fishing for pan fish and large mouth bass.

- When driving south out of Litchfield on Minnesota Highway 22, you drive approximately 7 miles and then turn east on County Highway 18 and drive one mile. The park is not open to the public at this time because it is still in development.

- The park will encompass most of Greenleaf Lake, several marshes and wetlands in the area, parts of Sioux Lake to the north and the rolling terrain of woods and fields to the south and east of Greenleaf Lake.

- The Parks Department plans to develop hiking and cross-country ski trails in the park. Along with the fishing pier and the boat landing, there will be a picnic area for visitors to use.

- At the intersection of Highway 22 and County Road 18 is a small collection of homes and buildings and the area is known as 'Greenleaf'.

(In flight)

Hayes Lake

48990 County Road 4
Roseau, Minnesota 56751
218-425-7504

- This park is located about 22 miles south and east of Roseau, MN. This is a fairly young park that was first dedicated in the 1970's after the dam was built on the Roseau River that led to the formation of Hayes Lake. The lake and the park are named after a family of settlers that lived on the land prior to the park being developed.

- The park is populated by species of red and white pine, with a smattering of aspens here and there. There are many bogs and muskegs in the area.

- This park is a small, but very beautiful park with a total of 35 camping sites, with a mix of electric and non-electric sites. There are vault toilets and a flush toilet/shower facility available to the campers.

- There are over ten miles of trails available for hiking, biking, snowmobile, and cross country skiing.

- There a couple of remote campsites along the Pine Ridge trail which would offer a camper a very primitive camping experience.

- Boat ramp with docks, picnic areas, swim beach, and a bog walk offer wonderful activities for all the family.

- The campground has a mix of large tall Red pines and Tall White pines. There is good under growth between the sites to help give some seclusion from your neighbors in the park. Our favorite sites were: # 9, 31, and 33. Easy access to the lake from the camping area, a short trail to the picnic and swim beach or to the bog walk.

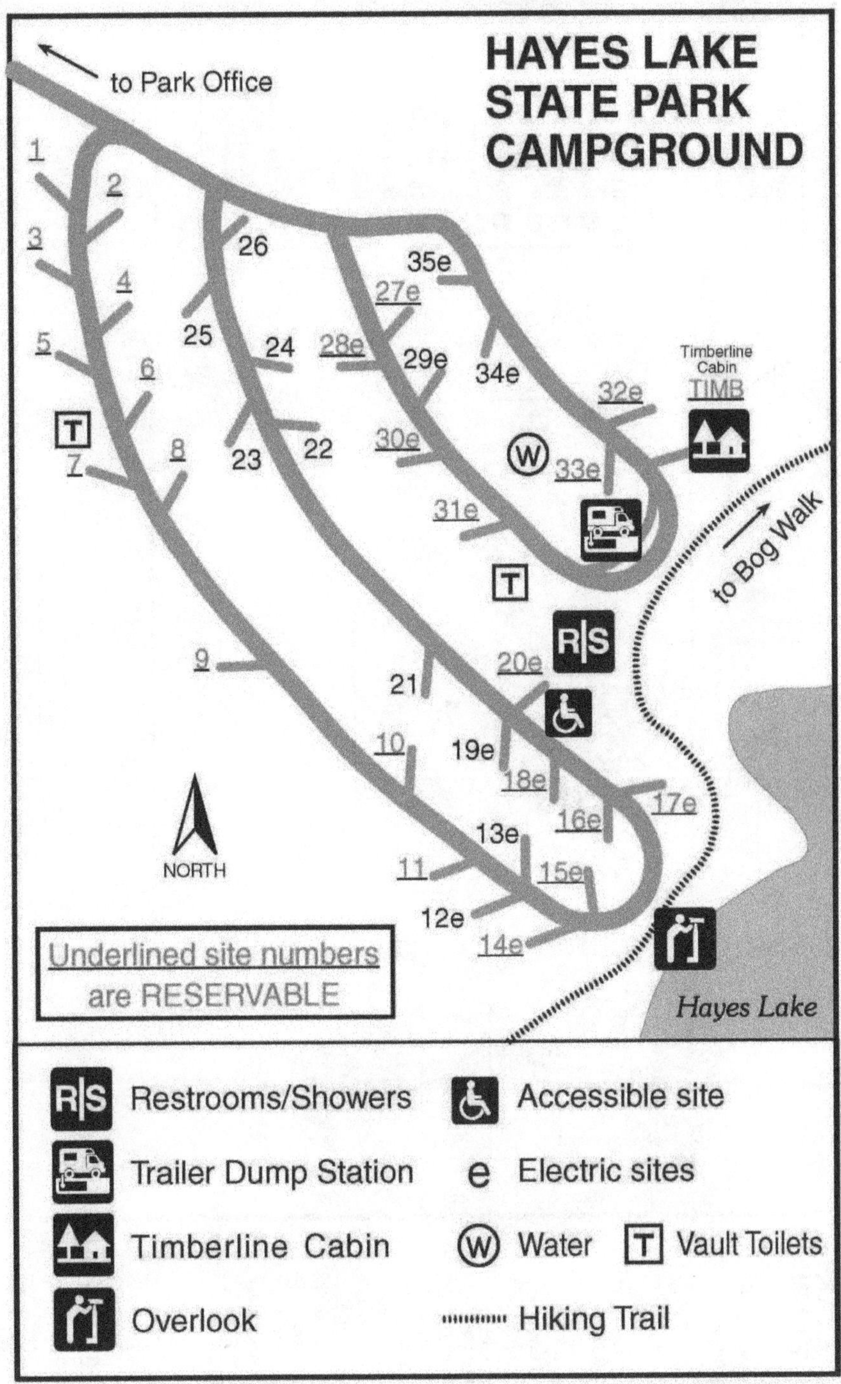
HAYES LAKE
STATE PARK
CAMPGROUND
to Park Office
1
2
3
4
5
6
7
8
9
10
11
12e
13e
14e
15e
16e
17e
18e
19e
20e
21
22
23
24
25
26
27e
28e
29e
30e
31e
32e
33e
34e
35e
Timberline Cabin
TIMB
to Bog Walk
NORTH
Hayes Lake
Underlined site numbers are RESERVABLE
Restrooms/Showers
Trailer Dump Station
Timberline Cabin
Overlook
Accessible site
e Electric sites
Water
Vault Toilets
Hiking Trail
Note: This park may have RESERVABLE sites other than in the main campground. See the main park map for the locations of any additional camping or lodging sites.
© 4/2010 by State of Minnesota, Department of Natural Resources

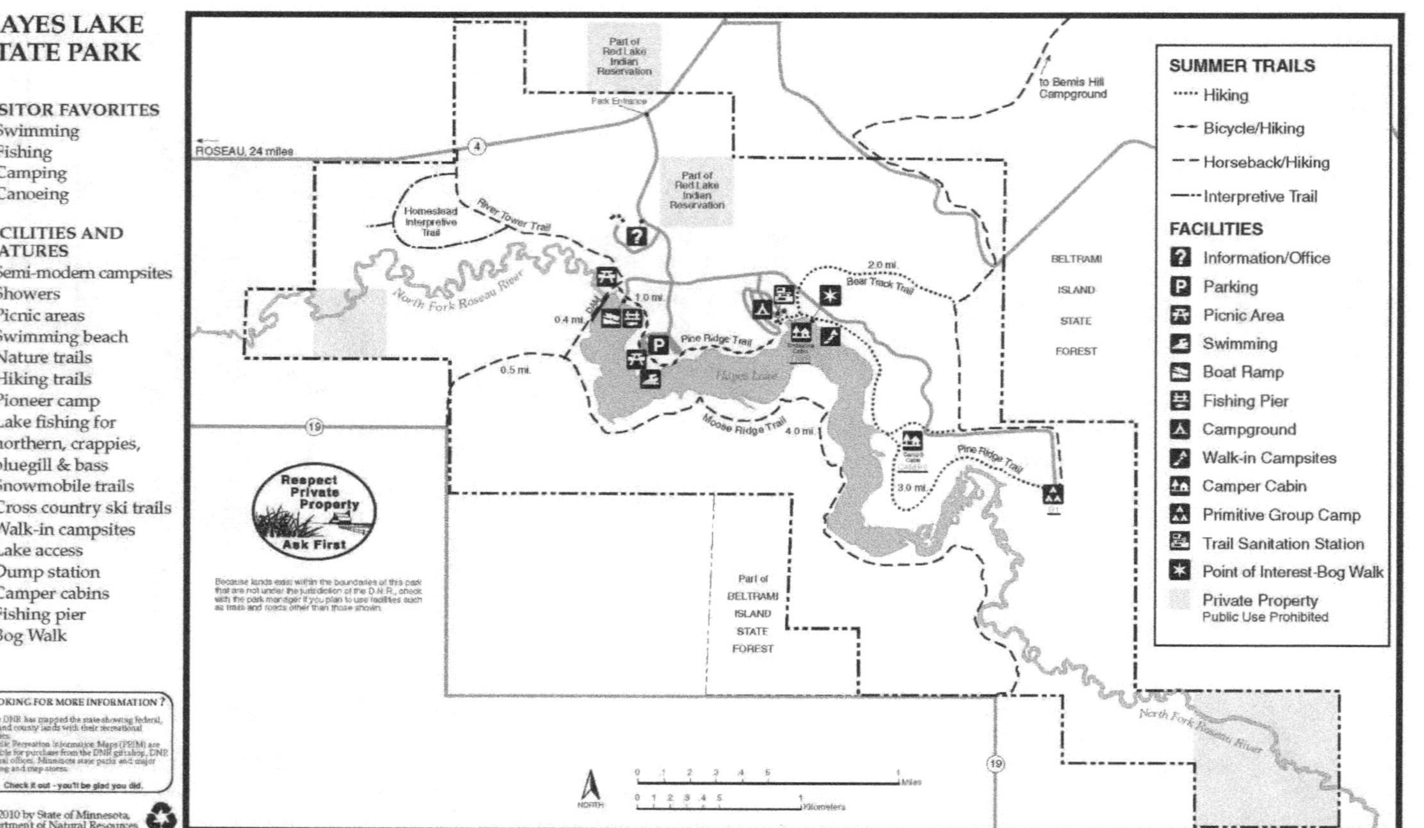
HAYES LAKE STATE PARK
VISITOR FAVORITES
• Swimming
• Fishing
• Camping
• Canoeing
FACILITIES AND FEATURES
• Semi-modern campsites
• Showers
• Picnic areas
• Swimming beach
• Nature trails
• Hiking trails
• Pioneer camp
• Lake fishing for northern, crappies, bluegill & bass
• Snowmobile trails
• Cross country ski trails
• Walk-in campsites
• Lake access
• Dump station
• Camper cabins
• Fishing pier
• Bog Walk
LOOKING FOR MORE INFORMATION?
Check it out - you'll be glad you did.
© 4/2010 by State of Minnesota, Department of Natural Resources
SUMMER TRAILS
Hiking
Bicycle/Hiking
Horseback/Hiking
Interpretive Trail
FACILITIES
Information/Office
Parking
Picnic Area
Swimming
Boat Ramp
Fishing Pier
Campground
Walk-in Campsites
Camper Cabin
Primitive Group Camp
Trail Sanitation Station
Point of Interest-Bog Walk
Private Property
Public Use Prohibited
ROSEAU, 24 miles
Part of Red Lake Indian Reservation
Park Entrance
Part of Red Lake Indian Reservation
to Bemis Hill Campground
Homestead Interpretive Trail
River Tower Trail
North Fork Roseau River
DAM
1.0 mi.
0.4 mi.
0.5 mi.
Pine Ridge Trail
Hayes Lake
Moose Ridge Trail
4.0 mi.
2.0 mi.
Bear Track Trail
Pine Ridge Trail
3.0 mi.
BELTRAMI ISLAND STATE FOREST
Part of BELTRAMI ISLAND STATE FOREST
North Fork Roseau River
Respect Private Property
Ask First
Because lands exist within the boundaries of this park that are not under the jurisdiction of the D.N.R., check with the park manager if you plan to use facilities such as trails and roads other than those shown.
NORTH
Miles
Kilometers
4
19
19

Hill Annex Mine

880 Gary Street
Calumet, Minnesota 55716
218-247-7215

- Located within the city limits of the small town of Calumet, Minnesota. The park is located along Hwy. 169 as it travels between Grand Rapids and Hibbing.

- This state park is a 'day-use' park. There is a visitor's center that is located on the south east edge of the Hill Annex Mine. Inside of the visitor's center, there is a gift shop and a small set up of historical items and story boards telling the story of the mine, the park and the local area.

- Bus tours of the mine can be arranged from the office area.

- There is a nice picnic area on the grounds near the office. Also, there is a large viewing tower that has been built near the edge of the pit and can afford a visitor a much better view of the mine pit.

Interstate

307 Milltown Road
Taylors Falls, Minnesota 55084
651-465-5711

- The northern portion of this state park lies within the city limits of Taylors Falls, Minnesota. The southern portion of the park can be found just ¾ of a mile drive up MN Hwy 8.

- The southern part of the park contains the park's main office. There are the campgrounds, boat and canoe landings, picnic area, and primitive group camp area.

- The north section of the park contains some hiking trails, visitor center, tour boat landing sites, and the glacial potholes for which this park is famous for having. The town of Taylors Falls is a nice small town with lots of unique shops and activities available for visitors.

- The campgrounds in the southern portion of the park has a nice toilet and shower facility along with vault toilets else where in the park. There are water spigots for fresh water. Canoe, kayak, and boat rental are available.

- There are 37 campsites in the campground and 22 of the sites have electrical hook-ups. The sites are close together; but, this is understandable when realizing that there is a large, steep basalt hillside to the west and the river to the east.

- There are over 4 miles of hiking trails and Excursion boats are available to take tours of the St. Croix Valley and The Dalles area.

- There is nice tree cover in the camp area and this allows good shade for camping. The sites in the campground we liked were: # 4, 6, 23, 26, and 30.

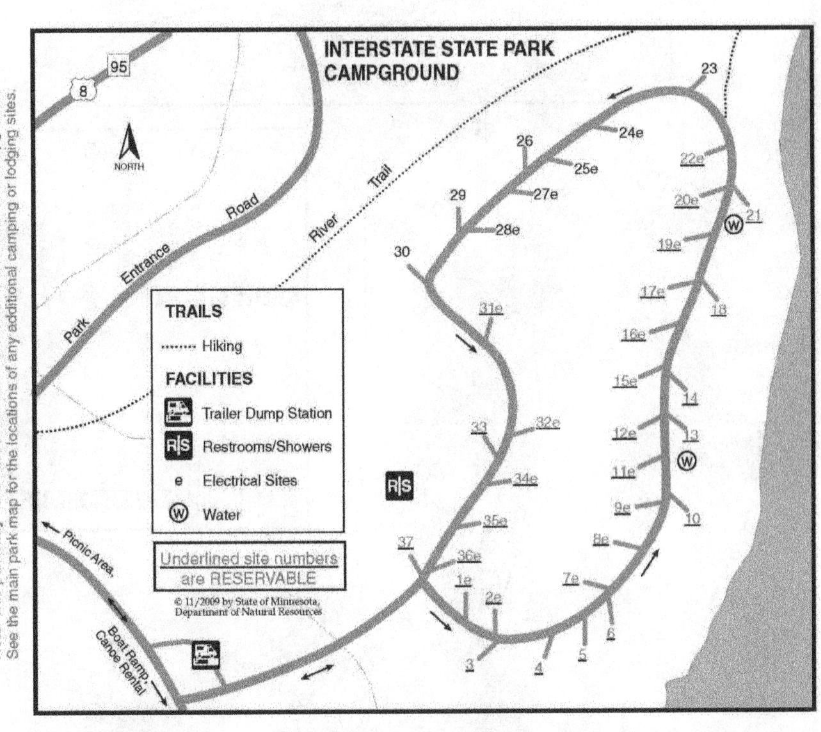
INTERSTATE STATE PARK CAMPGROUND
95
8
NORTH
Park Entrance Road
River Trail
TRAILS
Hiking
FACILITIES
Trailer Dump Station
Restrooms/Showers
e Electrical Sites
Water
Underlined site numbers are RESERVABLE
© 11/2009 by State of Minnesota, Department of Natural Resources
Picnic Area
Boat Ramp, Canoe Rental
1e 2e 3 4 5 6 7e 8e 9e 10 11e 12e 13 14 15e 16e 17e 18 19e 20e 21 22e 23 24e 25e 26 27e 28e 29 30 31e 32e 33 34e 35e 36e 37
Note: This park *may* have RESERVABLE sites other than in the main campground.
See the main park map for the locations of any additional camping or lodging sites.

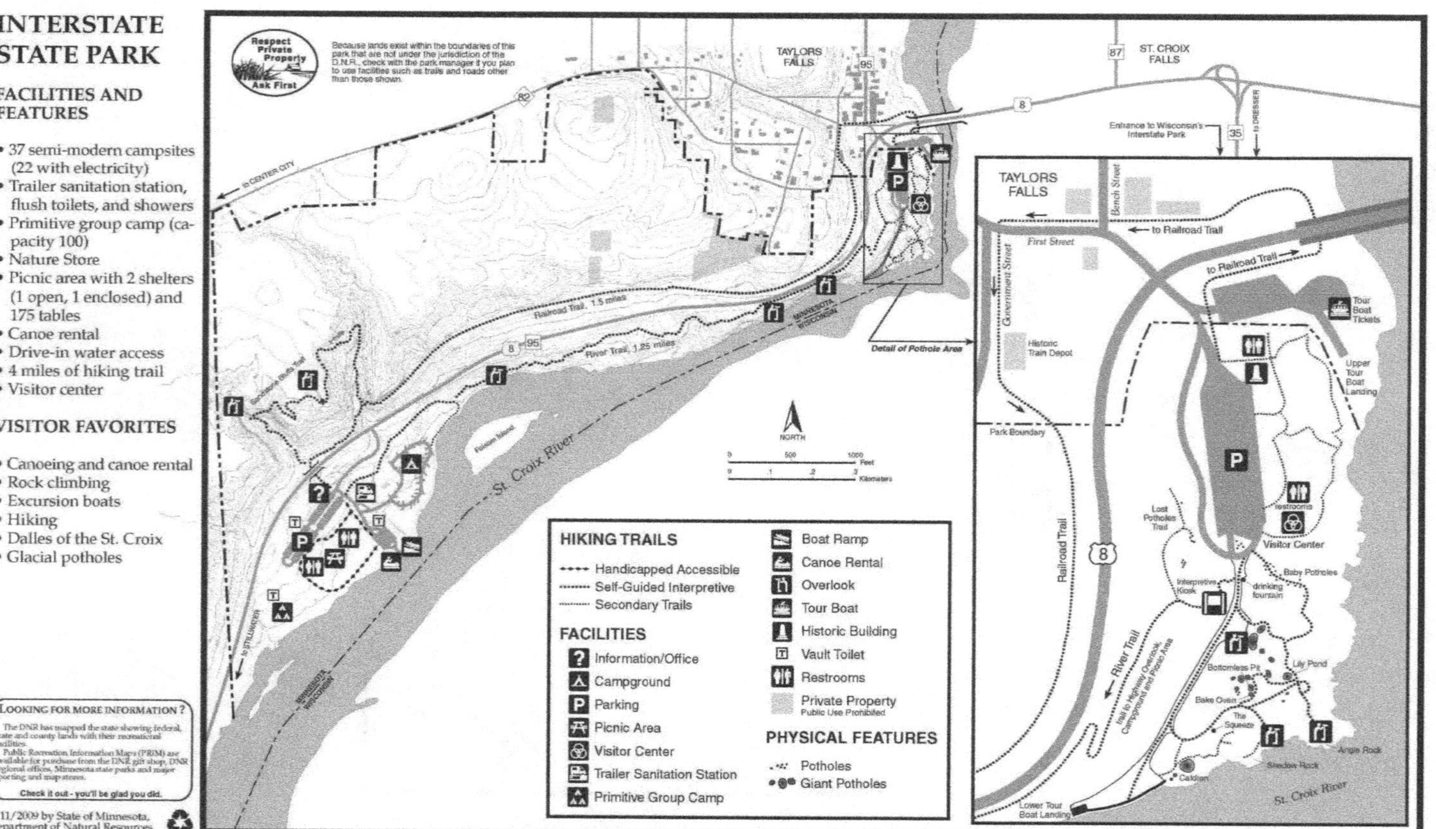
INTERSTATE
STATE PARK
FACILITIES AND
FEATURES
• 37 semi-modern campsites (22 with electricity)
• Trailer sanitation station, flush toilets, and showers
• Primitive group camp (capacity 100)
• Nature Store
• Picnic area with 2 shelters (1 open, 1 enclosed) and 175 tables
• Canoe rental
• Drive-in water access
• 4 miles of hiking trail
• Visitor center
VISITOR FAVORITES
• Canoeing and canoe rental
• Rock climbing
• Excursion boats
• Hiking
• Dalles of the St. Croix
• Glacial potholes
LOOKING FOR MORE INFORMATION?
Check it out - you'll be glad you did.
© 11/2009 by State of Minnesota, Department of Natural Resources
Respect Private Property Ask First
Because lands exist within the boundaries of this park that are not under the jurisdiction of the D.N.R., check with the park manager if you plan to use facilities such as trails and roads other than those shown.
TAYLORS FALLS
ST. CROIX FALLS
Entrance to Wisconsin's Interstate Park
to DRESSER
to CENTER CITY
to STILLWATER
Railroad Trail, 1.5 miles
River Trail, 1.25 miles
St. Croix River
MINNESOTA
WISCONSIN
Detail of Pothole Area
NORTH
Feet
Kilometers
HIKING TRAILS
Handicapped Accessible
Self-Guided Interpretive
Secondary Trails
FACILITIES
Information/Office
Campground
Parking
Picnic Area
Visitor Center
Trailer Sanitation Station
Primitive Group Camp
Boat Ramp
Canoe Rental
Overlook
Tour Boat
Historic Building
Vault Toilet
Restrooms
Private Property
Public Use Prohibited
PHYSICAL FEATURES
Potholes
Giant Potholes
Bench Street
to Railroad Trail
First Street
Government Street
Historic Train Depot
Park Boundary
Railroad Trail
River Trail
Tour Boat Tickets
Upper Tour Boat Landing
restrooms
Visitor Center
Lost Potholes Trail
Interpretive Kiosk
drinking fountain
Baby Potholes
Bottomless Pit
Lily Pond
Bake Oven
The Squeeze
Angle Rock
Shadow Rock
Cauldron
Lower Tour Boat Landing
St. Croix River

Itasca

36750 Main Park Drive
Park Rapids, Minnesota 56470
218-699-7251

- This park can be found on U.S. Hwy 71, 20 miles north of the city of Park Rapids, Minnesota. This is the Grand Daddy of all the Minnesota State Parks. It has everything that would be needed to have an enjoyable experience in the north woods. Whether you use tent, trailer, or prefer to do your camping in the comfort of a room in an Inn – you can find it here.

- Two different camping areas are inside the Park – Pine Ridge Camp and Bear Paw. There are155 sites in Pine Ridge and 65 are electric hook-ups. The Bear Paw camp has 79 sites, 34 are electric and 11 cart-in rustic camp sites. There are flush toilets/shower facilities at both of the camps. There are vault toilets, water spigots, picnic areas, boat ramps on numerous lakes, remote campsites along the miles and miles of hiking trails. Historic sites, scenic overlooks, an amphitheater, observation tower, shelters along the hiking and ski trails, a visitor center, an interpretive center, a swimming beach, canoe/boat rental, camper cabins to rent, and lodges that offer indoor comfort while staying at Itasca.

- Tour boat excursions' can be taken on Lake Itasca. Camper cabins are available by the camp grounds but other multi-room cabins are available to rent, also.

- There are 26 different trails for hiking in the park. They are of varying levels of difficulty and length.

- Itasca State Park is a small watershed all on its own and all the small lakes, ponds, marshes and streams flow to Lake Itasca. Then, the lake water exits at the spot on the north shore of the lake that is the recognized as the start of the Mississippi River.

- Huge pine groves, scenic lakes and marshes, and an overwhelming abundance of different wildlife and vegetation live within the park. This park is open throughout the year. Trails and activities are open for use during all seasons.

- In order to get the maximum usage out of the park for the maximum number of visitors, the camping areas are closely packed in with not a lot of space between the sites. However, there are sites in each of the camps that will allow for seclusion. Obviously, the remote campsites on the trails are more secluded than those sites in the two different camps.

- In the Bear Paw Camp we liked sites # 5, 14, 47, 61 and 62. In the Pine Ridge Camp, we thought that sites # 121, 150, 167, 222, 225, 232, and 247 would suit our needs.

- If you plan to stay at Itasca, please plan on taking a couple of days. There is so much to see at this state park, it would take more than just one day to take it all in.

(The Mississippi's beginning)

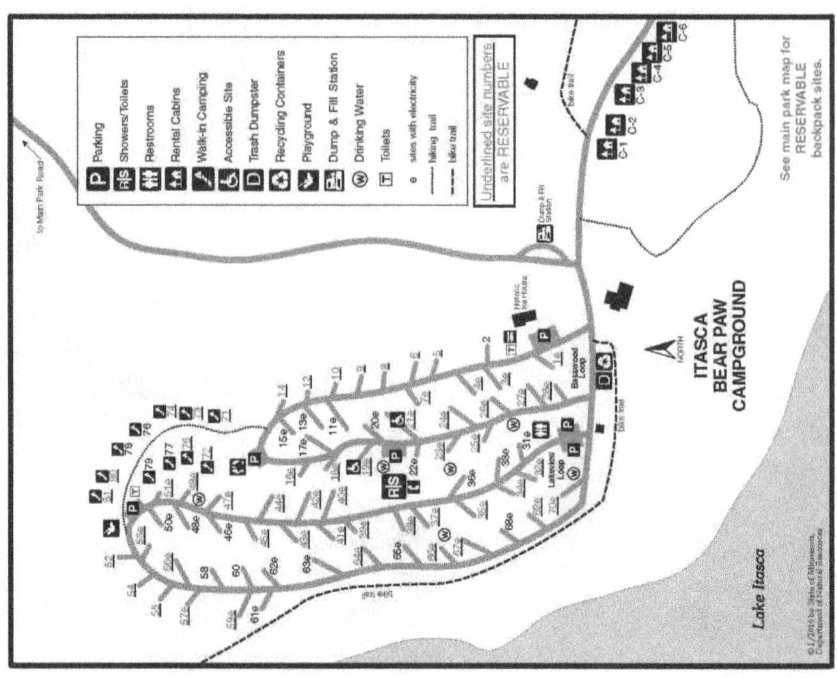
Parking
Showers/Toilets
Restrooms
Rental Cabins
Walk-in Camping
Accessible Site
Trash Dumpster
Recycling Containers
Playground
Dump & Fill Station
Drinking Water
Toilets
Underlined site numbers are RESERVABLE
Lake Itasca
ITASCA BEAR PAW CAMPGROUND
See main park map for RESERVABLE backpack sites.

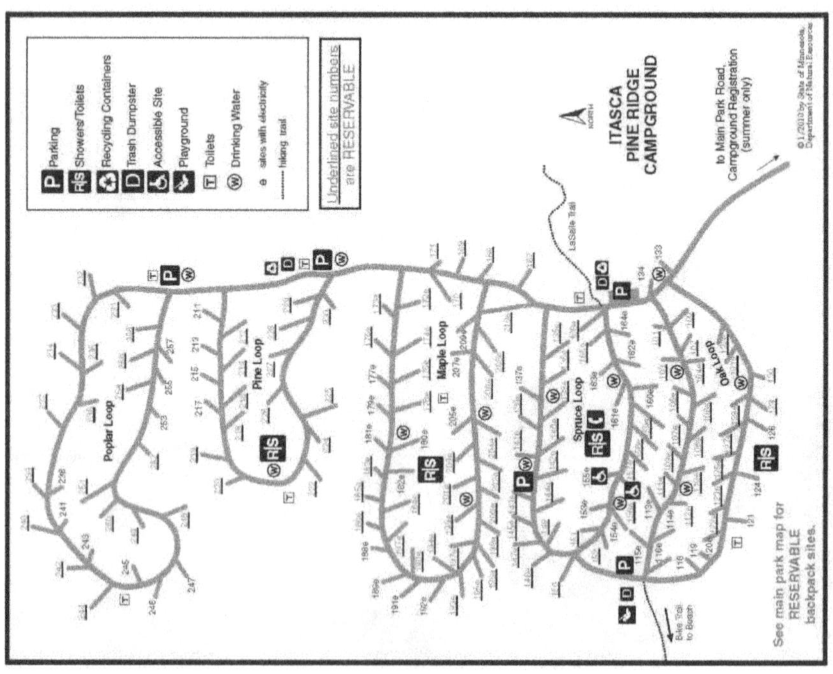
Parking
Showers/Toilets
Recycling Containers
Trash Dumpster
Accessible Site
Playground
Toilets
Drinking Water
Underlined site numbers are RESERVABLE
Poplar Loop
Pine Loop
Maple Loop
Spruce Loop
Oak Loop
LaSalle Trail
ITASCA PINE RIDGE CAMPGROUND
to Main Park Road, Campground Registration (summer only)
See main park map for RESERVABLE backpack sites.

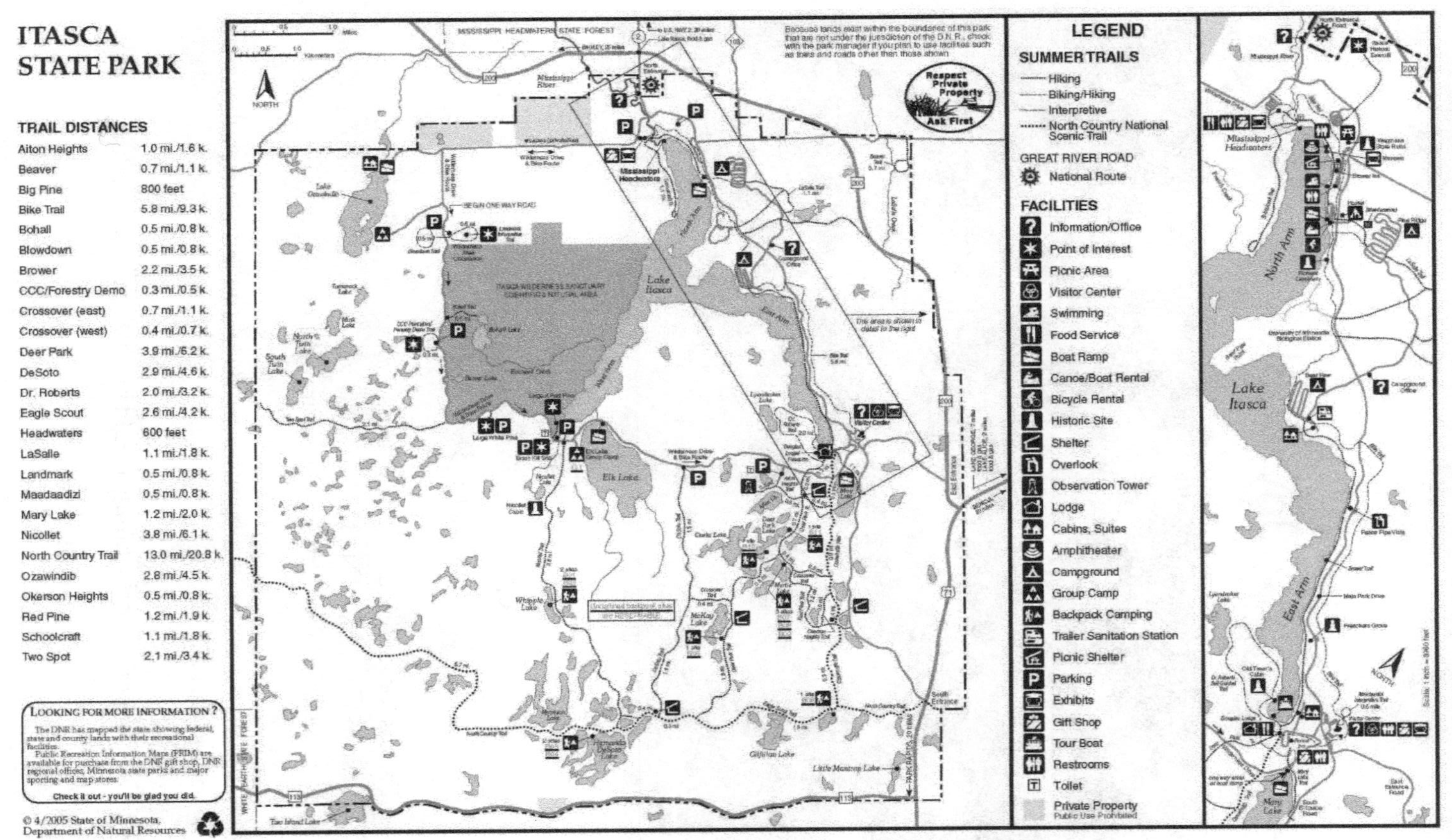
ITASCA
STATE PARK
TRAIL DISTANCES
Aiton Heights 1.0 mi./1.6 k.
Beaver 0.7 mi./1.1 k.
Big Pine 800 feet
Bike Trail 5.8 mi./9.3 k.
Bohall 0.5 mi./0.8 k.
Blowdown 0.5 mi./0.8 k.
Brower 2.2 mi./3.5 k.
CCC/Forestry Demo 0.3 mi./0.5 k.
Crossover (east) 0.7 mi./1.1 k.
Crossover (west) 0.4 mi./0.7 k.
Deer Park 3.9 mi./6.2 k.
DeSoto 2.9 mi./4.6 k.
Dr. Roberts 2.0 mi./3.2 k.
Eagle Scout 2.6 mi./4.2 k.
Headwaters 600 feet
LaSalle 1.1 mi./1.8 k.
Landmark 0.5 mi./0.8 k.
Maadaadizi 0.5 mi./0.8 k.
Mary Lake 1.2 mi./2.0 k.
Nicollet 3.8 mi./6.1 k.
North Country Trail 13.0 mi./20.8 k.
Ozawindib 2.8 mi./4.5 k.
Okerson Heights 0.5 mi./0.8 k.
Red Pine 1.2 mi./1.9 k.
Schoolcraft 1.1 mi./1.8 k.
Two Spot 2.1 mi./3.4 k.
LOOKING FOR MORE INFORMATION?
The DNR has mapped the state showing federal, state and county lands with their recreational facilities.
Public Recreation Information Maps (PRIM) are available for purchase from the DNR gift shop, DNR regional offices, Minnesota state parks and major sporting and map stores.
Check it out - you'll be glad you did.
© 4/2005 State of Minnesota, Department of Natural Resources
MISSISSIPPI HEADWATERS STATE FOREST
Because lands exist within the boundaries of this park that are not under the jurisdiction of the D.N.R., check with the park manager if you plan to use facilities such as trails and roads other than those shown.
Respect Private Property Ask First
NORTH
Mississippi River
Mississippi Headwaters
Lake Itasca
North Arm
East Arm
Elk Lake
BEGIN ONE WAY ROAD
ITASCA WILDERNESS SANCTUARY
Lake Ozawindib
South Twin Lake
North Twin Lake
Whipple Lake
McKay Lake
Gilfillan Lake
Little Mantrap Lake
Two Island Lake
Visitor Center
South Entrance
East Entrance
This area is shown in detail to the right
LEGEND
SUMMER TRAILS
Hiking
Biking/Hiking
Interpretive
North Country National Scenic Trail
GREAT RIVER ROAD
National Route
FACILITIES
Information/Office
Point of Interest
Picnic Area
Visitor Center
Swimming
Food Service
Boat Ramp
Canoe/Boat Rental
Bicycle Rental
Historic Site
Shelter
Overlook
Observation Tower
Lodge
Cabins, Suites
Amphitheater
Campground
Group Camp
Backpack Camping
Trailer Sanitation Station
Picnic Shelter
Parking
Exhibits
Gift Shop
Tour Boat
Restrooms
Toilet
Private Property
Public Use Prohibited
Mississippi Headwaters
North Arm
Lake Itasca
East Arm
Mary Lake

Jay Cooke

780 Highway 210
Carlton, Minnesota 55718
218-384-4610

- Park is located just outside of the small town of Thomson, which is next to Carlton, MN. The park has very easy access off of I-35 and is just 12 miles southwest of downtown Duluth.

- This state park, in my opinion, is one of the premiere parks in the entire state.

- Every member of the family would be able to find something to enjoy at this park.

- There are 82 campsites in the, main campground. There is wide variety to the camp sites and there are sites available to handle all sorts of vehicles, trailers, and RV's. There are numerous remote tent camping sites set up along the trails.

- There are 50 miles of hiking trails, 32 miles of cross country ski trail, and 12 miles of snowmobile trail.

- All amenities are available at Jay Cooke.

- Picnic Areas with shelter areas, shelters along the trails, scenic overlook sites along the trails, historic sites within the park, and then the St. Louis River. There is a swinging bridge that crosses the river. The Thomson Dam that is up the river from the rapids and the river gorge that channels all the melted snow in the spring creating a huge rapid that would rival any of the big rivers out west for rafting.

- The beauty of the area with the rock outcrops, the pines, cedars, and hardwood species all around the park, help to enhance the geologic significance of the area. Many geology classes from both Wisconsin and Minnesota come to Jay Cooke to study the rocks and soils.

- The main campground is built onto a hillside and there is varying degrees of slope and pitch to some of the sites. However, as with all the state parks, the DNR has attempted to level the sites as much as possible and it is not difficult to find a spot in the campground that wouldn't be able to handle any vehicle or trailer.

- Toilets/showers are centrally located in the campground. There are vault toilets to use all over the rest of the park. There are water spigots for fresh potable water. 21 of the camp sites have electrical hook-ups available.

- When we visited the park, we were impressed by sites -#17, 43, 44, and 59.

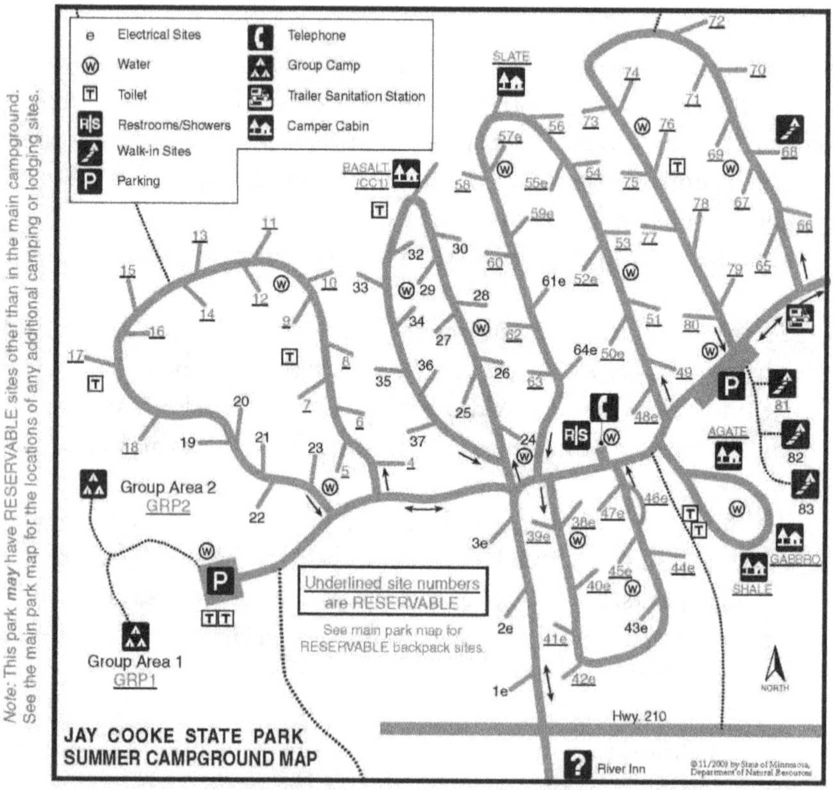

Note: This park *may* have RESERVABLE sites other than in the main campground.
See the main park map for the locations of any additional camping or lodging sites.
e Electrical Sites
Water
Toilet
Restrooms/Showers
Walk-in Sites
Parking
Telephone
Group Camp
Trailer Sanitation Station
Camper Cabin
SLATE
BASALT (CC1)
AGATE
GABBRO
SHALE
Group Area 2
GRP2
Group Area 1
GRP1
Underlined site numbers are RESERVABLE
See main park map for RESERVABLE backpack sites.
Hwy. 210
River Inn
NORTH
JAY COOKE STATE PARK
SUMMER CAMPGROUND MAP
©11/2009 by State of Minnesota, Department of Natural Resources

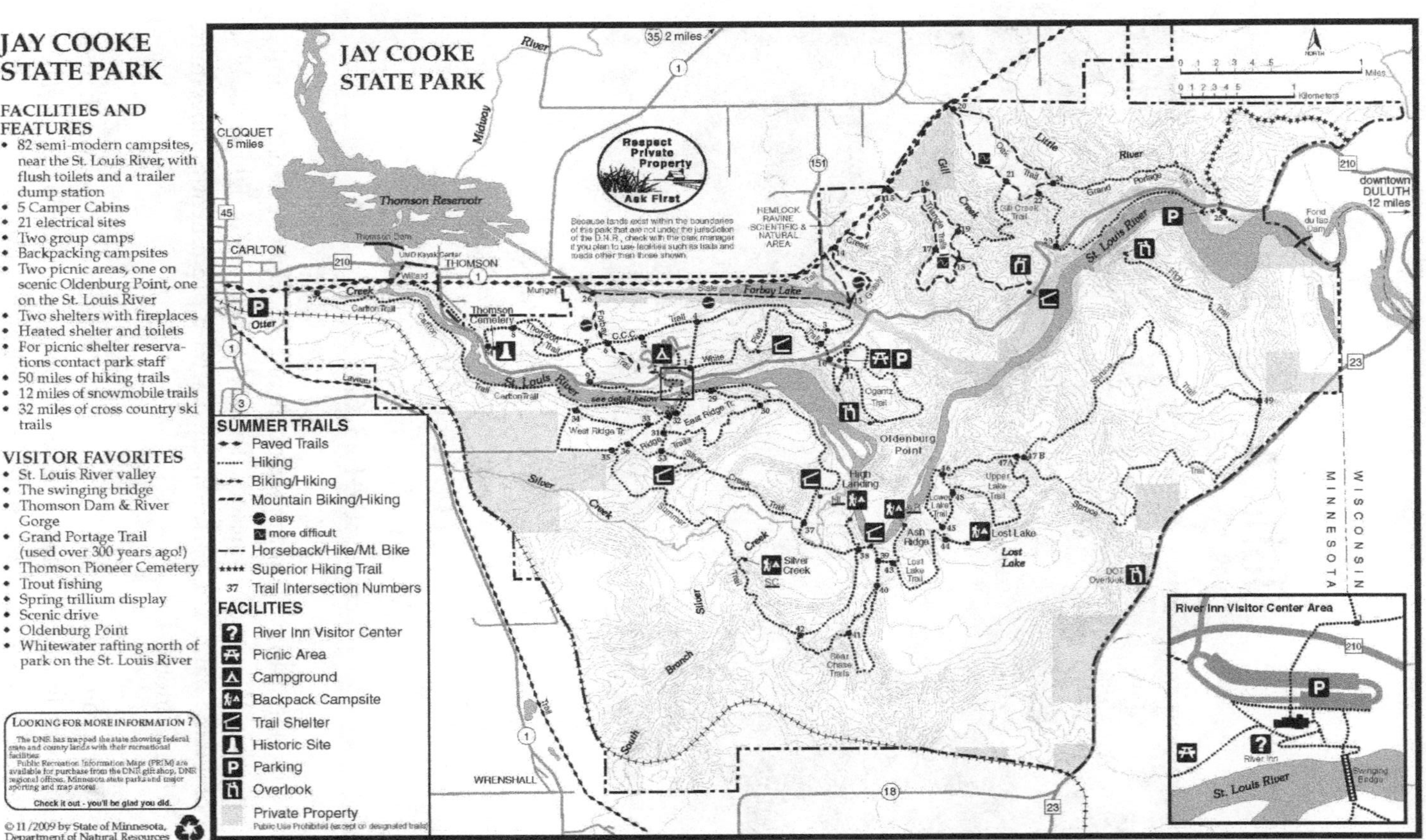
JAY COOKE STATE PARK
FACILITIES AND FEATURES
• 82 semi-modern campsites, near the St. Louis River, with flush toilets and a trailer dump station
• 5 Camper Cabins
• 21 electrical sites
• Two group camps
• Backpacking campsites
• Two picnic areas, one on scenic Oldenburg Point, one on the St. Louis River
• Two shelters with fireplaces
• Heated shelter and toilets
• For picnic shelter reservations contact park staff
• 50 miles of hiking trails
• 12 miles of snowmobile trails
• 32 miles of cross country ski trails
VISITOR FAVORITES
• St. Louis River valley
• The swinging bridge
• Thomson Dam & River Gorge
• Grand Portage Trail (used over 300 years ago!)
• Thomson Pioneer Cemetery
• Trout fishing
• Spring trillium display
• Scenic drive
• Oldenburg Point
• Whitewater rafting north of park on the St. Louis River
LOOKING FOR MORE INFORMATION?
The DNR has mapped the state showing federal state and county lands with their recreational facilities.
Public Recreation Information Maps (PRIM) are available for purchase from the DNR gift shop, DNR regional offices, Minnesota state parks and major sporting and map stores.
Check it out - you'll be glad you did.
© 11/2009 by State of Minnesota, Department of Natural Resources
JAY COOKE STATE PARK
Respect Private Property Ask First
Because lands exist within the boundaries of this park that are not under the jurisdiction of the D.N.R., check with the park manager if you plan to use facilities such as trails and roads other than those shown.
CLOQUET 5 miles
CARLTON
THOMSON
Thomson Reservoir
35 2 miles
HEMLOCK RAVINE SCIENTIFIC & NATURAL AREA
St. Louis River
Forbay Lake
Oldenburg Point
High Landing
Silver Creek
Lost Lake
Ash Ridge
Thomson Cemetery
WRENSHALL
WISCONSIN
MINNESOTA
downtown DULUTH 12 miles
Fond du lac Dam
DOT Overlook
SUMMER TRAILS
Paved Trails
Hiking
Biking/Hiking
Mountain Biking/Hiking
easy
more difficult
Horseback/Hike/Mt. Bike
Superior Hiking Trail
37 Trail Intersection Numbers
FACILITIES
River Inn Visitor Center
Picnic Area
Campground
Backpack Campsite
Trail Shelter
Historic Site
Parking
Overlook
Private Property
Public Use Prohibited (except on designated trails)
River Inn Visitor Center Area
River Inn
Swinging Bridge
St. Louis River

John A. Latsch

John A. Latsch State Park
c/o Great River Bluffs State Park
43605 Kipp Drive
Winona, Minnesota 55987
507-643-6849

- This state park sits on the west side of U.S. Hwy 61 about 11 miles north of Winona, Minnesota. The park entrance sits right at the base of a large bluff. The park is named after a prominent businessman from Winona.

- When you pull into the entrance, there is a small picnic area there to use with five or six tables and several elevated charcoal grills. There is a water spigot and a vault toilet at the picnic area.

- There is a trail that leads up along the steep incline of the bluff for hikers – if they were to wish to try and get a better view of the Mississippi River Valley. Another trail leads away from the picnic area and that will take you to 6 or 7 remote campsites along the base of the hill.

JOHN A. LATSCH STATE PARK

FOR MORE INFORMATION:
Whitewater State Park
Route 1, Box 256
Altura, MN 55910
(507)-932-3007

FACILITIES AND FEATURES

- 7 walk-in campsites
- Picnic area
- Water (hand pump)
- Toilet

VISITOR FAVORITES

- Trail to Mount Charity
- Panoramic views of the Mississippi River valley

LOOKING FOR MORE INFORMATION?

The DNR has mapped the state showing federal, state and county lands with their recreational facilities.

Public Recreation Information Maps (PRIM) are available for purchase from the DNR gift shop, DNR regional offices, Minnesota state parks and major sporting and map stores.

Check it out - you'll be glad you did.

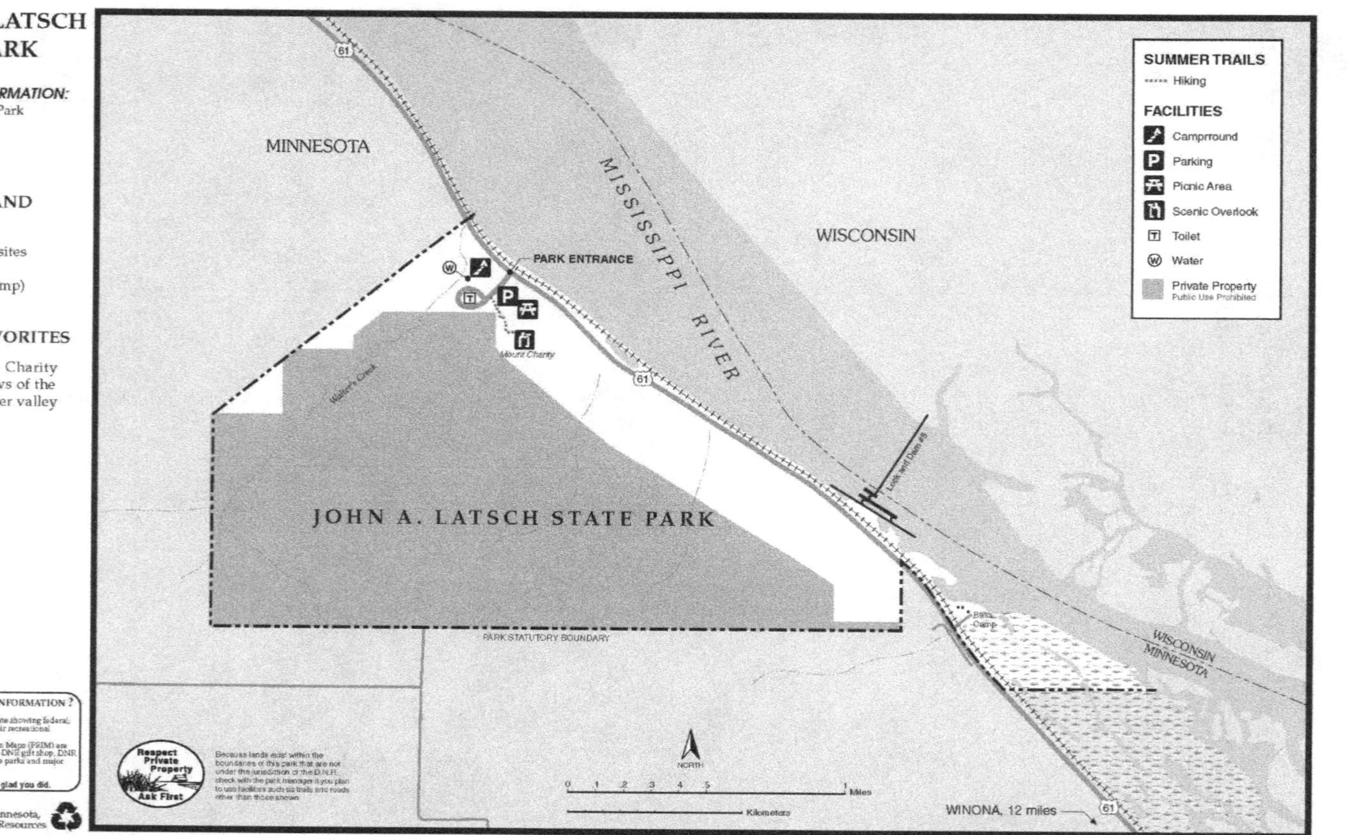

Judge C. R. Magney

4051 East Highway 61
Grand Marais, Minnesota 55604
218-387-3039

- This state park is located approximately 14 miles northeast of Grand Marais, Minnesota, on Hwy. 61.
- There are 27 campsites in the park. There are toilet/shower facilities, vault toilets, water spigots, and nine miles of hiking trail in the park. These trails hook into the Lake Superior Hiking Trail.
- There are two bridges in the park – the first is the bridge over the Brule River on Hwy. 61 and the second is a foot bridge that crosses the river about 200 yards up river from the highway.

- There are two major waterfalls on the Brule River and both are within easy hiking distance of the park. There are two picnic areas – one near the foot bridge and one near the parking area for the trails.

- Julie and I both agree that this is one fantastic park and we will be returning to it in the future to hike the trails, enjoy the camping, and to wonder around on the shore of Lake Superior.

- Nice tall White Pines, lots of shade and undergrowth between the sites. We liked the following camp sites - # 7, 8, 9, 17, 20, and 21. These sites are the ones we thought would best meet our needs with our pick-up and small trailer.

(A view across the water of Lake Superior)

JUDGE C.R. MAGNEY STATE PARK CAMPGROUND

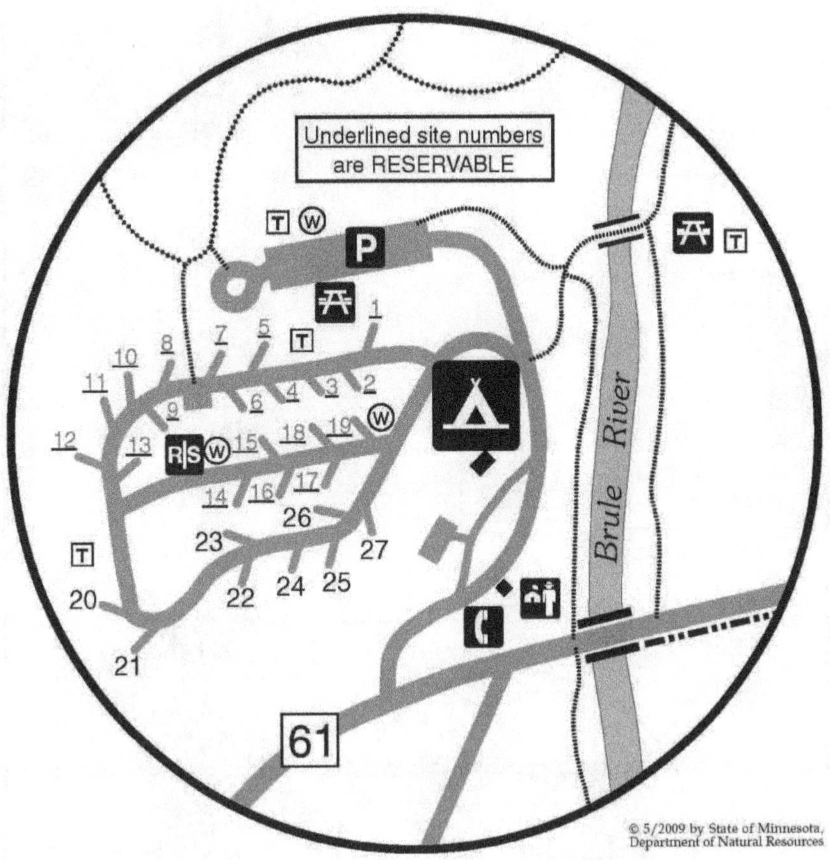

JUDGE C.R. MAGNEY STATE PARK

FACILITIES AND FEATURES:

- Semi-modern campground with 27 sites
- Picnic area on the Brule River
- 9 miles of hiking trail

VISITOR FAVORITES:

- The Devil's Kettle of the Brule River
- Superior Hiking Trail
- Camping
- Hiking
- Trout fishing
- Birdwatching
- Picnicking

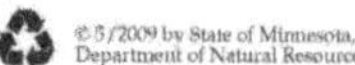

TRAILS

Hiking

Superior Hiking Trail

FACILITIES

Ranger Station

Campground

Restrooms/Showers

Parking

Picnic Area

Telephone

Toilets

Drinking Water

Private Property
Public Use Prohibited

LOOKING FOR MORE INFORMATION?

The DNR has mapped the state showing federal, state and county lands with their recreational facilities.

Public Recreation Information Maps (PRIM) are available for purchase from the DNR gift shop, DNR regional offices, Minnesota state parks and major sporting and map stores.

Check it out - you'll be glad you did.

Brule River

Superior Hiking Trail

Devil's Kettle

Upper Falls

Campground Area

to HOVLAND, 5 miles

to GRAND MARAIS, 14 miles

Lake Superior

Respect Private Property Ask First

Because lands exist within the boundaries of this park that are not under the jurisdiction of the D.N.R., check with the park manager if you plan to use facilities such as trails and roads other than those shown.

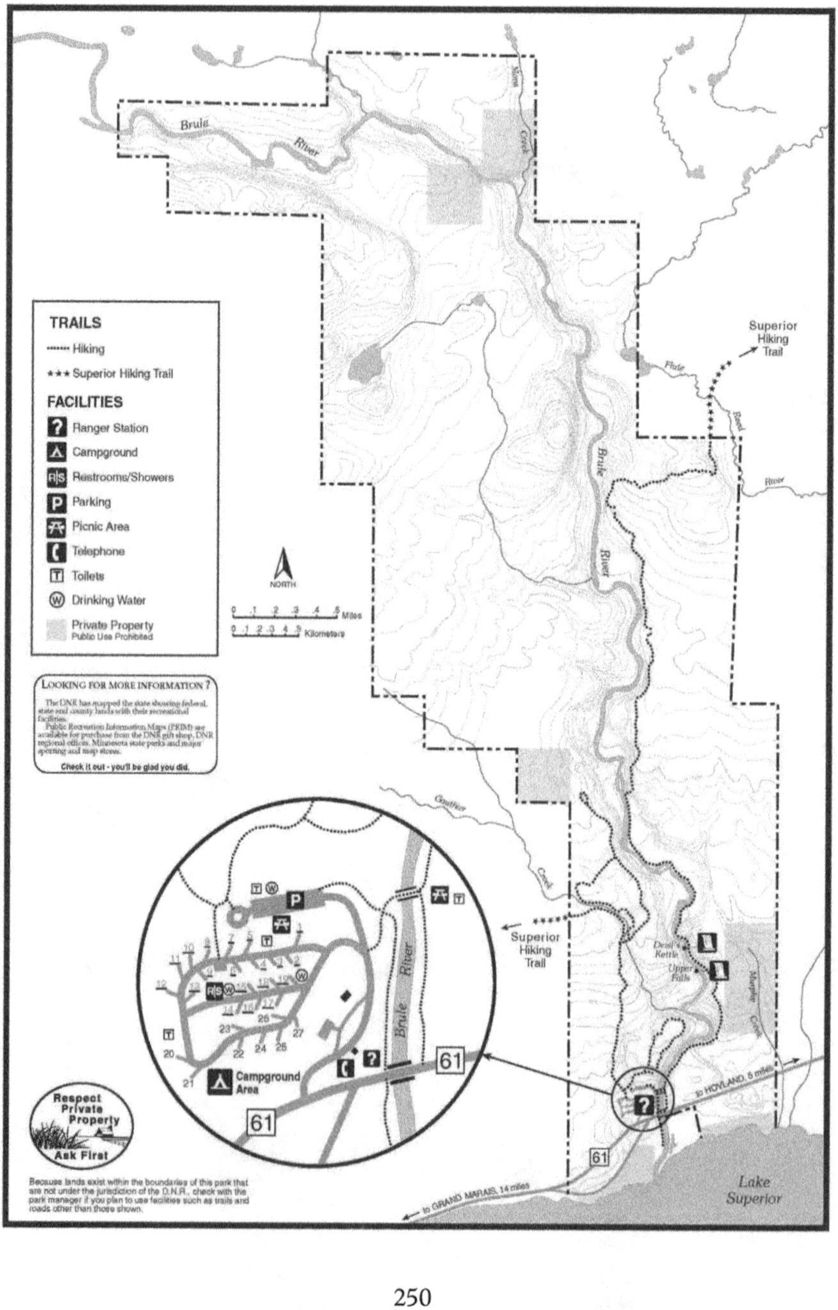

Kilen Woods

50200 860th Street
Lakefield, Minnesota 56150
507-662-6258

- This park is located nine miles northeast of the town of Lakefield, Minnesota. This is a small state park, only 200 acres. There are 33 campsites in the campground. Eleven of those sites have electrical hook-ups. There are 4 walk-in campsites along the trails.

- This park is located along the west shore of the Des Moines River.

- 5 miles of hiking trail. A very nice picnic area, water spigots and vault toilets available. This Park has one of the nicest toilet/shower buildings that we have seen in any of the state parks. There is a public canoe access to the Des Moines River in the park. Amphitheater and scenic overlook sites are also available to the campers.

- The campground has two loops with numerous pull-through sites for big campers and trailers. There are lots of oaks and ash trees for shade in the camp. Sites one through eight are open sites with few or little trees near them. We liked site # 9, 11, 13, 17, 21, and 29.

- A very wonderful, small state park that would allow a great camping experience.

(Farm country wind turbines)

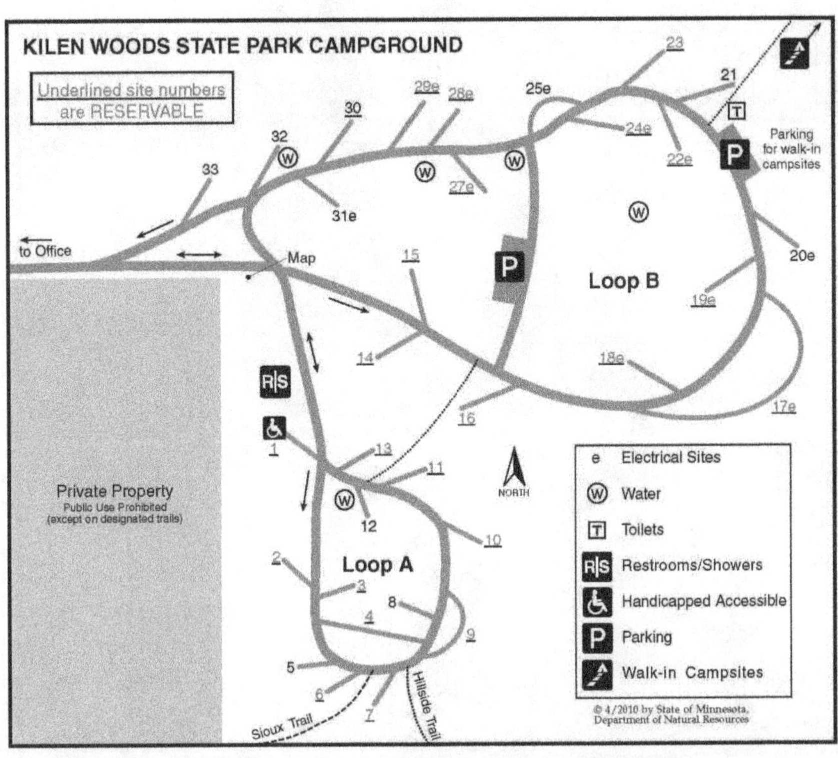
KILEN WOODS STATE PARK CAMPGROUND
Underlined site numbers are RESERVABLE
to Office
Map
Loop A
Loop B
Private Property
Public Use Prohibited
(except on designated trails)
Parking for walk-in campsites
Sioux Trail
Hillside Trail
NORTH
e Electrical Sites
Water
Toilets
Restrooms/Showers
Handicapped Accessible
Parking
Walk-in Campsites
© 4/2010 by State of Minnesota, Department of Natural Resources

KILEN WOODS STATE PARK

FACILITIES AND FEATURES

- 32 semi-modern campsites with tables, water, showers, toilets & fire rings
- 11 of above campsites with electric hookups
- 4 walk-in campsites
- Camping reservations
- Picnic area
- Multipurpose year-round shelter building with water, kitchen, reservations accepted
- 5 miles of hiking trail
- Public canoe access on the Des Moines River

VISITOR FAVORITES

- Des Moines River overlook
- Tallgrass prairie
- Canoeing on the Des Moines River
- Oak woods

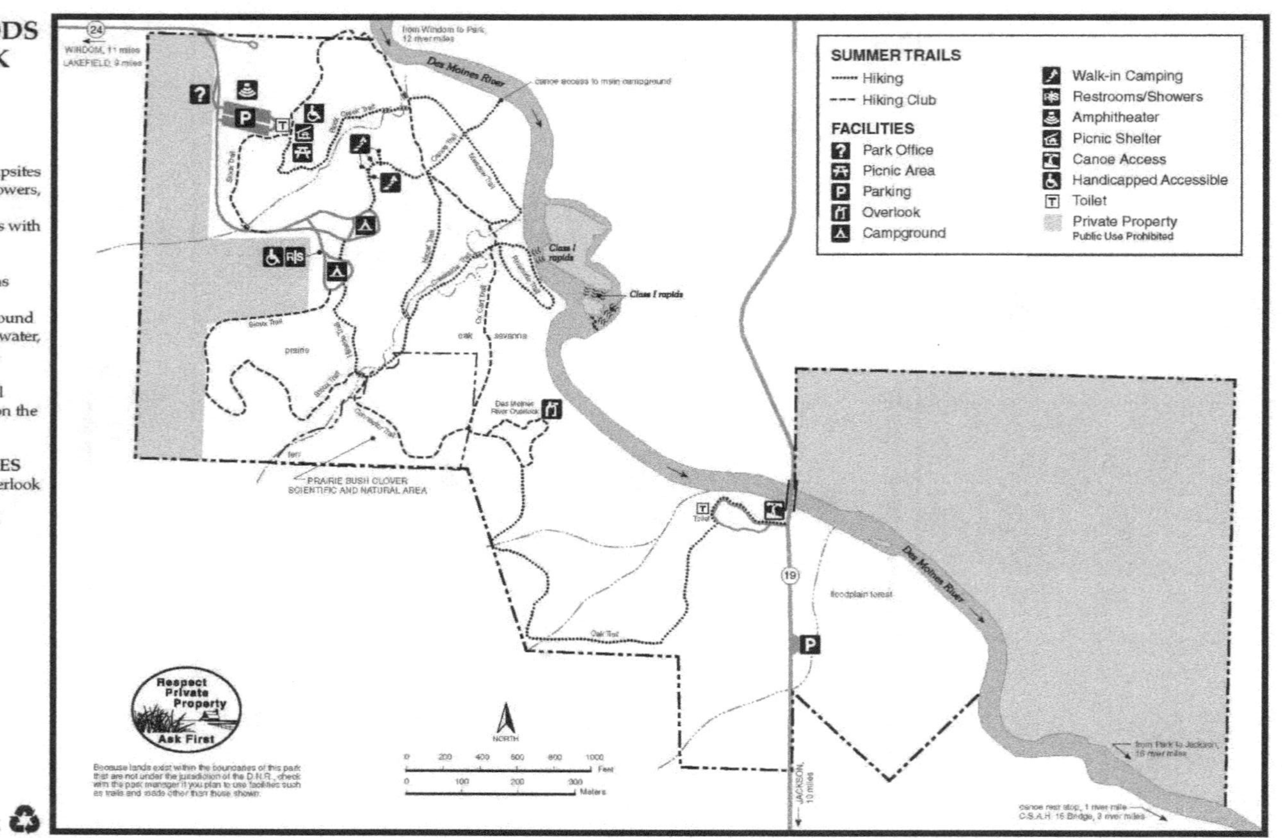

Lac Qui Parle

14047 20th Street NW
Watson, Minnesota 56295
320-734-4450

- This state park is located about 12 miles north of Montevideo, MN to the west of Hwy. 59 or just a couple of miles from the town of Watson, on Hwy. 59.

- The park straddles the Minnesota River at the dam that helps to create Lac Qui Parle Lake. The park is over 1000 acres and has one camping area on the east side of the lake, The Upper Camp, and the Lower Camp on the west side.

- There are many features to be seen at this nice park. There is a collection of many different bird species that are on display at the main park office. There are two different historical sites along the road leading to the main office. Also, Minnesota's largest Cottonwood tree is located within the park.

- At the site of the dam on the river, is a picnic area. There are two different boat ramps, a canoe carry in launch site, horse trails, hiking trails, and a swimming beach. Another picnic area is located near the swim beach on the west side of the lake.

- The camping areas have vault toilets, water spigots, and each camp has a separate building with showers in it.

- The sites are nice and level with good picnic tables and fire rings. There are seventy campsites total in the park, 24 in the Lower Camp, the rest in the upper camp. There are also three sites at the Upper Camp that can be reached by hiking in to them. There are many sites with electric hook-ups in both camps.

- Lac Qui Parle – 'the lake that speaks'. A fur trader named Joseph Renville built a stockade at the foot of the lake in 1826. Later, the first church established in Minnesota was built a short distance from the stockade.

- The sites at the upper campground are very open and sit atop of the terrace overlooking the lake. These sites are open and don't have a lot of shading.

- The lower Campground has much more cover overhead and brush and undergrowth between the campsites. They are nicely spaced apart. All the sites are nice and level.

- We liked sites #11, 13, 14, 16, and 22.

(The Mission at Lac Qui Parle State Park)

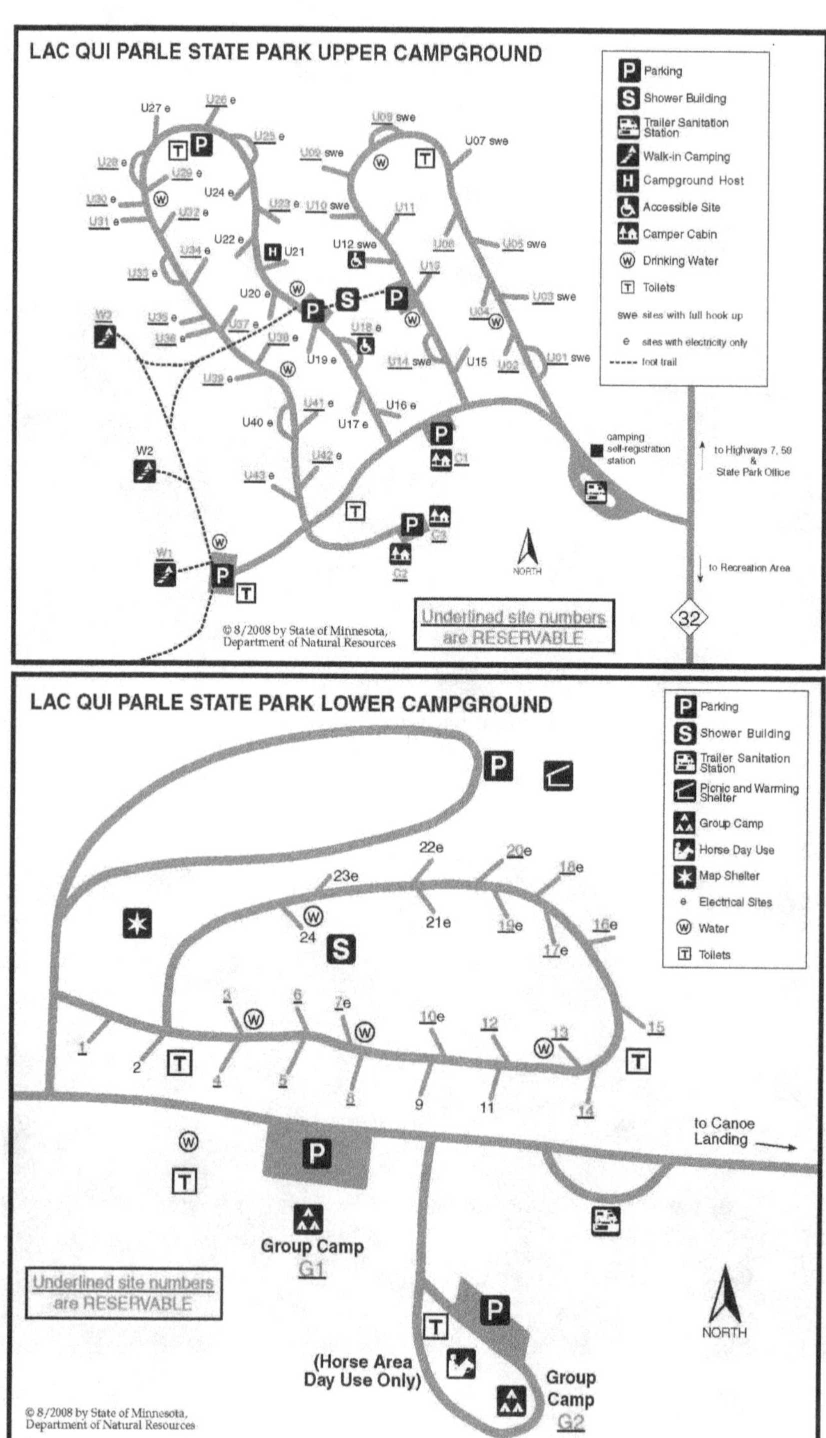
LAC QUI PARLE STATE PARK UPPER CAMPGROUND
Parking
Shower Building
Trailer Sanitation Station
Walk-in Camping
Campground Host
Accessible Site
Camper Cabin
Drinking Water
Toilets
swe sites with full hook up
e sites with electricity only
foot trail
camping self-registration station
to Highways 7, 59 & State Park Office
to Recreation Area
Underlined site numbers are RESERVABLE
© 8/2008 by State of Minnesota, Department of Natural Resources
LAC QUI PARLE STATE PARK LOWER CAMPGROUND
Parking
Shower Building
Trailer Sanitation Station
Picnic and Warming Shelter
Group Camp
Horse Day Use
Map Shelter
Electrical Sites
Water
Toilets
to Canoe Landing
Group Camp G1
(Horse Area Day Use Only)
Group Camp G2
Underlined site numbers are RESERVABLE
© 8/2008 by State of Minnesota, Department of Natural Resources

LAC QUI PARLE STATE PARK

FACILITIES AND FEATURES

- Upper Campground (showers and flush toilets)
- Lower Campground (showers but no flush toilets)
- 3 Camper Cabins
- Primitive group camp (50 capacity) in lower unit
- Horseback riders day-use area
- 20 picnic sites
- Swimming beach
- Drive in boat launch to Lac qui Parle Lake
- 5 miles of hiking trail
- 5 miles of horseback riding
- 5 miles of ski trail
- 2 trailer dump stations
- Canoe access to Lac qui Parle River
- Public telephones

LOOKING FOR MORE INFORMATION?

The DNR has mapped the state showing federal, state and county lands with their recreational facilities.

Public Recreation Information Maps (PRIM) are available for purchase from the DNR gift shop, DNR regional offices, Minnesota state parks and major sporting and map stores.

Check it out - you'll be glad you did.

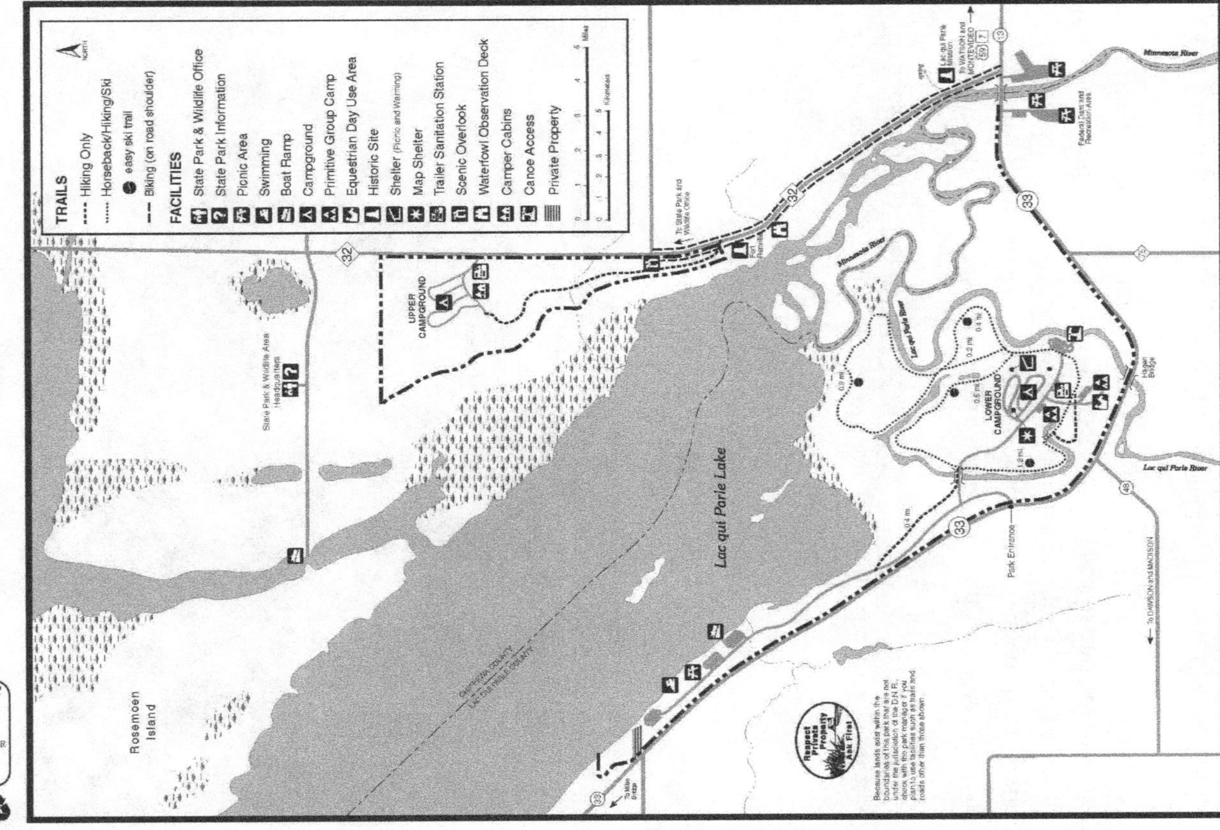

Lake Bemidji

3401 State Park Road NE
Bemidji, Minnesota 56601
218-308-2300

- Park located on the north side of Lake Bemidji. The park is located 6 miles north of Bemidji off Hwy. 71.

- The park has 95 sites with a mix of electric and non-electric sites. There are picnic areas, swimming beach, boat launch, fresh water spigots, vault toilets, flush toilets and showers, too. There is a scenic overlook and an amphitheater on site. Hiking trails and board walks for those who like to stroll around.

- The park also has an access point for the Paul Bunyan State Trail.

- This park is a great place for family oriented activities. The campgrounds are open with little to no underbrush between the sites.

- The first two camping areas - Oak Lane and Pine lane are on relatively flat to rolling terrain.

- The second two camping areas - Birch Lane and Aspen Lane - are built up on higher, hill and ridge terrain. These areas are still very open with nice sites - they just might be a little more challenging to back a large camper or trailer into.

- From our perspective, the nicer sites we saw were those up on top of the hill in the Aspen Lane area - # 85, 87, and 95.

- A nice picnic area with shelters, play areas, fish cleaning shack, a large dock to fish from. Boat and canoe rental is available at the park.

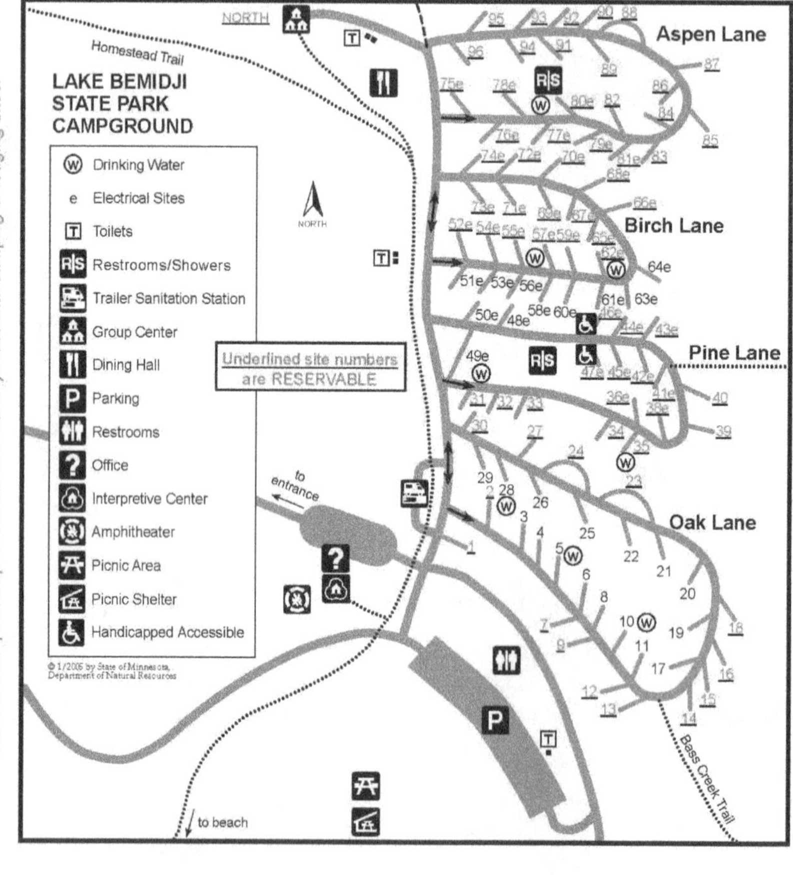

LAKE BEMIDJI
STATE PARK
CAMPGROUND
Drinking Water
Electrical Sites
Toilets
Restrooms/Showers
Trailer Sanitation Station
Group Center
Dining Hall
Parking
Restrooms
Office
Interpretive Center
Amphitheater
Picnic Area
Picnic Shelter
Handicapped Accessible
NORTH
Homestead Trail
Underlined site numbers are RESERVABLE
to entrance
to beach
Aspen Lane
Birch Lane
Pine Lane
Oak Lane
Bass Creek Trail
Note: This park *may* have RESERVABLE sites other than in the main campground.
See the main park map for the locations of any additional camping or lodging sites.

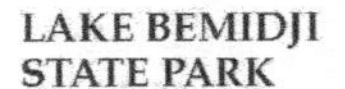

LAKE BEMIDJI STATE PARK

SUMMER FACILITIES AND FEATURES

- 95 semi-modern campsites
- Hot showers
- Group areas
- Picnic area
- Swimming beach
- Public boat access/marina
- Boat/canoe rentals
- Lake fishing
- Visitor center/trail center
- Naturalist programs
- Nature trails
- Trailer dump station
- Paul Bunyan State Trail
- Fishing pier

SPECIAL FEATURE

The Lake Bemidji Bog Walk is a boardwalk into the spruce-tamarack bog. See orchids, insect-eating plants and a hidden lake.

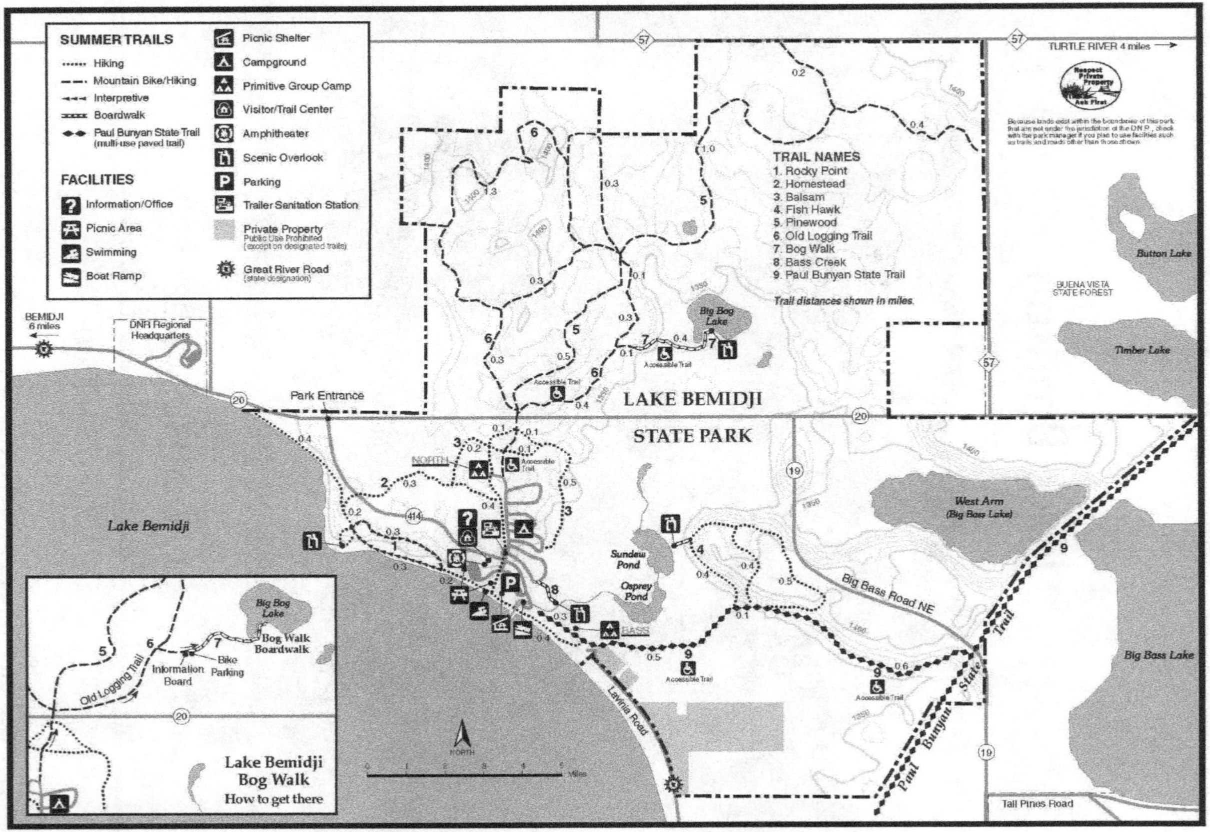

SUMMER TRAILS

Hiking
Mountain Bike/Hiking
Interpretive
Boardwalk
Paul Bunyan State Trail (multi-use paved trail)

FACILITIES

Information/Office
Picnic Area
Swimming
Boat Ramp
Picnic Shelter
Campground
Primitive Group Camp
Visitor/Trail Center
Amphitheater
Scenic Overlook
Parking
Trailer Sanitation Station
Private Property (Public Use Prohibited, except on designated trails)
Great River Road (state designation)

TRAIL NAMES

1. Rocky Point
2. Homestead
3. Balsam
4. Fish Hawk
5. Pinewood
6. Old Logging Trail
7. Bog Walk
8. Bass Creek
9. Paul Bunyan State Trail

Trail distances shown in miles.

LAKE BEMIDJI STATE PARK
Lake Bemidji
Park Entrance
BEMIDJI 6 miles
DNR Regional Headquarters
Big Bog Lake
Sundew Pond
Osprey Pond
West Arm (Big Bass Lake)
Big Bass Lake
Big Bass Road NE
Lavinia Road
Paul Bunyan State Trail
Tall Pines Road
TURTLE RIVER 4 miles
Button Lake
Timber Lake
BUENA VISTA STATE FOREST
Respect Private Property Ask First

Because lands exist within the boundaries of this park that are not under the jurisdiction of the DNR, check with the park manager if you plan to use facilities such as trails and roads other than those shown.

Lake Bemidji Bog Walk
How to get there

Big Bog Lake
Bog Walk Boardwalk
Bike Parking
Information Board
Old Logging Trail

LOOKING FOR MORE INFORMATION?

The DNR has mapped the state showing federal, state and county lands with their recreational facilities.
Public Recreation Information Maps (PRIM) are available for purchase from the DNR gift shop, DNR regional offices, Minnesota state parks and major sporting and map stores.
Check it out - you'll be glad you did.

Lake Bronson

County Highway 28
Lake Bronson, Minnesota 56734
218-754-2200

- Located one mile east of the city of Lake Bronson, MN. This is the site of a WPA project that built the dam that created the lake the city is named after.

- This park is located on the border region between the prairie in the west and the forests in the east. There are 194 campsites split between two camping areas. Lakeside Camp has 61 sites, with 23 electric sites. Two Rivers Camp is a large campground with near 100 sites, a dozen of them having electrical hook up.

- There are two different boat launch sites on the lake, piers and docks at the lakeside to fish from, fish cleaning shacks, picnic areas, there are 5 archeological/historical sites along the trails, remote sites for camping that can be reached from water or trail, and 14 miles of trail to use for hiking, cross country skiing, or biking.

- The large Observation Tower in the park is a National Historic site.

- The terrain of the park is flat to slightly rolling hills. There are many trees in the park of which the majority of them are deciduous. Scrub oaks, white and red oaks, aspen, and some birch can be found. The camping areas are nicely tree covered and there is little vegetation growing up from the ground.

- There are very nice toilets and showers set up at each of the camps. Vault toilets and water spigots are also well dispersed throughout the park. There are playgrounds near each of the campgrounds. All of the sites in the park campgrounds are nice and level; however, some sites are crowded together.

- This is a beautiful state park, family oriented and has many of the amenities to allow comfortable camping and recreation for everyone.

- Camp sites that we liked were: 8, 28, 36, 40, 47, 100, 116, 135, 141, and 169.

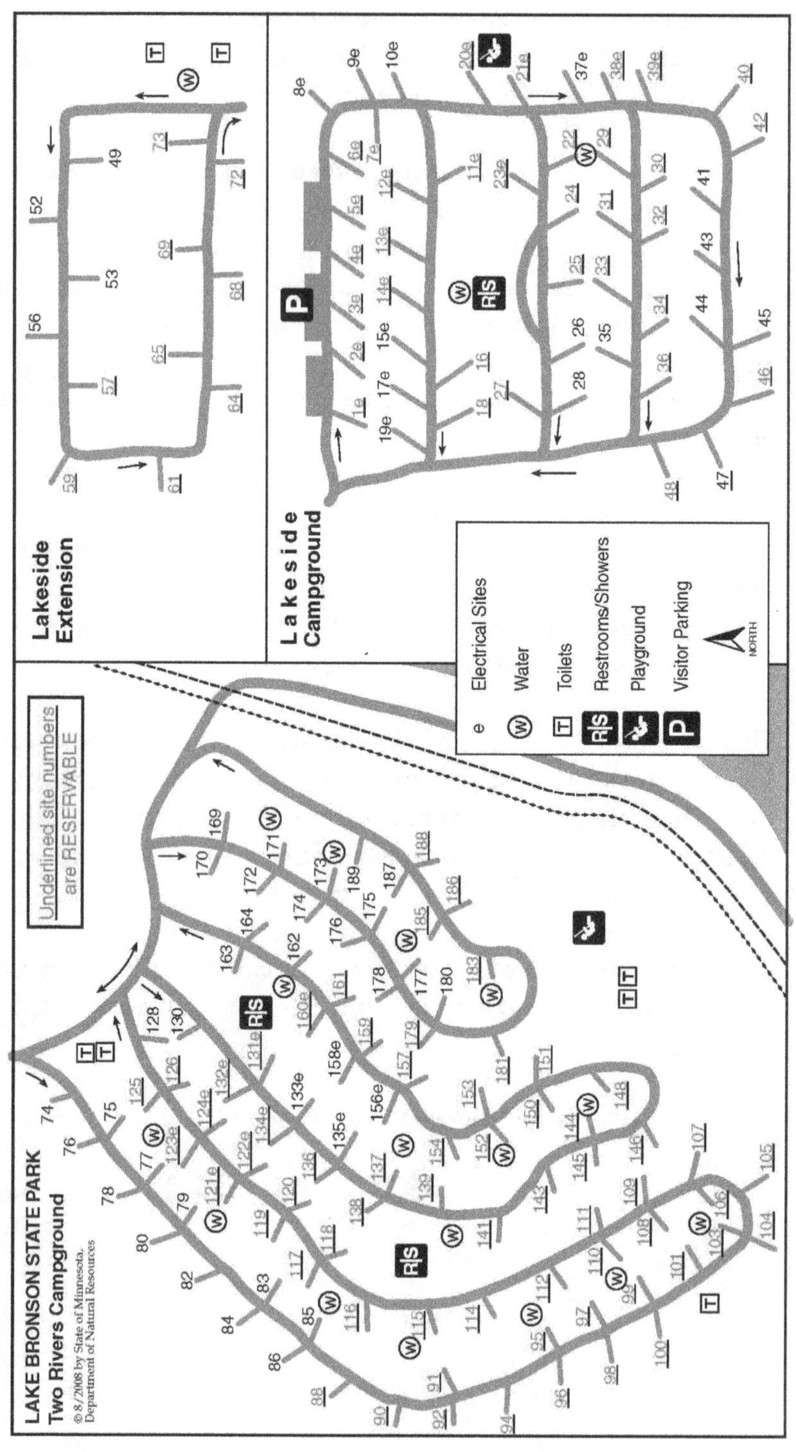
LAKE BRONSON STATE PARK
Two Rivers Campground
© 8/2008 by State of Minnesota, Department of Natural Resources
Underlined site numbers are RESERVABLE
Lakeside Extension
Lakeside Campground
e Electrical Sites
Water
Toilets
Restrooms/Showers
Playground
Visitor Parking
NORTH

LAKE BRONSON STATE PARK

SUMMER FACILITIES AND FEATURES

- 194 semi-modern campsites (35 sites with electricity)
- 3 hike-in campsites
- 2 canoe-in campsites
- Dump station, flush toilets and showers
- Primitive group camp with an enclosed shelter (capacity 50)
- Picnic area with an open picnic shelter and 110 tables
- Observation tower
- Snack bar
- Boat and canoe rentals
- Drive-in water accesses
- Lake fishing: northern pike, walleye, perch, bass, crappies
- 14 miles of hiking trails
- 1 mile self-guided interpretive trail
- 5 miles of bike trail
- Summer interpretive programs

VISITOR FAVORITES

- Fishing
- Swimming
- Wildlife observation
- Hiking

LOOKING FOR MORE INFORMATION?

The DNR has mapped the state showing federal, state and county lands with their recreational facilities. Public Recreation Information Maps (PRIM) are available for purchase from the DNR gift shop, DNR regional offices, Minnesota state parks and major sporting and map stores.

Check it out - you'll be glad you did.

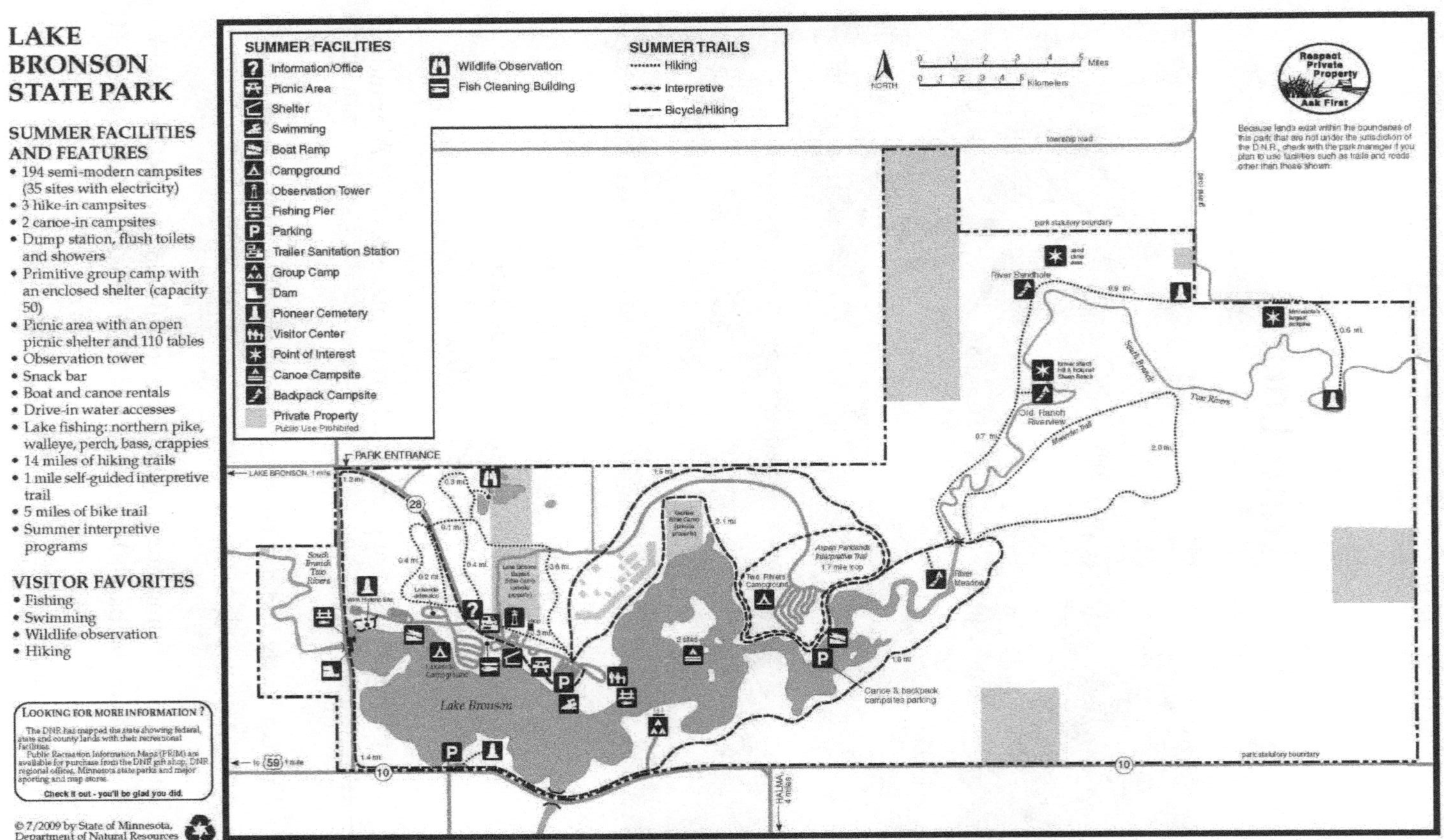

Lake Carlos

2601 County Road 38 NE
Carlos, Minnesota 56319
320-852-7200

- This park is located approximately ten miles north of Alexandria, Minnesota on Hwy. 29.

- This is a lovely and diverse state park that offers all the amenities to create an enjoyable atmosphere for the entire family.

- There 121 camping sites available in two different camps. The Upper camp has more than 40 campsites and 22 of those sites have electrical hook-ups. The lower campground which is next to the lake has over 80 sites and over 55 sites that have electrical hook-ups available.

- There are group camping areas available; a horseback riders campground; a long beautiful, sandy swimming beach; picnic area, amphitheater, and interpretive center. Water spigots, vault toilets, flush toilet/shower facilities, and fish cleaning shack.

- There are 14 miles of hiking trail, 9 miles of horse trail, cross country and snowmobile trails are available during the winter. Snow shoes can be rented at the park office.

- Lake Carlos is an exceptional lake for all sorts of recreation: Boating, sailing, skiing, and fishing.

- Great tree cover, lots of shade. We liked sites # 12, 14, 15 to 23.

- Lake Carlos would be a fine campground for the whole family to enjoy.

(General Store at the Kensington Rhunestone Museum, Alexandria, Minnesota.)

(South view from the top of Inspiration Peak, 25 miles northwest of Lake Carlos.)

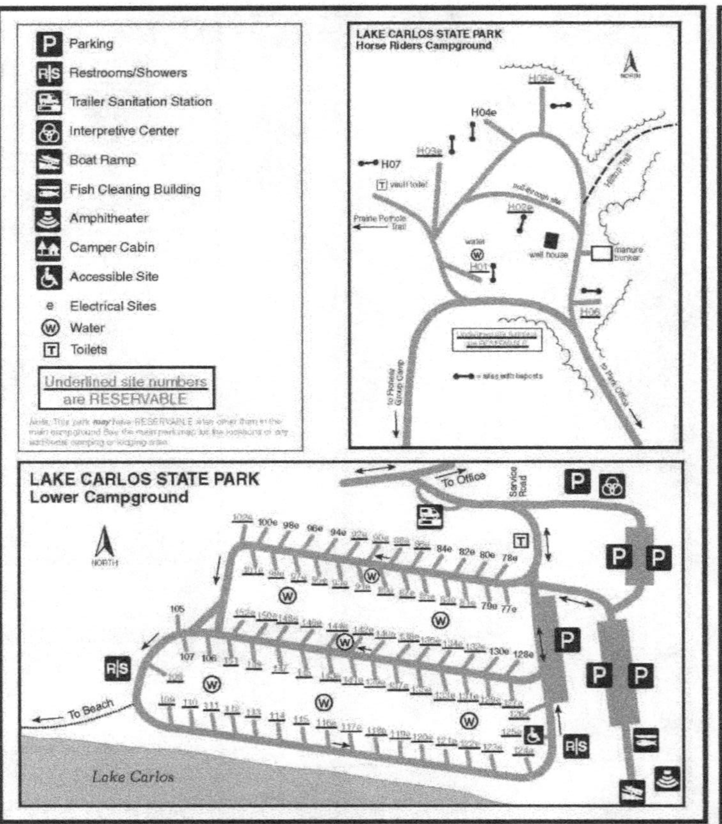
Parking
Restrooms/Showers
Trailer Sanitation Station
Interpretive Center
Boat Ramp
Fish Cleaning Building
Amphitheater
Camper Cabin
Accessible Site
e Electrical Sites
Water
Toilets
Underlined site numbers are RESERVABLE
LAKE CARLOS STATE PARK
Horse Riders Campground
NORTH
H05e
H04e
H03e
H07
vault toilet
Prairie Pothole Trail
H02e
water
H01
well house
manure bunker
H06
to Park Office
LAKE CARLOS STATE PARK
Lower Campground
NORTH
To Office
Service Road
To Beach
Lake Carlos

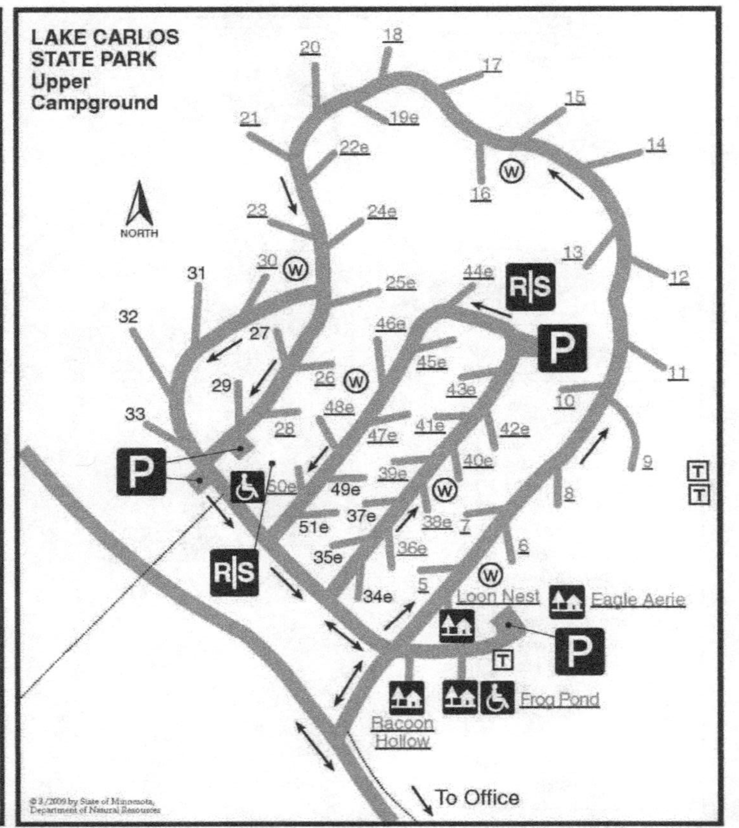
LAKE CARLOS
STATE PARK
Upper
Campground
NORTH
Loon Nest
Eagle Aerie
Frog Pond
Racoon Hollow
To Office
© 3/2009 by State of Minnesota, Department of Natural Resources

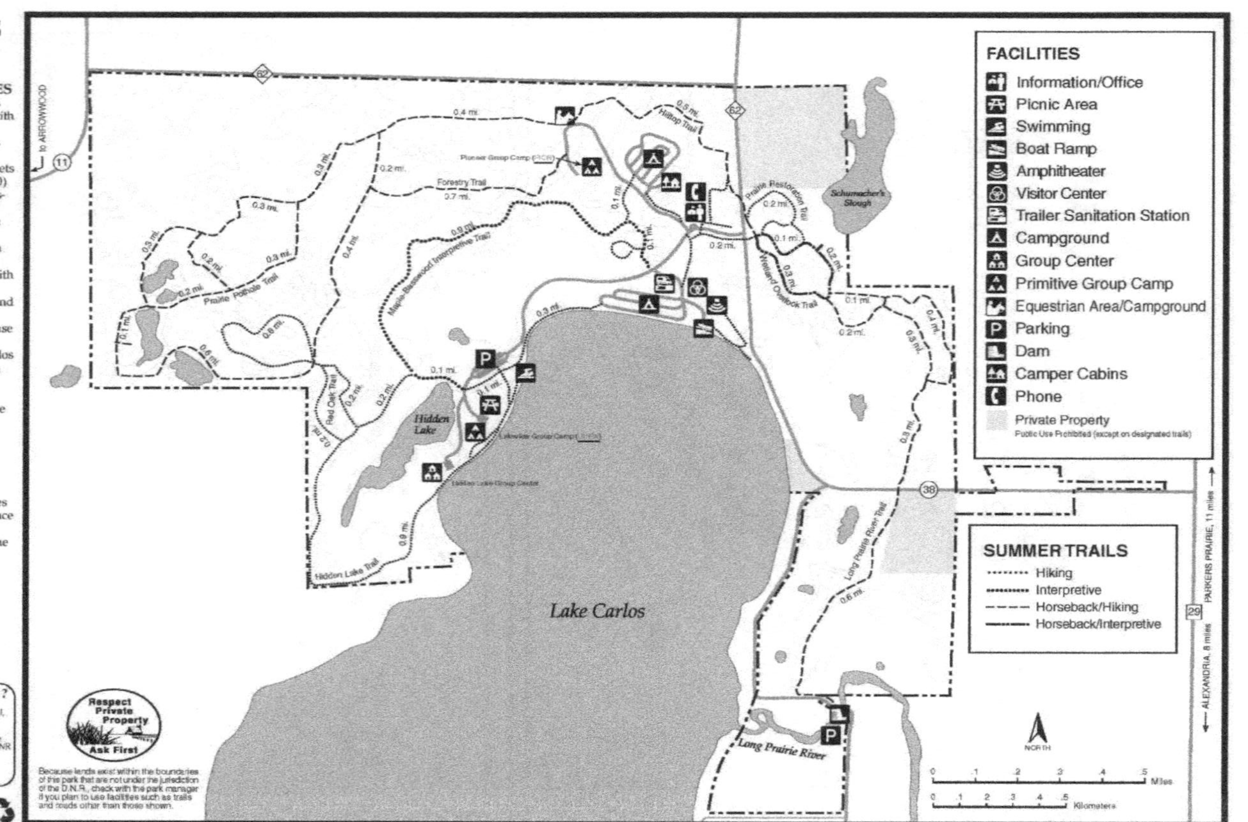
LAKE CARLOS
STATE PARK
FACILITIES AND FEATURES
• Two semi-modern campgrounds with a total of 121 campsites (81 with electricity)
• Four year-round Camper Cabins with electricity
• Dump station, showers, flush toilets
• Modern group camp (capacity 60) with cabins, a dining hall, a classroom building, and a sanitation building with showers and flush toilets
• Two primitive group camps with vault toilets, shelter, and water
• Horseback riders campground with running water and pit toilets
• Day use picnic area with tables and fire rings
• Swimming beach with a bathhouse
• Fish cleaning building
• Drive-in water access on Lake Carlos
• Carry-in water access on Hidden Lake
• 14 miles of hiking trail
• 3 miles of self-guided interpretive trail
• 9 miles of horseback riding trail
• 5 miles of cross-country ski trail
• 9 miles of snowmobile trail
• The park has a public telephone. Laundry and lodging facilities, groceries, and other conveniences are available within a short distance of the park.
• Snowshoes available to rent at the park office
Emergency Telephone Numbers:
Park: 320-852-7200
County Sheriff: 320-762-8151
Conservation Officer: 320-762-1046
LOOKING FOR MORE INFORMATION?
Check it out - you'll be glad you did.
636/2009 by State of Minnesota, Department of Natural Resources
FACILITIES
Information/Office
Picnic Area
Swimming
Boat Ramp
Amphitheater
Visitor Center
Trailer Sanitation Station
Campground
Group Center
Primitive Group Camp
Equestrian Area/Campground
Parking
Dam
Camper Cabins
Phone
Private Property
Public Use Prohibited (except on designated trails)
SUMMER TRAILS
Hiking
Interpretive
Horseback/Hiking
Horseback/Interpretive
NORTH
Miles
Kilometers
Lake Carlos
Hidden Lake
Long Prairie River
Schumacher's Slough
Hilltop Trail
Forestry Trail
Prairie Pothole Trail
Red Oak Trail
Hidden Lake Trail
Prairie Restoration Trail
Wetland Overlook Trail
Long Prairie River Trail
Maple-Basswood Interpretive Trail
Pioneer Group Camp
Lakeview Group Camp
Hidden Lake Group Center
to ARROWWOOD
PARKERS PRAIRIE, 11 miles
ALEXANDRIA, 8 miles
Respect Private Property Ask First
Because lands exist within the boundaries of this park that are not under the jurisdiction of the D.N.R., check with the park manager if you plan to use facilities such as trails and roads other than those shown.

Lake Louise

Lake Louise State Park
21071 County Road 118
Preston, Minnesota 55965
507-352-5111
(contact c/o Forestville-Mystery Cave State Park)

- The park is located about 1.5 miles north of LeRoy, Minnesota on County Highway 14. LeRoy is about 5 miles west of U.S. Highway 63 on Hwy 56, just after it enters Minnesota from Iowa.

- There is a special monument built on the south side of town that is dedicated to the large wind generator farm that is just inside of Iowa, south of Leroy. The display at the monument discusses the use of alternate energy sources like wind energy and it explains and describes the wind generators that can be seen from the site.

- This park, like Kilen Woods near Jackson, is sometimes referred to as an 'oasis' in the middle of rich farmland. The park has a very long history as does the town of Leroy. The park was named after a member of the family that donated the land to the town. The park was known as Wildwood Park before it became a state park.

- There twenty sites to camp at and eleven have electrical hookup. There is a separate camp set up for those that want to bring horses for trail riding. There are two remote group camps, a boat landing, swimming beach, and a picnic area. There are 10 miles of horse trail, 12 miles of hiking trail and there is access to the paved Shooting Star Bicycle trail.

- This is a lovely park nestled along two small streams that combine to form the Iowa River. There is a small dam at the end of the park which creates the lake.

- In the campground area there is a toilet and shower building. There are water spigots and vault toilets available for use. There is nice tree cover and undergrowth around all of the camping sites. A restroom/ shower building is on site as well as water spigots and vault toilets for camper use.

- Camp sites that we thought were nice are: 8, 9, 10, 11, 14, and 19.

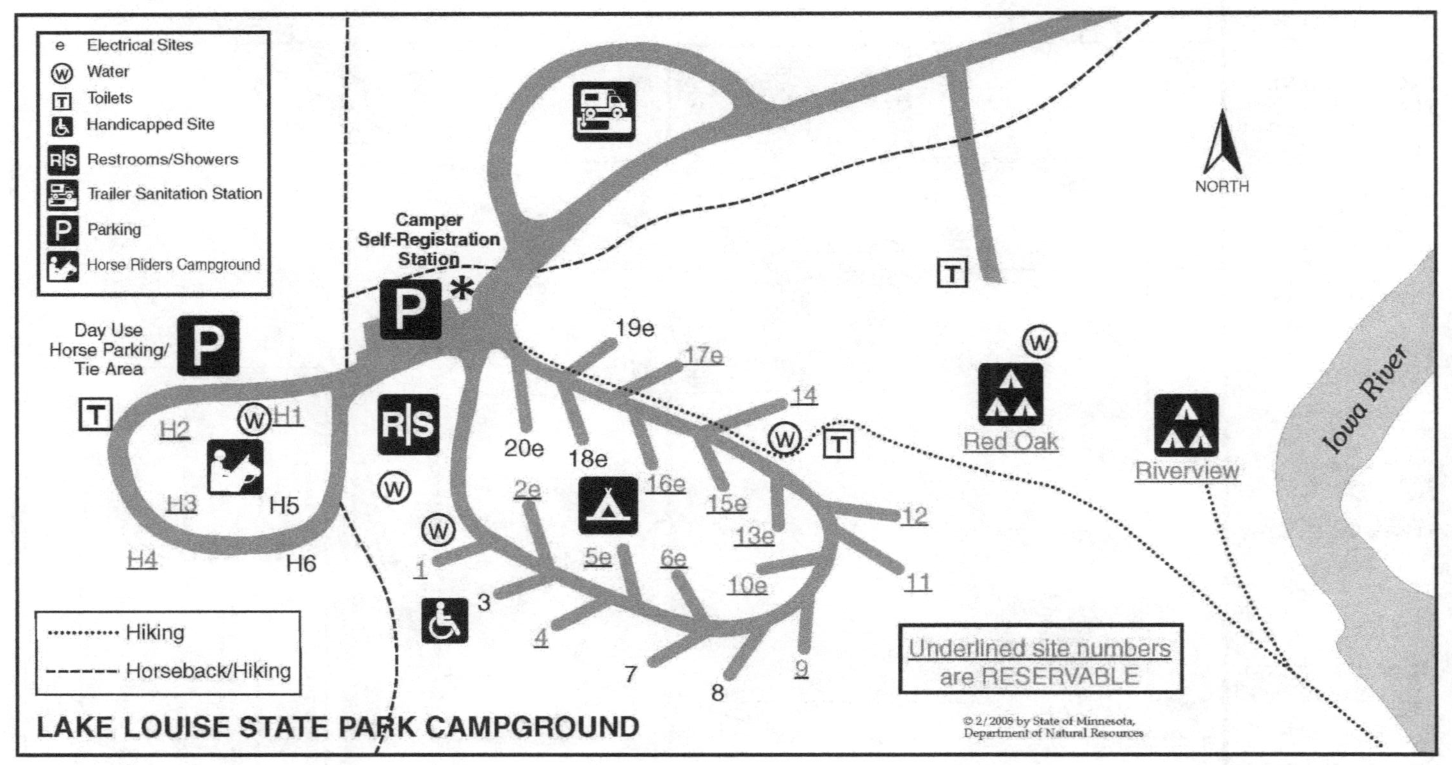

e Electrical Sites
Water
Toilets
Handicapped Site
Restrooms/Showers
Trailer Sanitation Station
Parking
Horse Riders Campground
Day Use
Horse Parking/
Tie Area
Camper
Self-Registration
Station
NORTH
Iowa River
Red Oak
Riverview
H1
H2
H3
H4
H5
H6
1
2e
3
4
5e
6e
7
8
9
10e
11
12
13e
14
15e
16e
17e
18e
19e
20e
Hiking
Horseback/Hiking
Underlined site numbers
are RESERVABLE
LAKE LOUISE STATE PARK CAMPGROUND
© 2/2008 by State of Minnesota,
Department of Natural Resources

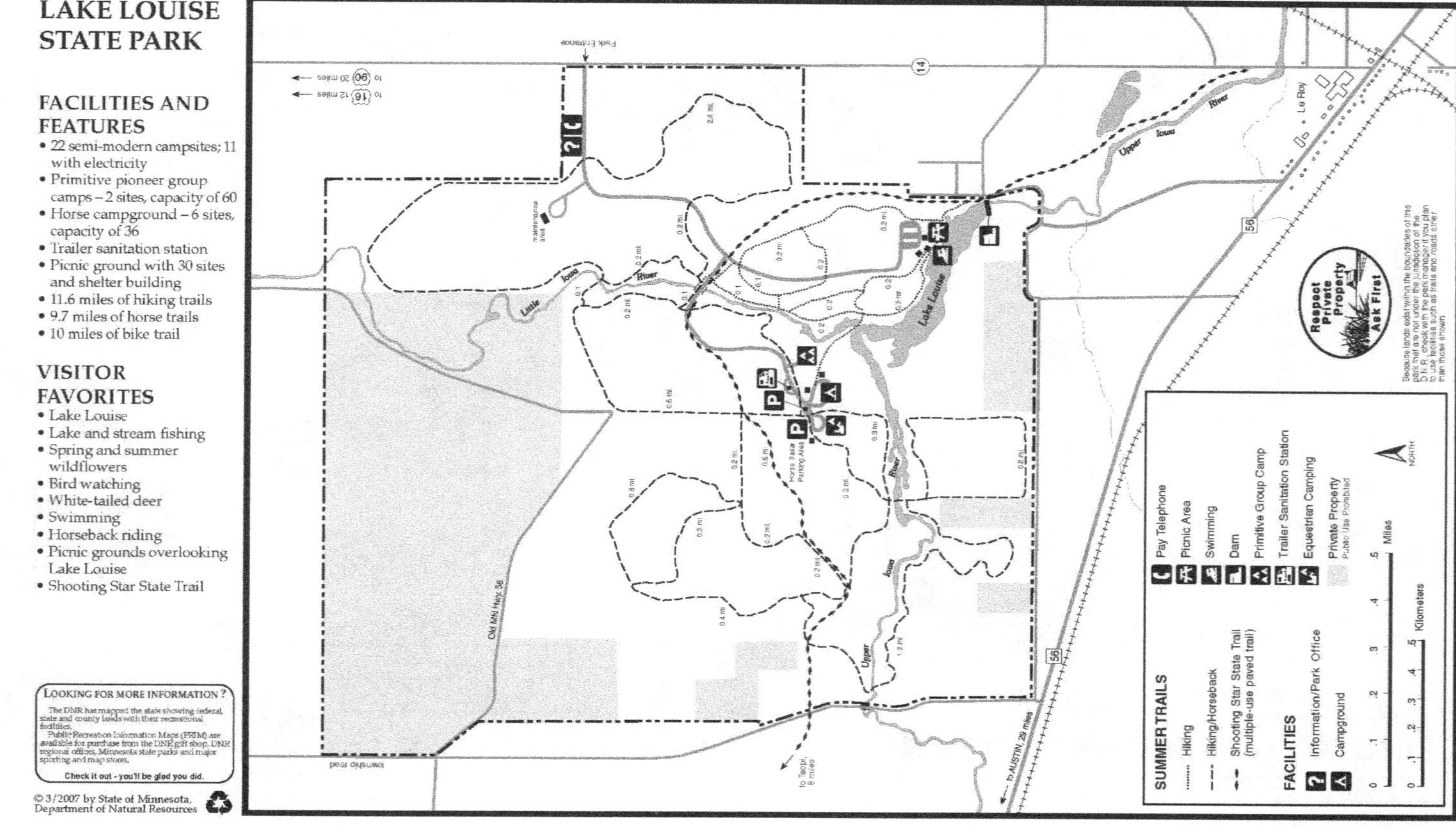
LAKE LOUISE STATE PARK
FACILITIES AND FEATURES
• 22 semi-modern campsites; 11 with electricity
• Primitive pioneer group camps – 2 sites, capacity of 60
• Horse campground – 6 sites, capacity of 36
• Trailer sanitation station
• Picnic ground with 30 sites and shelter building
• 11.6 miles of hiking trails
• 9.7 miles of horse trails
• 10 miles of bike trail
VISITOR FAVORITES
• Lake Louise
• Lake and stream fishing
• Spring and summer wildflowers
• Bird watching
• White-tailed deer
• Swimming
• Horseback riding
• Picnic grounds overlooking Lake Louise
• Shooting Star State Trail
LOOKING FOR MORE INFORMATION?
The DNR has mapped the state showing federal, state and county lands with their recreational facilities.
Public Recreation Information Maps (PRIM) are available for purchase from the DNR gift shop, DNR regional offices, Minnesota state parks and major sporting and map stores.
Check it out - you'll be glad you did.
© 3/2007 by State of Minnesota, Department of Natural Resources
Park Entrance
to 16 12 miles
to 90 20 miles
14
maintenance area
Little Iowa River
Old MN Hwy 56
township road
Horse Trailer Parking Area
Lake Louise
Upper Iowa River
to Taopi, 8 miles
to AUSTIN, 29 miles
56
Le Roy
Respect Private Property Ask First
Because lands exist within the boundaries of this park that are not under the jurisdiction of the D.N.R., check with the park manager if you plan to use facilities such as trails and roads other than those shown.
SUMMER TRAILS
Hiking
Hiking/Horseback
Shooting Star State Trail (multiple-use paved trail)
FACILITIES
Information/Park Office
Campground
Pay Telephone
Picnic Area
Swimming
Dam
Primitive Group Camp
Trailer Sanitation Station
Equestrian Camping
Private Property
Public Use Prohibited
Miles
Kilometers
NORTH

Lake Maria

11411 Clementa Avenue NW
Monticello, Minnesota 55362
763-878-2325

- Located about 7 miles from Monticello, MN. This park is exclusive to those people who want to get out and do some remote camping. All the sites in the park (17 of them) can only be reached by hiking the trails to get to them.
- There are 14 miles of hiking trails, 22 kilometers of ski trails, horse back trails and skate-skiing trails.
- There is a boat launch and dock for fishing on Lake Maria.

- Wildlife abounds in this small park. There are over 200 species of birds, deer, fox, and beaver. Lake Maria is also the home to many Blanding's Turtles - a threatened species.

- This park is very popular for cross country skiing and hiking in the winter. A very large owl flew over our truck twice as we drove through the woods toward the boat landing.

- This state park is easily accessible from anywhere in the Twin Cities Metro Area, but it still retains its wildness and the sense of being close to nature.

LAKE MARIA STATE PARK

FACILITIES AND FEATURES

- 17 backpack campsites
- 2 primitive group camps, capacity 50
- 3 camper cabins
- Picnic area
- Public boat access
- Boat & canoe rental
- Trail/interpretive center
- 14 miles of hiking trails
- 1 mile interpretive trails
- 22 kilometers of ski trails
- 5 kilometers skate-ski trails
- 6 miles of horseback trails

VISITOR FAVORITES

- Hiking
- Cross-country skiing
- Bird watching
- Backpack camping
- Canoeing
- Lake fishing – northern pike, bluegill, crappie, perch, bullhead, carp
- Interpretive programs & displays

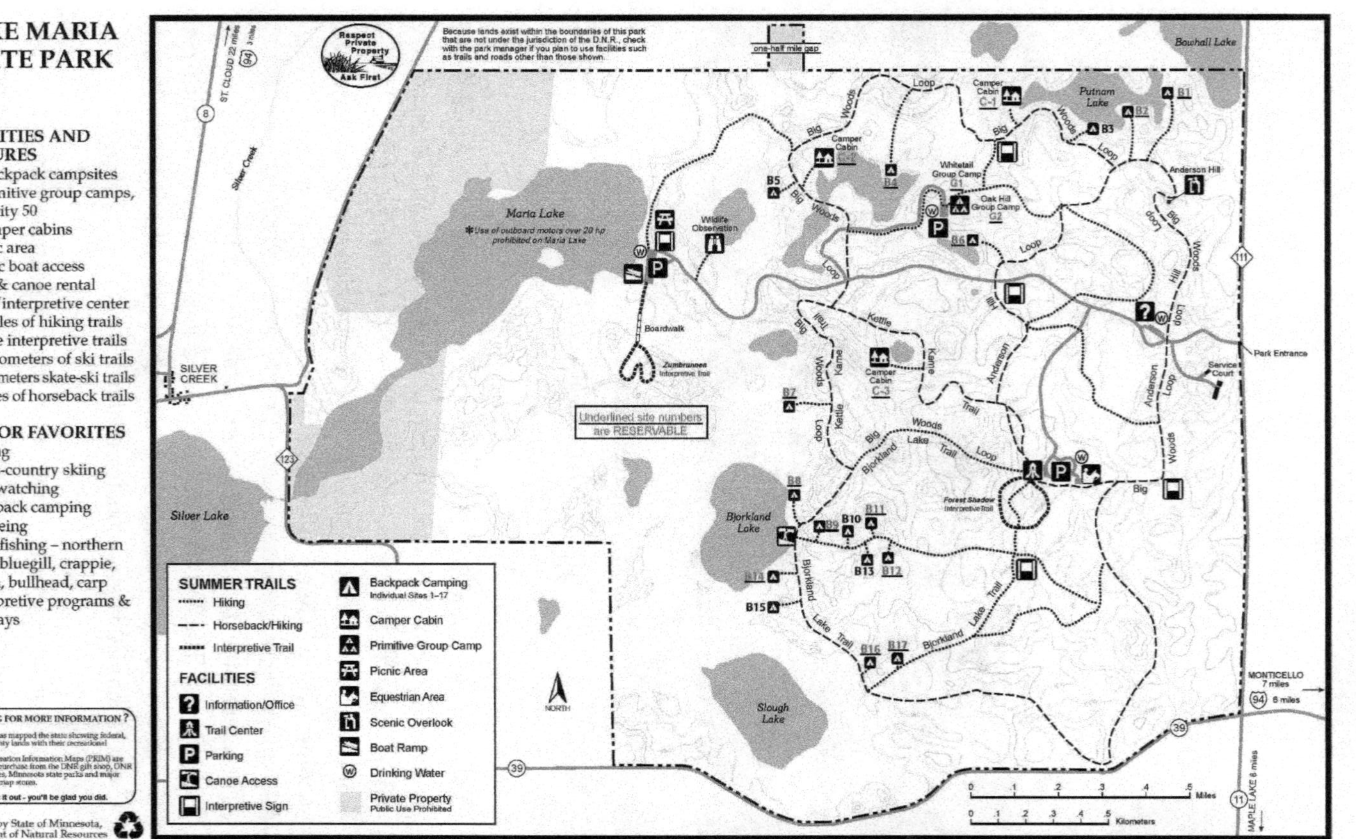

LOOKING FOR MORE INFORMATION?

The DNR has mapped the state showing federal, state and county lands with their recreational facilities.

Public Recreation Information Maps (PRIM) are available for purchase from the DNR gift shop, DNR regional offices, Minnesota state parks and major sporting and map stores.

Check it out - you'll be glad you did.

Lake Shetek

163 State Park Road
Currie, Minnesota 56123
507-763-3256

- This park is located 14 miles northeast of Slayton, Minnesota. It is a few miles north of the small town of Currie, MN, on County Hwy. 38. A park created by the WPA. Lake Shetek is the largest lake in southwestern Minnesota. The lake is the headwaters of the Des Moines River. 'Shetek' in native Ojibwe means – pelican.

- There are over 110 campsites available at this park, split between two camps. The Wolfpoint Camp area has 77 sites of which 67 of the sites have electrical hook-up available. The other camp – Prairie Camp – has 20 rustic sites for tents.

- There is a large group camp area, camper cabins, remote cart-in campsites along the trails, an amphitheater, swim beach, interpretive center, a couple historic sites to visit, over 22 miles of different trails for hiking, biking, ski and snowmobile.

- A large beautiful picnic area with two different covered shelters.
- The lake is aerated during the winter to stop the fish kill. So, there is great fishing on the lake with northern, crappies, bass, walleyes, and channel catfish. Fish cleaning shack near the main campground.
- Lots of good tree cover and shade. These campsites at Wolfpoint are all in a close area and there is not a lot of room between the sites. The camp roads can get congested from time to time due to how close the neighbors are. Two nice flush toilet/shower facilities at this camp.
- We liked site # 13, 14, 74 and 76. All the amenities needed for a great family camping experience are here.

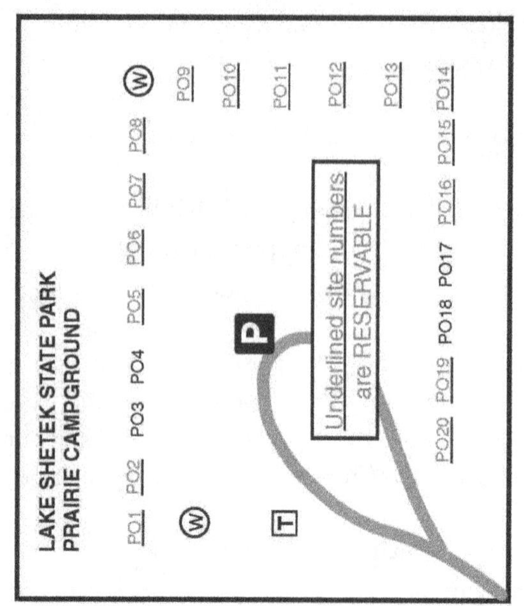

LAKE SHETEK STATE PARK
WOLF POINT CAMPGROUND

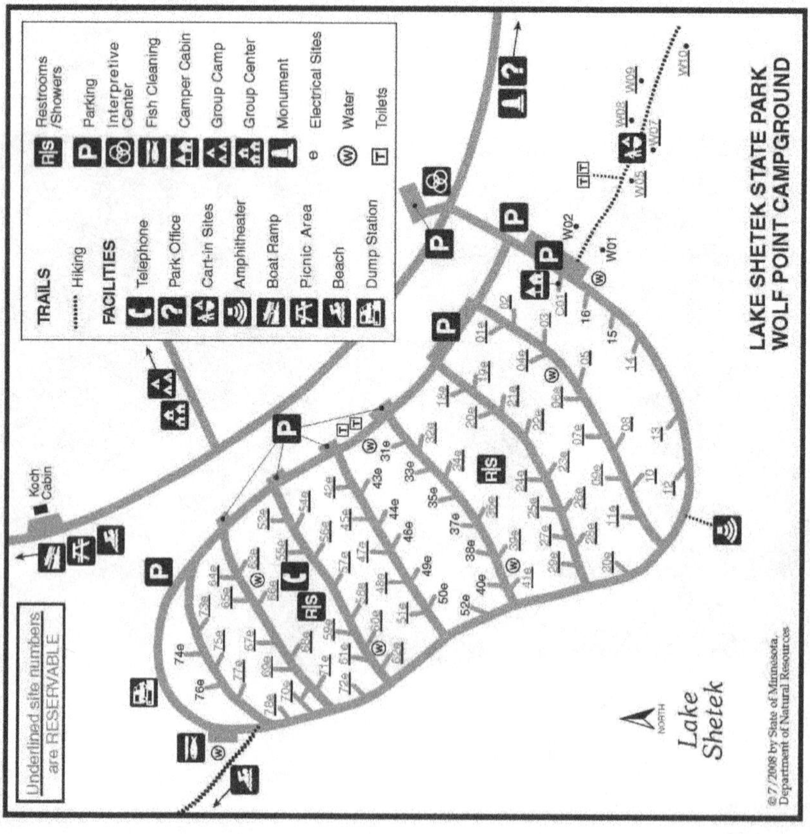

TRAILS
Hiking

FACILITIES
Telephone
Park Office
Cart-in Sites
Amphitheater
Boat Ramp
Picnic Area
Beach
Dump Station
Restrooms /Showers
Parking
Interpretive Center
Fish Cleaning
Camper Cabin
Group Camp
Group Center
Monument
e Electrical Sites
Water
Toilets

Underlined site numbers
are RESERVABLE

Koch Cabin

Lake Shetek

NORTH

© 7/2008 by State of Minnesota,
Department of Natural Resources

LAKE SHETEK STATE PARK

FACILITIES AND FEATURES:

- 77 semi-modern campsites; 67 electrical (Wolf Point Campground)
- 10 rustic cart-in sites
- 20 rustic campsites (Prairie Campground)
- 1 primitive group camp (Wilderness camp)
- Zuya Group Center; 80-person capacity
- Camper Cabin
- Picnic area with 2 shelters (1 winter warming shelter)
- Boat and canoe launch
- Rowboat,canoe and kayak rental
- 8 miles of hiking trails
- 6 mikes of paved bike trail
- 5 miles of snowmobile trails
- 3 miles of ski trails

VISITOR FAVORITES:

- Swimming beach
- Koch Cabin
- Loon Island
- Fishing ponds
- Interpretive center
- Nature Store
- Shetek Monument
- Eastlick Marsh observation deck and spotting scope
- Woodland, marsh, and prairie hiking trails

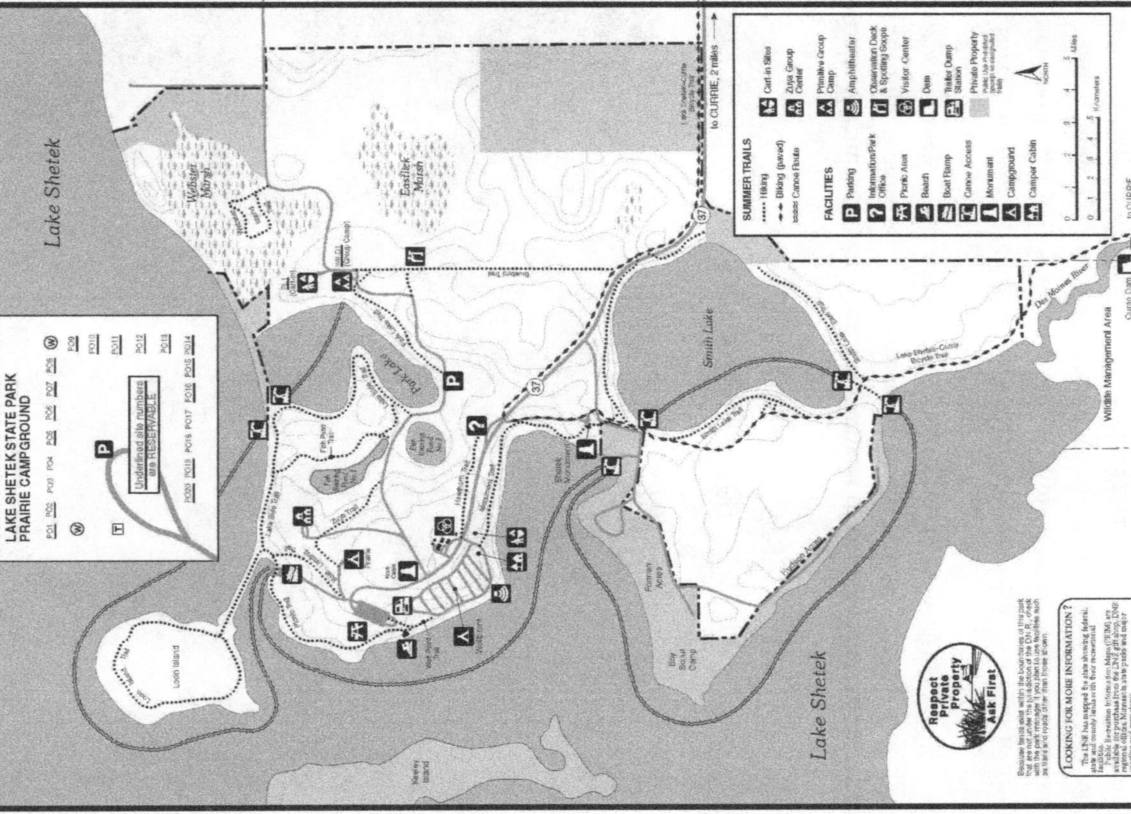

Lake Vermillion

U.S. Highway 169
Soudan, Minnesota 55782

- Lake Vermilion State Park is the newest of the all of the state parks. The final requisition and agreement for the purchase of the property was completed and announced by the Governor in 2010.

- There are over three thousand acres that will be included in the new park. The new state park will sit immediately to the east of the Soudan Underground Mine State Park, as can be seen on the map on the next page. Nearly ten miles of the east shore of Lake Vermilion are now under the protection of the Park Service, thus ensuring the area will be enjoyed by visitors for years to come.

- The park is still in the developmental stage; however, there are several day-use sites for visitors to use. A trail from the Soudan Park leads into the new park from the west, there is a picnic area for day-use in the northeast corner of the new park, and there are several campsites along the shoreline that can be reached by canoe or boat.

- Lake Vermilion State Park will be an important addition to the area giving visitors to the Boundary Waters Canoe Area (BWCA) another state park to use for camping and recreation.

- The map on this page is of the current facilities open for use at Lake Vermilion State Park. This map does an excellent job of showing the new state park's location in relation to Soudan Underground Mine State Park.

Areas Open for Day Use Activities

Lake Vermilion State Park—August 2010

The Lakeside day use area is accessible only by lake, and includes picnic tables, fire ring and portable toilet.
The 2.4-mile Alaska Shaft hiking trail is accessible by parking at Soudan Underground Mine State Park.

Maplewood

39721 Park Entrance Road
Pelican Rapids, Minnesota 56572
218-863-8383

- This park is located about 8 miles east of Pelican Rapids, MN, on Hwy. 108.

- This is a large park of 9,000 acres. It is situated among tall hills and valleys. There are numerous lakes, ponds and streams in the park.

- There are 61 campsites split between four different camping areas near Grass Lake and Lake Lida. There is also a horse camp with access to the horse riding trails and that camp has 24 sites. Electric sites are at the Grass Lake Camp.

- There are 25 miles of hiking trails and there is mountain biking trails. All the trails are multi-use trails and during the winter the trails make up many miles of cross country ski and snowmobile trail. There are remote campsites and scenic overlooks along the trails.

- There are boat ramps on Lake Lida and Beers Lake. There is a third boat ramp for small boats and canoes located on one of the other small lakes in the park.

- Campsites that are canoe/boat accessible only, picnic areas, fishing docks and piers, swimming beaches, the miles of trails and all of the surrounding beautiful scenery allow for a wonderful camping experience here.

- The park has many different trees species that give great shade and cover.

- There are flush toilet/showers available only at the main campground at Grass Lake. There are water spigots and vault toilets at all the other camps and throughout the park at different locales.

- We enjoyed all of the sites at the Lake Lida camping area.

- We enjoyed sites # 35, 42, 43 and 45 of the Hollow Loop camping area. All the sites in the Grass Lake camping area are easily accessible, even for very big trailers. All of the sites have a lot of room and space around them.

- Lots of good secluded camping at the Knoll Loop. Small trailers can access this area but not large trailers. We liked sites # 53, 57, 58, and 59.

(Forested landscape)

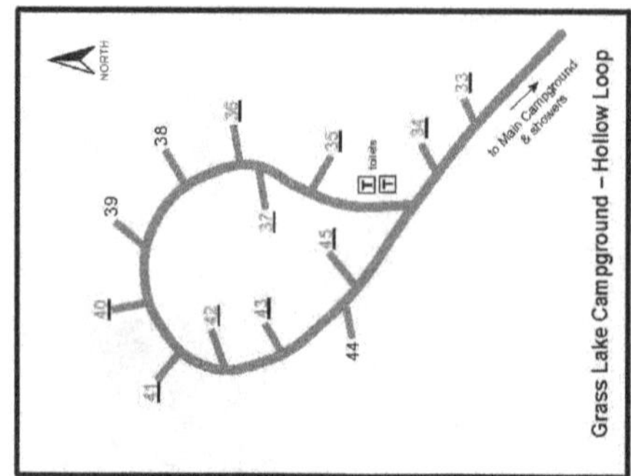

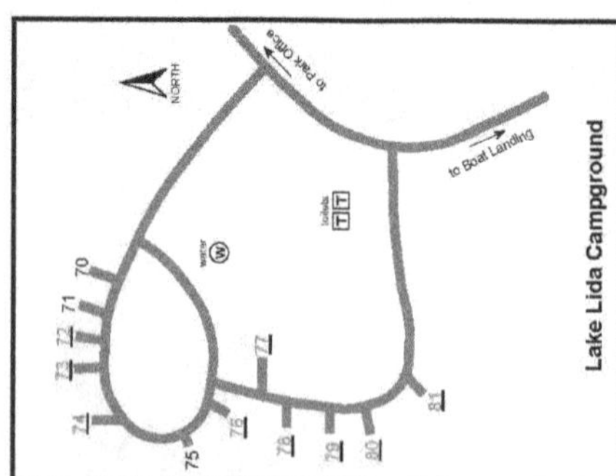

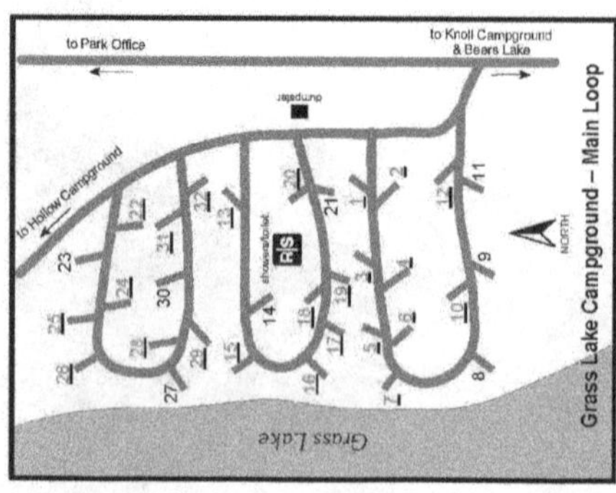

Note: This park *may* have RESERVABLE sites other than in the main campground.
See the main park map for the locations of any additional camping or lodging sites.

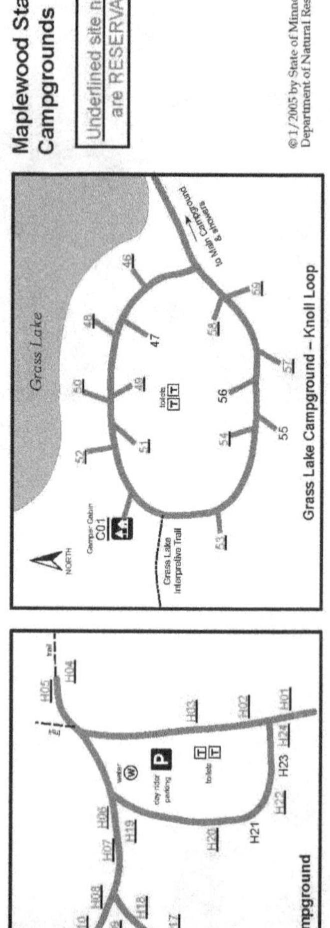

MAPLEWOOD STATE PARK

FACILITIES AND FEATURES

- Campgrounds: Sixty-one family campsites are provided in three locations around Grass Lake. Showers and flush toilets are available.
- Swimming Beach. Located on Lake Lida, the area provides a changing house and sanitation building. A nearby picnic area makes this an ideal location for family recreation. No motor boats are allowed in the swimming area.
- Boat Launching Ramps. Two ramps are provided in the park, one on South Lake Lida and one on Beers Lake. Both lakes offer good fishing for walleye, northern, and panfish.
- Lake Lida Group Picnic Area. An excellent view is afforded from this rustic picnic location. Water, pit toilets, and a large parking area.
- Forest Demonstration Area. A self-guiding trail leads visitors through the area where they can identify trees.
- Park Drive. Two way traffic with sharp curves. Drive slowly and watch for parked cars. Many glimpses of wildlife can be expected.
- Overlooks. High hills provide dramatic vistas. Interpretive signs at major points of interest.
- Trails. Multiple-use trails are available throughout the year. Summer trails include 25 miles of hiking trails and 15 miles for horseback riding. For persons returning in the winter, there are 17 miles of ski trails and 14 miles of snowmobile trails. The winter trails are groomed weekly.
- Maplewood Church and Cemetery. These are active-watch service notices.
- Firewood. Purchase at the contact station.
- Laundry, Groceries, Gas. Obtain locally outside the park.

LOOKING FOR MORE INFORMATION ?

The DNR has mapped the state showing federal, state and county lands with their recreational facilities.
Public Recreation Information Maps (PRIM) are available for purchase from the DNR gift shop, DNR regional offices, Minnesota state parks and major sporting and map stores.

Check it out - you'll be glad you did.

SUMMER TRAILS

Hiking
Horseback / Hiking
Interpretive
Mountain Biking
0.5 miles
Trail Distance Reference Points
Distances shown are between reference points
Private Property
Public Use Prohibited

FACILITIES

Information/Office
Picnic Area
Swimming
Trail Center
Boat Ramp
Campground
Primitive Group Camp
Backpack Campsites
Canoe Camping
Horse Campground
Wildlife Observation

McCarthy Beach

7622 McCarthy Beach Road
Side Lake, Minnesota 55781
218-254-7979

- The park is located about 15 miles north and slightly west of Hibbing. MN. Taking Hwy. 169 north from Hibbing, you drive toward the town of Chisholm, MN. St. Louis County Road 5 goes north (left) just before reaching Chisholm. Follow this road north for 15 miles until you reach the small town of Side Lake, MN; then, follow the signs.

- This park winds around between two major lakes – Side Lake and Sturgeon Lake. There are numerous other small bodies of water contained within the park.

- There are two different camping areas available for visitors. The main campground is located on the south end of the park. There are 59 campsites, 17 have electrical hook-ups, with access to flush toilets and showers, vault toilets, water spigots, boat/canoe/kayak rental available, boat docks and a large fishing pier out into Side Lake.

- There is also a fish cleaning shack close to the fishing pier and many small trails and picnic tables set up along the west shoreline of Side Lake.

- Across the road from the campground is Sturgeon Lake. There is boat access on Sturgeon Lake and a very large swimming beach with picnic tables, fire pits, and a small shack to change clothes in. Vault toilets and water spigots are available there, too.

- The second camping area is about 7 miles north of the main camp. It sits along the shoreline of Beatrice Lake. There is a boat landing at Beatrice Lake and all the campsites at this campground are remote. There are vault toilets and water spigots are available at Beatrice Lake.

- The entire park has beautiful tall red and white pines mixed in with a variety of other species – spruces, birch, ironwood, small maples and other hardwood species. All the trees and under growth allow for nice seclusion between sites. Many miles of trails for hiking, snowmobiling, cross country skiing, horse back riding, an observation tower, and a group camp are available. The Taconite State Trail travels through the park.

- The campsites we liked were - # 8, 12, 13, 17, 23, 28, 29, 30, 34, 39, 47, 50, and 56 – all of these sites are at the main campground. The sites at Beatrice Lake that we liked were - # 5, 6, 8, 9, 21, and 29.

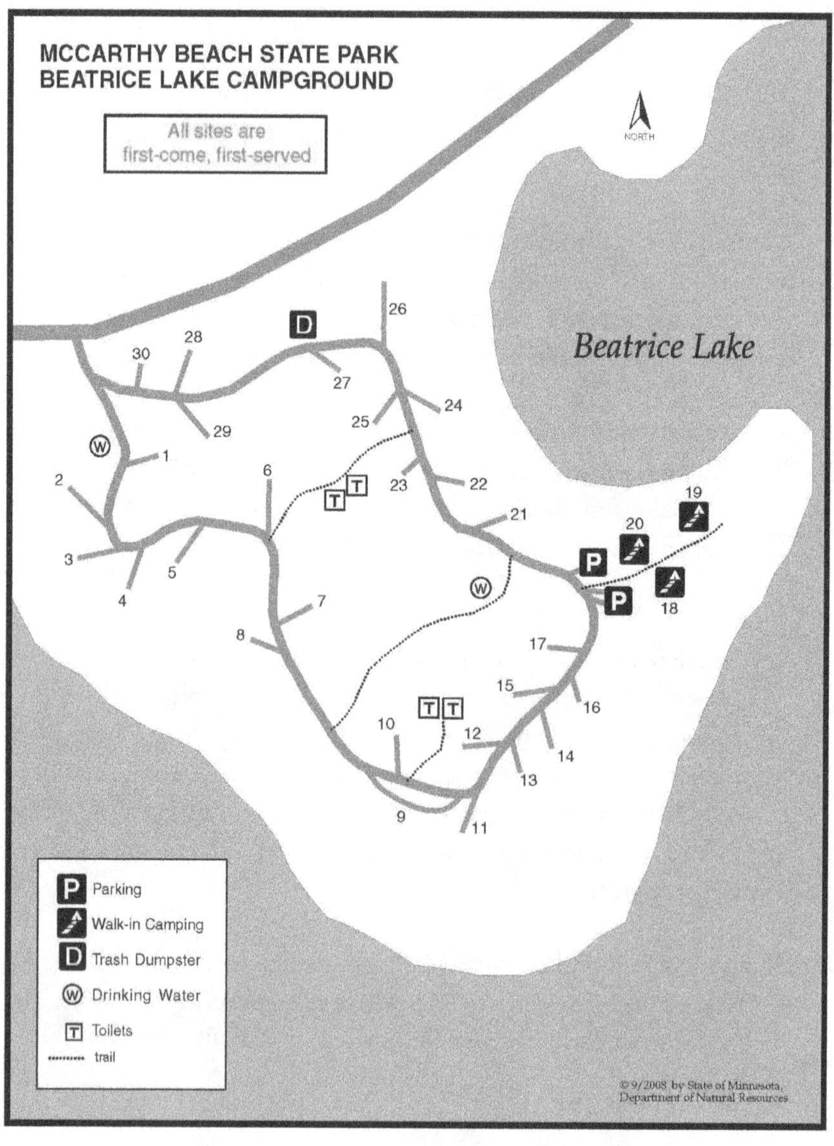
MCCARTHY BEACH STATE PARK
BEATRICE LAKE CAMPGROUND
All sites are
first-come, first-served
NORTH
Beatrice Lake
1
2
3
4
5
6
7
8
9
10
11
12
13
14
15
16
17
18
19
20
21
22
23
24
25
26
27
28
29
30
Parking
Walk-in Camping
Trash Dumpster
Drinking Water
Toilets
trail
© 9/2008 by State of Minnesota,
Department of Natural Resources

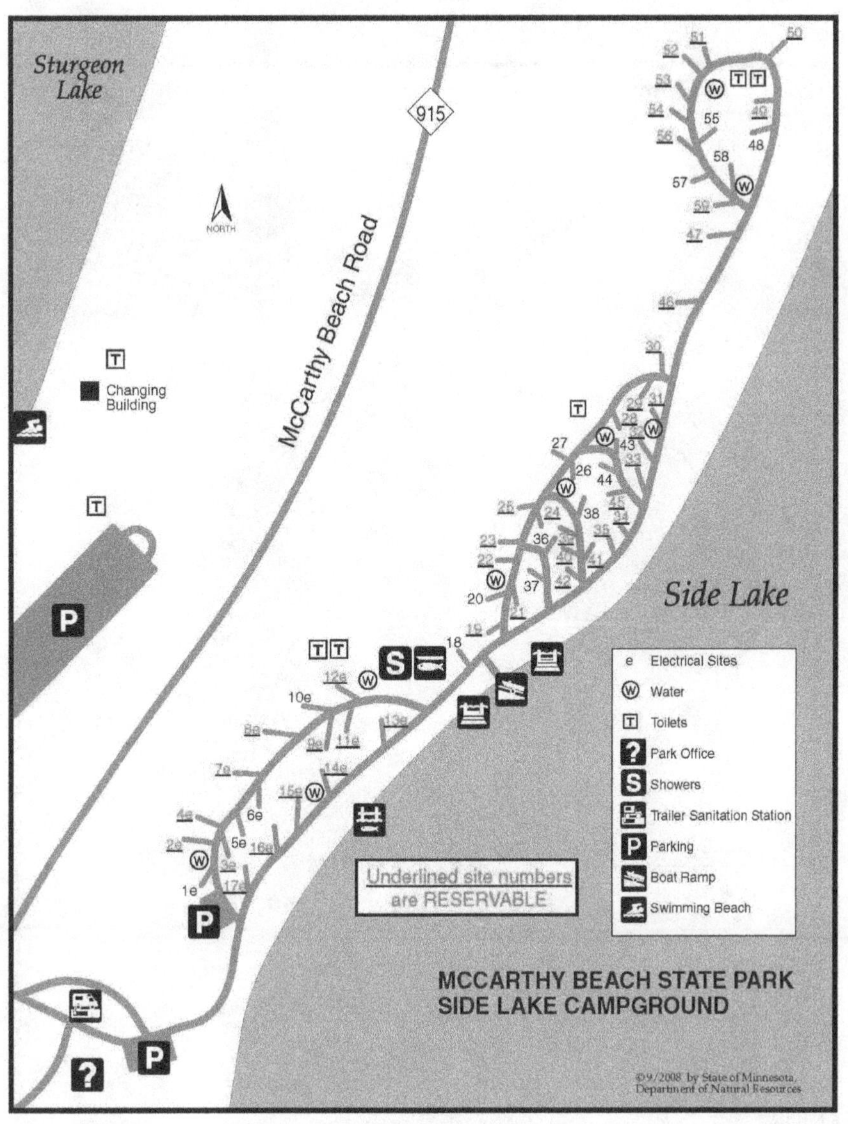
Sturgeon Lake
915
McCarthy Beach Road
NORTH
Changing Building
Side Lake
e Electrical Sites
Water
Toilets
Park Office
Showers
Trailer Sanitation Station
Parking
Boat Ramp
Swimming Beach
Underlined site numbers are RESERVABLE
MCCARTHY BEACH STATE PARK
SIDE LAKE CAMPGROUND
©9/2008 by State of Minnesota, Department of Natural Resources

McCARTHY BEACH STATE PARK

VISITOR FAVORITES

- Sandy swimming beach with changing house and boat access on Sturgeon Lake.
- Majestic red and white pines.
- Trails along ridge tops and valley floors.
- A chain of clear lakes for a variety of water recreation.
- Seven lakes for fishing—trout, walleye, northern pike, bass, and panfish.

FACILITIES AND FEATURES

- 59 semi-modern campsites (17 with electricity) with showers and flush toilets, trailer dump station, and fish-cleaning house on Side Lake.
- 30 rustic campsites with vault toilets and hand-pump water on Beatice Lake.
- Class III group camp on Sturgeon Lake.
- Trails: 18 miles of hiking trails, 12 miles of snowmobile and horseback trails, 9 miles of cross-country ski trails.
- Picnic area and shelter on Sturgeon Lake.
- Midpoint of Taconite Trail.
- Boat docks & fishing pier.

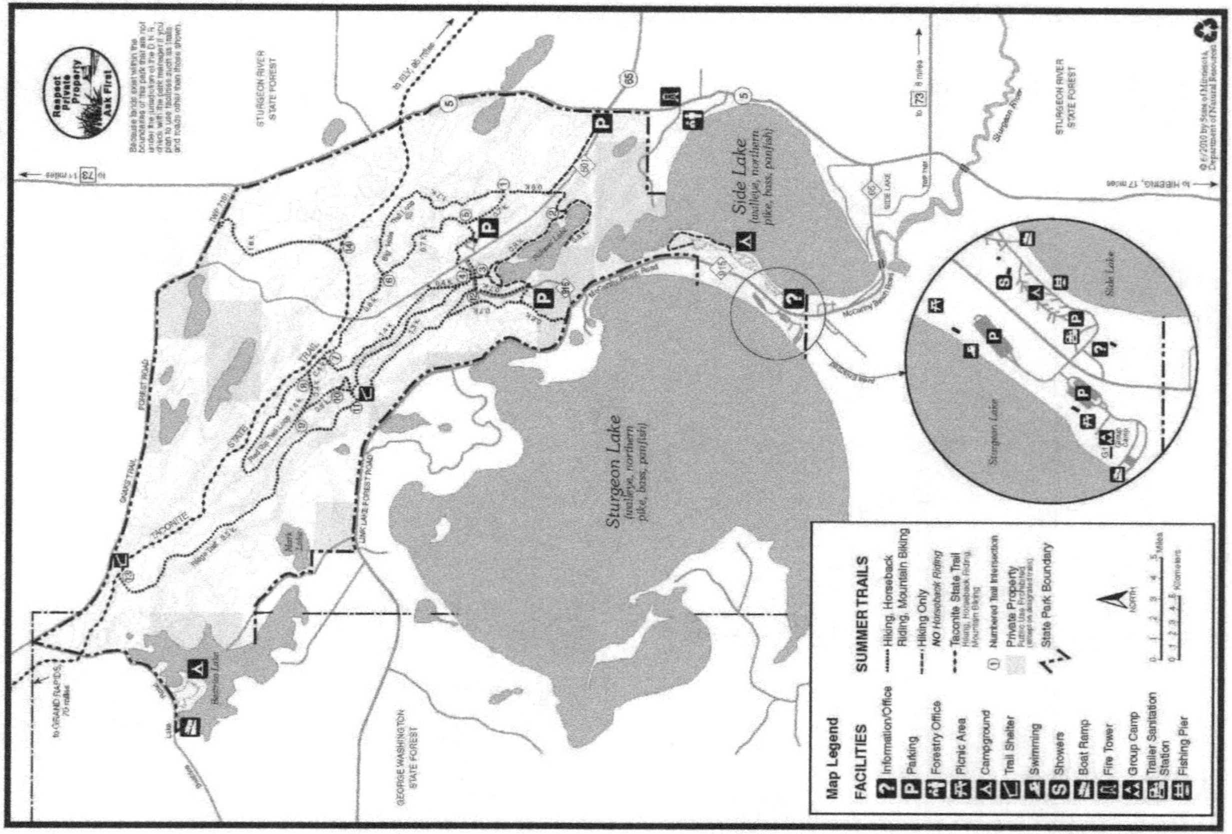

Mille Lacs Kathio

15066 Kathio State Park Road
Onamia, Minnesota 56359
320-532-3523

- This state park is the 4th largest of all the state parks, encompassing just over 10,000 acres. It is located one mile west of Hwy. 169, a couple miles south of Grand Casino - Mille Lacs.

- This state park has a great deal of history around it concerning the length of time that human inhabitants have lived in the area around the park and Mille Lacs Lake. This park has all the amenities to allow for comfortable camping by all the members of the family.

- Toilet/showers at the campground, playground, swimming beach, two boat launch sites, fish cleaning shacks, 35 miles of hiking trails, cross country ski trails, snowmobile trails, horse trails and a separate camp for the horses and their owners, remote campsites along the hiking trails, group camp areas, and an interpretive center. Canoe and boat rentals are available.

- Historic sites to see along the trails along with scenic overlook sites.

- The Main campground - Petaga Camp - has 41 sites that are in the camp proper and three sites that are a short hike into the woods from the parking area. Toilet/shower facility, fresh water sites and vault toilets are all available in the camping area. Close access to the picnic area, playground, and the trails.

- The second campground - Ogeechee - is a more remote camp. There are no electrical sites available here and there are only vault toilets.

- The camp grounds are open underneath a good cover of trees. Very little undergrowth in either of the campgrounds and would not lend too much seclusion while camping. All the sites are on good level terrain and would be very accessible to trailers and RV's.

- Camp sites that we liked were: 4, 16, 26, 38, 39, 41, 52, and 63.

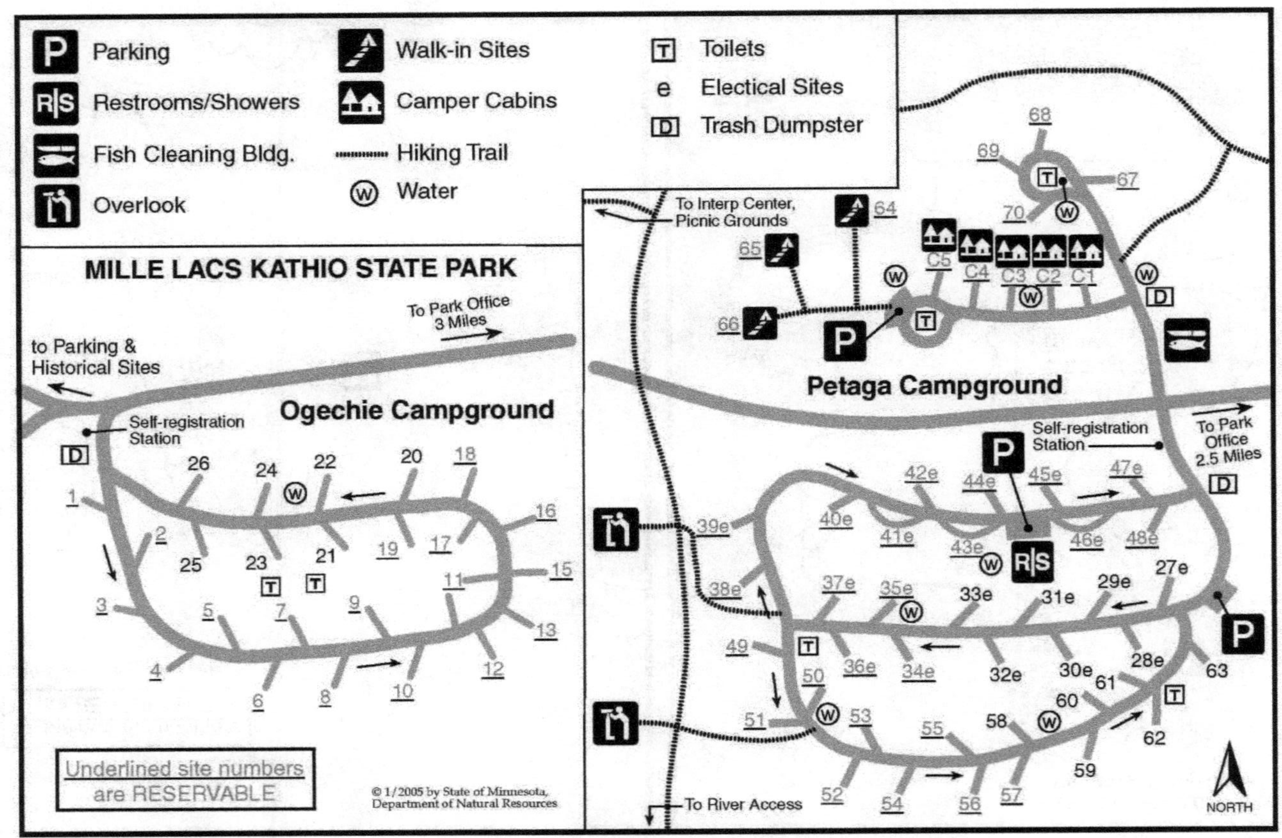
Parking
Restrooms/Showers
Fish Cleaning Bldg.
Overlook
Walk-in Sites
Camper Cabins
Hiking Trail
Water
Toilets
Electical Sites
Trash Dumpster
MILLE LACS KATHIO STATE PARK
To Park Office 3 Miles
to Parking & Historical Sites
Ogechie Campground
Self-registration Station
Petaga Campground
To Interp Center, Picnic Grounds
Self-registration Station
To Park Office 2.5 Miles
To River Access
Underlined site numbers are RESERVABLE
© 1/2005 by State of Minnesota, Department of Natural Resources
NORTH

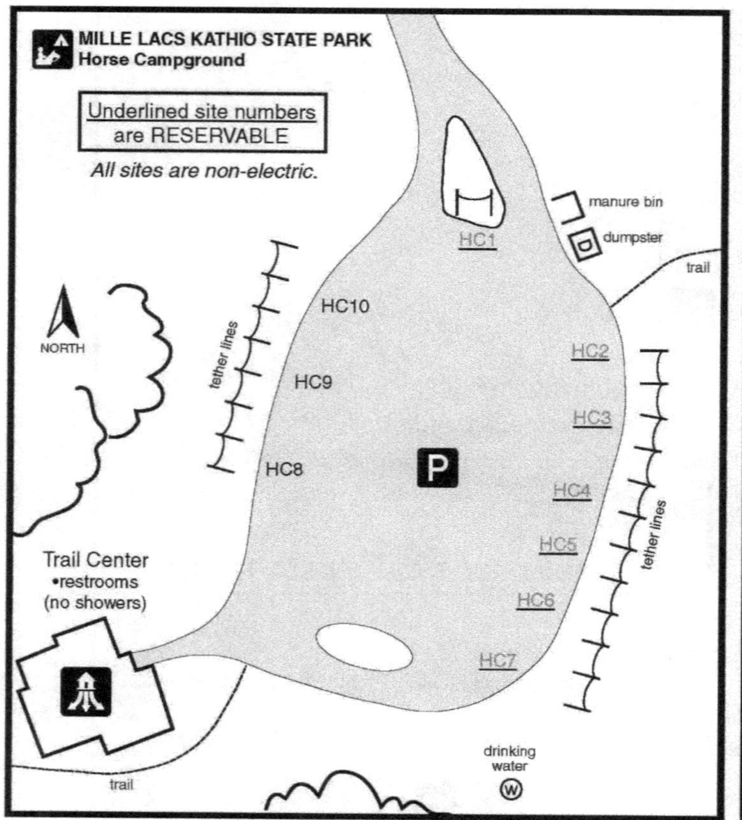
MILLE LACS KATHIO STATE PARK
Horse Campground
Underlined site numbers
are RESERVABLE
All sites are non-electric.
NORTH
HC1
manure bin
dumpster
D
trail
HC10
HC9
HC8
tether lines
P
HC2
HC3
HC4
HC5
HC6
HC7
tether lines
Trail Center
•restrooms
(no showers)
trail
drinking
water
W

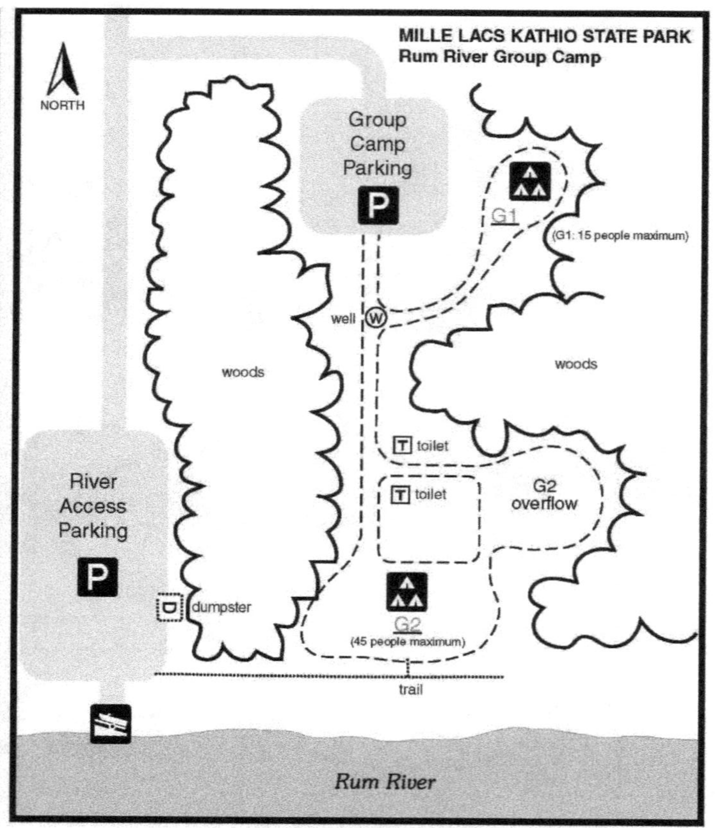
MILLE LACS KATHIO STATE PARK
Rum River Group Camp
NORTH
Group
Camp
Parking
P
G1
(G1: 15 people maximum)
well
W
woods
woods
toilet
toilet
G2
overflow
River
Access
Parking
P
D
dumpster
G2
(45 people maximum)
trail
Rum River

MILLE LACS KATHIO STATE PARK

FACILITIES AND FEATURES

- 20 electric campsites.
- 2 accessible electric campsites.
- 19 semi-modern campsites.
- 26 rustic campsites (showers available, 1.5 mile drive).
- 3 semi-modern walk-in campsites.
- 4 backpack sites.
- 5 camper cabins w/electricity and heat.
- 10 rustic horse campsites (no showers).
- Primitive group camp w/hand pump and vault toilets (60 capacity, no showers)
- Bundled firewood, ice, pop.
- Picnic grounds.
- Modern playground.
- Swimming beach.
- Canoe, kayak, and rowboat rental.
- Cross-country ski and snowshoe rental.
- 2 boat/canoe water accesses (Rum River, Shakopee Lake).
- 35 miles of hiking trail.
- 1 mile of self-guided trail.
- 22 miles of horseback trail.
- 30 kilometers of cross-country ski trail.
- 19 miles of snowmobile trail.
- Modern trail center/winter chalet.
- Year-round visitor center, interpretive center.
- 100-foot observation tower (available in summer only).

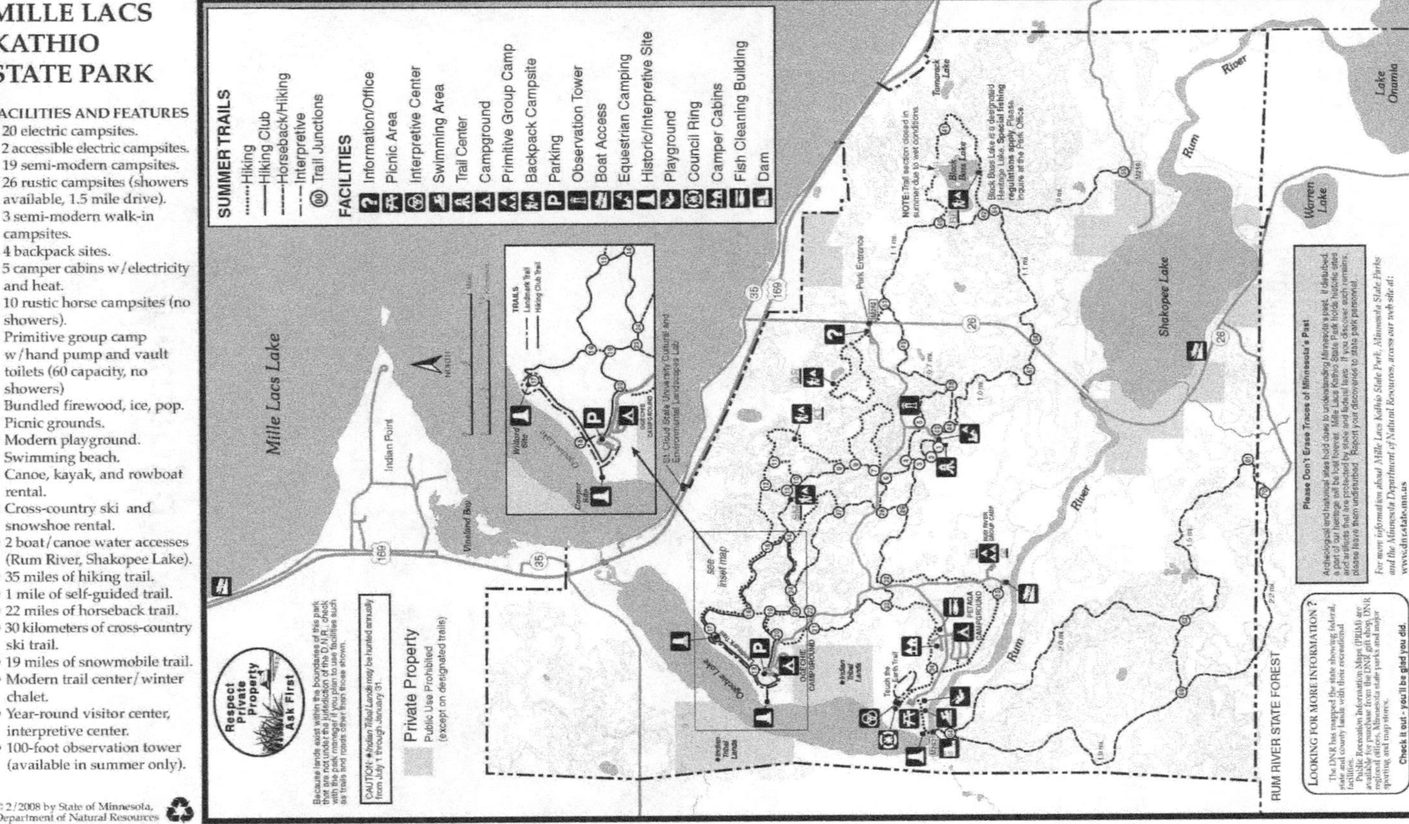

Minneopa

54497 Gadwall Road
Mankato, Minnesota 56001
507-389-5464

- This state park is 5 miles west on U.S. Hwy. 169 from Mankato, Minnesota. The name of the park is derived from the Dakota which means – water falling twice. This is reference to the two waterfalls within the park. The second part of the falls is the tallest water fall in southern Minnesota.

- This state park straddles MN Hwy. 68 that goes west out of Mankato and heads toward Judson and New Ulm. The larger portion of the park sits along the south bank of the Minnesota River and just west of the confluence of Minneopa Creek and the Minnesota River.

- There are 4 or 5 miles of trails for hiking and skiing. There are picnic areas, group camps, scenic overlooks of the river, historic sites and the beautiful water falls.

- Red Fox Campground is the main camp. All the sites are nicely spaced and have good shade and cover. There is good undergrowth to allow for seclusion. - The sites are spaced nicely. There are water spigots, Vault toilets and a restroom/shower building within easy walking of the sites.

- We liked sites# 14, 22, and 23 of Loop A. Loop B sites # 3, 12, 22, 24, and 30. All of the sites are nice and level and allow great camping.

- A beautiful very old historic cemetery is atop the hill between the two sections of the park. This is a very worth while site to see while in the area.

- A great state park with lots to offer and virtually on the doorstep of a major metropolitan area.

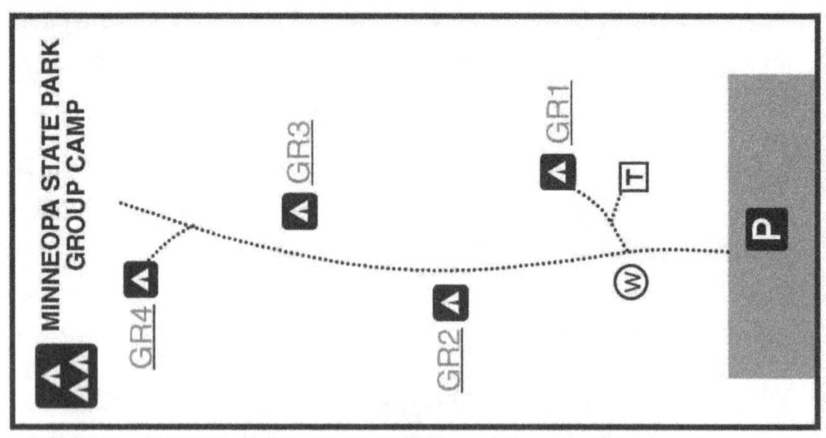

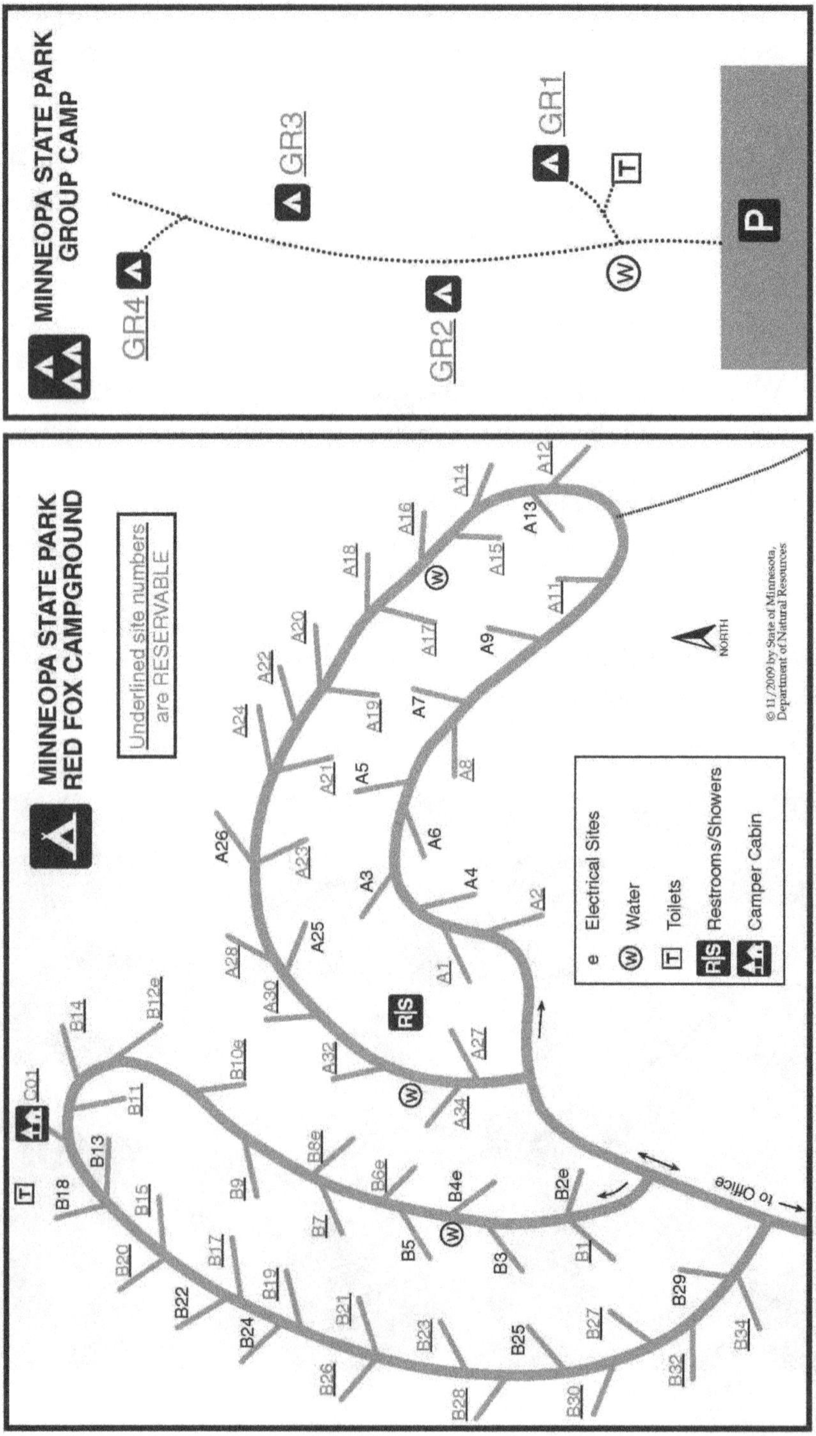

MINNEOPA STATE PARK
RED FOX CAMPGROUND

Underlined site numbers are RESERVABLE

e Electrical Sites
W Water
T Toilets
R|S Restrooms/Showers
Camper Cabin

to Office

NORTH

© 11/2009 by State of Minnesota, Department of Natural Resources

MINNEOPA STATE PARK

FACILITIES AND FEATURES:
- 2 picnic areas
- Picnic shelter w/electricity
- Semi-modern campground
- Heated camper cabin with electricity
- Hiking/Ski trails
- Primitive group camp
- Historic site
- Native prairie
- Visitor center
- Geologic formations
- Cross-country ski trails
- Volleyball court
- Horseshoe pit
- RV dump station

VISITOR FAVORITES:
- Twin waterfall
- Seppmann Windmill
- Stream fishing
- Wildlife viewing
- Hiking
- Photography

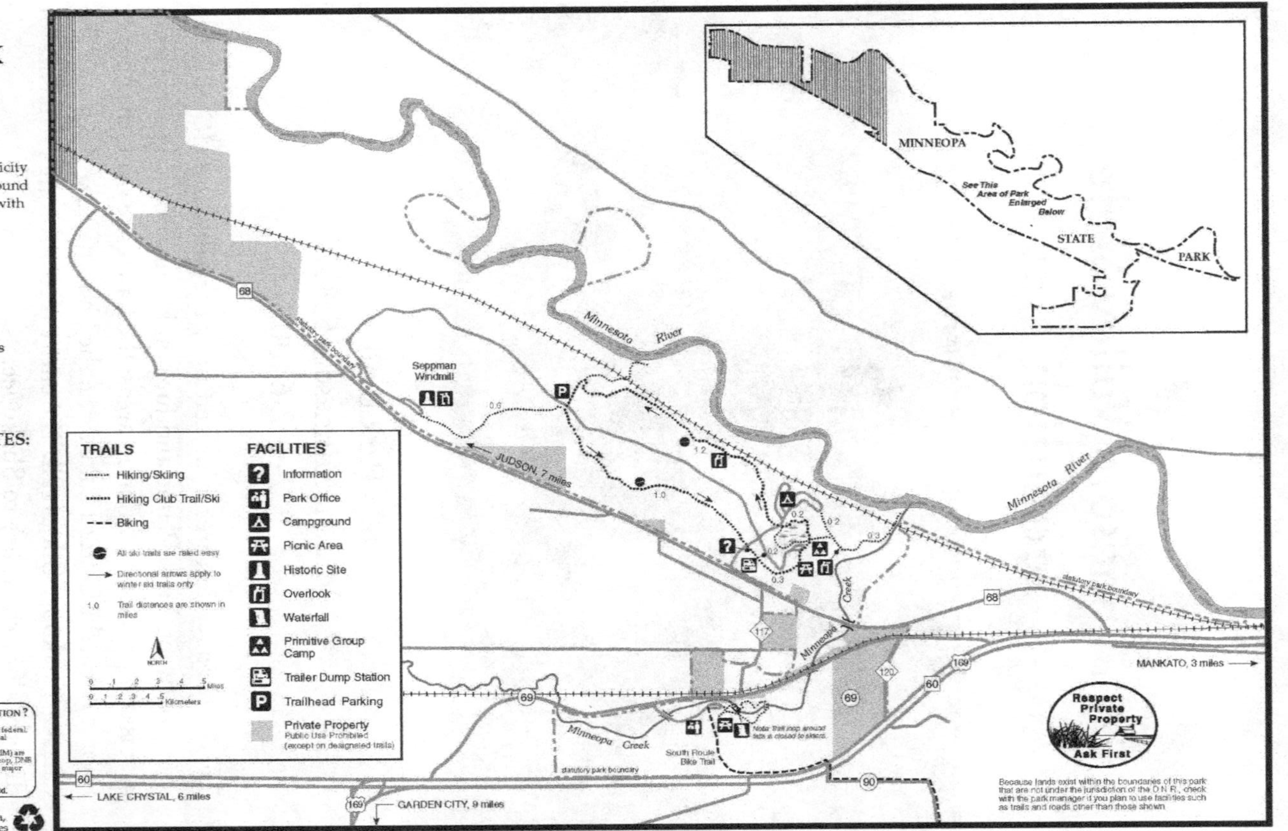

LOOKING FOR MORE INFORMATION?

The DNR has mapped the state showing federal, state and county landswith their recreational facilities.

Public Recreation Information Maps (PRIM) are available for purchase from the DNR gift shop, DNR regional offices, Minnesota state parks and major sporting and map stores.

Check it out - you'll be glad you did.

Minnesota Valley State Recreation Area

19825 Park Boulevard
Jordan, Minnesota 55352
952-492-6400

- This state recreation area is located along the Minnesota River in the valley between Belle Plaine and Jordan, Minnesota. The recreation area is comprised of 5 different areas: the Lawrence Unit, the Carver Rapids Area, the Gifford Lake Area, the Nyssen's Lake Area, and the Chaska/Shakopee Bike Trail. The entire recreation area stretches all the way along the valley to Shakopee.

- There is in excess of 35 miles of trails for hiking, biking, skiing, horseback, and snowmobiles in this recreation area. There are numerous shelters along the trails, there are a couple of boat launches along the river, there are two historic sites, picnic areas, vault toilets, water spigots, and the camping area that can be found at the Lawrence Unit.

- The Quarry Campground is located in the Lawrence Unit. It has 25 sites suitable for campers and trailers, 8 rustic walk-in sites, 6 horse camp sites and a large rustic group camp site.

- The campsites are nicely separated and secluded by undergrowth that exists between the sites. We liked Sites # 6, 13, 14, 15, 17, 20, 22, 24, and 25.

(Minnesota River Valley)

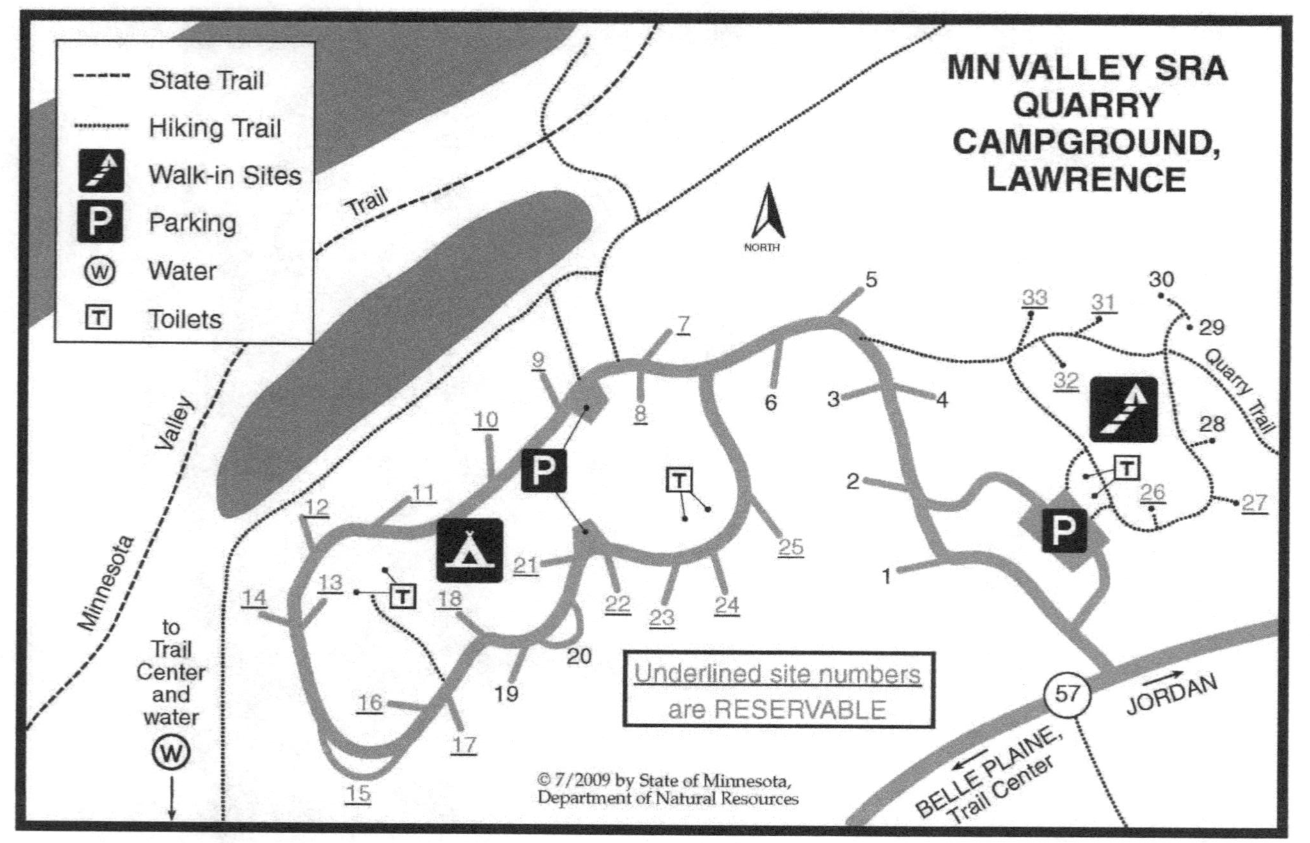
MN VALLEY SRA
QUARRY
CAMPGROUND,
LAWRENCE
State Trail
Hiking Trail
Walk-in Sites
Parking
Water
Toilets
NORTH
Minnesota
Valley
Trail
Quarry Trail
to Trail Center and water
57
JORDAN
BELLE PLAINE, Trail Center
Underlined site numbers
are RESERVABLE
© 7/2009 by State of Minnesota,
Department of Natural Resources

MINNESOTA VALLEY STATE RECREATION AREA

FACILITIES AND FEATURES

Lawrence Unit:
- 25 scenic drive-in campsites
- 8 secluded walk-in campsites
- 6 horse camp sites
- Rustic group camp
- Picnic area
- Trail center and trail access to 35 miles of horseback, mountain biking and hiking trails
- Fishing at Beason Lake and Minnesota River
- Historic S. B. Strait House

Carver Rapids Area:
- 7 miles of hiking on the Mazomani Trail
- Historic Jabs Farm
- "Little Rapids" campsites

Gifford Lake Area:
- Fishing at Gifford Lake
- Trail access

Nyssen's Lake Area:
- Trail access for snowmobiling, horseback riding, mountain biking, and hiking

Chaska/Shakopee Bike Trail
- 4-mile paved hiking/biking trail
- Interpretive signs
- Wildlife observation

Note: the trail no longer crosses the Minnesota River at Chaska.

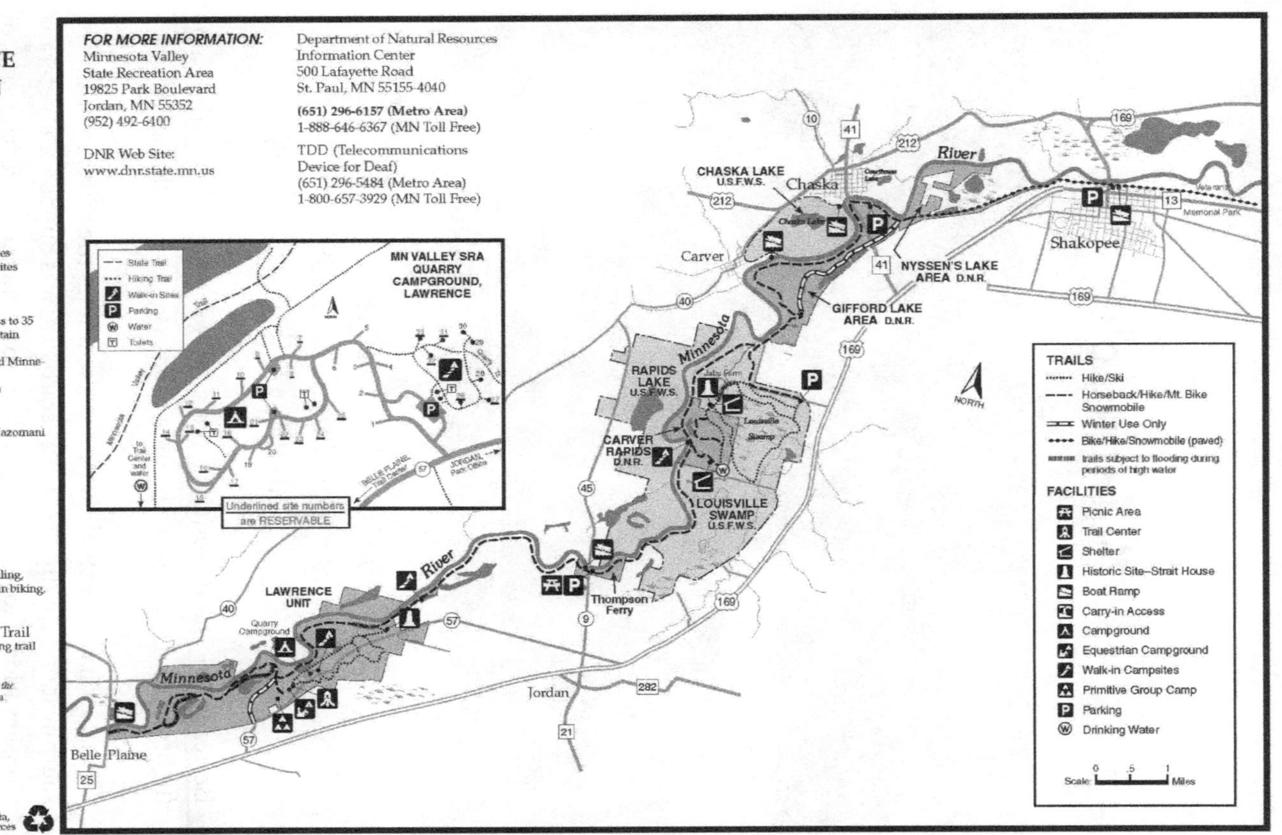

Monson Lake

1690 15th Street NE
Sunburg, Minnesota 56289
320-366-3797

- Be ready for the diversity of the wildlife around this park. Large flights of bird species - to include pelicans, geese, ducks, etc.

- This is a very nice, small park nestled among the trees. It is located southwest of Sunburg, MN. The state park was built by the Veterans Conservation Corps. It was built to commemorate the site of a massacre of white settlers by the Dakota Sioux Tribe in 1862. There is a Granite marker at the camp and two shallow dig sites that archeologists have created digging for artifacts. There are other bill boards up by the parking area, which help to tell the story of the massacre.

- This is a small park and not well known to the general public. However, it is used a lot by residents of the area and it would be a good idea to call ahead and make reservations for a site. Only 20 sites, sites 15 thru 20 have electric. There is about one mile of hiking trail in the park.

- The lake has a good variety of fish species - northern, crappie, bass and walleyes. In the campground, there is nice undergrowth between sites which would allow for more seclusion from your neighbors.

- Sites # 16 and 18 are nicely tucked back into the woods and secluded from other campers.

(Broberg Monument – Monson Lake State Park)

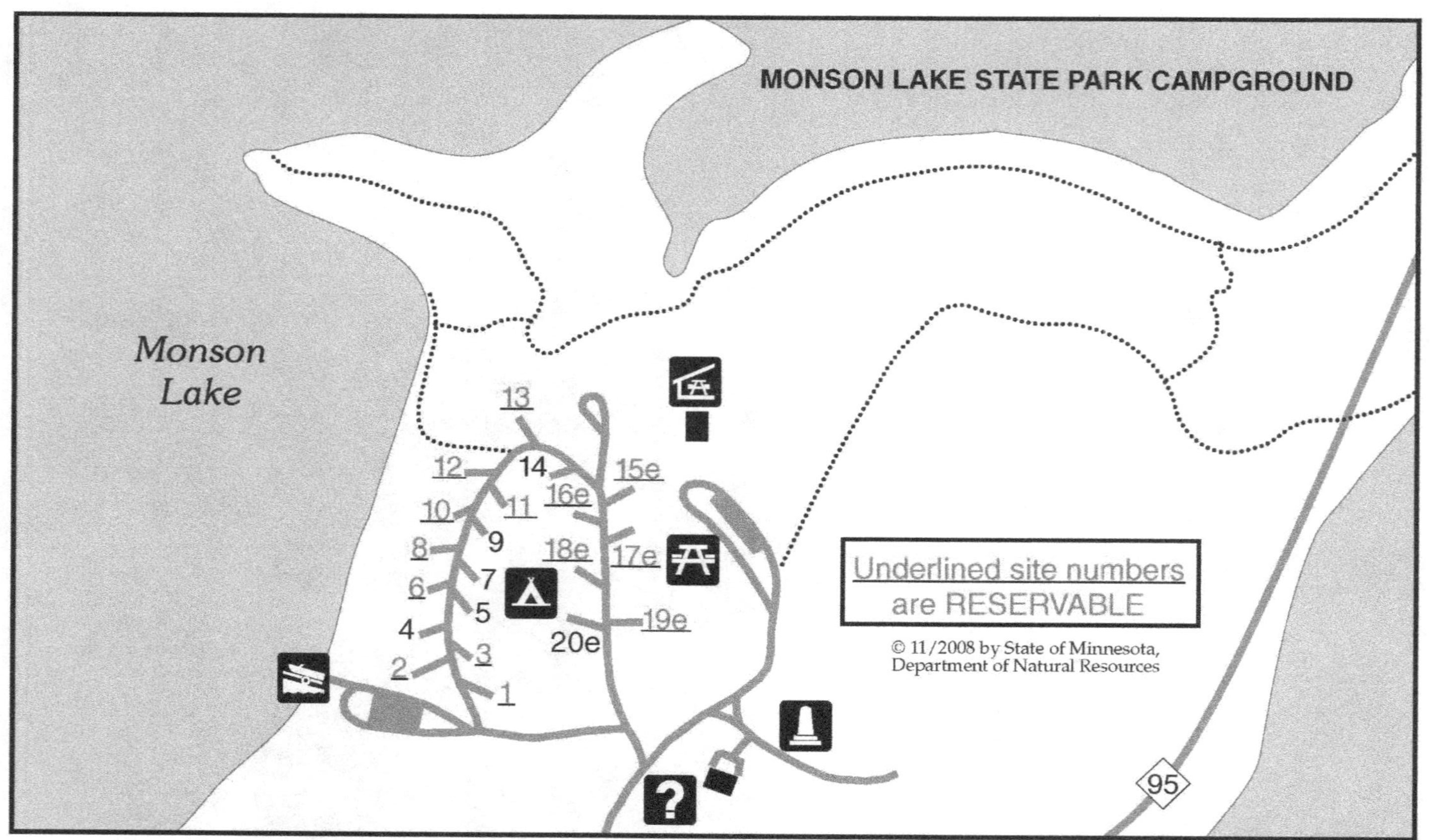
MONSON LAKE STATE PARK CAMPGROUND
Monson
Lake
13
12
14
15e
16e
10
11
9
8
18e
17e
7
6
5
19e
4
20e
3
2
1
Underlined site numbers
are RESERVABLE
© 11/2008 by State of Minnesota,
Department of Natural Resources
95

MONSON LAKE STATE PARK

FACILITIES AND FEATURES
- 1 mile hiking trail
- 20 campsites (6 with electricity)
- Boat ramp
- Wooded picnic area
- Stone shelter building
- Toilets
- Lake fishing
- Canoe route
- Historic site

VISITOR FAVORITES
- Excellent fishing
- Hiking
- Birdwatching
- Canoeing

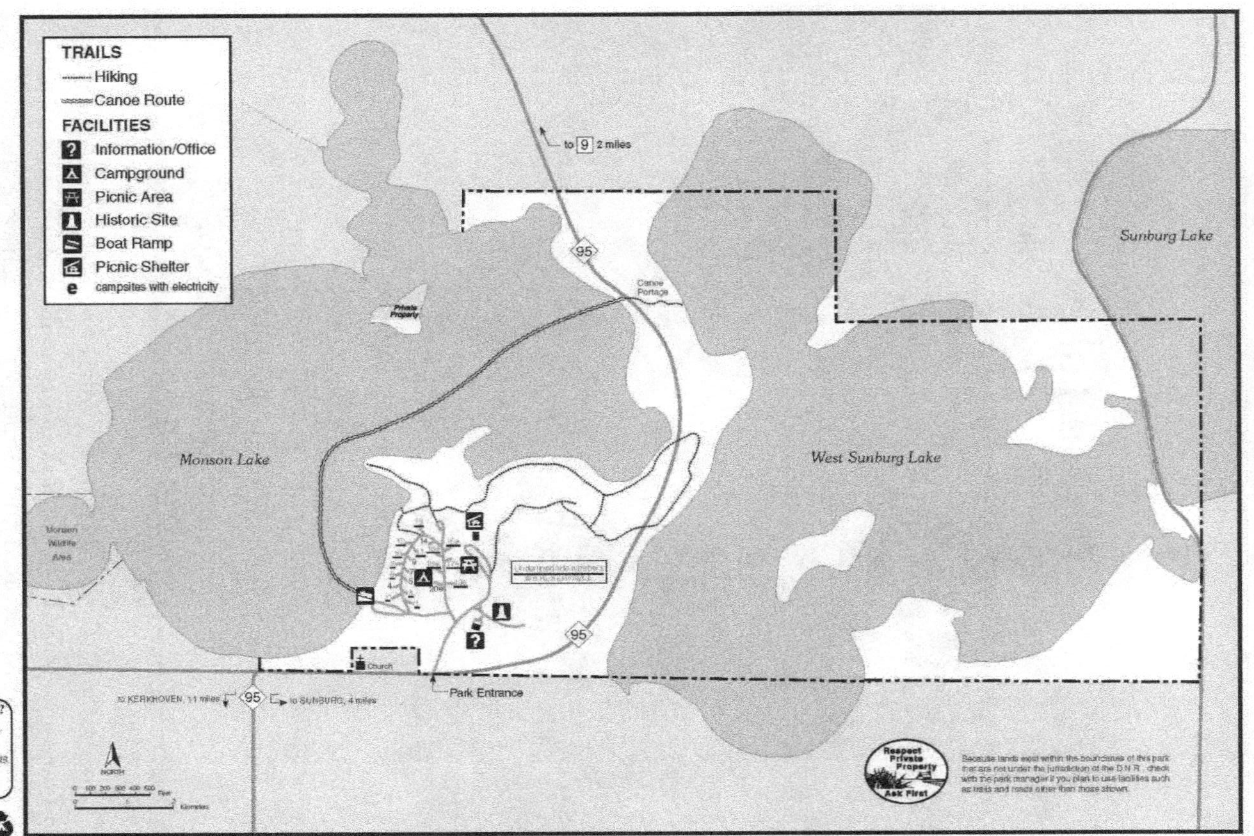

LOOKING FOR MORE INFORMATION ?

The DNR has mapped the state showing federal, state and county lands with their recreational facilities.

Public Recreation Information Maps (PRIM) are available for purchase from the DNR gift shop, DNR regional offices, Minnesota state parks and major sporting and map stores.

Check it out - you'll be glad you did.

Moose Lake

4252 County Road 137
Moose Lake, Minnesota 55767
218-485-5420

- This state park is located just .5 miles east of I-35 near the city of Moose Lake, MN. This park is situated among stands of Aspen, Birch and Maple. Red and White pines which were the dominant species here 150 years ago were logged off. Today, these species have been re-planted throughout the park.

- There are 35 sites in the campground and 20 sites have electrical hook-up capability. The campground is situated on rolling terrain;

however, the campsites themselves have been situated in a fashion to allow for trailers and RV's to have relatively level sites to park on.

- There is a fair amount of undergrowth beneath the tops of the Aspens and Birch trees. This allows for good seclusion between sites. Two of the tent sites in the campground have been set back from the road and are accessible by a short hiking trail for those who want to get even more seclusion.

- There is a nice lake - Echo Lake - which has a swimming beach and good fishing for northern, bass, walleye and other pan fish. Toilet/showers available at the campground along with vault toilets, fresh water spigots, and picnic area.

- There are approximately 7 miles of hiking trails that can be used for hiking, cross country skiing, and snowmobiling. There are boat and canoe rentals available.

- The most unique feature of the park is the Geological display at the main office. The display describes the geology of Minnesota and there is a fabulous display of Lake Superior Agates.

- Sites that we liked were - # 5, 14, 29, and 32.

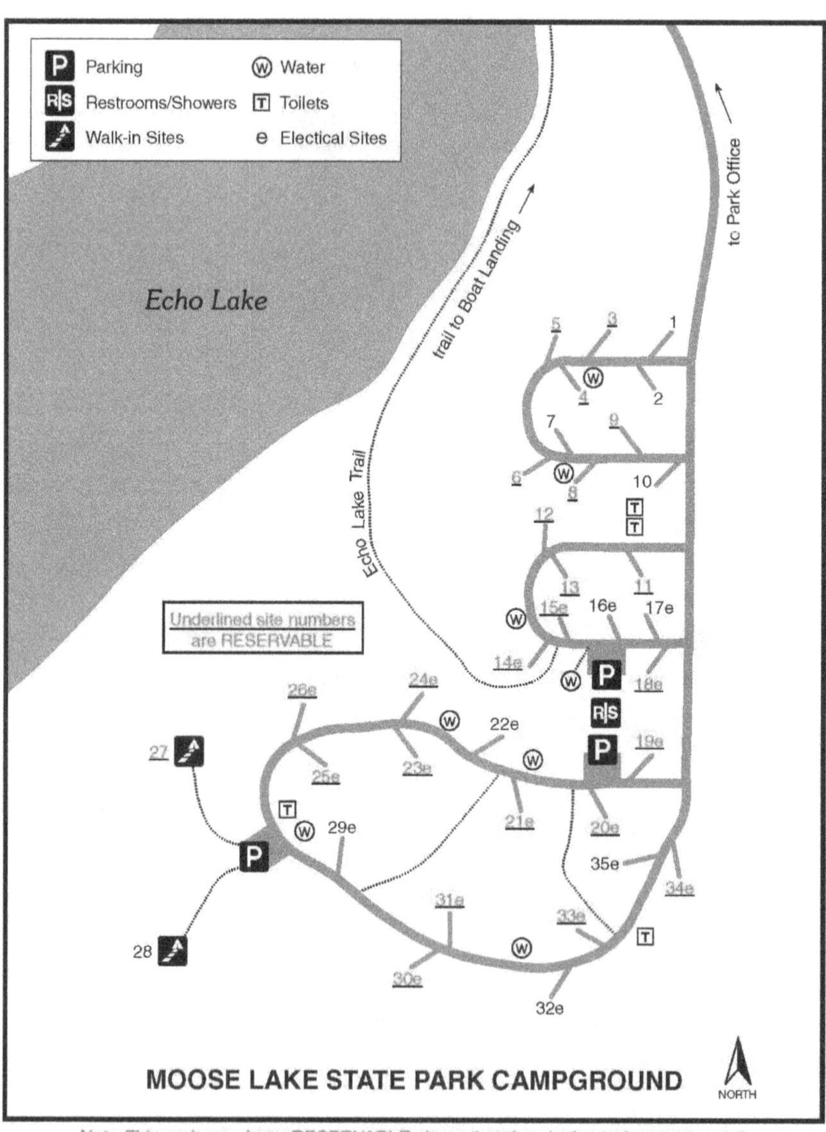

Note: This park *may* have RESERVABLE sites other than in the main campground. See the main park map for the locations of any additional camping or lodging sites.

MOOSE LAKE STATE PARK

FACILITIES AND FEATURES:

- 35 semi-modern campsites
- 20 electric sites
- Picnic grounds
- Hiking, cross-country and snowmobile trails
- Swimming beach
- Drive-in boat access on Echo Lake
- Boat rental
- Agate/Geological Interpretive Center

VISITOR FAVORITES:

- Swimming
- Fishing
- Hiking trails
- Snowmobile & cross-country ski trails.
- Exhibition hall with geological displays and gem and mineral collections

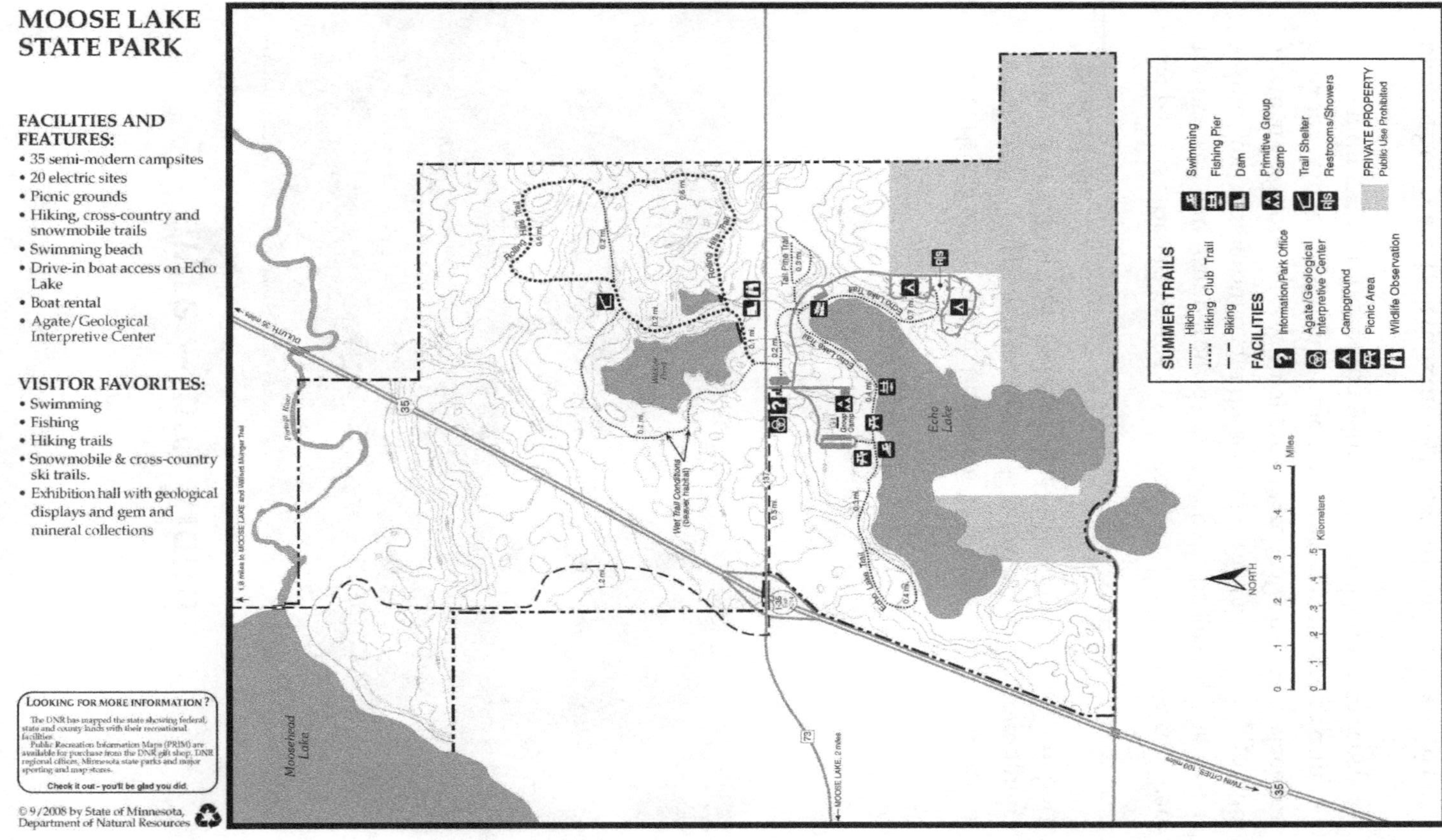

LOOKING FOR MORE INFORMATION?

The DNR has mapped the state showing federal, state and county lands with their recreational facilities.

Public Recreation Information Maps (PRIM) are available for purchase from the DNR gift shop, DNR regional offices, Minnesota state parks and major sporting and map stores.

Check it out - you'll be glad you did.

Myre – Big Island

19499 780th Avenue
Albert Lea, Minnesota 56007
507-379-3403

- The park is located off of Interstate 35 to the east and south of Interstate 90. The park is located on County Hwy. 38 about 3 miles southeast of Albert Lea. Access to the park can be made from both I-35 and I-90.

- The park is situated on the north side of Albert Lea Lake. There are two separate campgrounds on the park property. The first is White Fox Campground and the second is Big Island Campground. There are 98 total sites with approximately 30 that have electrical hookups. There are several picnic areas, two remote group camps, a boat landing site on Big Island with canoes and kayaks to rent.

- Blazing Star State Trail runs through the park and there are 16 miles of other multi-use trails available in the park. There is opportunity to do lots of bird watching in the park due to the variety of habitats that exist within the boundaries. Rolling hills with sparse tree cover, open fields, wooded areas, and shore land are some of the different habitats.

- There are restrooms with showers at both campgrounds. There are water spigots and vault toilets for use throughout the park.

- The White Fox campground has trees and vegetation all around – oaks, maples, sumac, and many other species. There is a fair amount of undergrowth between the sites to allow for a little seclusion from the neighbors. The campground on Big Island has very thick tree cover; so much so, that it is very dark in the campground even in the mid day. With the heavy canopy above, there is not a lot of undergrowth between the sites. Both campgrounds have very nice level sites that are easily accessible to all manner of camping rig.

- At White Fox, the sites we liked the best were: 39, 47, 60, 75, 86, and 94.

- At Big Island Campground, the sites we liked were: 4, 7, 9, 15, 22, and 30.

- There is a single camper cabin that is available for reservation.

- This park has all of the amenities that any family would look for in order to have an enjoyable experience for everyone. Add that to the fact that there is a large city less than five miles away. Myre – Big Island State Park would be a great park to bring the entire family to visit.

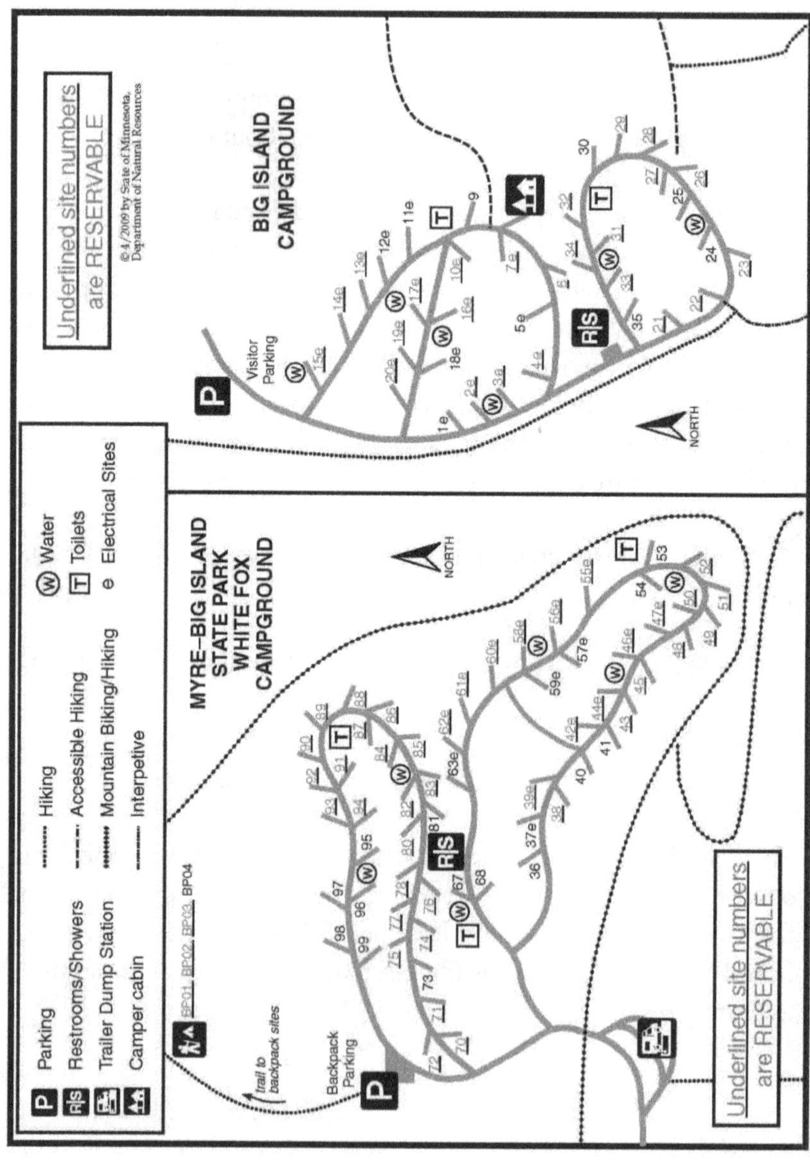
Parking
Restrooms/Showers
Trailer Dump Station
Camper cabin
Hiking
Accessible Hiking
Mountain Biking/Hiking
Interpretive
Water
Toilets
e Electrical Sites
BP01, BP02, BP03, BP04
trail to backpack sites
Backpack Parking
MYRE–BIG ISLAND STATE PARK WHITE FOX CAMPGROUND
NORTH
Underlined site numbers are RESERVABLE
Visitor Parking
BIG ISLAND CAMPGROUND
©4/2009 by State of Minnesota, Department of Natural Resources
Underlined site numbers are RESERVABLE
Note: This park may have other RESERVABLE sites not shown on this page. See the main park map for the locations of any additional camping or lodging sites.

MYRE–BIG ISLAND STATE PARK

FACILITIES AND FEATURES

- 98 semi-modern campsites in two campgrounds
- 4 remote backpack camping sites
- 1 camper cabin
- 45 picnic sites
- 16 miles of hiking trails
- 8 miles of cross-country ski trails
- 7 miles of snowmobile trails
- 7 miles of mountain bike trails

VISITOR FAVORITES

- Wildflowers on Big Island
- Bird watching on the oak savanna
- Hiking the esker
- Canoeing on Albert Lea Lake

LOOKING FOR MORE INFORMATION?

The DNR has mapped the state showing federal, state and county lands with their recreational facilities.

Public Recreation Information Maps (PRIM) are available for purchase from the DNR gift shop, DNR regional offices, Minnesota state parks and major sporting and map stores.

Check it out - you'll be glad you did.

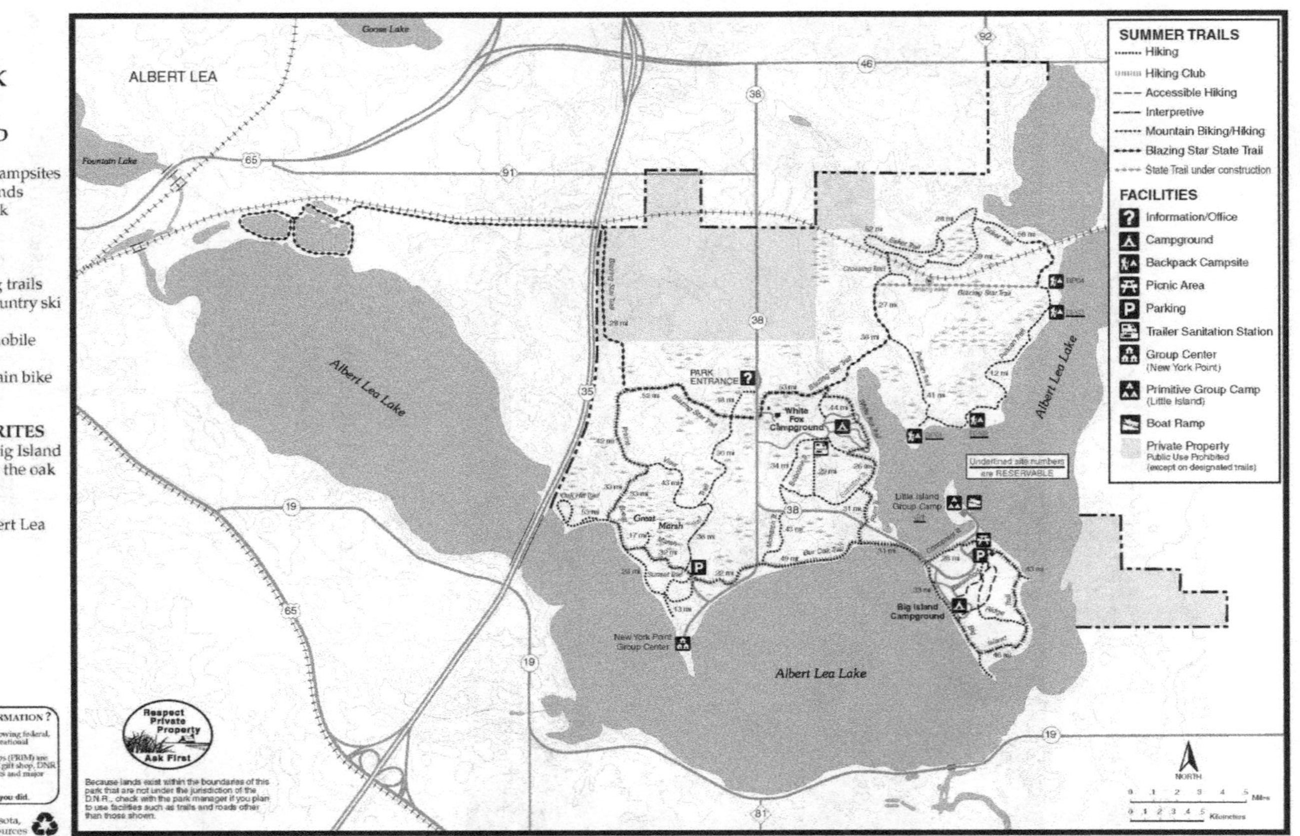

Nerstrand Big Woods

9700 170th Street East
Nerstrand, Minnesota 55053
507-333-4840

- This state park is approximately 45 miles south of the Twin Cities Metro area. It can be reached by taking Hwy. 246 south out of Northfield for eleven miles. The park is located twelve miles northeast of Faribault, Minnesota.

- This is a very special park in the state because within the park is one of the last stands of 'Big Woods'. Prior to white settlement in Minnesota, this wooded area was the southern most extent of the maple, basswood, elm, ash, ironwood type of forest. This was the same type of forest that existed in a larger band that crossed the state from the area of the Twin Cities, through the St. Cloud region and then up to Fargo and Grand Forks.

- The item that makes this forest special when compared the woods to the north is that this forest also has oak species in it. Red, white, and scrub oaks can be found among the other species of trees in the park and these oaks are the clue to why this section of 'Big Woods' developed this far south.

- This park is a 'full service' park with regards to varieties of activities for the whole family. There are miles and miles of trails for hiking, cross country skiing, and snowmobiling. There is a small waterfall that can be viewed from the trails 0.3 miles north of the main campground. There is a large picnic area with playground, tables and elevated char coal grills and two large picnic shelters. There is a remote group camp area with several walk in campsites nearby. There is an amphitheater in the park where programs are regularly held and a volley ball court.

- The main camping area is made up of the main road dividing into three different lanes: Lane A, Lane B, and Lane C. The electrical sites are located at the sites that are on the inside of the lanes. There is a large flush toilet/shower building, extra parking for additional vehicles, vault toilets, and water spigots available for use.

- Obviously, in this park, there is lots of tree cover and shading available at the campsites. Site that we liked were: 6, 14, 17, 22, 28, 30, 35, 37, and 50.

- One site to see along the trails in the park was relayed to us by the Park Ranger. He stated that along beaver trail, just north of Prairie Creek, there can be seen two trees that are growing very close together. Someone, a number of years ago placed a piece of wood between the two trunks and now the trees are growing over and around the board, creating a natural bench.

(Spider webs in the morning sun.)

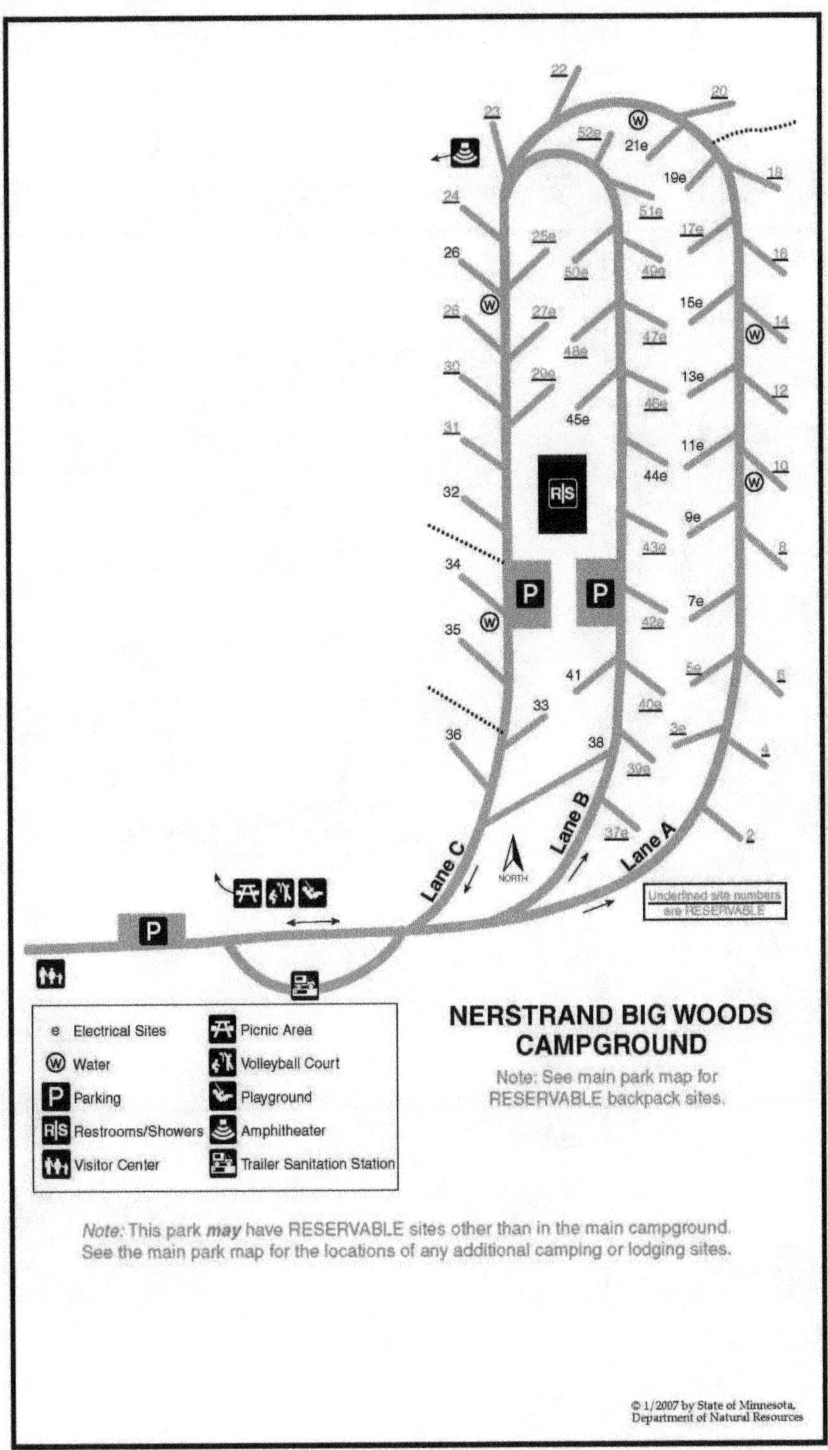
NERSTRAND BIG WOODS
CAMPGROUND
Note: See main park map for RESERVABLE backpack sites.
Underlined site numbers are RESERVABLE
Lane A
Lane B
Lane C
NORTH
e Electrical Sites
Water
Parking
Restrooms/Showers
Visitor Center
Picnic Area
Volleyball Court
Playground
Amphitheater
Trailer Sanitation Station
Note: This park may have RESERVABLE sites other than in the main campground. See the main park map for the locations of any additional camping or lodging sites.
© 1/2007 by State of Minnesota, Department of Natural Resources

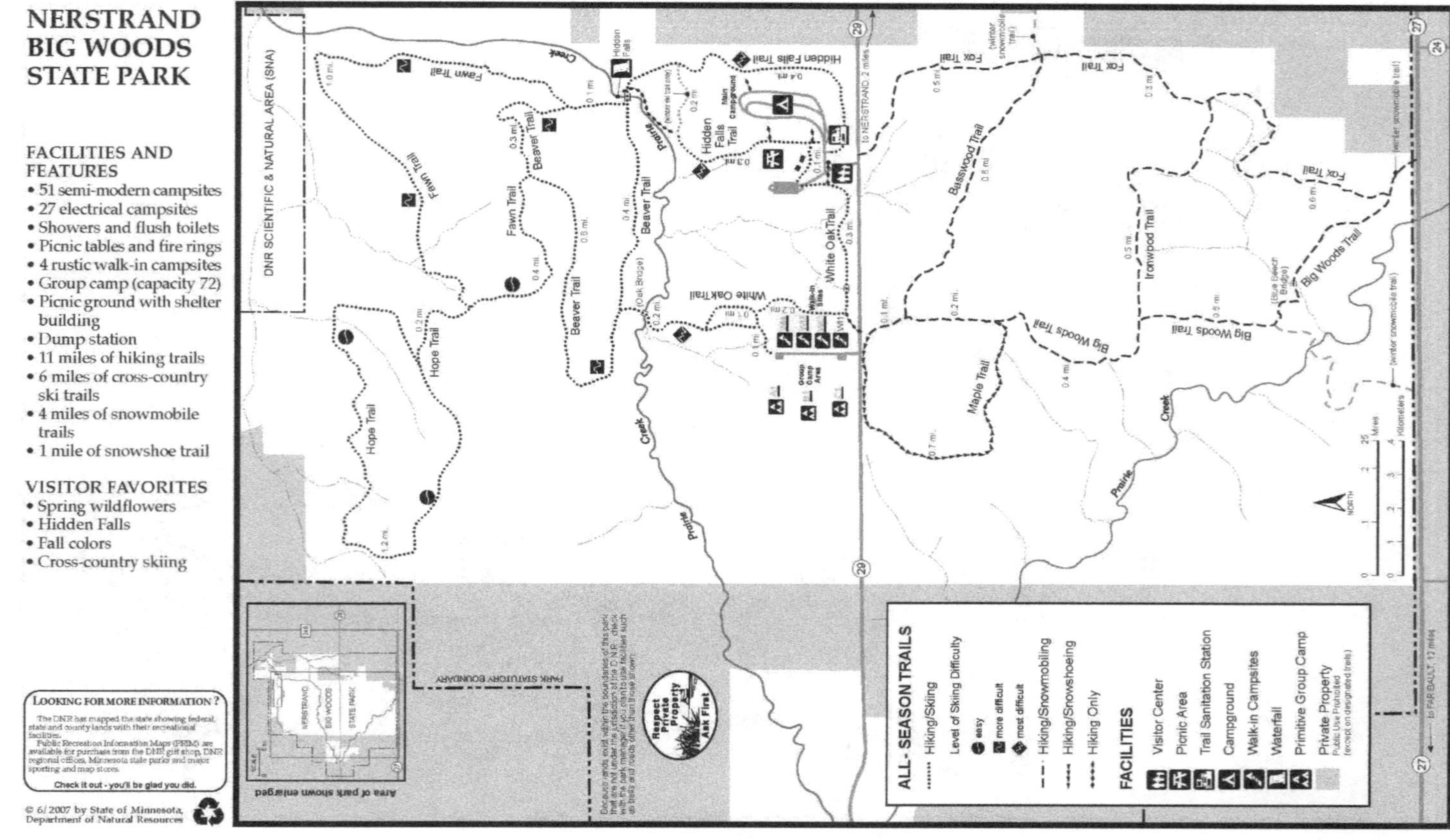
NERSTRAND BIG WOODS STATE PARK
FACILITIES AND FEATURES
• 51 semi-modern campsites
• 27 electrical campsites
• Showers and flush toilets
• Picnic tables and fire rings
• 4 rustic walk-in campsites
• Group camp (capacity 72)
• Picnic ground with shelter building
• Dump station
• 11 miles of hiking trails
• 6 miles of cross-country ski trails
• 4 miles of snowmobile trails
• 1 mile of snowshoe trail
VISITOR FAVORITES
• Spring wildflowers
• Hidden Falls
• Fall colors
• Cross-country skiing
LOOKING FOR MORE INFORMATION?
The DNR has mapped the state showing federal, state and county lands with their recreational facilities.
Public Recreation Information Maps (PRIM) are available for purchase from the DNR gift shop, DNR regional offices, Minnesota state parks and major sporting and map stores.
Check it out - you'll be glad you did.
© 6/2007 by State of Minnesota, Department of Natural Resources
DNR SCIENTIFIC & NATURAL AREA (SNA)
Hope Trail
Fawn Trail
Beaver Trail
Hidden Falls
Hidden Falls Trail
White Oak Trail
Main Campground
Group Camp Area
Walk-in Sites
Prairie Creek
(Oak Bridge)
(Blue Beech Bridge)
Maple Trail
Basswood Trail
Big Woods Trail
Ironwood Trail
Fox Trail
(winter snowmobile trail)
to NERSTRAND, 2 miles
to FARIBAULT, 12 miles
PARK STATUTORY BOUNDARY
Area of park shown enlarged
NERSTRAND BIG WOODS STATE PARK
Because lands exist within the boundaries of this park that are not under the jurisdiction of the D.N.R., check with the park manager if you plan to use facilities such as trails and roads other than those shown.
Respect Private Property Ask First
NORTH
Miles
Kilometers
ALL-SEASON TRAILS
Hiking/Skiing
Level of Skiing Difficulty
easy
more difficult
most difficult
Hiking/Snowmobiling
Hiking/Snowshoeing
Hiking Only
FACILITIES
Visitor Center
Picnic Area
Trail Sanitation Station
Campground
Walk-in Campsites
Waterfall
Primitive Group Camp
Private Property
Public Use Prohibited (except on designated trails)

Old Mill

33489 240th Avenue NW
Argyle, Minnesota 56713
218-437-8174

- This is a lovely state park located 13 miles east of the city of Argyle. It is nestled in an area of ravine forest surrounded by prairie and farm fields.

- Originally this site was the homestead of a Swedish immigrant family that built a mill to process grains from the local area. After a time, it became tradition to camp along the river near the mill. This tradition continues today in this lovely little park.

- There are 26 campsites in the campground and a mix of electric and non-electric. There are toilets with showers, fresh water spigots, picnic area, swimming beach, and 3 or 4 miles of hiking trail with scenic overlook sites along the path.

- There is an old WPA Dam on site in the park that used to create a small lake. However, the dam was opened in order to allow for the reclamation of the original river valley and settler sites.

- The trails in the park are available for hiking, cross country skiing, snowmobiles, and snow shoeing.

- There are trees all around and small amount of undergrowth between sites in the campground which will afford campers some privacy and seclusion. The sites are nice and level and can easily accommodate trailers and RV's.

- There are dates during the summer when re-enactments around the old mill site occur. This little park is a jewel of a spot and will fast become a favorite for anyone who chooses to stay or visit there.

- One last note, the Park is just south of the town of Karlstad, MN, - The Moose Capitol of Minnesota.

- Camp sites we liked were: 4, 18, 20, 21, and 28.

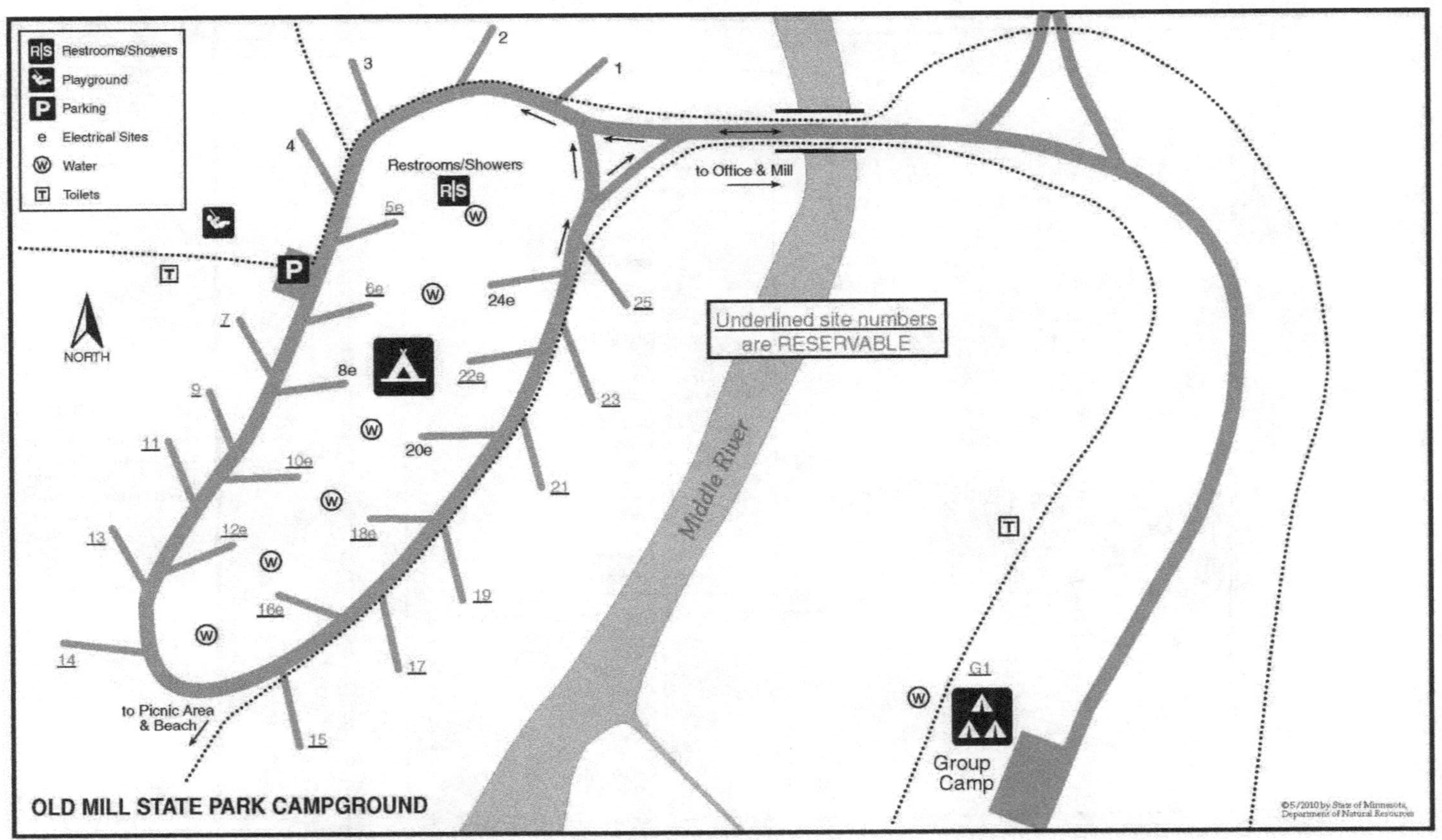
Restrooms/Showers
Playground
Parking
e Electrical Sites
Water
Toilets
NORTH
Restrooms/Showers
to Office & Mill
Underlined site numbers
are RESERVABLE
Middle River
G1
Group
Camp
to Picnic Area
& Beach
OLD MILL STATE PARK CAMPGROUND
©5/2010 by State of Minnesota,
Department of Natural Resources

OLD MILL STATE PARK

FACILITIES AND FEATURES

- 26 semi-modern campsites
- Primitive group camp
- Showers & electric sites
- Picnic area
- Picnic shelter
- Swimming pond
- Fishing
- Historic site
- Hiking trails
- Snowmobile trails
- Cross-country ski trails
- Sliding area
- Warming house
- Snowshoe rental

VISITOR FAVORITES

- Swimming
- Picnicking
- Camping
- Hiking

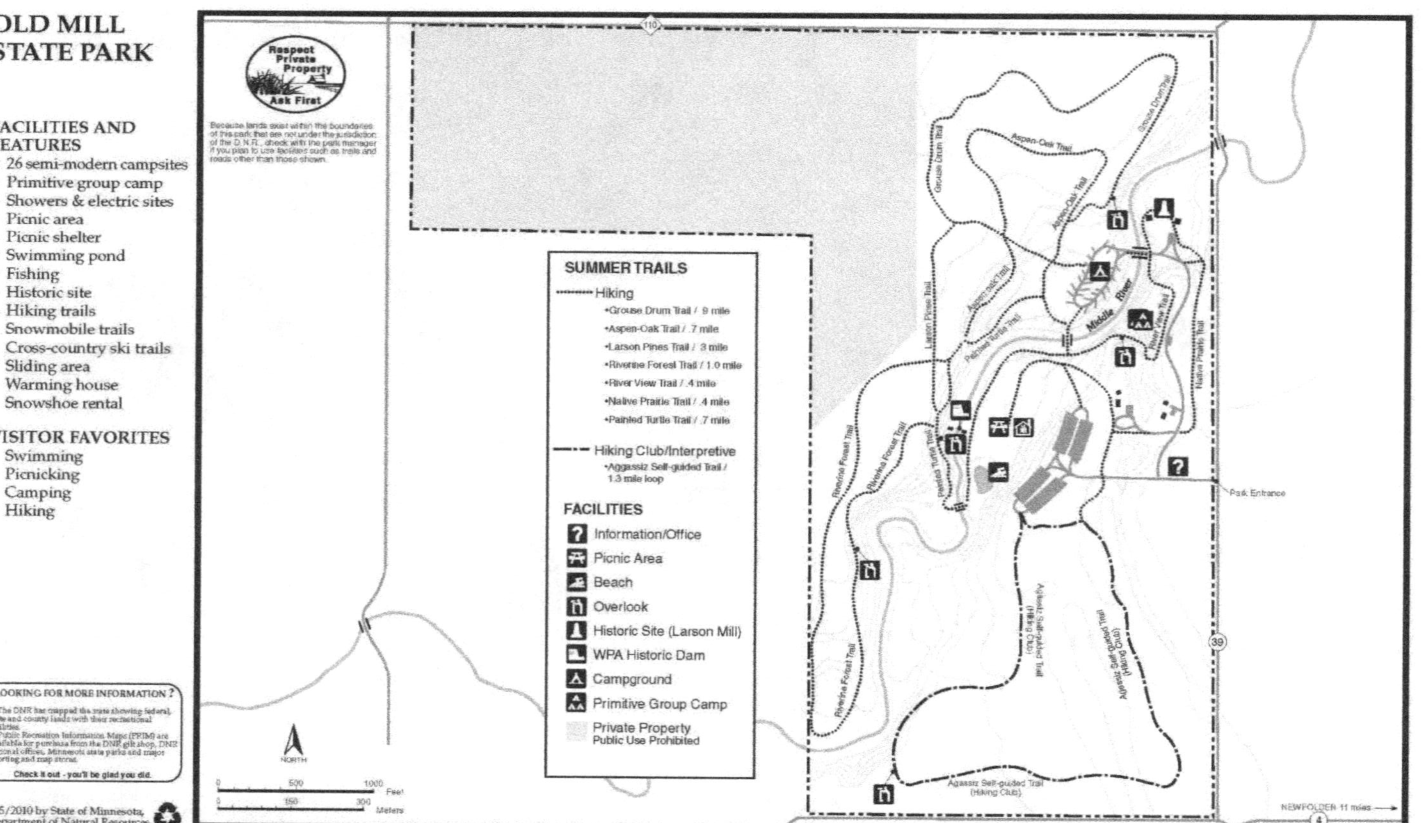

LOOKING FOR MORE INFORMATION?

The DNR has mapped the state showing federal, state and county lands with their recreational facilities.

Public Recreation Information Maps (PRIM) are available for purchase from the DNR gift shop, DNR regional offices, Minnesota state parks and major sporting and map stores.

Check it out - you'll be glad you did.

Red River State Recreational Area

515 2nd Street NW
East Grand Forks, Minnesota 56721
218-773-4950

- This park exists on the site of reclaimed property in East Grand Forks after the terrible flooding of 1997. This is a relatively new park and it is located within the city of East Grand Forks.

- This park has all the amenities available - toilets and showers, fresh water spigots, and remote camping down by the river. Access to the river is close by. The sites are large and many of them are quite open. Some sites have trees close by and are well shaded. Access to Downtown is just a short walk away.

- Hiking and biking along the trails next to the river.

- All of the campsites are nice and level and have good gravel pads for parking RV's or trailers on.

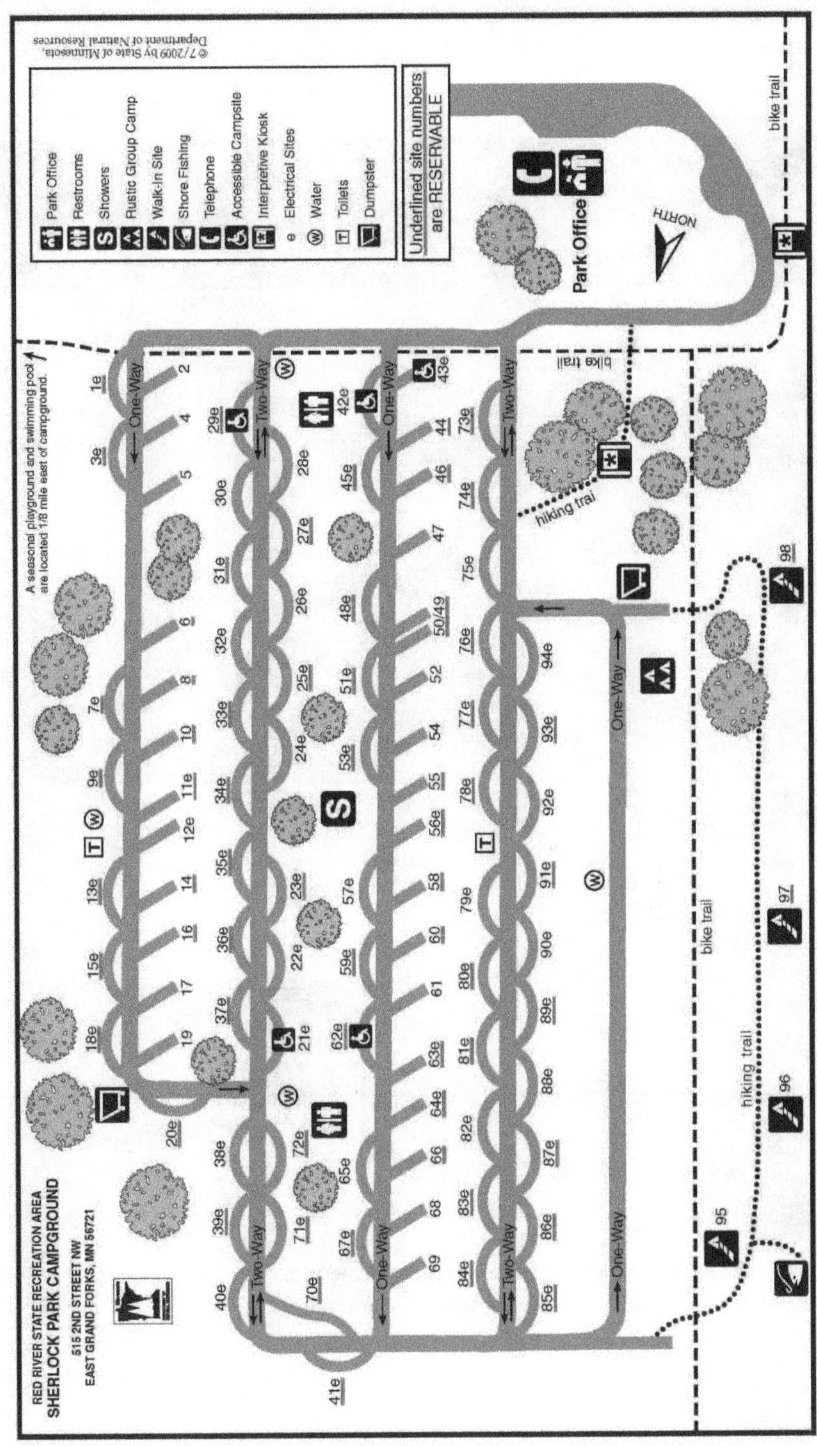
RED RIVER STATE RECREATION AREA
SHERLOCK PARK CAMPGROUND
515 2ND STREET NW
EAST GRAND FORKS, MN 56721
Park Office
Restrooms
Showers
Rustic Group Camp
Walk-In Site
Shore Fishing
Telephone
Accessible Campsite
Interpretive Kiosk
Electrical Sites
Water
Toilets
Dumpster
Underlined site numbers are RESERVABLE
© 7/2009 by State of Minnesota, Department of Natural Resources
A seasonal playground and swimming pool are located 1/8 mile east of campground.
Park Office
NORTH
One-Way
Two-Way
bike trail
hiking trail

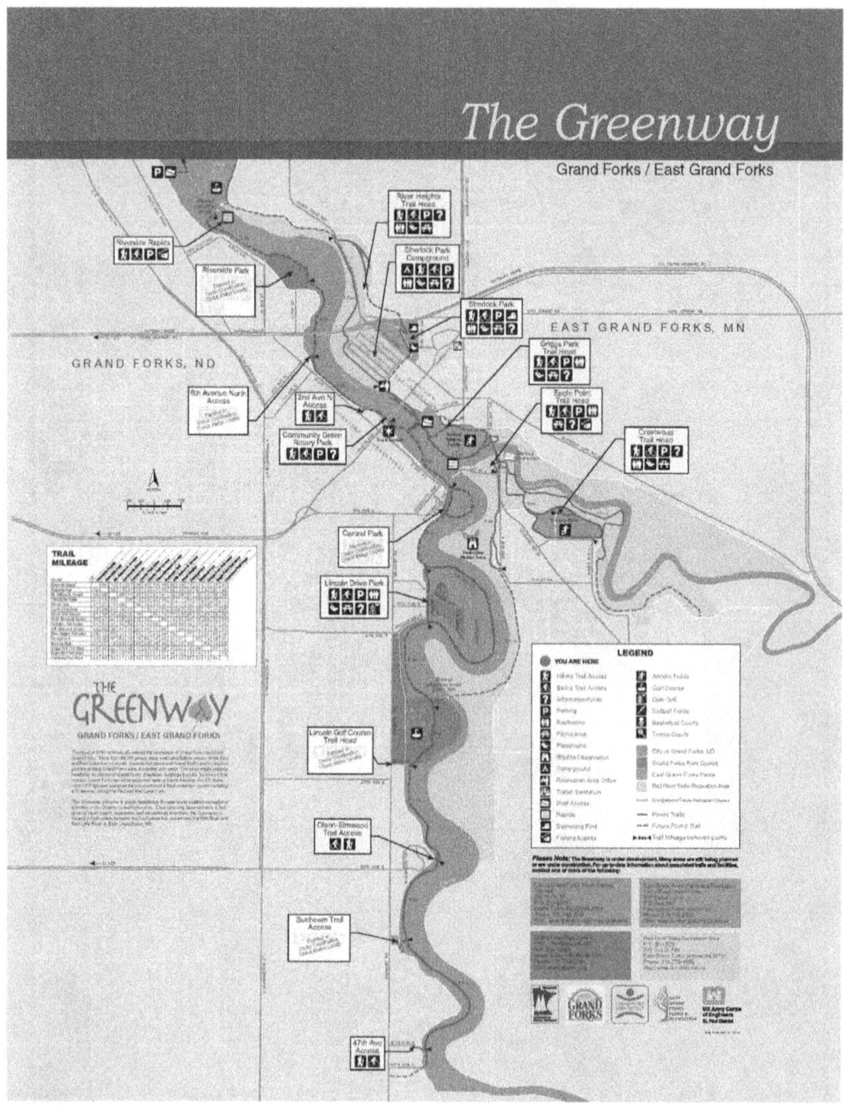
The Greenway
Grand Forks / East Grand Forks
EAST GRAND FORKS, MN
GRAND FORKS, ND
Riverside Rapids
Riverside Park
River Heights Trail Head
Sherlock Park Campground
Sherlock Park
Griggs Park Trail Head
Eagle Point Trail Head
Greenwood Trail Head
8th Avenue North Access
2nd Ave N Access
Community Green Rotary Park
Central Park
Lincoln Drive Park
Lincoln Golf Course Trail Head
47th Ave Access
TRAIL MILEAGE
THE GREENWAY
GRAND FORKS / EAST GRAND FORKS
LEGEND
YOU ARE HERE
US Army Corps of Engineers St. Paul District

Rice Lake

8485 Rose Street
Owatonna, Minnesota 55060
507-455-5871

- This park is located about seven miles east of Owatonna, Minnesota, on Steele County Highway 19.

- The state park property completely surrounds the lake. All of the facilities for the park are located on the north shore of the lake. Rice Lake, itself, is one of the headwater sources for the Zumbro River. The lake and this area attracted settlers to it very early in the states history.

- The lake and the area are prime locations for wildlife and migratory bird species. There have been seven different species of woodpeckers observed in the park. The lake is shallow and has marsh grasses growing up nearly all the way around its shoreline, thus the lake is a fantastic source to see swans, Canada geese, blue and snow geese, egrets, herons, and all manner of duck species.

- There are 42 semi-modern camping sites in the park, a large remote group camp, eight or nine hike-in/cart-in camp sites, a large picnic area, playground, boat landing, and over 4 miles of multi-use trail in the park. There are several shelters along the trails and a covered shelter at the picnic area and several vault toilets along the trails. Sixteen of the campsites in the main camping area have electrical hook up available.

- All of the camp sites in the main camping area and at the group camp site have picnic tables and fire rings available. The picnic area has several dozen picnic tables. There is a flush toilet/shower building, vault toilets, and water spigots available at the main campground.

- The boat landing is a little rough for any boats larger than a canoe. As stated before, there is marsh grass growing up all around the lake shore and this boat landing was literally hacked and dredged out from among that marsh grass. There are canoes and kayaks available for rent at the landing.

- The camping area is heavily wooded and because of that there is not a lot of under growth between the campsites. Two loops make up the camp grounds: Loop A and Loop B. Loop B has the electrical sites. Sites we liked were: A4, A5, A12, A17, A21, B4, B13, B15, and B20.

- There is a set of five remote campsites that are located at the south tip of the lake. They are reached by canoe and there is a vault toilet and fire rings available at those sites.

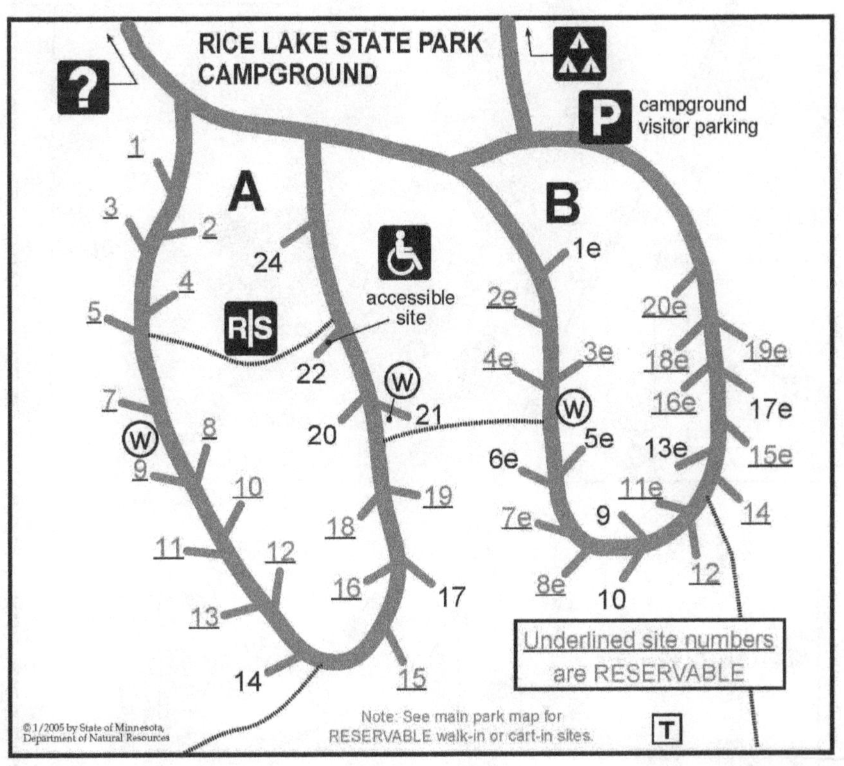
RICE LAKE STATE PARK
CAMPGROUND
campground
visitor parking
A
B
accessible
site
Underlined site numbers
are RESERVABLE
Note: See main park map for
RESERVABLE walk-in or cart-in sites.
© 1/2005 by State of Minnesota,
Department of Natural Resources

RICE LAKE STATE PARK

FACILITIES AND FEATURES

• **Campgrounds:**
Rice Lake has a variety of camping facilities: a semi-modern campground with 42 sites to accommodate individual and family-sized groups; a primitive group camp to accommodate large groups (60+); 5 canoe-in sites, 5 walk-in sites; and 4 cart-in sites.

Semi-modern campsites have a picnic table, fire ring and parking space. Many sites also have a tent pad. Rice Lake's campgrounds are served by flush toilets, showers, and 16 electrical sites. Running water is supplied at the sanitation building.

The primitive group camp has picnic tables, tent sites, and a fire ring.

• **Picnic Grounds:**
Rice Lake's picnic grounds have tables, fire rings, running water, toilets, playground equipment and a picnic shelter.

• **Public Water Access:**
A water access to Rice Lake is available in the park. A parking lot is provided.

• **Phone:**
A public pay phone is available outside the park office.

VISITOR FAVORITES:

- Spring wildflowers
- Waterfowl migrations (spring & fall)
- Wildlife observation

LOOKING FOR MORE INFORMATION?

The DNR has mapped the state showing federal, state and county lands with their recreational facilities.

Public Recreation Information Maps (PRIM) are available for purchase from the DNR gift shop, DNR regional offices, Minnesota state parks and major sporting and map stores.

Check it out - you'll be glad you did.

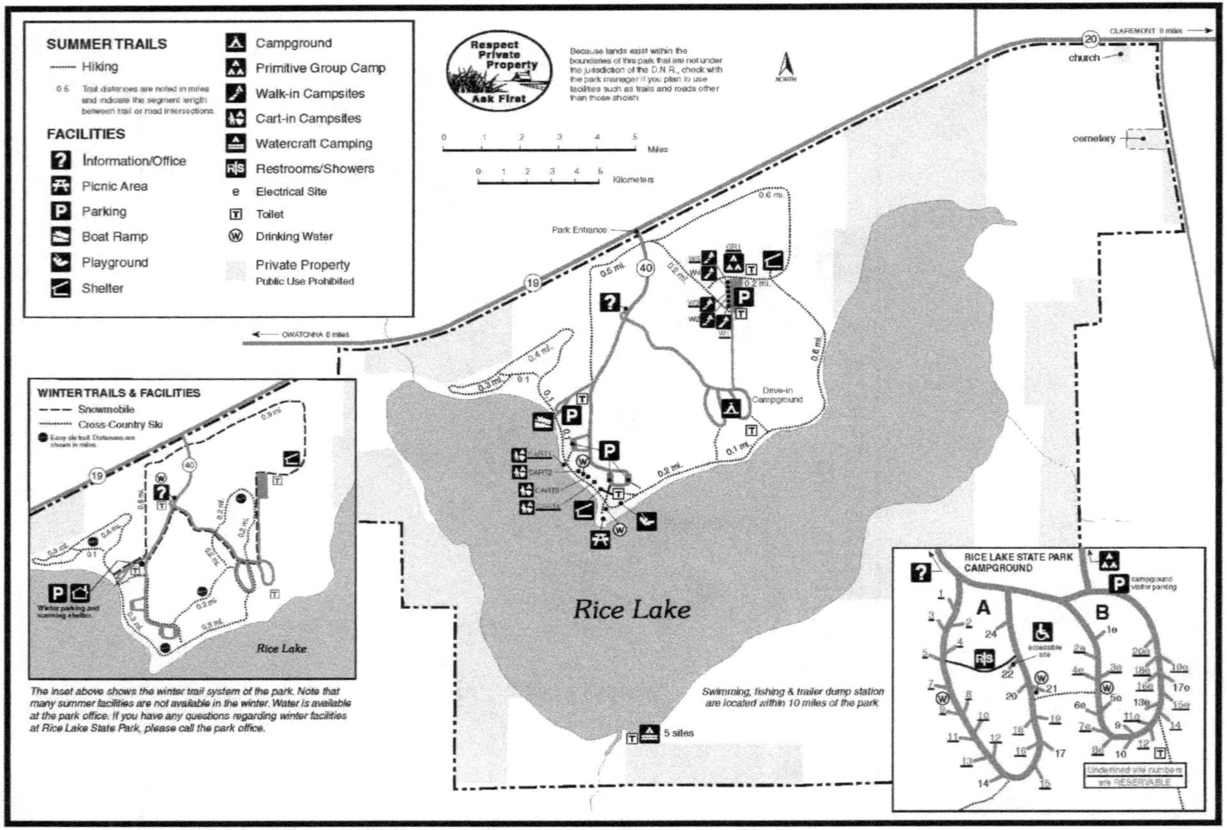

The inset above shows the winter trail system of the park. Note that many summer facilities are not available in the winter. Water is available at the park office. If you have any questions regarding winter facilities at Rice Lake State Park, please call the park office.

St. Croix

30065 St. Croix Park Road
Hinckley, Minnesota 55037
320-384-6591

- This park is located just 15 miles east of Hinckley, MN, on Hwy. 48. This state park is among the largest of the state parks. There is over 33,000 acres in the park. The park follows the western shore of the St. Croix River.

- This park has all the amenities to allow for very comfortable camping for everyone. The camping areas are nice and level and are able to accommodate tents, trailers, and RV's of all shapes and sizes.

- The camps, 3 of them - Riverview, Paint Rock Springs, and Old Logging Trail - are all nicely tree covered and allow for nice shade. The camp sites are close together and there is little underbrush to allow for seclusion. There is even a camp store on site between the camp areas that is open until 10 p.m. with food, snacks, and drinks available.

- There are 215 campsites in the park. 42 of the sites have electric hook-ups. There are toilet/showers in each of the separate camping areas, water spigots for fresh water, and vault toilets dispersed throughout the park.

- There are numerous spots to carry in a canoe to the river. There are a couple of boat launch sites. Swimming beaches, picnic areas, shelters on the trails, hiking trails, horse riding trails, snowmobile trails, cross country ski trails, over 80 miles of trails and there are remote camping sites along those trails. There are two Group Centers and primitive group camps.

- Numerous scenic overlook spots along the trails, a tall observation tower that is located on the Willard Munger State Trail which runs through the park.

- St. Croix is a wonderful park with many family oriented activities and miles and miles of some very beautiful trail and riverbank to explore.

- Camp sites we liked were: 4, 22, 52, 64, 114, 124, 125, 141, 166, 191, 210, 211, and 215.

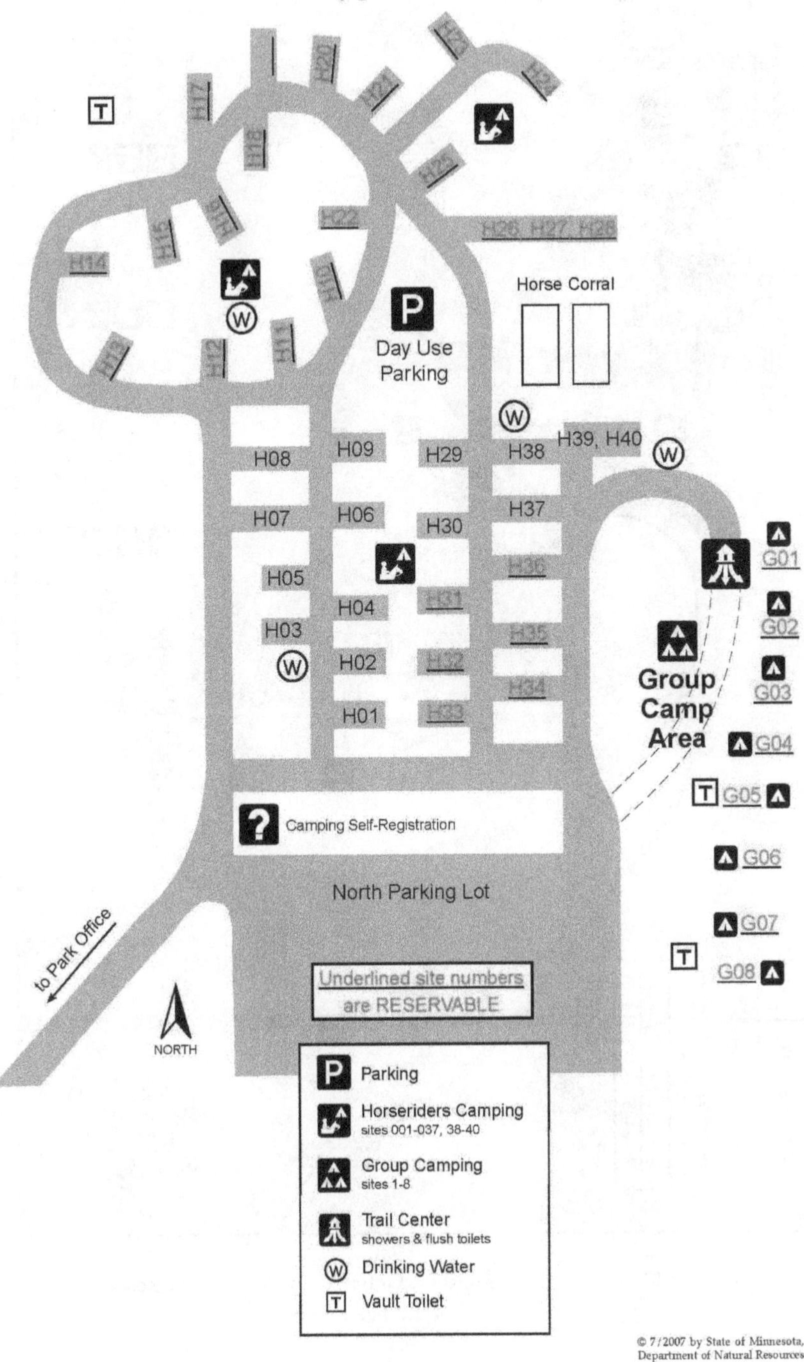
ST. CROIX STATE PARK ALL SEASON TRAIL CENTER
Horse Campground & Group Camp
Horse Corral
Day Use Parking
H08
H09
H29
H38
H39, H40
H07
H06
H30
H37
H05
H04
H03
H02
H01
Group Camp Area
G01
G02
G03
G04
G05
G06
G07
G08
Camping Self-Registration
North Parking Lot
to Park Office
NORTH
Underlined site numbers are RESERVABLE
Parking
Horseriders Camping
sites 001-037, 38-40
Group Camping
sites 1-8
Trail Center
showers & flush toilets
Drinking Water
Vault Toilet
© 7/2007 by State of Minnesota, Department of Natural Resources

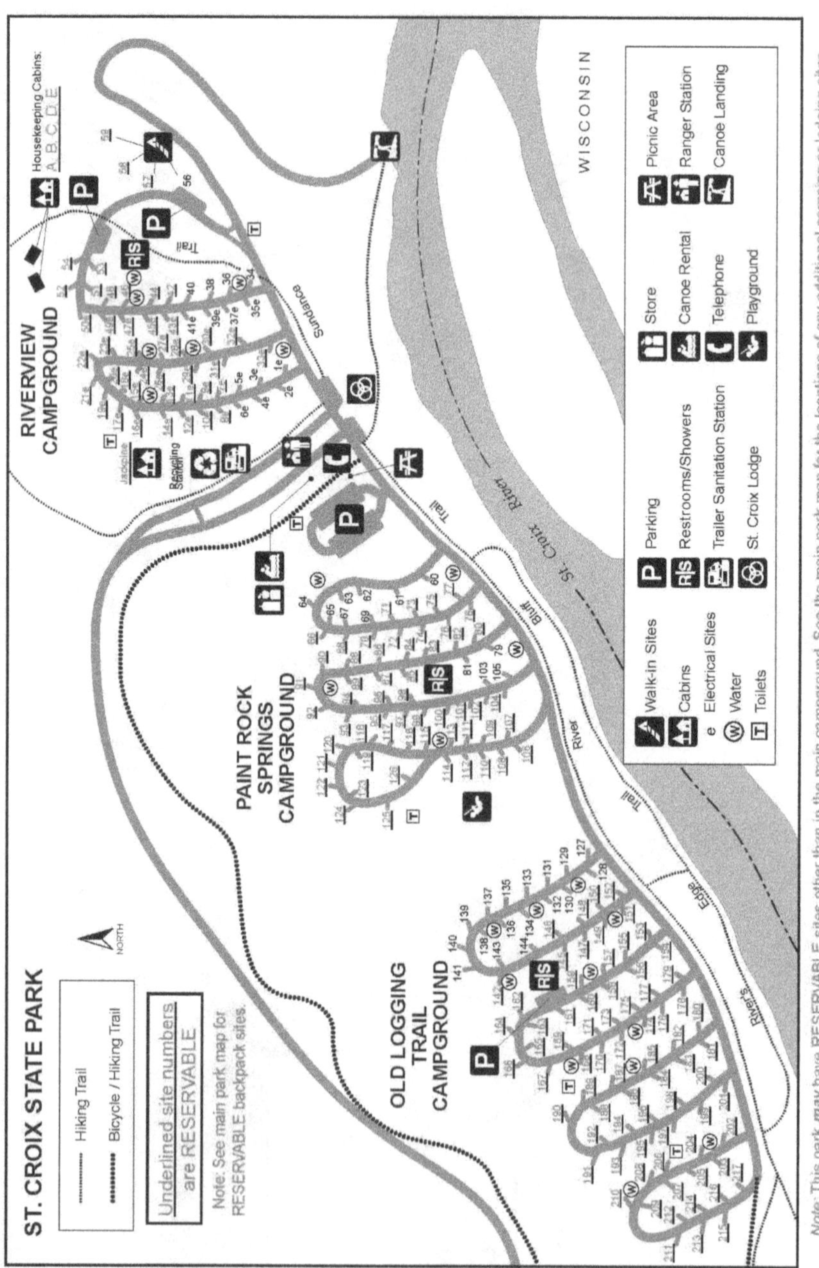
ST. CROIX STATE PARK
Hiking Trail
Bicycle / Hiking Trail
Underlined site numbers are RESERVABLE
Note: See main park map for RESERVABLE backpack sites.
NORTH
RIVERVIEW CAMPGROUND
PAINT ROCK SPRINGS CAMPGROUND
OLD LOGGING TRAIL CAMPGROUND
Housekeeping Cabins:
Jackpine
Recycling Station
Sundance Trail
Bluff Trail
River Trail
River's Edge Trail
St. Croix River
WISCONSIN
Walk-in Sites
Cabins
Electrical Sites
Water
Toilets
Parking
Restrooms/Showers
Trailer Sanitation Station
St. Croix Lodge
Store
Canoe Rental
Telephone
Playground
Picnic Area
Ranger Station
Canoe Landing
Note: This park may have RESERVABLE sites other than in the main campground. See the main park map for the locations of any additional camping or lodging sites.

ST. CROIX STATE PARK

FACILITIES AND FEATURES

Winter:

- 80 miles of groomed and well-marked snowmobile trails
- Snowmobile trails connect the park with state forests and several communities
- Enclosed shelter with two fireplaces and flush toilets
- 11 miles of ski trails
- 2 modern guest houses, each accommodating up to 15 people
- Winter camping

Summer:

- 215 campsites (42 electric)
- 2 modern group centers
- Primitive tent area for groups
- Horse camp area
- Canoe and backpack campsites
- Picnic ground with enclosed shelter
- Swimming beach and playgrounds
- Hiking, horseback and bicycle trails
- Canoe and kayak rental
- 5 housekeeping cabins (seasonal)

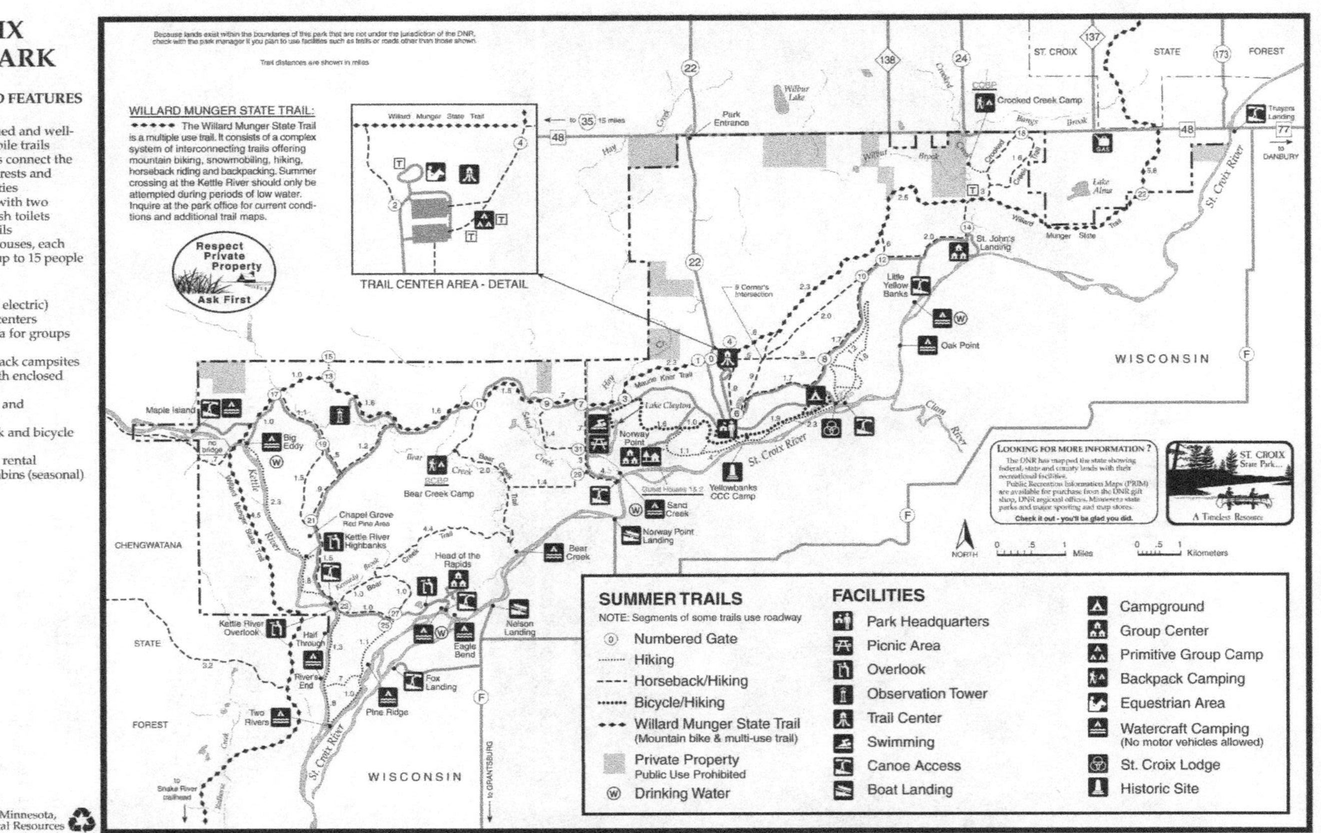

Sakatah Lake

50499 Sakatah Lake State Park Road
Waterville, Minnesota 56096
507-362-4438

- Park is located 14 miles west of Faribault, Minnesota, on MN Hwy 60. The nearest town is a small town one mile further west on Hwy 60 – Waterville.

- Sakatah Lake is actually made up of two lakes that can be found along the Cannon River, between Faribault and Mankato. The lake further to the west is the larger of the two bodies of water that are included in the park.

- The state of Minnesota has also created a 39 mile long multi-use state trail between Faribault and Mankato and the trail is called the Sakatah State Trail. This trail was created on top of the old rail line that ran between Faribault and Mankato. Access to the trail can be made from the park.

- Within the park there is a picnic area and boat landing down near the water. There are two group camp areas in the park and there is a bicycle camping site set up along the state trail. There is approximately 4 kilometers of other hiking trails, along with the state trail, in the park for campers to enjoy.

- The camping area is dived into four loops, two on each side of the road leading down to the lake. There are vault toilets and water spigots located throughout the camping area. There is as toilet/shower facility situated between the two loops on the north side of the road. There are 14 sites that have electrical hookups and they are also on the loops on the north side of the road. The sites are level and there is an abundance of shade created by all the trees – oaks, ash, poplar, birch, and cottonwoods. Plenty of under growth growing up between the sites will help to create some seclusion between campsites.

- There is also a fishing pier out in the lake for campers to use and is located along the road leading down to the boat landing. There is a fish cleaning shack located at the RV dump station. One camper cabin is available for reservation at this park.

- There are many wonderful sites to camp at in this state park. Most are nicely leveled and easy to access, even with all the trees. Each site has a fire pit, picnic table and a pad area for a tent. The sites we liked the most were: 3, 4, 8, 12, 15, 26, 31, 38, 40, 41, and 54.

SAKATAH LAKE STATE PARK CAMPGROUND

NORTH

········· Hiking Trail
------ Campground Access to State Trail

to Picnic Grounds, Boat Ramp, Bike Trail

to Park Entrance

Recycling Center

Hiking Club Trailhead

Underlined site numbers are RESERVABLE

e Electrical Sites	P Parking	Camper Cabin
Ⓦ Water	R/S Restrooms/Showers	Park Office
T Toilets	Trailer Sanitation Station	? Information
Trash Dumpster	Fish Cleaning House	
H Horseshoe Pit		

Note: This park *may* have RESERVABLE sites other than in the main campground. See the main park map for the locations of any additional camping or lodging

SAKATAH LAKE STATE PARK

FACILITIES AND FEATURES

- 62 semi-modern campsites
- Showers (seasonal)
- Trailer sanitation station (seasonal)
- Boat ramp
- Picnic grounds
- Access to 39 miles of hiking, biking, skiing and snowmobiling trails
- 14 electrical sites
- Bicycle touring camp
- Primitive group camps
- Camper Cabin

VISITOR FAVORITES

- Shaded campsites
- Fishing and boating on Sakatah Lake
- Hiking/biking/snowmobiling the State Trail
- Picnicking at the lake
- Canoeing
- Horseshoes

LOOKING FOR MORE INFORMATION?

The DNR has mapped the state showing federal, state and county lands with their recreational facilities.

Public Recreation Information Maps (PRIM) are available for purchase from the DNR gift shop, DNR regional offices, Minnesota state parks and major sporting and map stores.

Check it out - you'll be glad you did.

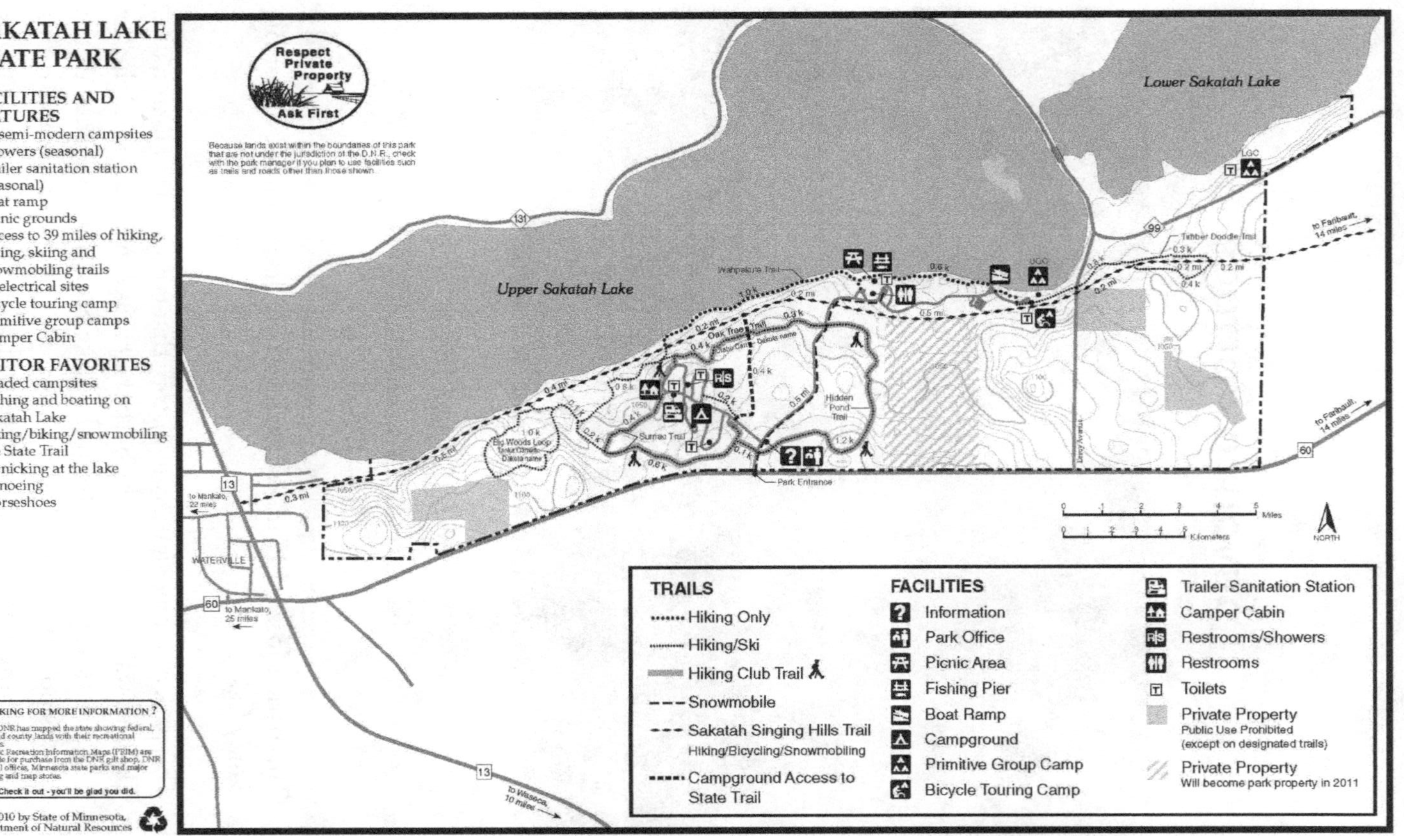

Savanna Portage

55626 Lake Place
McGregor, Minnesota 55760
218-426-3271

- This park is located 17 miles northwest of McGregor, MN, near Big Sandy Lake.

- This park has some significant history that is pointed out in its name. The area was heavily used by both the natives in the area and the fur trappers as a spot to get from the Lake Superior watershed to the Mississippi watershed. The trail that was used to accomplish this followed the small rivers, swamps and lakes that are located in the park and then lead to Big Sandy Lake.

- Savanna Portage encompasses over 15,000 acres and much of this is very remote, densely wooded, hills and valleys. Small lakes and creeks run throughout the area. The area is covered in aspen, birch, maple and basswood. On higher ridges, you will find groves of pine growing tall and slender.

- The roadways in the park are not paved, they are gravel. However, don't let this stop you from coming to visit this beautiful state park. There are 61 campsites in the main camping areas and 18 of the sites have electrical hook-ups.

- Three different lakes in the park have boat launch sites and docks. Two other lakes have carry-in access for canoes. There is over 22 miles of hiking trail in the park, 10 miles of mountain bike trails. There are several remote camping areas set up along the hiking trails. Many shelters are set up along the trails, too.

- There are several piers set up on the shores of the lakes to allow for fishing from shore. Boat and canoe rental is available. Picnic areas, swimming beaches, fish cleaning shacks, toilets/shower facility and playground for children are all available here at Savanna.

- The sites at the main campgrounds are nicely wooded with some ground cover to allow for some seclusion. The sites at the campgrounds that we felt were very nice sites were - # 20, 29, 45 and 49.

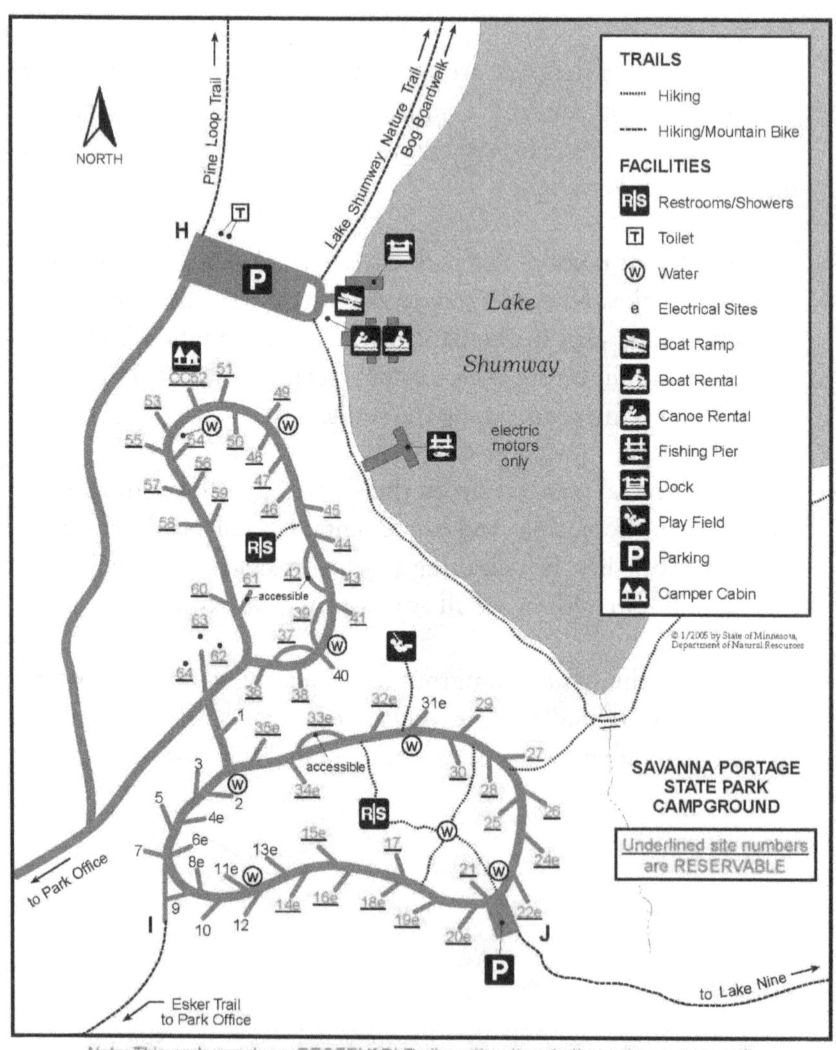
NORTH
Pine Loop Trail
Lake Shumway Nature Trail
Bog Boardwalk
H
I
J
Lake Shumway
electric motors only
accessible
to Park Office
Esker Trail to Park Office
to Lake Nine
TRAILS
Hiking
Hiking/Mountain Bike
FACILITIES
Restrooms/Showers
Toilet
Water
e Electrical Sites
Boat Ramp
Boat Rental
Canoe Rental
Fishing Pier
Dock
Play Field
Parking
Camper Cabin
© 1/2005 by State of Minnesota, Department of Natural Resources
SAVANNA PORTAGE STATE PARK CAMPGROUND
Underlined site numbers are RESERVABLE
Note: This park may have RESERVABLE sites other than in the main campground.
See the main park map for the locations of any additional camping or lodging sites.

SAVANNA PORTAGE STATE PARK

FACILITIES AND FEATURES

- 61 semi-modern campsites with modern sanitation building with showers.
- 5 backpack campsites
- 2 canoe-in/backpack sites (1 on Wolf Lake & 1 on Lake Shumway)
- A primitive group camp
- Picnic shelter on Loon Lake
- Lake fishing for northerns, bass, trout, and panfish
- Boat, motor, and canoe rental
- 22 miles of good hiking trails
- 10 miles of mountain bike trails
- 18 campsites with electricity

VISITOR FAVORITES

- Camping on beautiful Lake Shumway
- Swimming at the beautiful pine-covered swimming beach at Loon Lake
- Snowmobiling on 36 miles of snowmobile trails
- Hiking the Savanna Portage
- Cross-country skiing on 12 miles of well-groomed trails
- Wildlife photography
- Children's playground at Loon Lake picnic grounds
- Continental Divide interpretive overlook

LOOKING FOR MORE INFORMATION?

The DNR has mapped the state showing federal, state and county lands with their recreational facilities.
Public Recreation Information Maps (PRIM) are available for purchase from the DNR gift shop, DNR regional offices, Minnesota state parks and major sporting and map stores.

Check it out - you'll be glad you did.

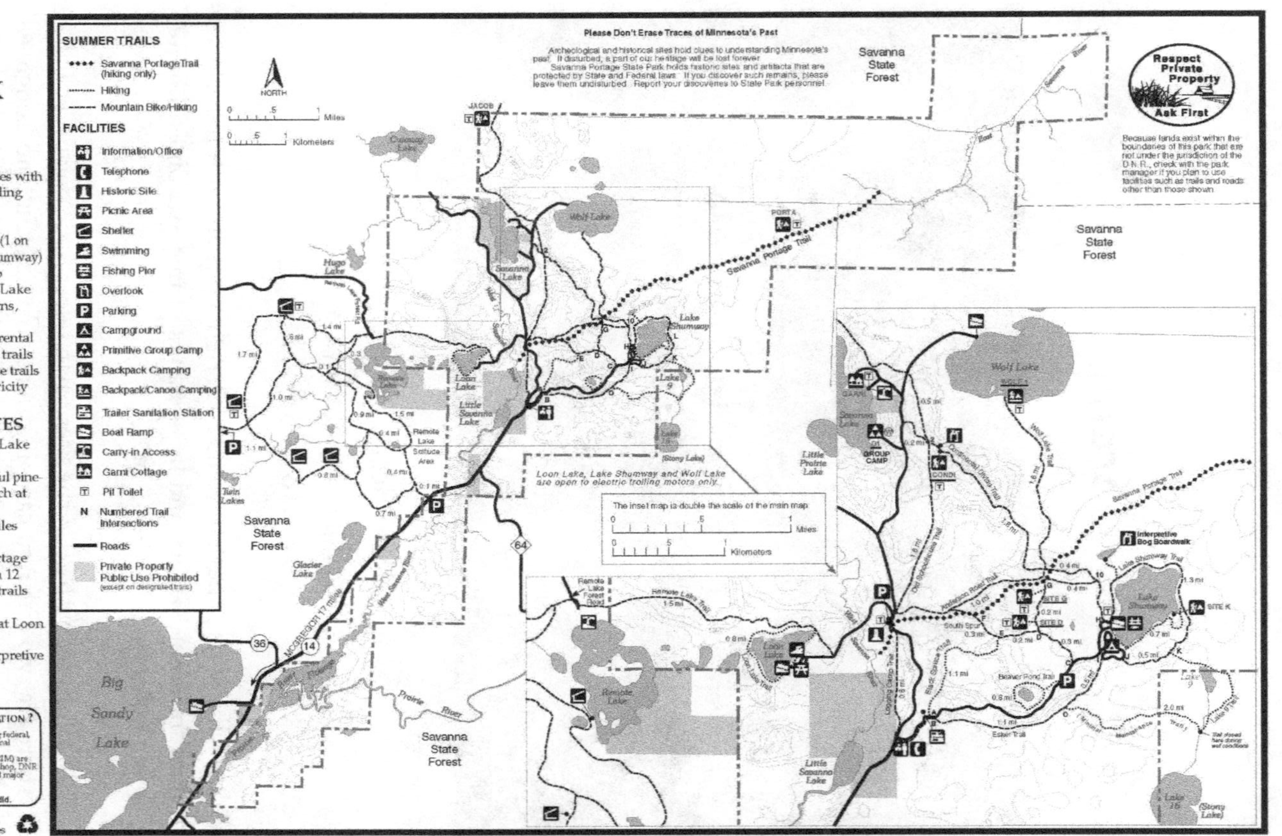

Scenic

56956 Scenic Highway 7
Big Fork, Minnesota 56628
218-743-3362

- Beautiful state park that would rank right up there with Itasca State Park for scenic beauty and large stands of majestic pines. Located seven miles from Big Fork, MN.

- 106 campsites with 20 of the sites having electrical hook up available. There are two different camping areas - Chase Point and Lodge. All of the electric sites are in the Chase Point Camp. There is one electric site available in the Lodge Camp and that is near the Toilets and showers and it is a handicap accessible site.

- Flush toilets, showers, vault toilets, picnic areas, fish cleaning shacks, boat landings and docks, boat and canoe rentals, and miles and miles of trail for cross country skiing, snowmobiling, and hiking.

- There are seven camp sites that are accessible only by hiking and/or canoeing to them. These sites are very remote; however, they would also allow you to have the most unique experience and appreciation for the absolute beauty of this area.

- Six lakes are within the boundaries of the park and these allow a camper to fish for walleyes, northern, crappies and bass.

- Most of the sites in the Chase Point Campground are better suited to tents. However, sites # 43 and 50 could accommodate shorter trailers.

- The CCC was responsible for the development of the park. One of the picnic areas in the park is on the National Registry of Historic sites due to the construction.

- Tall majestic red and white pines with spruce undergrowth abound all over the park. This allows for good seclusion from the other campers.

- We preferred sites # 43 and 50 in the Chase Point camp and sites # 18, 19, 20 and 21 in the Lodge Camp.

(A northern Minnesota lake.)

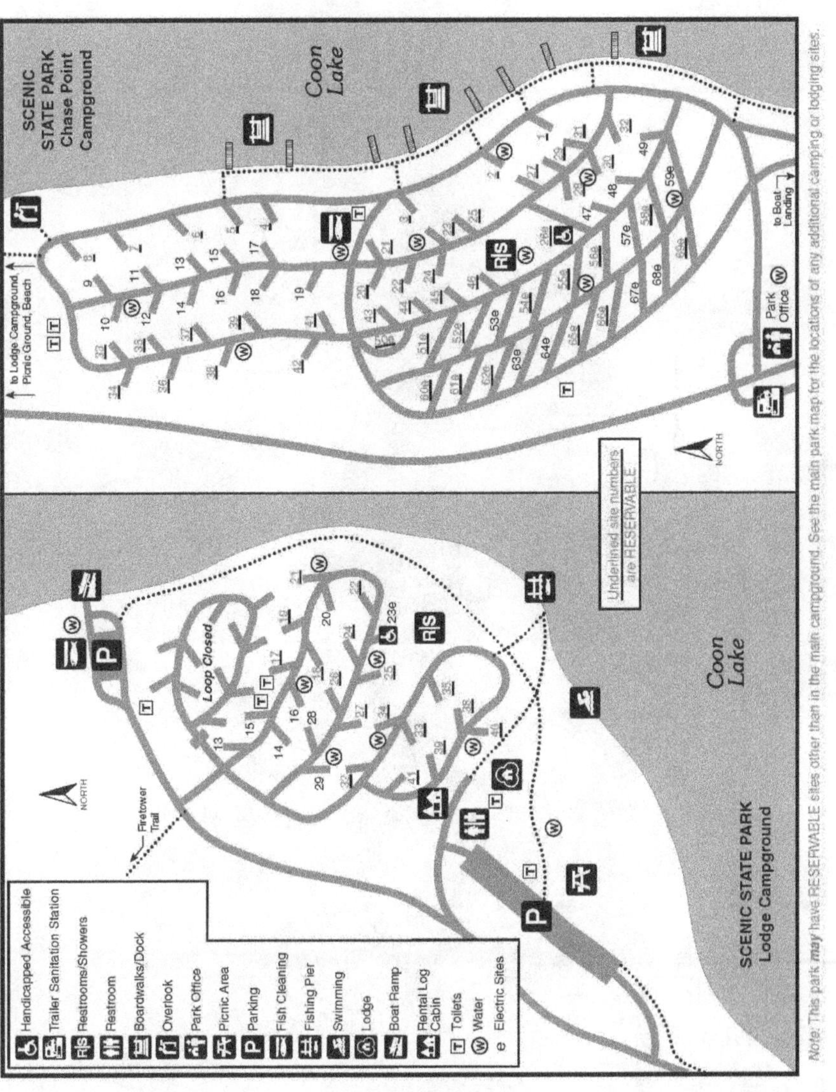
SCENIC STATE PARK Chase Point Campground
Coon Lake
to Lodge Campground, Picnic Ground, Beach
to Boat Landing
Park Office
Underlined site numbers are RESERVABLE
NORTH
SCENIC STATE PARK Lodge Campground
Loop Closed
Firetower Trail
Handicapped Accessible
Trailer Sanitation Station
Restrooms/Showers
Restroom
Boardwalks/Dock
Overlook
Park Office
Picnic Area
Parking
Fish Cleaning
Fishing Pier
Swimming
Lodge
Boat Ramp
Rental Log Cabin
Toilets
Water
Electric Sites
Note: This park *may* have RESERVABLE sites other than in the main campground. See the main park map for the locations of any additional camping or lodging sites.

SCENIC STATE PARK

FACILITIES AND FEATURES

- 106 modern campsites – 20 with electric hook ups.
- Large picnic grounds among old, giant pines.
- Sandy swimming beach.
- Boat and canoe rental.
- Fishing for walleye, northern, and panfish.
- 10 miles of hiking trails.
- 5 miles of interpretive trails.
- 5 miles of cross-country skiing trails.
- 10 miles of snowmobiling trails.
- 7 backpacking and canoe-in sites.
- Sewage dump station.
- CCC log cabin: Built by the Civilian Conservation Corps in the 1930s, this restored cabin is available for rent from April 15 – October 31. It has one small bedroom and sleeps up to 4 people. Toilet facilities are located nearby.
- Rustic group camp.

VISITOR FAVORITES

- Camping.
- Fishing in three lakes.
- Chase Point Trail.
- Coon Lake swimming beach.
- Hiking.
- Fishing pier.

LOOKING FOR MORE INFORMATION?

The DNR has mapped the state showing federal, state and county lands with their recreational facilities.
Public Recreation Information Maps (PRIM) are available for purchase from the DNR gift shop, DNR regional offices, Minnesota state parks and major sporting and map stores.

Check it out - you'll be glad you did.

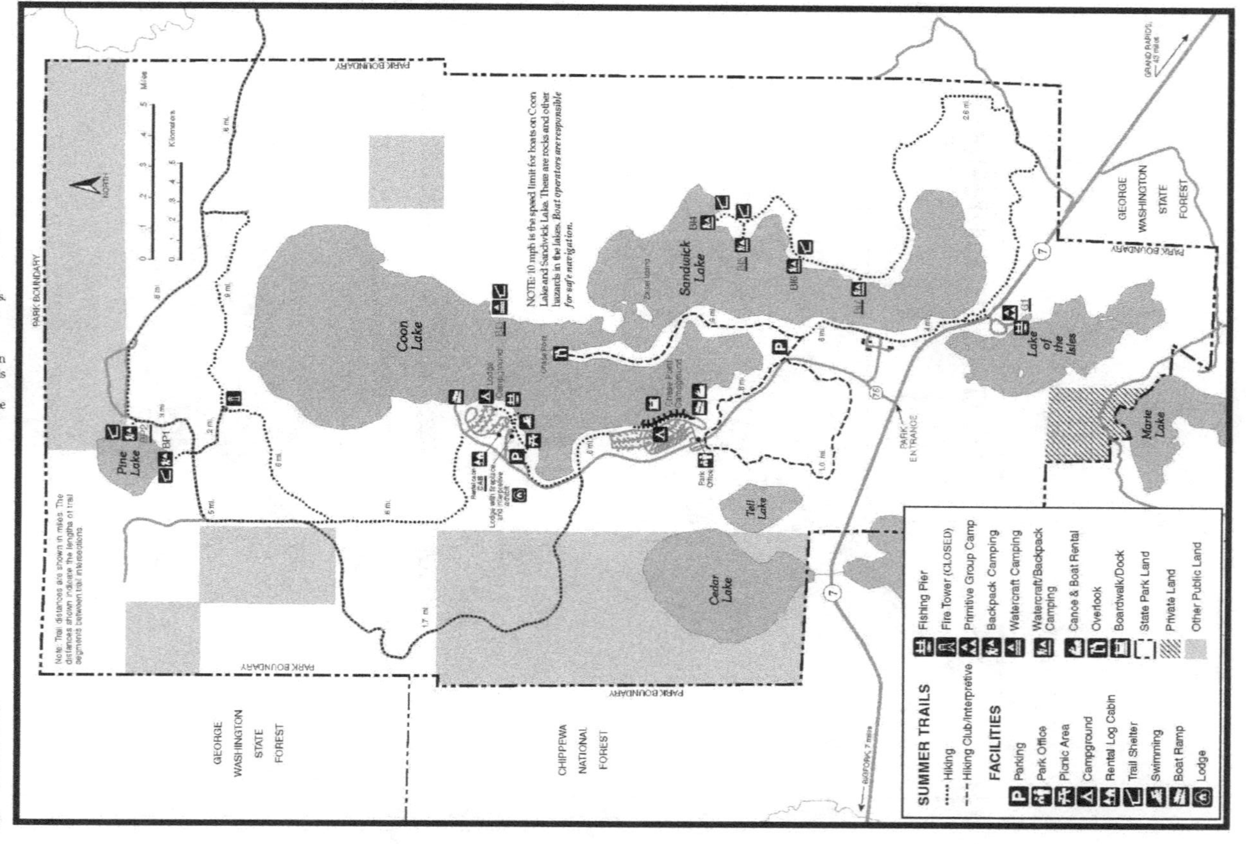

Schoolcraft

9042 Schoolcraft Lane NE
Deer River, Minnesota 56636

Contact c/o Hill Annex Mine
P.O. Box 376
Calumet, Minnesota 55716
218-247-7215

- Park named after Henry Schoolcraft for all of his explorations in the area of central Minnesota and the upper Mississippi River. This park is close to the cities of Calumet, MN and Cohasset, MN.

- There are 24 non-electric sites in the main campground. There are 4 other sites available that can be reached by hiking trail or water.

- Two miles of hiking trails, picnic areas, a boat launch that gives access to the Mississippi, vault toilets, and historical sites give this state park a great deal of ambiance. It is reported that at the picnic area there is a pine tree that stands that is over 300yrs. Old.

- There are many nice sites that are large enough to accommodate trailers and RV's. There are many large trees all around the campground with a mixture of pine and hardwoods.

- Site # 19 is a very nice site with big pines and roomy. Many of the sites have decent seclusion with adequate undergrowth between the sites to keep them semi-private.

- Exceptional picnic area with tall standing pines and open space. Fresh water and toilets close by.

- Other campsites we liked were: 2, 6, 9, 17, and 22.

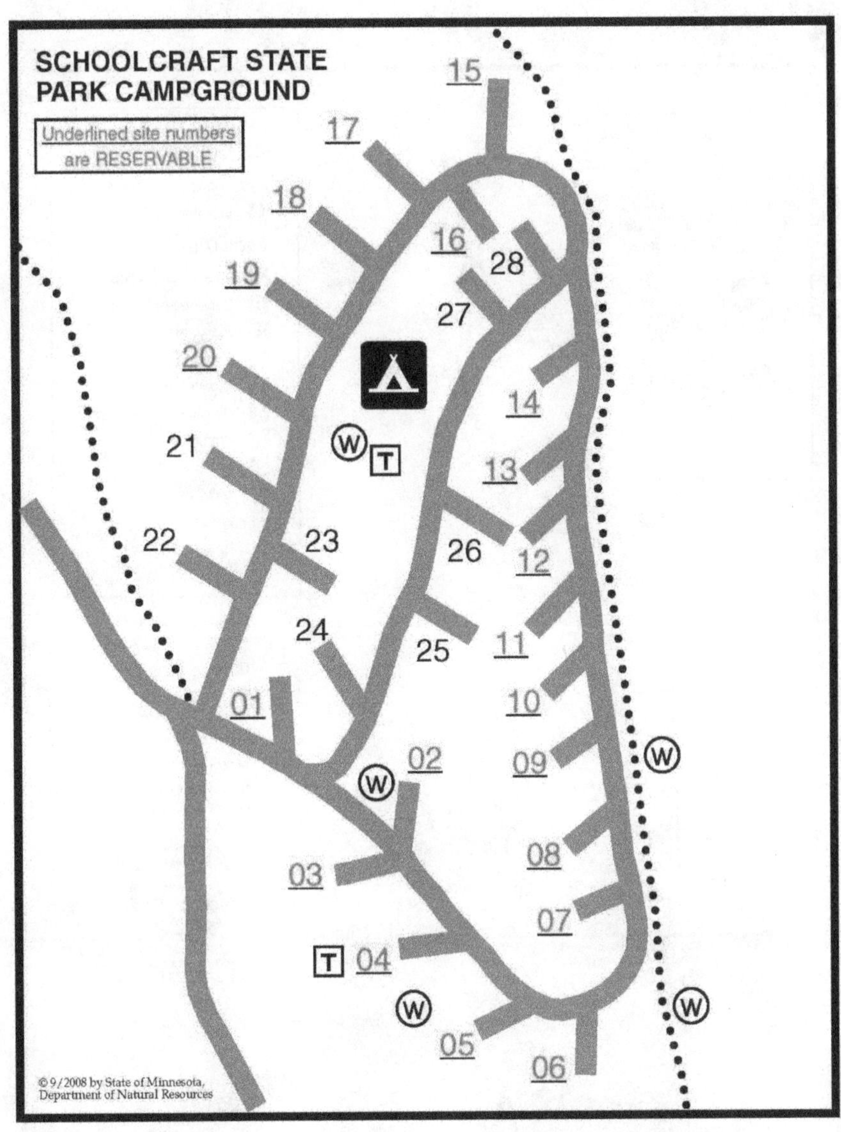
SCHOOLCRAFT STATE
PARK CAMPGROUND
Underlined site numbers
are RESERVABLE
15
17
18
16
28
19
27
20
14
21
13
22
23
26
12
24
25
11
01
10
02
09
03
08
07
04
05
06
© 9/2008 by State of Minnesota,
Department of Natural Resources

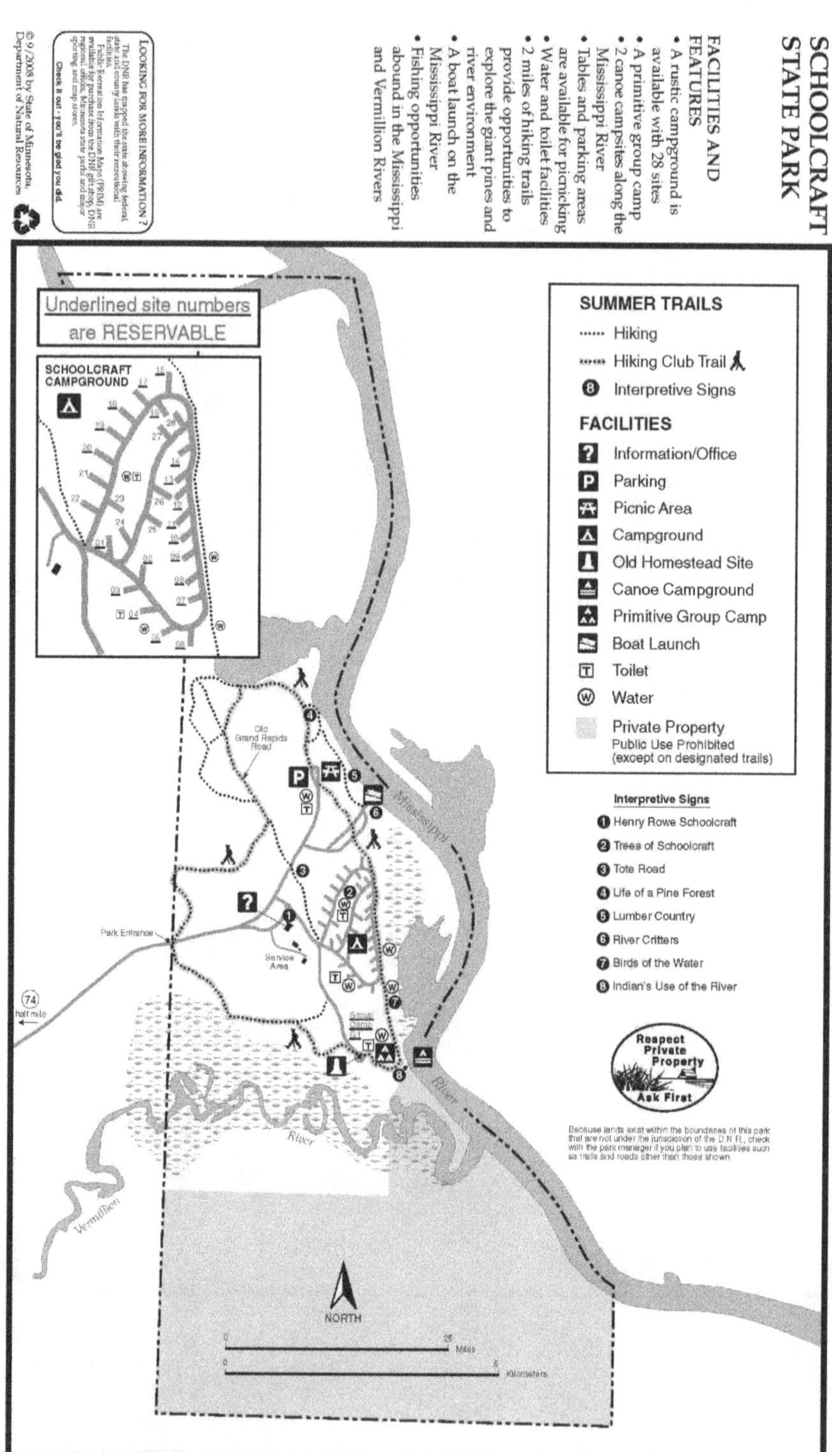
SCHOOLCRAFT STATE PARK
FACILITIES AND FEATURES
• A rustic campground is available with 28 sites
• A primitive group camp
• 2 canoe campsites along the Mississippi River
• Tables and parking areas are available for picnicking
• Water and toilet facilities
• 2 miles of hiking trails provide opportunities to explore the giant pines and river environment
• A boat launch on the Mississippi River
• Fishing opportunities abound in the Mississippi and Vermillion Rivers
LOOKING FOR MORE INFORMATION ?
The DNR has mapped the state showing federal, state and county lands with their recreational facilities.
Public Recreation Information Maps (PRIM) are available for purchase from the DNR gift shop, DNR regional offices, Minnesota state parks and major sporting and map stores.
Check it out - you'll be glad you did.
© 9/2008 by State of Minnesota, Department of Natural Resources
Underlined site numbers are RESERVABLE
SCHOOLCRAFT CAMPGROUND
SUMMER TRAILS
Hiking
Hiking Club Trail
Interpretive Signs
FACILITIES
Information/Office
Parking
Picnic Area
Campground
Old Homestead Site
Canoe Campground
Primitive Group Camp
Boat Launch
Toilet
Water
Private Property
Public Use Prohibited (except on designated trails)
Interpretive Signs
1 Henry Rowe Schoolcraft
2 Trees of Schoolcraft
3 Tote Road
4 Life of a Pine Forest
5 Lumber Country
6 River Critters
7 Birds of the Water
8 Indian's Use of the River
Respect Private Property Ask First
Because lands exist within the boundaries of this park that are not under the jurisdiction of the D.N.R., check with the park manager if you plan to use facilities such as trails and roads other than those shown.
Old Grand Rapids Road
Mississippi
River
Park Entrance
Service Area
Group Camp
Vermillion
River
74
half mile
NORTH
Miles
Kilometers

Sibley

800 Sibley Park Road NE
New London, Minnesota 56273
320-354-2055

- About 5 miles from new London, MN. This is a very large park with all of the amenities on the same level as Itasca State Park. This park was built in 1919, by the Veterans Conservation Corps. This park is also on the Glacial Ridges Scenic Route.

- Miles and miles of trails for hiking, biking, horseback, cross country ski, and snowmobile. There is a horse camp specifically for those who bring their horses, 9 camp sites available in that area.

- A gift shop is located on site. Flush toilets and showers, boat ramps, docks, swimming area, fish cleaning stations, and an interpretive center with activities every weekend are just a few of the things to see and do at this state park.

- 132 total sites with 53 that are electric. Lakeview Campgrounds is a very open camp and there is little underbrush. Many of the sites are right next to each other. There is very undergrowth between the campsites – so, little seclusion. Has great bathroom and shower facility. This campground is very amenable to the family, family groups and family activities.

- The best sites for seclusion in the Lakeview Camp are sites - # 55, 65, 66, 73, and 74.

- Oakridge Campground is situated around an open field area and then up onto a wooded ridge. There are Oak and Basswoods for tree species in the park, but up on the ridge there are more cedar trees. Some small trailers can be parked up on the ridge. Site # 80 is a good site. Also, sites - #87, 88, 89, and 90. Sites 99 thru 132 are in the lower area of Oakridge campground - more open, field like conditions.

- This park even has a baseball field set up by one of the boat landings.

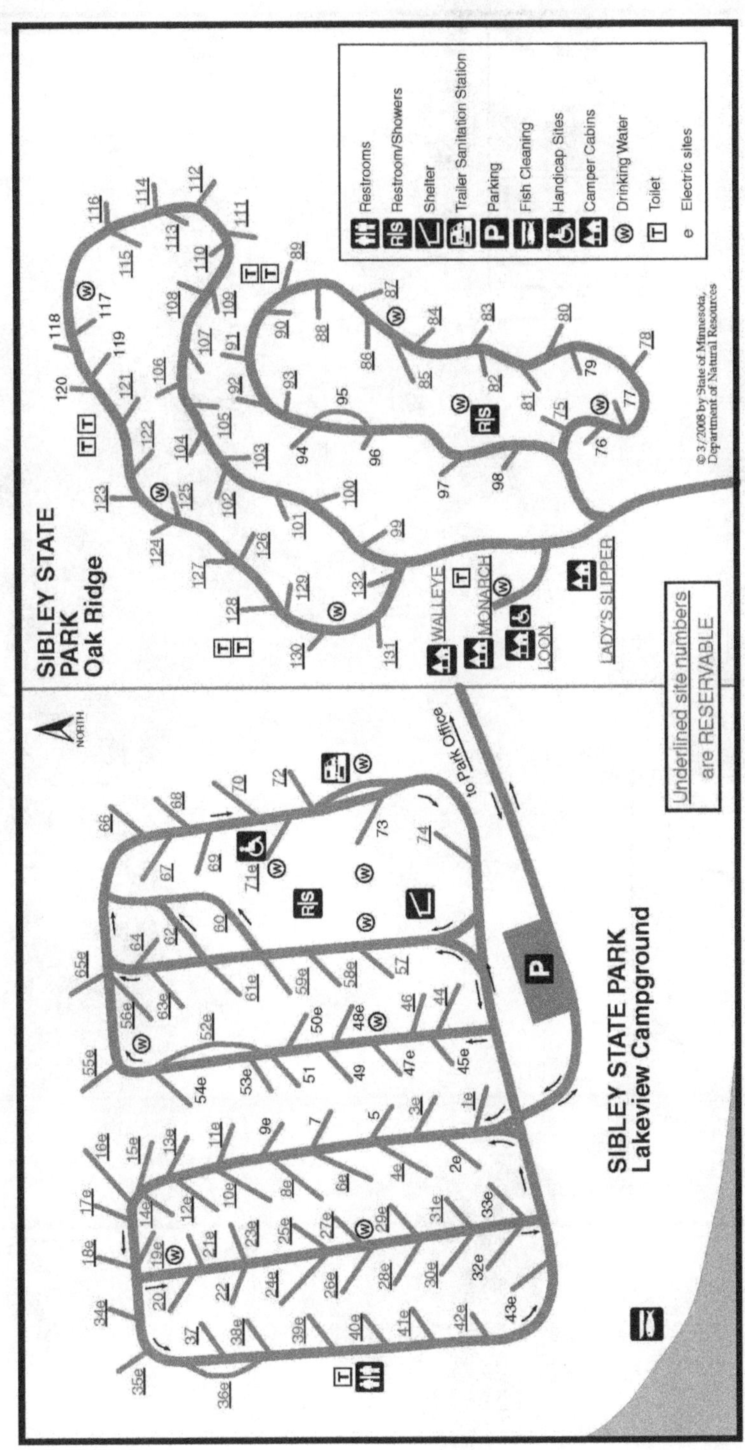
SIBLEY STATE PARK
Oak Ridge
SIBLEY STATE PARK
Lakeview Campground
NORTH
to Park Office
WALLEYE
MONARCH
LOON
LADY'S SLIPPER
Underlined site numbers are RESERVABLE
Restrooms
Restroom/Showers
Shelter
Trailer Sanitation Station
Parking
Fish Cleaning
Handicap Sites
Camper Cabins
Drinking Water
Toilet
Electric sites
© 3/2008 by State of Minnesota, Department of Natural Resources

SIBLEY STATE PARK

FACILITIES AND FEATURES

- 132 semi-modern campsites (53 with electricity)
- 4 Camper cabins
- Dump station, flush toilets and showers
- Modern group center (capacity 128)–reservations required
- 3 primitive group camp sites (capacity 20, 30, 50 each)
- Horseback riders camp (9 campsites)
- Picnic area with 70 tables and an open shelter (capacity 100)
- Swimming beach
- Camping reservations
- Lake fishing
- Boat and canoe rentals and water access
- Interpretive center
- Gift Shop
- 18 miles of hiking trail
- 8.7 miles of horseback riding trail
- 5 miles bicycle trail
- 8.0 miles of cross-country ski trail
- 6.1 miles snowmobile trail
- 2.5 miles of skate-ski trail

LOOKING FOR MORE INFORMATION?

The DNR has mapped the state showing federal, state and county lands with their recreational facilities.

Public Recreation Information Maps (PRIM) are available for purchase from the DNR gift shop, DNR regional offices, Minnesota state parks and major sporting and map stores.

Check it out - you'll be glad you did.

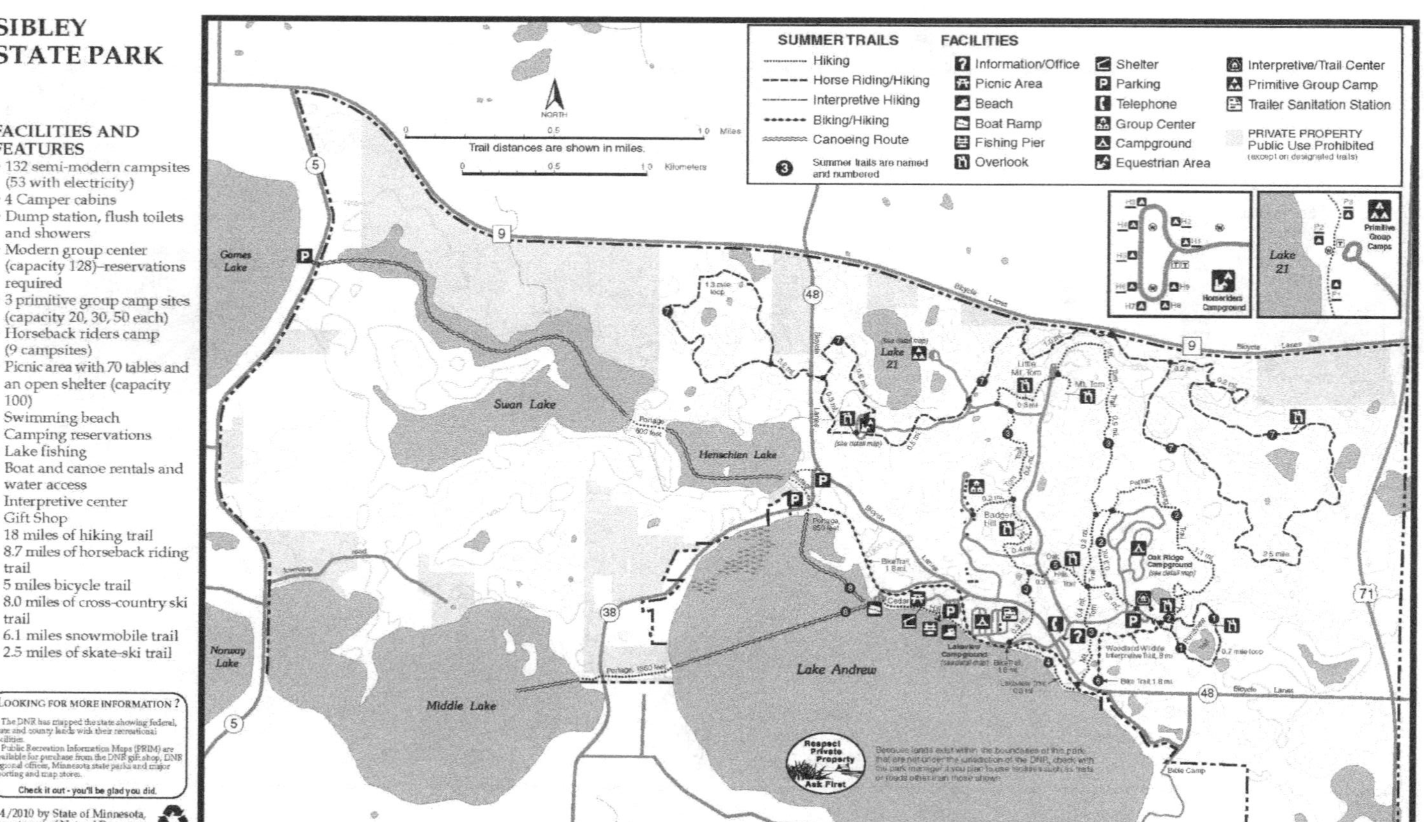

Soudan Underground Mine

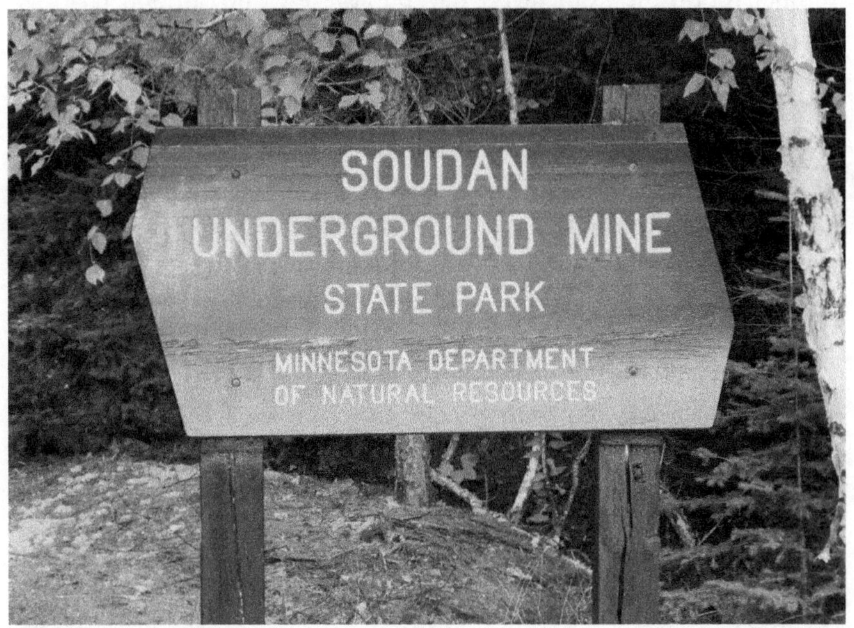

P.O. Box 335
Soudan, Minnesota 55782
218-753-2245

- This state park is located in the town of Soudan, MN. Take Hwy. 169 north, as if on the way to the Boundary Waters Canoe Area, drive to the towns of Tower and Soudan. The state park is located at the top of the hill above the town of Soudan. Both of these small towns are located on the south end of Lake Vermillion.

- The park is there to allow visitors to enjoy the remains of the very unique mining operation that existed there until the 1960's. There are tours that are available for visitors to go on down into the mine.

An interpretive center on top of the hill near the shaft opening, the wheel house, picnic areas, and five miles of hiking trails that visitors can use to see many of the other open pits and sites to see at the park.

- This is a 'day park', much like Fort Snelling and Grand Portage, it is open for business during the day; but, there are no camping facilities at the mine site.

- The hiking trails are all over on the hill on which the mine sits; so, be aware that some of the trails can be challenging to amateur hikers.

- The geology of the area, the mine and its history and this region of the state are all important parts of what helped create the state of Minnesota and this park would be a wonderful learning experience to all members of the family.

- There is a group of primitive campsites that are accessible from the waters of Lake Vermillion. The rules regarding the use of these campsites with regard to Soudan State Park can be picked up at the park headquarters building.

(Looking up the hill toward the Soudan Mine site.)

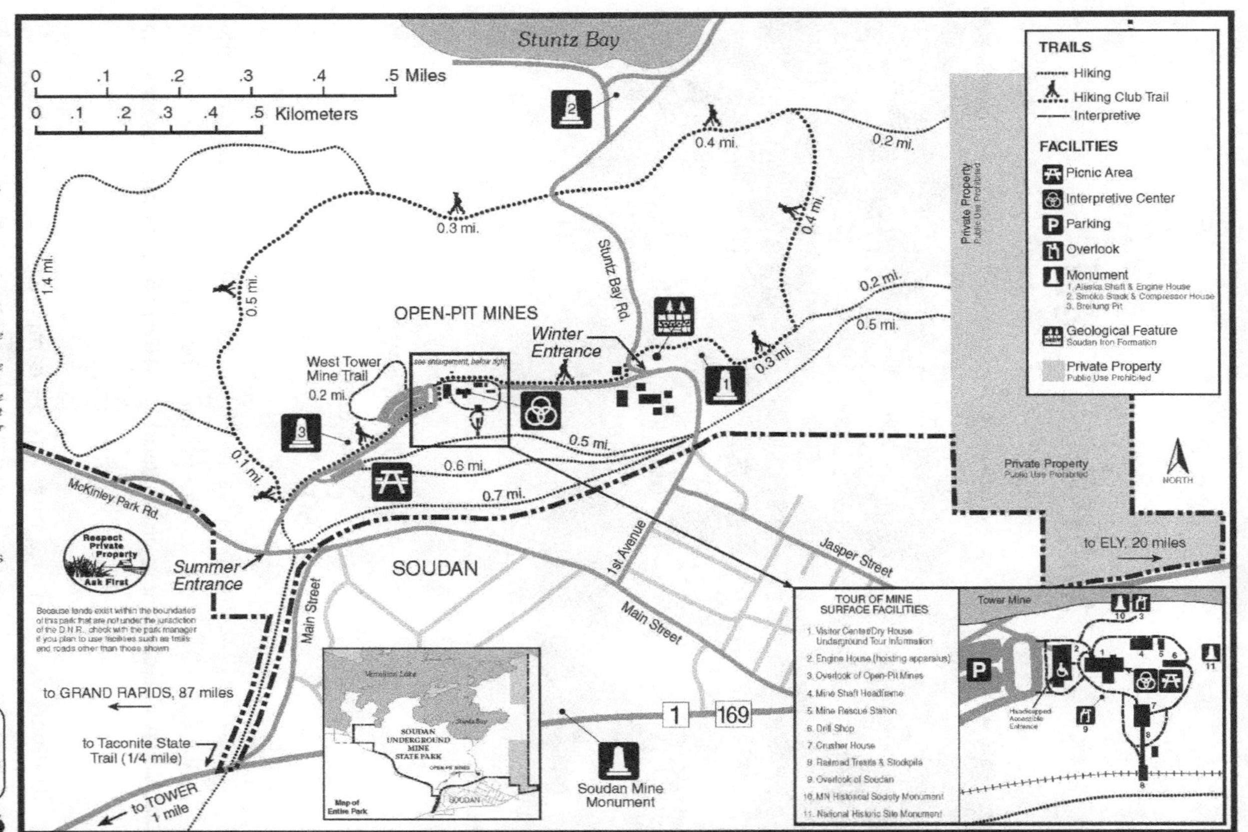

SOUDAN UNDERGROUND MINE STATE PARK

The Soudan Mine is designated a National Historic Landmark due to its significance in American history.

VISITOR FAVORITES

- Underground mine tour
- Interpretive center
- High energy physics lab

Since the early 1980s, scientists have conducted high energy experiments at the bottom of the Soudan Mine. The depth of the mine shields the experiments from cosmic rays found on the earth's surface. Information on current experiments is available in the Visitor Center.

FACILITIES AND FEATURES

- Picnic area
- Interpretive trail
- Five miles of hiking trails among open-pit mines

LOOKING FOR MORE INFORMATION?

The DNR has mapped the state showing federal, state and county lands with their recreational facilities.

Public Recreation Information Maps (PRIM) are available for purchase from the DNR gift shop, DNR regional offices, Minnesota state parks and major sporting and map stores.

Check it out - you'll be glad you did.

Split Rock Creek

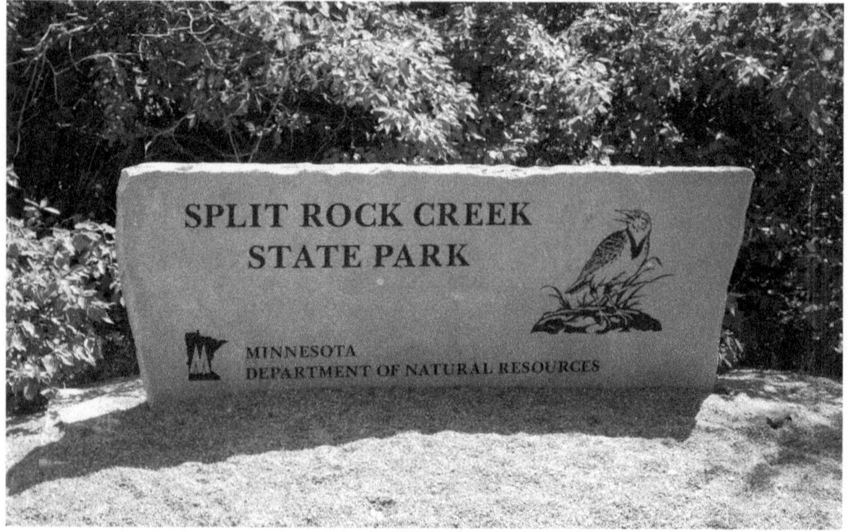

336 50th Avenue
Jasper, Minnesota 56144
507-348-7908

- The park is located 6 miles south of the city of Pipestone on MN. Hwy. 23. This park is very popular because it is the only sizeable lake in the county so it is used by many residents and visitors year round.

- The park is small and only has 34 campsites total. Twenty of the sites have electrical hook-up available. There is a small loop near the main camp area that is set up to handle tents only. All the campsites are close to the lake.

- There are fresh water spigots, vault toilets and a nice flush toilet/ shower building that is located in the center of the camping area.

- There is a couple of miles of hiking trails, picnic area, boat landing, swimming beach, fishing pier, fish cleaning shack, interpretive center, and a small piece of ground that is preserved as natural prairie. This parcel, 10 acres in size, is a 'virgin' piece of prairie. No plow has ever turned the soil on this small plot and the DNR and the university system comes to the plot to retrieve species of native prairie plants to re-plant in other areas of the state.

- Camp area has some under growth beneath large cottonwoods, oaks, and maples. The sites are spaced nicely apart. We liked sites # 3, 4, 9, 14, 22, and 24. But, I would venture to say that all of the sites here at this park are exceptional and would allow a great camping experience whether you were in a tent or a trailer.

(Prairie Dinosaur)

Note: This park *may* have RESERVABLE sites other than in the main campground.
See the main park map for the locations of any additional camping or lodging sites.

Hiking
Parking
Restrooms/Showers
Walk-in Campsites
Electrical Sites
Water
Toilets

Underlined site numbers are RESERVABLE

to Group Camp
to Office
Campground Host
NORTH

Split Rock Lake

SPLIT ROCK CREEK
STATE PARKCAMPGROUND

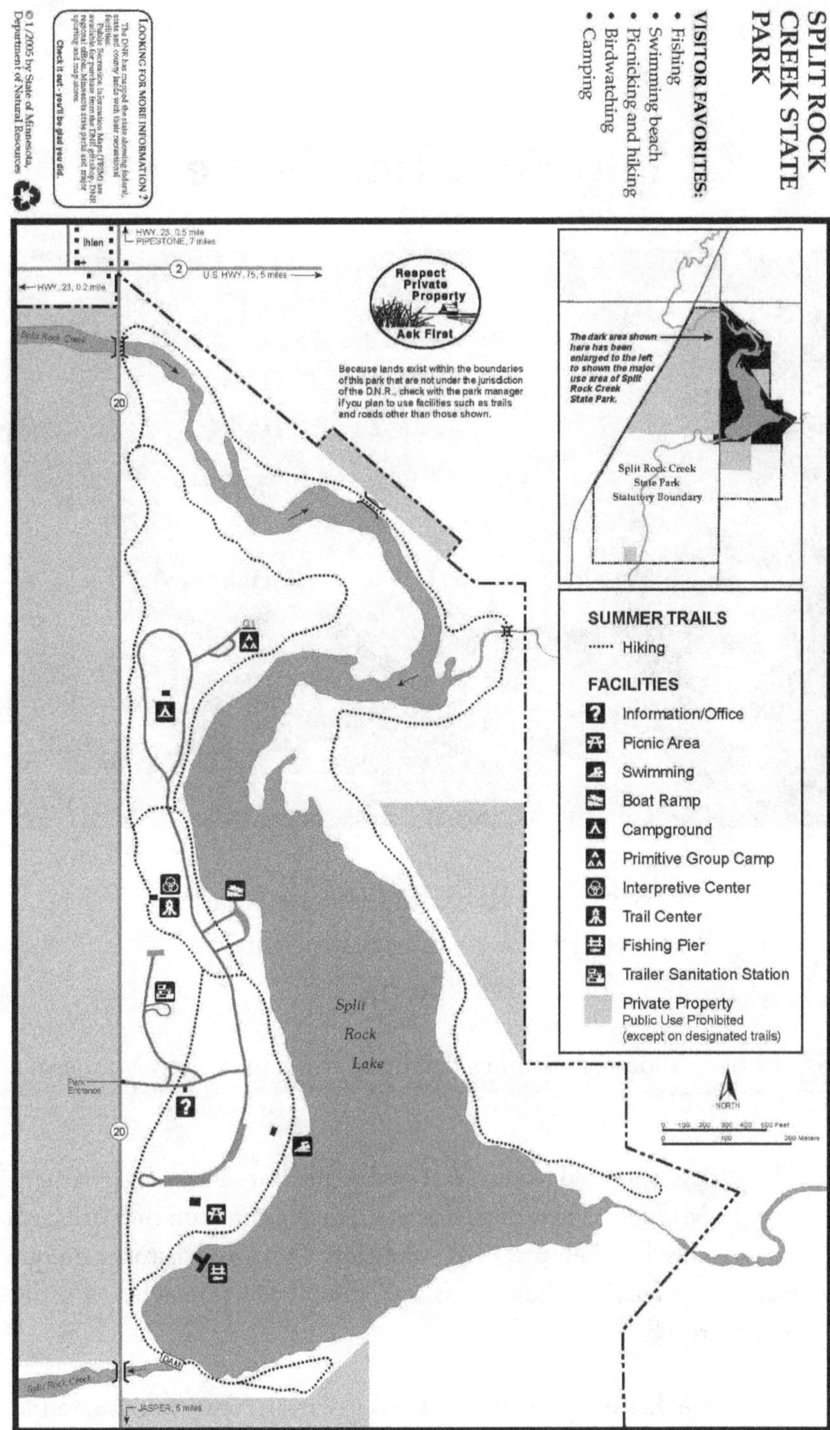
SPLIT ROCK CREEK STATE PARK
VISITOR FAVORITES:
• Fishing
• Swimming beach
• Picnicking and hiking
• Birdwatching
• Camping
LOOKING FOR MORE INFORMATION?
Check it out - you'll be glad you did.
© 1/2005 by State of Minnesota, Department of Natural Resources
Ihlen
HWY. 23, 0.5 mile
PIPESTONE, 7 miles
U.S. HWY. 75, 5 miles
HWY. 23, 0.2 mile
Respect Private Property Ask First
Because lands exist within the boundaries of this park that are not under the jurisdiction of the D.N.R., check with the park manager if you plan to use facilities such as trails and roads other than those shown.
The dark area shown here has been enlarged to the left to shown the major use area of Split Rock Creek State Park.
Split Rock Creek State Park Statutory Boundary
Split Rock Creek
SUMMER TRAILS
Hiking
FACILITIES
Information/Office
Picnic Area
Swimming
Boat Ramp
Campground
Primitive Group Camp
Interpretive Center
Trail Center
Fishing Pier
Trailer Sanitation Station
Private Property
Public Use Prohibited
(except on designated trails)
Split Rock Lake
Park Entrance
NORTH
DAM
JASPER, 6 miles

Split Rock Lighthouse

3755 Split Rock Lighthouse Road
Two Harbors, Minnesota 55616
218-226-6377

- The park is located 20 miles northeast of Thunder Bay, Minnesota, on Hwy. 61.

- The park is operated in cooperation by the State Parks Department and the Minnesota historical Society. The buildings on the park have been restored to their pre-1924 condition. This gives visitors a unique view of the facility when it was operational at a time when it could only be reached by boat.

- There are historical facts and information that can be found throughout the park concerning its being built in 1909 and its years of operation afterward. The Historical Center on site offers much information to visitors.

- There is a camping area available to visitors of the park but it is a cart-in/hike-in type camping area. Nineteen sites are available there. There are vault toilets and water spigots available. Near the parking area, there is a toilet/shower facility.

- There are over thirteen miles of trail in the park that will take a hiker over the diverse topography of the park and around to the 3 or 4 rivers and creeks that flow through parts of the park. Many of these trails are multi-use trails. There are many camping sites located along the trails, too. There is a canoe launch site on the lake shore and several campsites that can be reached by kayak and/or canoe.

- A long portion of the Gitchi-Gami State Trail runs through the park. There is a nice picnic area available for use in the park.

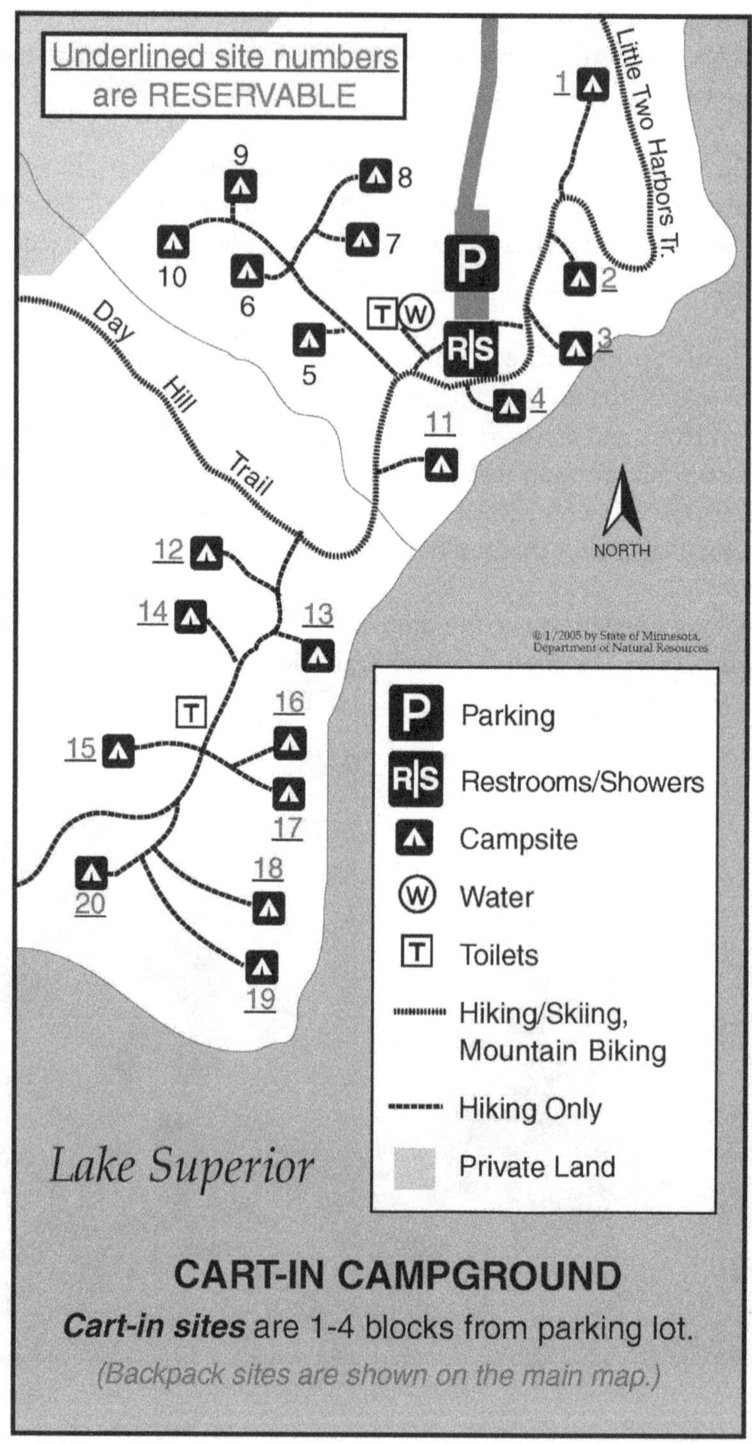
Underlined site numbers
are RESERVABLE
Little Two Harbors Tr.
Day Hill Trail
1
2
3
4
5
6
7
8
9
10
11
12
13
14
15
16
17
18
19
20
NORTH
© 1/2005 by State of Minnesota, Department of Natural Resources
Parking
Restrooms/Showers
Campsite
Water
Toilets
Hiking/Skiing, Mountain Biking
Hiking Only
Private Land
Lake Superior
CART-IN CAMPGROUND
Cart-in sites are 1-4 blocks from parking lot.
(Backpack sites are shown on the main map.)

SPLIT ROCK LIGHTHOUSE STATE PARK

VISITOR FAVORITES

- Touring the historic Split Rock Lighthouse & Visitor Center.
- Skipping stones at Pebble Beach and the mouth of the Split Rock River.
- Walking the trails along the steep cliffs of Lake Superior.
- Split Rock Lighthouse State Park offers hiking trails, cross-country ski trails, stream and lake fishing, picnicking, camping and kayak access to Lake Superior.
- Split Rock River waterfalls along the Superior Hiking Trail.
- The Gitchi-Gami State Trail is under construction on the North Shore. The longest completed segment (13.2 miles) passes through Split Rock Lighthouse State Park.

LOOKING FOR MORE INFORMATION?

The DNR has mapped the state showing federal, state and county lands with their recreational facilities.
Public Recreation Information Maps (PRIM) are available for purchase from the DNR gift shop, DNR regional offices, Minnesota state parks and major sporting and map stores.

Check it out - you'll be glad you did.

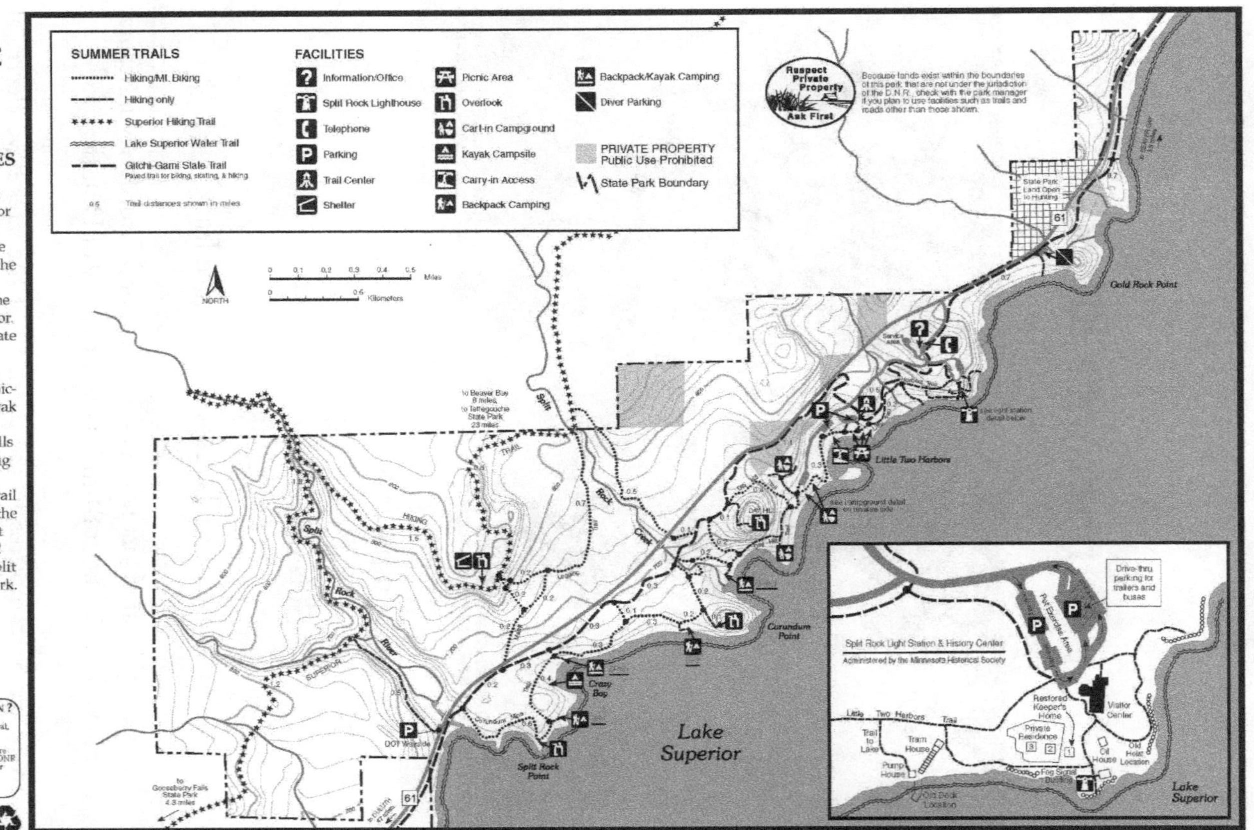

Temperance River

Temperance River State Park
5702 Highway 61
Silver Bay, Minnesota 55614
218-663-7476
(contact c/o Tettegouche State Park)

- This park is located just north of the town of Schroeder, Minnesota, on Hwy. 61. It is about 81 miles from the city of Duluth.

- There are 55 campsites in the park. 18 of the sites have electrical hook-up. The park is set up on either side of the Temperance River. The north side campground has 39 sites and the electric sites are located on this side of the river. The other campground, on the south side of the river doesn't have any electric sites but the camp is set nearer the lake shore and some of the camp sites are within a stone's throw of the water.

- Besides the big bridge that crosses the river at the highway, there is also a smaller foot bridge that crosses the river between the two camps.

- There are three remote cart-in sites off the trails on the south side of the park. There is access to the Superior Hiking Trail besides the 8 miles of hiking and snowmobile trail and 12 miles of cross country ski trail.

- There is a toilet shower facility on site at the north camp and there are vault toilets and water spigots throughout the park. Extra parking areas are available in the park and here is a boat launch on the south end of the park and a picnic area by the shore near the south campground.

- There are four different water falls in the park – two on the Temperance and two on the Cross River. There are scenic overlook sites on the trails and the beautiful, rocky north shore of Lake Superior to enjoy.

- Sportsmen can attempt to fish the rivers for trout or steelhead.

- We liked Sites # 4, 7, 17, 18, 22, 26, 28, 44, 45, 53, and 54.

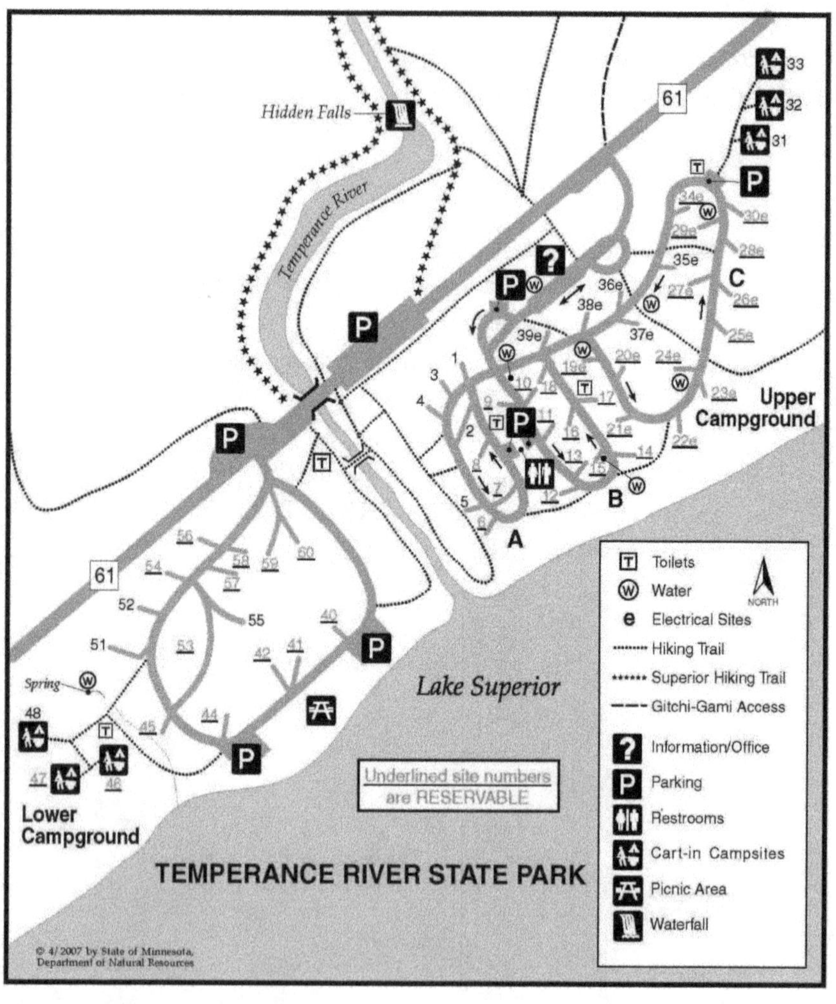
Hidden Falls
Temperance River
61
Lower Campground
Upper Campground
Lake Superior
Spring
Underlined site numbers are RESERVABLE
TEMPERANCE RIVER STATE PARK
Toilets
Water
Electrical Sites
Hiking Trail
Superior Hiking Trail
Gitchi-Gami Access
Information/Office
Parking
Restrooms
Cart-in Campsites
Picnic Area
Waterfall
NORTH
© 4/2007 by State of Minnesota, Department of Natural Resources

TEMPERANCE RIVER STATE PARK

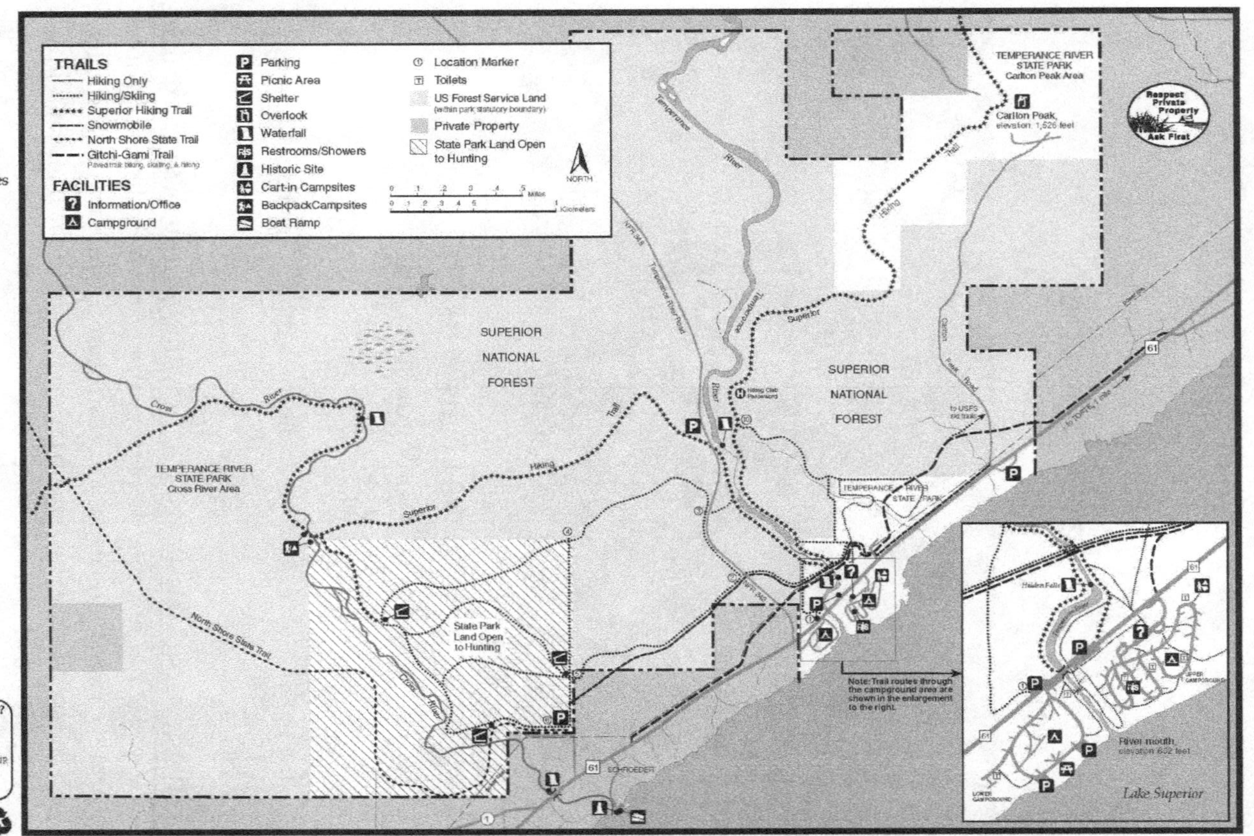

FACILITIES AND FEATURES

- 55 semi-modern campsites (18 with electricity)
- 3 cart-in camping sites
- Modern sanitation building
- Picnic grounds
- 8 miles of hiking trails
- 12 miles of ski trails
- 8 miles of snowmobile trails

VISITOR FAVORITES

- Hiking the river gorge trails
- Fishing for trout and steelhead
- Camping along Lake Superior
- Scenic sites
- Picnic grounds on Lake Superior shore
- Major trail head to the Superior Hiking Trail

LOOKING FOR MORE INFORMATION ?

The DNR has mapped the state showing federal, state and county lands with their recreational facilities.

Public Recreation Information Maps (PRIM) are available for purchase from the DNR gift shop, DNR regional offices, Minnesota state parks and major sporting and map stores.

Check it out - you'll be glad you did.

Tettegouche

5702 Highway 61
Silver Bay, Minnesota 55614
218-226-6365

- This park is located 4.5 miles northeast of Silver Bay, Minnesota, on Hwy. 61.

- This state park has almost too many things to do and partake in to be enjoyed in just one short stay. There are two different camping areas – a small 13 site cart-in rustic camp area down near the lake and a second camping area up on the hill above the highway with 34 campsites (6 of these sites are walk-in).

- Within the park, there are 6 lakes, the Baptism River, Palisade Creek, 4 waterfalls to include the tallest waterfall in Minnesota, many miles of trails for hiking, cross country skiing, and snowmobiling. There are several major hiking trails, cross country ski trails and snowmobile trail that run through the park – the Sawtooth Trail, the Lake Superior Trail and the Red Dot Trail.

- The trails by the Wayside and near the visitor's center allow beautiful views of Palisade Head which is just 1 mile down the shoreline.

- There are remote campsites down by the shore where the Baptism River empties into Lake Superior. These sites can be reached by canoe and are very rustic.

- There are many observation spots along all the trails, there are protected shelters along the trails and in the picnic areas and these trails range from easy to difficult.

- The camping areas have many trees and give good shade and seclusion. There are vault toilets and water spigots throughout the park in the camping areas. The Camp area on the hill above the highway has a toilet/shower building. Four camper cabins are also available in the park.

- The sites which we liked were - # 4, 10, 14, 20, 22, and 31. All the sites are nice and level and have good gravel pads to park a trailer on.

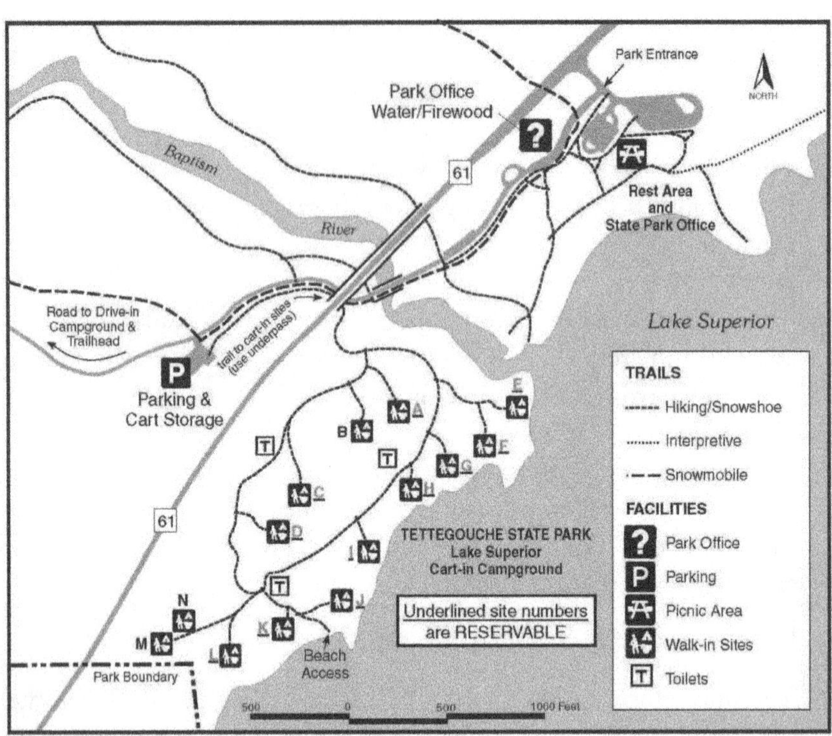

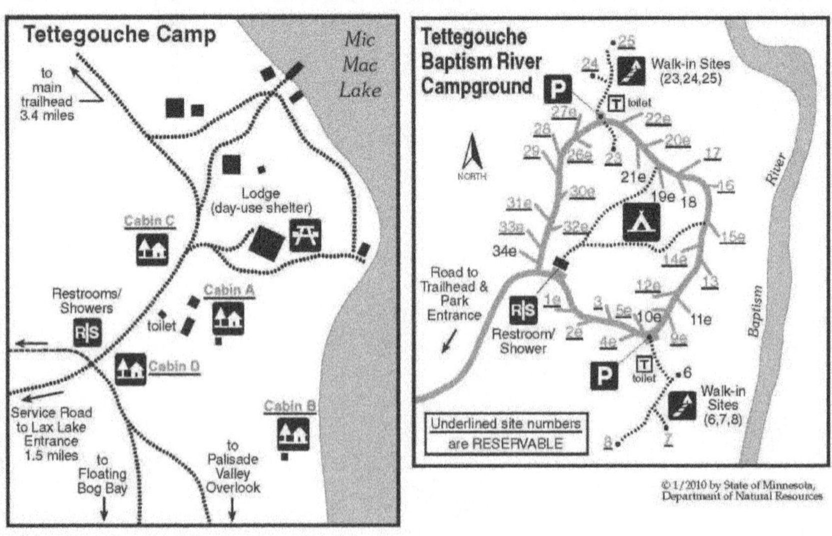

© 1/2010 by State of Minnesota,
Department of Natural Resources

TETTEGOUCHE STATE PARK

FACILITIES AND FEATURES

- 23 miles of hiking trails with numerous scenic overlooks, including a self-guided interpretive trail to Shovel Point
- 34 semi-modern campsites (flush toilets and showers)
- 13 cart-in campsites
- Five picnic areas—Baptism River, Nipisquit Lake, Bean Lake, Tettegouche Camp and Trailhead
- Class I Wayside Rest Area at Baptism River
- Trout and salmon fishing in both the Baptism River and Lake Superior
- Northern pike and walleye fishing in four inland lakes (access by foot trail only)
- Four waterfalls on the Baptism River, including Minnesota's highest waterfall
- 12 miles of designated ski trails

The park's main winter attractions are skiing, snowshoeing, hiking, camping and snowmobiling.

Snowmobiles may unload in the wayside rest parking lots. Trails from there allow the snowmobilers to go to Finland, Silver Bay and the North Shore State Trail.

LOOKING FOR MORE INFORMATION?

The DNR has mapped the state showing federal, state and county lands with their recreational facilities.

Public Recreation Information Maps (PRIM) are available for purchase from the DNR gift shop, DNR regional offices, Minnesota state parks and major sporting and map stores.

Check it out - you'll be glad you did.

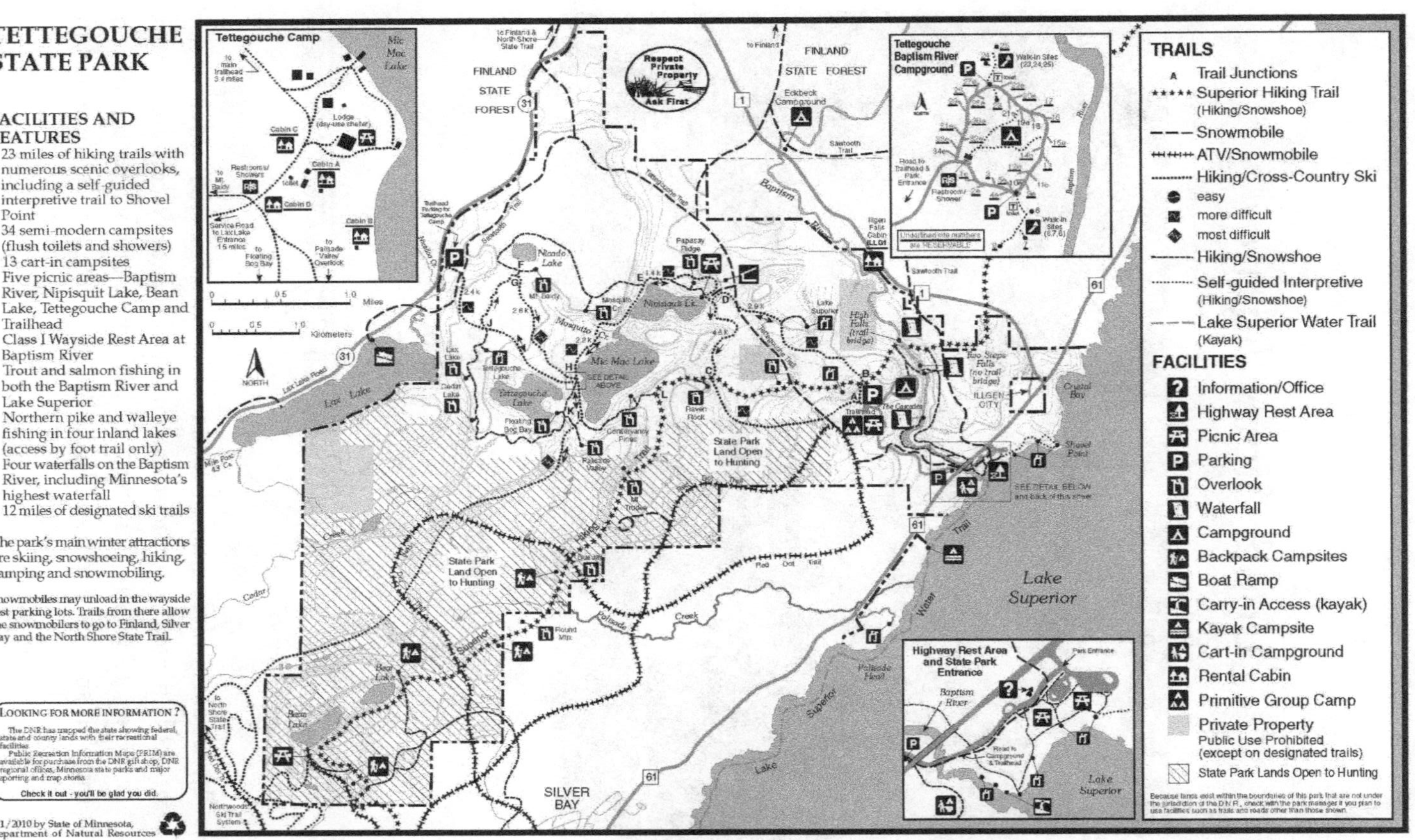

Upper Sioux Agency

5908 Highway 67
Granite Falls, Minnesota 56241
320-564-4777

- Park is located about 8 miles southeast of Granite Falls, Minnesota on State Hwy. 67.

- This is a very nice park with loads of history associated with it. It can be easily passed by without knowing it. There are picnic areas, boat launches, 19 miles of hiking trails, 16 miles of horseback trail and miles of snowmobile trail. Two different camping areas are within the park.

- The first Campground is the Yellow medicine River Camp. It has 31 sites that are nicely shaded and separated from each other, 14 of the sites with electric hook-up. Two sites have a permanent Tipi set up to use. There is a restroom/shower facility, vault toilets, water spigots and parking areas available. This camp is accessed by a road that is about ¾ of a mile further east on Hwy. 67 from the park office.

- The second campground is the Riverside camp. There are six sites and they are right next to the river, the sites are small and are basically used by tents; but, a small trailer could be parked in some of the spots. One vault toilet is available at this camp.

- Both camps are at the base of a very steep hill leading to the river. The horse camp area is about ½ mile west on Hwy. 67 from the main office.

- There is a nice interpretive center located at the main office and is devoted to the history of the native tribes and the mission of the Upper Sioux Agency.

- The park has a sledding hill set up during the winter to use. This would promise to be a very nice run on a sled due to the slope of the hill.

- Camp sites in the Yellow medicine River Camp allow for nice camping and shade on most of the spots. We liked sites # 5, 7, 14, 19, and 21. Sites #24 and 26 have a Tipi set up at them.

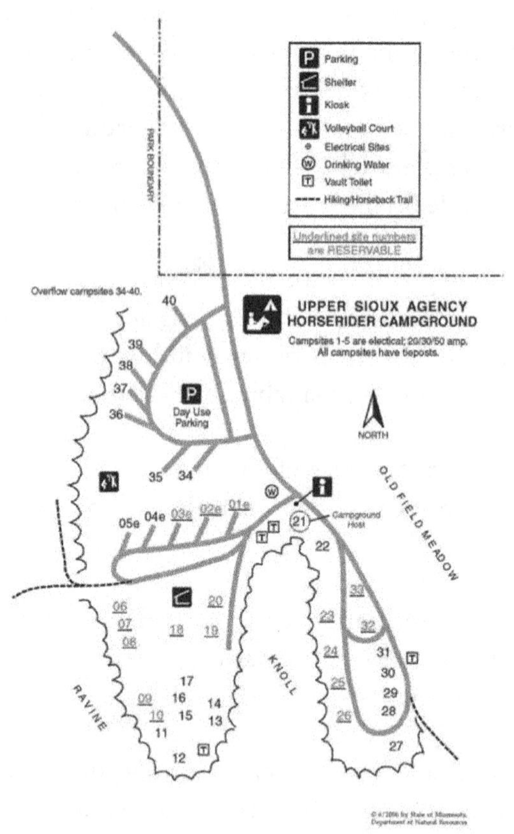
Parking
Shelter
Kiosk
Volleyball Court
Electrical Sites
Drinking Water
Vault Toilet
Hiking/Horseback Trail
Underlined site numbers are RESERVABLE
PARK BOUNDARY
Overflow campsites 34-40.
UPPER SIOUX AGENCY
HORSERIDER CAMPGROUND
Campsites 1-5 are electical; 20/30/50 amp.
All campsites have tieposts.
Day Use Parking
NORTH
OLD FIELD MEADOW
Campground Host
KNOLL
RAVINE

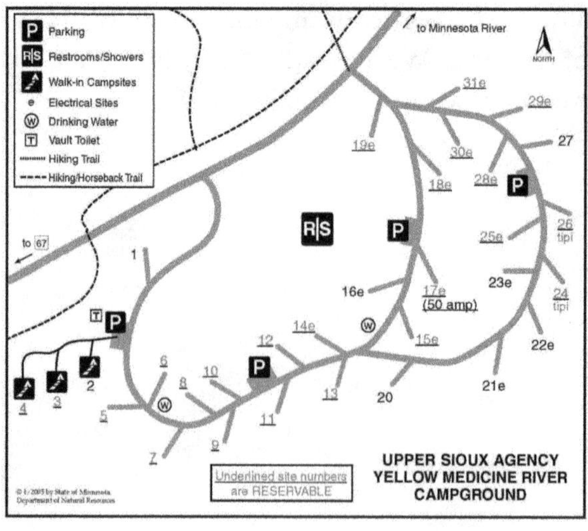
Parking
Restrooms/Showers
Walk-in Campsites
Electrical Sites
Drinking Water
Vault Toilet
Hiking Trail
Hiking/Horseback Trail
to Minnesota River
NORTH
to 67
(50 amp)
tipi
Underlined site numbers are RESERVABLE
UPPER SIOUX AGENCY
YELLOW MEDICINE RIVER
CAMPGROUND

RIVERSIDE CAMPGROUND
Watercraft Sites

UPPER SIOUX AGENCY STATE PARK

VISITOR FAVORITES
- River fishing
- Minnesota River overlook
- Interpretive center
- Historic Upper Sioux Agency site
- Winter sliding hill

FACILITIES AND FEATURES
- Public canoe access to Minnesota River
- Picnic area
- Equestrian camp
- Picnic shelter building
- Interpretive center
- Trails:
  19 miles hiking
  16 miles snowmobiling
  16 miles horseback

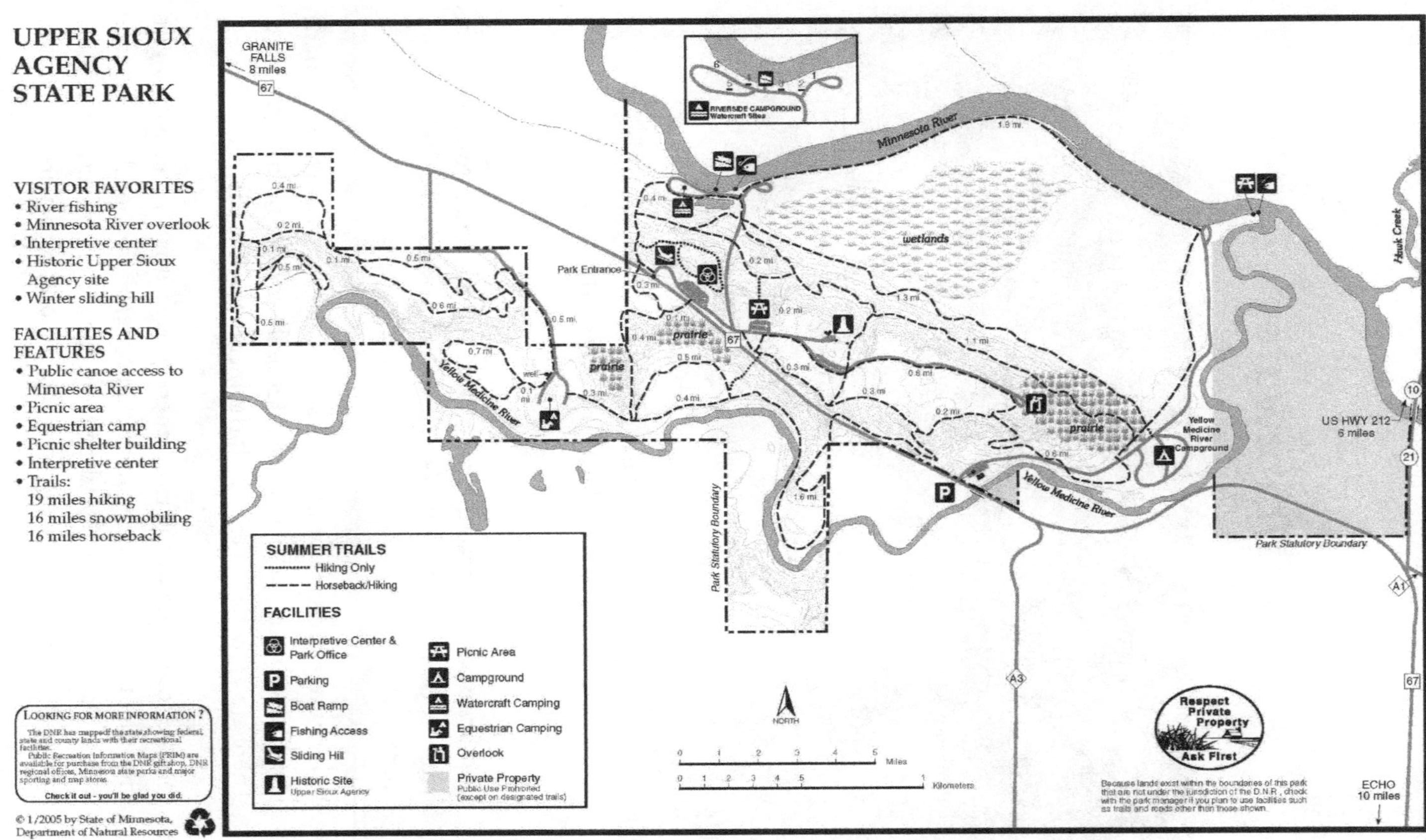

LOOKING FOR MORE INFORMATION?

The DNR has mapped the state showing federal, state and county lands with their recreational facilities.

Public Recreation Information Maps (PRIM) are available for purchase from the DNR gift shop, DNR regional offices, Minnesota state parks and major sporting and map stores.

Check it out - you'll be glad you did.

Whitewater

19041 State Highway 74
Altura, Minnesota 55910
507-932-3007

- This state park is located 3 miles south of the small town of Elba, Minnesota, on MN Hwy. 74. The park straddles the Whitewater River.

- Whitewater is every bit of a full service, family oriented state park just like so many others: Itasca, Gooseberry Falls, and St. Croix. There are activities to entice all the members of the family.

- On the south side of the river, there is a Visitor Center with a gift shop and there are two separate picnic areas. The South picnic area is at the end of the road leading from the visitor center. There is as fishing pier near this picnic area. The second picnic area is located near an old oxbow in the river. There is a swimming area near this picnic site. There is one loop of camp sites on the south side of the park; this is the Gooseberry Glen Campground.

- On the north side of the river - there is another Visitor Center with an interpretive display and an amphitheater. There are two remote group camps, several overlooks, and the larger of the two campgrounds on the north side. This campground, Cedar Hill, is divided into 4 different loops.

- There are a total of 110 campsites in the park, 47 of the sites have electric hook ups and there are 6 remote walk-in sites. There are miles and miles of trails for all sorts of use: hiking, self-guided tour, and cross-country skiing. One of the prime sites to see along the trails is 'Chimney Rock'. It can be accessed by several of the hiking trails near the river.

- Another site to see is the Elba Fire Tower which is two miles north of the Visitor Center on Hwy. 74. Many of the hiking trails in the park lead to the peaks on some of the bluffs in and around the park. From these vantage points it is easy to see much of the park and the surrounding area.

- Sites in the campgrounds we liked are as follows: 6, 9, 20, 25, 26, 44, 47, 51, 56, 61, and 63.

- All of the camp sites have been worked to give a nice, nearly level parking spot. All sites have picnic tables and fire pits. There is good over head shading from all the trees. Many of the campsites are close together and that doesn't allow for much under brush to exist to create any seclusion.

WHITEWATER STATE PARK

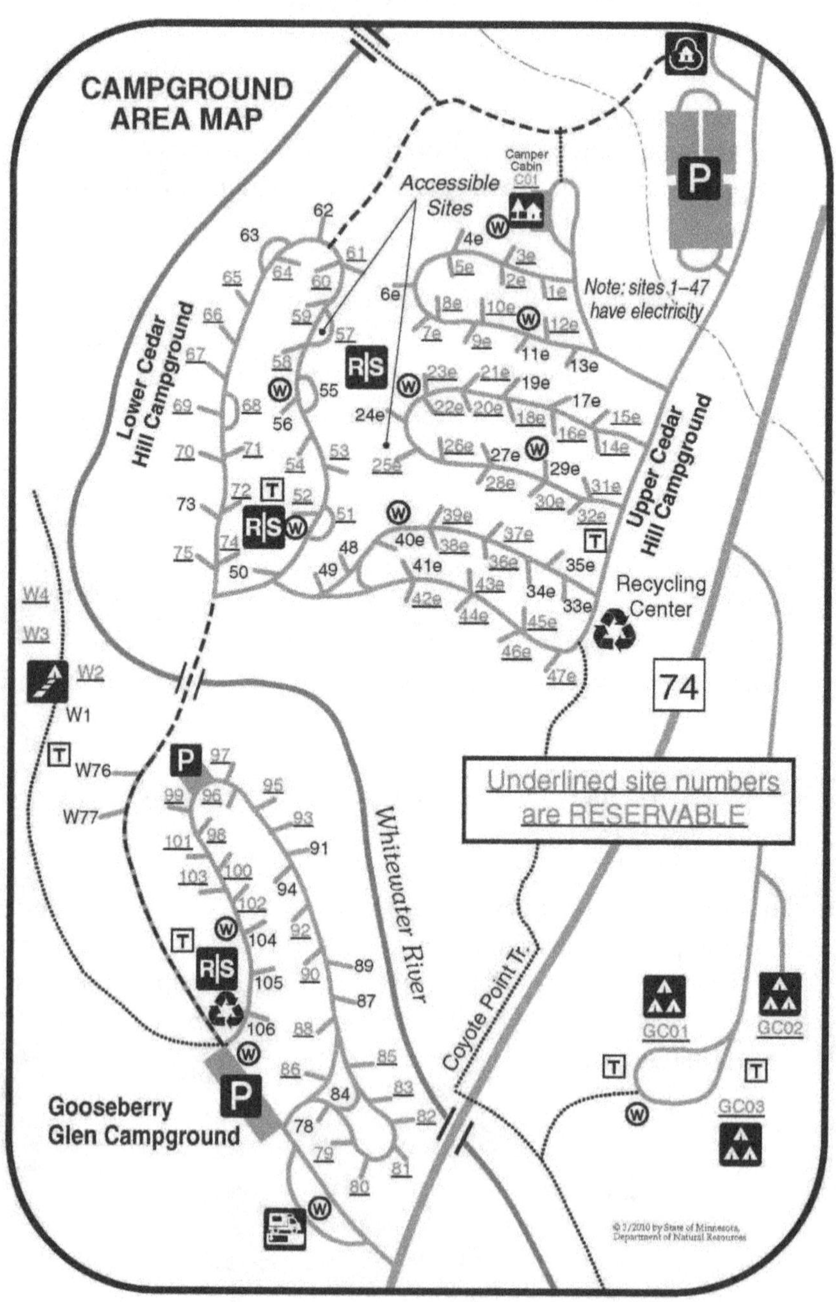

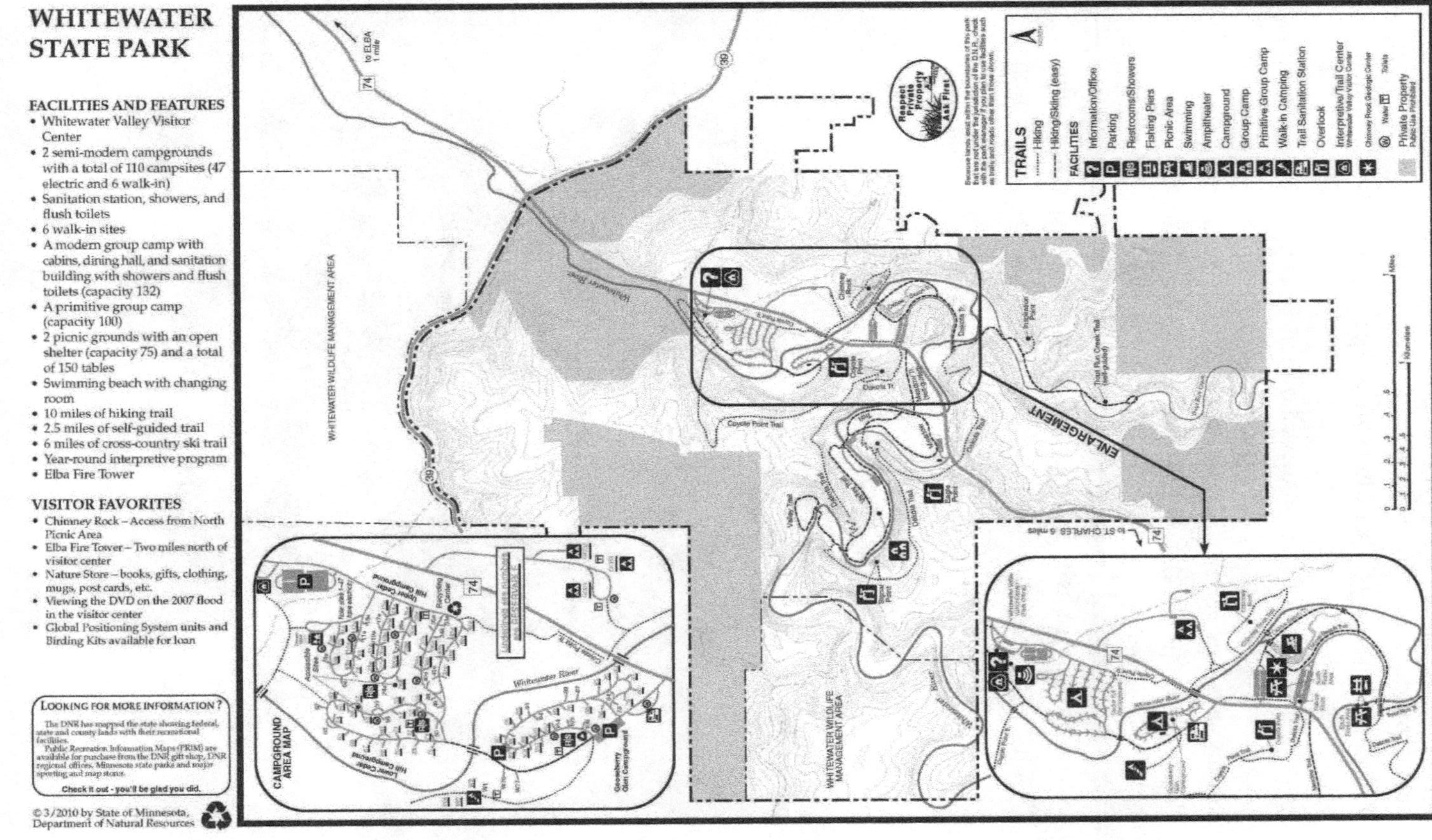
WHITEWATER STATE PARK
FACILITIES AND FEATURES
• Whitewater Valley Visitor Center
• 2 semi-modern campgrounds with a total of 110 campsites (47 electric and 6 walk-in)
• Sanitation station, showers, and flush toilets
• 6 walk-in sites
• A modern group camp with cabins, dining hall, and sanitation building with showers and flush toilets (capacity 132)
• A primitive group camp (capacity 100)
• 2 picnic grounds with an open shelter (capacity 75) and a total of 150 tables
• Swimming beach with changing room
• 10 miles of hiking trail
• 2.5 miles of self-guided trail
• 6 miles of cross-country ski trail
• Year-round interpretive program
• Elba Fire Tower
VISITOR FAVORITES
• Chimney Rock – Access from North Picnic Area
• Elba Fire Tower – Two miles north of visitor center
• Nature Store – books, gifts, clothing, mugs, post cards, etc.
• Viewing the DVD on the 2007 flood in the visitor center
• Global Positioning System units and Birding Kits available for loan
LOOKING FOR MORE INFORMATION?
The DNR has mapped the state showing federal, state and county lands with their recreational facilities.
Public Recreation Information Maps (PRIM) are available for purchase from the DNR gift shop, DNR regional offices, Minnesota state parks and major sporting and map stores.
Check it out - you'll be glad you did.
© 3/2010 by State of Minnesota, Department of Natural Resources
WHITEWATER WILDLIFE MANAGEMENT AREA
to ELBA 1 mile
74
39
Whitewater River
CAMPGROUND AREA MAP
Gooseberry Glen Campground
Recycling Center
ENLARGEMENT
to ST. CHARLES 6 miles
Coyote Point Trail
Valley Trail
Dakota Trail
Chimney Rock
Coyote Point
Signal Point
Eagle Point
Inspiration Point
Trout Run Creek Trail (self-guided)
Respect Private Property Ask First
TRAILS
Hiking
Hiking/Skiing (easy)
FACILITIES
Information/Office
Parking
Restrooms/Showers
Fishing Piers
Picnic Area
Swimming
Ampitheater
Campground
Group Camp
Primitive Group Camp
Walk-in Camping
Trail Sanitation Station
Overlook
Interpretive/Trail Center
Whitewater Valley Visitor Center
Chimney Rock Geologic Center
Water
Toilets
Private Property
Public Use Prohibited
Miles
Kilometers

Wild River

39797 Park Trail
Center City, Minnesota 55012
651-583-2125

- Taking MN Hwy. 95 to the town of Almelund, MN. Take Chisago County Hwy. 12 three miles north. The park sits along the terrace above the west bank of the St. Croix River.

- The park is a long narrow piece of property that follows along the bank of the river for 15 miles. This lovely park has all the amenities to create a great camping experience for the family. There are miles of hiking, horse back, cross country skiing, and snowmobiling trails.

- There are 96 campsites at the main camp area, 17 sites have electrical hook ups. There are camper cabins available and a guest house to rent. The park has facilities that are available and open all year around.

- There are flush toilets/showers available at the camp area. There are vault toilets, water spigots, a large amphitheater, picnic areas, boat ramps, a visitor center, shelters and remote campsites along the hiking trails, cross country skis and snow shoes are available for rent. There are canoes and kayaks available, too.

- The main campground is divided into 5 different loops. The sites are located along each loop and the sites are spaced nicely apart, there are tall trees all around with lots of undergrowth growing up between. Mixed tree species of pines and hardwoods make up the forests in the area.

- There is a large picnic area set up near a trail that leads down to Nevers Dam, a historical site along the river.

- There is a very nice camping facility set up for those people who bring their horses along to ride the trails. Like the sites in the regular campground, these sites are large with many trees to give cover and shade.

- We liked sites #A8, A10, B13, B14, B20, C2, C9, C15, D3, D8, D14, E10, E12, and E22.

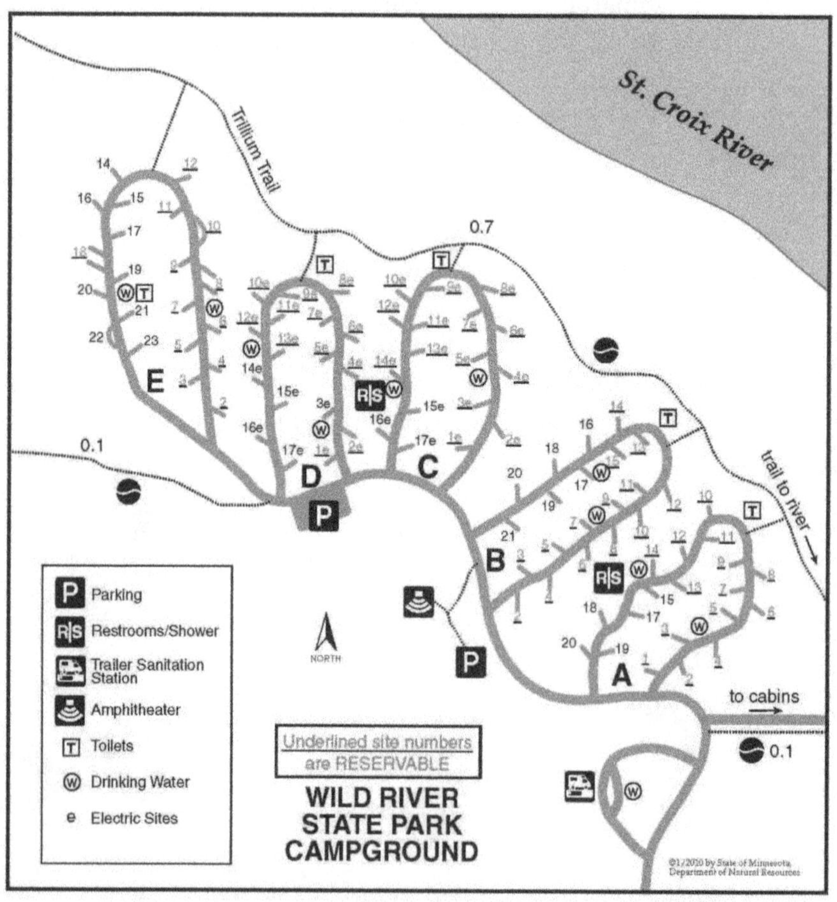

Note: This park ***may*** have RESERVABLE sites other than in the main campground. See the main park map for the locations of any additional camping or lodging sites.

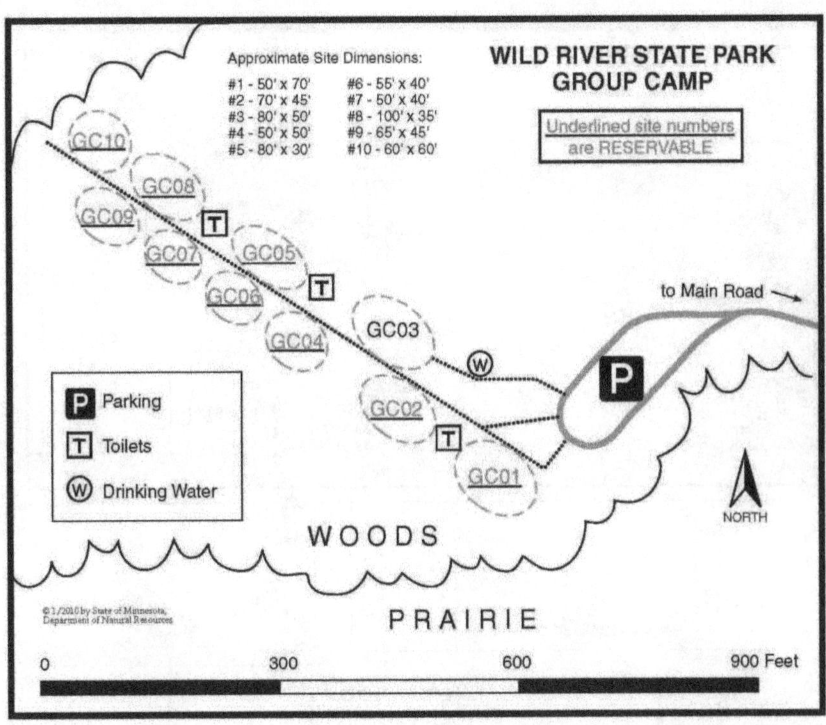
WILD RIVER STATE PARK
GROUP CAMP
Underlined site numbers are RESERVABLE
Approximate Site Dimensions:
#1 - 50' x 70'
#2 - 70' x 45'
#3 - 80' x 50'
#4 - 50' x 50'
#5 - 80' x 30'
#6 - 55' x 40'
#7 - 50' x 40'
#8 - 100' x 35'
#9 - 65' x 45'
#10 - 60' x 60'
GC10
GC08
GC09
GC07
GC05
GC06
GC04
GC03
GC02
GC01
to Main Road
Parking
Toilets
Drinking Water
NORTH
WOODS
PRAIRIE
© 1/2010 by State of Minnesota, Department of Natural Resources
0
300
600
900 Feet

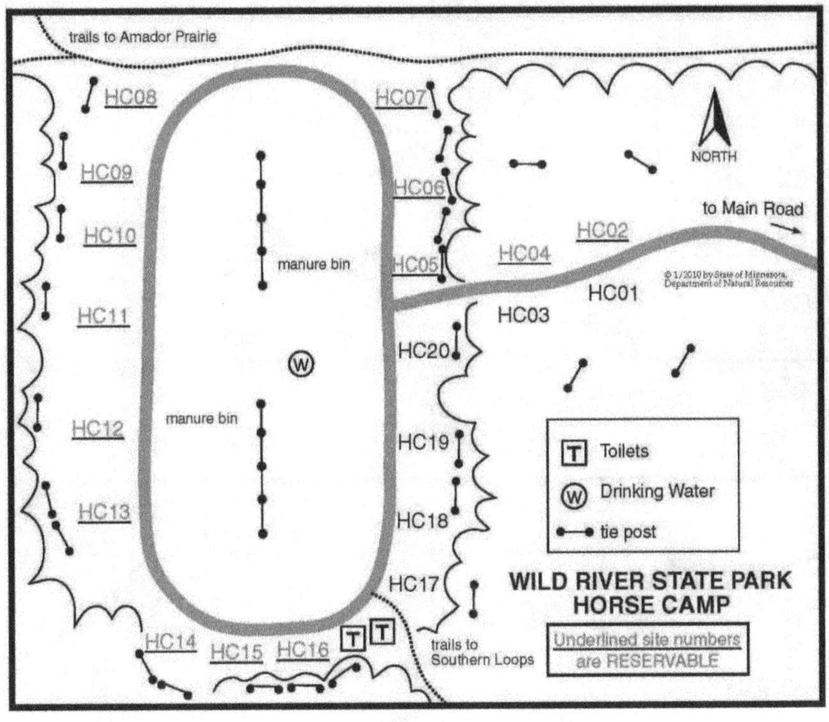
trails to Amador Prairie
HC08
HC07
HC09
HC06
HC10
HC05
HC04
HC02
HC01
HC03
HC11
HC20
HC12
HC19
HC13
HC18
HC17
HC14
HC15
HC16
manure bin
manure bin
NORTH
to Main Road
© 1/2010 by State of Minnesota, Department of Natural Resources
Toilets
Drinking Water
tie post
WILD RIVER STATE PARK
HORSE CAMP
Underlined site numbers are RESERVABLE
trails to Southern Loops

WILD RIVER STATE PARK

FACILITIES AND FEATURES

- Information station/gift shop
- 96 semi-modern campsites
- Guest house (6 capacity)
- 6 camping cabins
- Modern shower buildings
- 34 electrical sites
- Trailer dump station
- 9 primitive group campsites (18 people per site)
- Horse campground (20 campsites)
- Amphitheater (300 capacity)
- Wood, ice and souvenir sales
- Cross-country ski and snowshoe rental/concessions
- All-season trail center (reservations accepted 4/15 to 11/15)
- Year-round visitor center
- Picnic area with shelter building (reservations accepted 5/1 to 10/1)
- 4 canoe campsites
- 7 backpack sites
- Sunrise River picnic area
- River accesses (2)
- Hiking/ski trails (35 miles)
- Horse trails (20 miles)
- River fishing
- Canoe rental/shuttle concession

VISITOR FAVORITES

- McElroy Visitor Center
- Nevers Dam scenic overlook
- Self-guided trails
- Building architecture
- Canoeing
- Wildflowers, deer, birds
- Logging era outdoor exhibit
- Naturalist programs
- Guest house/Camping cabins
- Geocaching opportunities

LOOKING FOR MORE INFORMATION?

The DNR has mapped the state showing federal, state and county lands with their recreational facilities.

Public Recreation Information Maps (PRIM) are available for purchase from the DNR gift shop, DNR regional offices, Minnesota state parks and major sporting and map stores.

Check it out - you'll be glad you did.

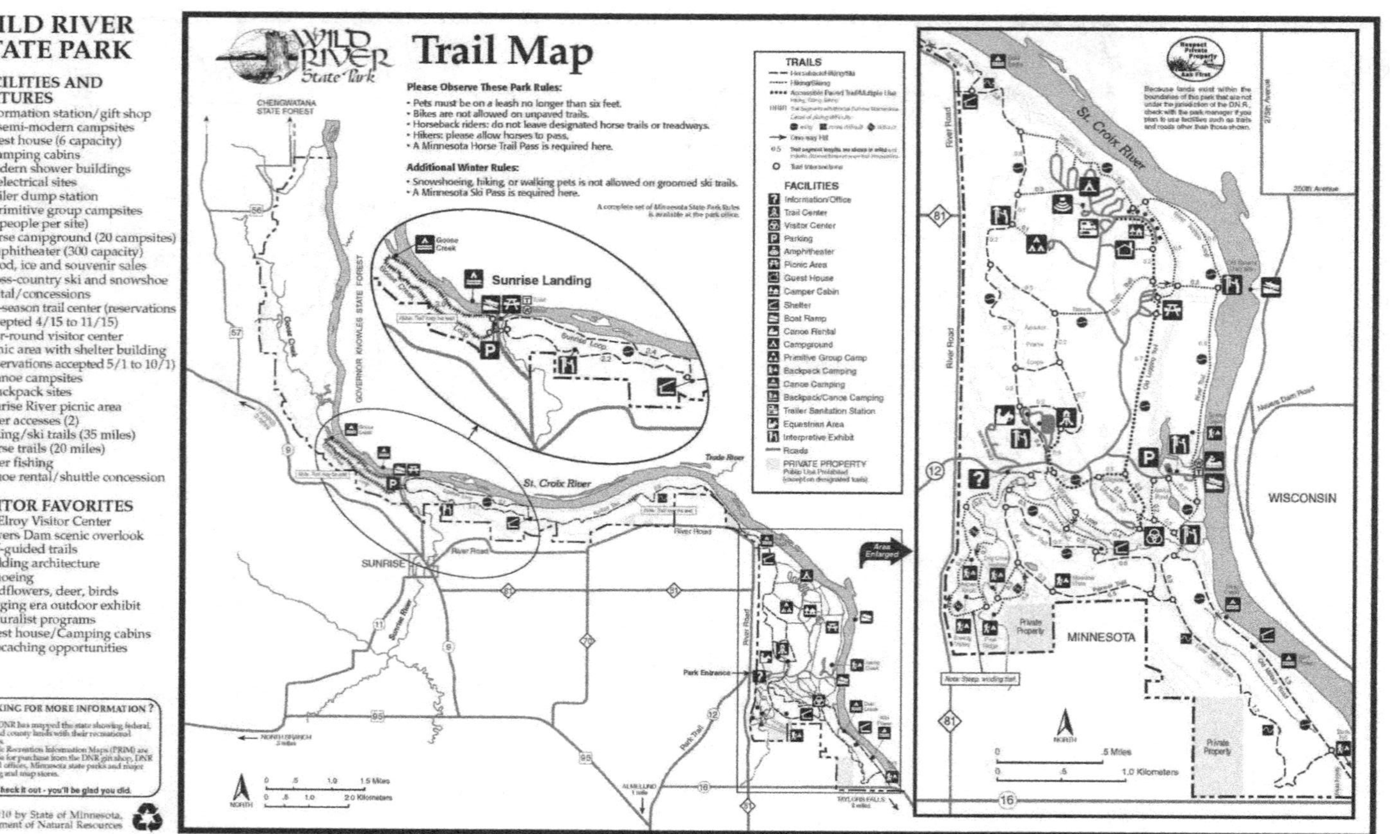

William O'Brien

16821 O'Brien Trail North
Marine on St. Croix, Minnesota 55047
651-433-0500

- The park is located just north of the town of Marine-on-St. Croix, Minnesota. Marine-on-St. Croix is the oldest logging settlement in the state.

- Two separate camp grounds in the park – Riverway, which is down near the river and the Savanna Campground, which sits on the terrace away from the river.

- Riverway Camp has 60 sites and Savanna Camp has 47 sites. There are 60 sites that have electrical hook-ups split between the two camps.

- The Riverway Camp is located near the river and the sites in this camp tend to be close together with some undergrowth between the sites. There are trees all around and give good shade in the camping area. This camping area is also close to Lake Alice and there is a fishing pier, swimming, a couple of open and sheltered picnic areas, a boat and canoe launch site, and trails all around the area.

- Savanna Camp has two or three small ponds and marshes near it plus access to the hiking trails. The camper cabins are also located up in the Savanna Camp. The Interpretive Center in the park is located near the Savanna Camp.

- Both of the camps have access to flush toilets/shower facilities. There are vault toilets and water spigots available for use throughout the park. The picnic area has volleyball nets, shelters, lots of tables, horseshoe throwing pits, and very nice tree cover and shade. Canoe rentals are available at the boat landing.

- There are two different group camps in the park – Riverside, down by the river and Wedge Hill, which sits above on the terrace.

- There are 12 miles of hiking and cross country skiing or skating trails. The park is open for year around use and winter camping.

- Sites in the Campgrounds that we liked were - # 11, 13, 47, 53, 59, 69, 70, 74, 85, 87, 95, 103, 109, 121, and 123.

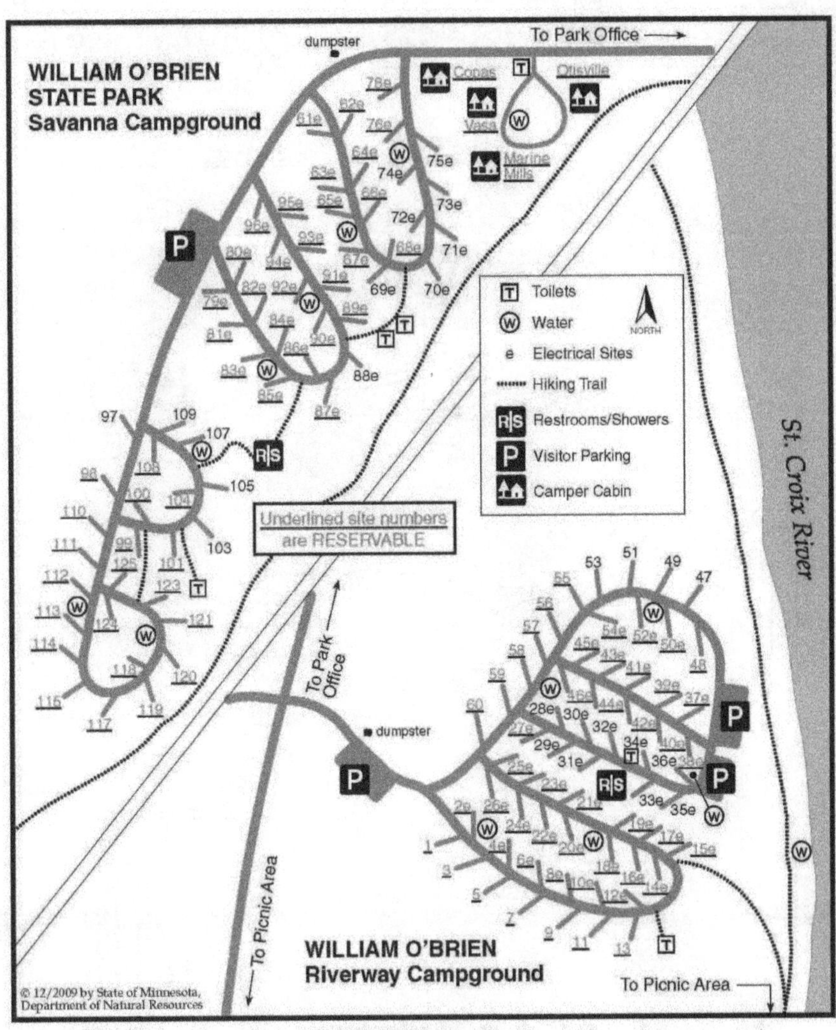

Note: This park *may* have RESERVABLE sites other than in the main campground. See the main park map for the locations of any additional camping or lodging sites.

WILLIAM O'BRIEN STATE PARK

FACILITIES AND FEATURES

- Visitor center with wood stove and displays
- 2 semi-modern campgrounds with a total of 124 sites (77 with electrical hookup)
- 4 camper cabins
- Showers, flush toilets, and trailer sanitation facility
- Riverside group campground (capacity 50)
- Wedge Hill group campground (capacity 105)
- Picnic grounds with 200 tables, 3 picnic shelters, and modern restrooms
- Swimming beach
- Lake and river fishing
- Boat launching ramp
- Canoe rental (summer)
- 12 miles of hiking trails
- 12 miles of cross-country ski trails (classic & skate)
- Year-round interpretive program
- Winter camping–rustic toilets provided, water available at park office
- Firewood and ice for sale at park office

LOOKING FOR MORE INFORMATION ?

The DNR has mapped the state showing federal, state and county lands with their recreational facilities.

Public Recreation Information Maps (PRIM) are available for purchase from the DNR gift shop, DNR regional offices, Minnesota state parks and major sporting and map stores.

Check it out - you'll be glad you did.

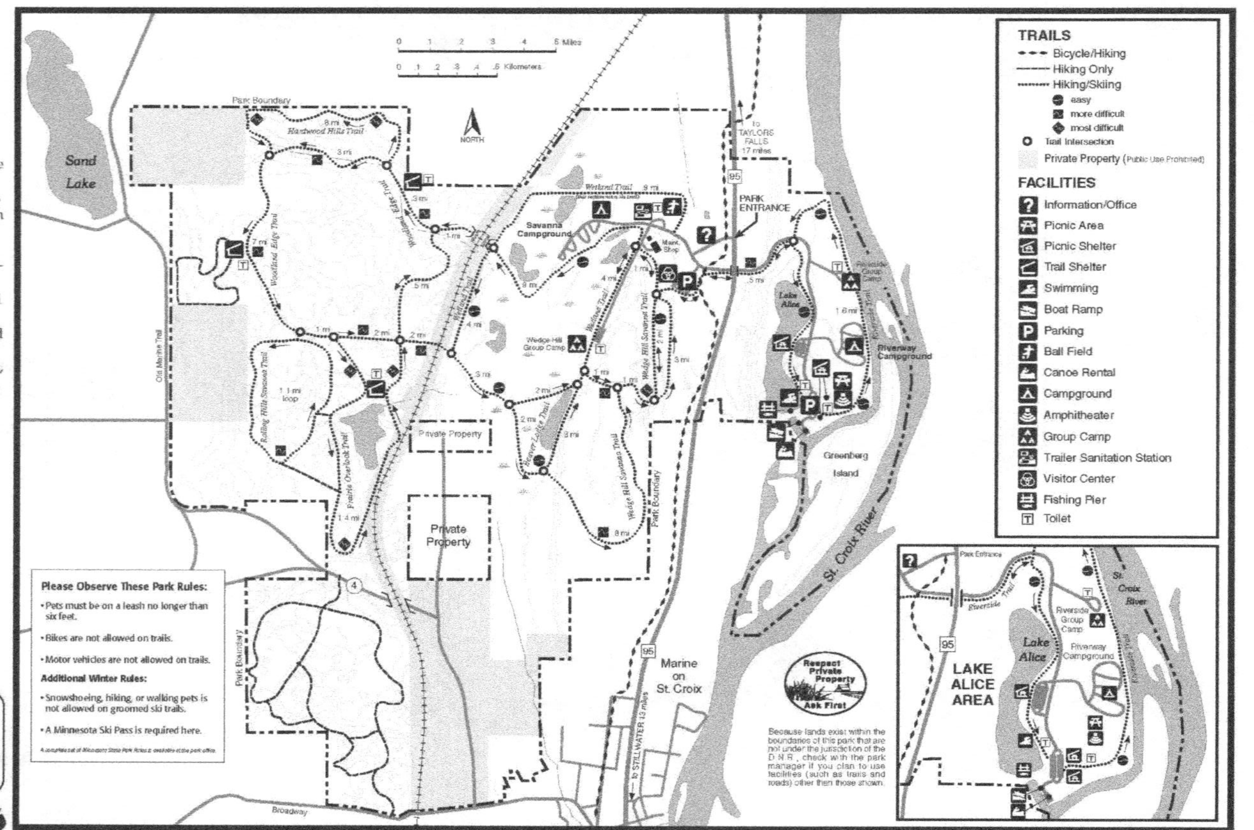

Zippel Bay

3684 54th Avenue NW
Williams, Minnesota 56686
218-783-6252

- Park is located ten miles northeast of Williams, MN, on the south shore of Lake of the Woods. It looks in some spots as if this park were actually cut out from inside the large red pine, jack pine and birch forest in the area. The roads in the park are predominantly gravel and dirt. In some spots, the roads get narrow.

- The park is frequently used by fisherman. From the park, they can gain access to the big lake. There is a camping area set up specifically for the angler's that visit the park. These sites are somewhat bigger to allow for boat trailers.

- There are three other campgrounds that are available for camping. All the sites in the Park are non-electric. One of the staff at the park mentioned that in a year or two, there is a plan to attempt to develop some electric sites on some high ground on the road leading to the boat landing.
- There are a couple of remote sites for camping along one of the trails
- Hiking trails, snowmobile trails, and horse trails are available for use. At the boat landing there are fish cleaning facilities, spots to moor boats, a fishing pier and a picnic area.
- There are three separate campgrounds beside the angler's camp. The closest to the lake is Lady's-slipper Camp, 11 sites. Up the road from there is the Birch Camp. These campgrounds are nice and do offer some seclusion from other campers due to all the trees and undergrowth. The Ridge Campground had the nicest sites available to pop-up campers and small pull-behinds.
- There is a site of an old fish processing plant on the park property.
- An absolutely beautiful picnic area on the shore of Lake of the Woods. A swimming beach is nearby and from the white sandy beach you can get a slight appreciation for how large the lake is.
- There is a shower facility available for campers; but, it is up by the Ranger's office and is quite a hike from any of the campgrounds.
- Camp sites that we liked were: 11, 12, 17, 33, and 39.

(Lake of the Woods)

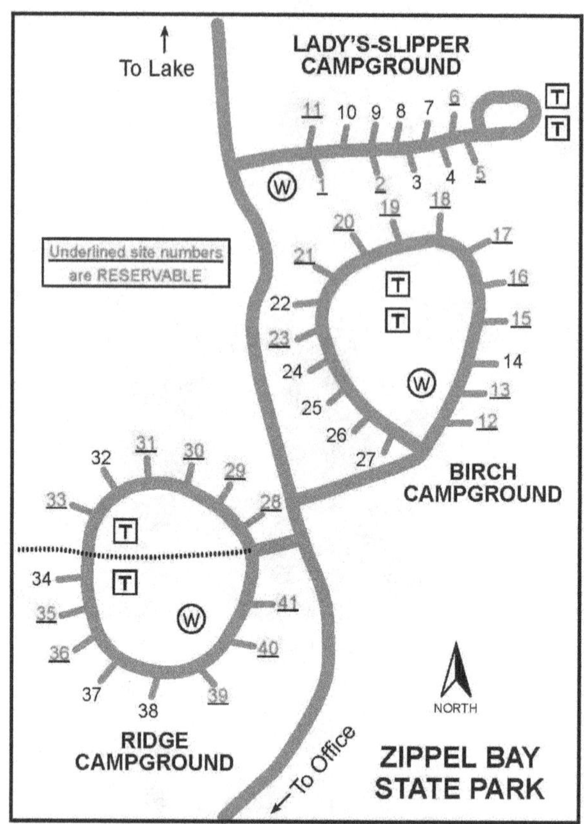

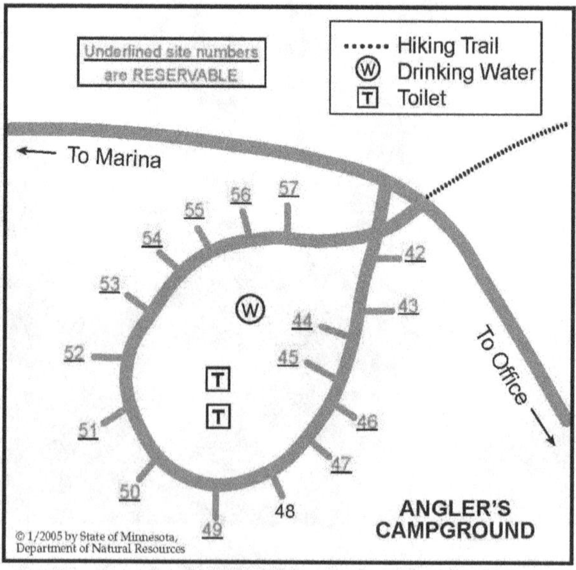

Note: This park *may* have RESERVABLE sites other than in the main campground. See the main park map for the locations of any additional camping or lodging sites.

ZIPPEL BAY STATE PARK

FACILITIES AND FEATURES

- Swimming beach on Lake of the Woods
- Nature trails
- Group camping area
- Beachcombing
- Public boat harbor, launching ramp and docks on Zippel Bay with access to Lake of the Woods
- Picnic area on Lake of the Woods
- Lake fishing with sightseeing and fishing launch service from the boat harbor (by arrangement)
- Fish-cleaning facility
- 60 drive-in campsites in birch and pine forests
- Trailer sanitation station
- Snowmobile trails
- Cross-country ski trails
- Horseback riding trails

SERVICE INFORMATION

- Firewood available at park headquarters
- Ice available at all nearby resorts
- Groceries and gas available eight miles east from the park entrance and at most nearby resorts
- Launch services, both half and full-day fishing excursions, can be arranged through nearby resorts
- Public telephone available in the park
- Fishing license, bait and tackle available at resorts and in Baudette and Williams, MN

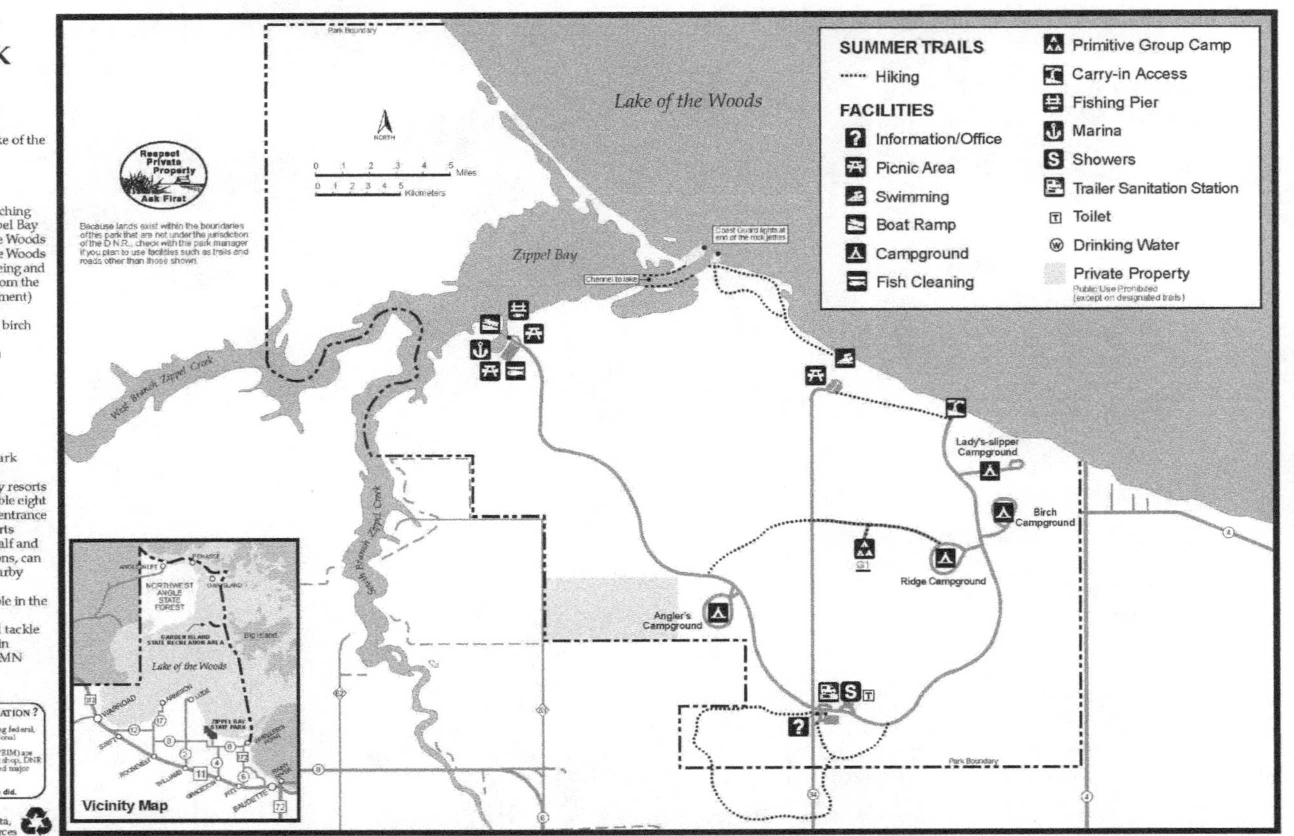

LOOKING FOR MORE INFORMATION?

The DNR has mapped the state showing federal, state and county lands with their recreational facilities.

Public Recreation Information Maps (PRIM) are available for purchase from the DNR gift shop, DNR regional offices, Minnesota state parks and major sporting and map stores.

Check it out - you'll be glad you did.

Other Sites to See –

As Julie and I criss-crossed the state on our travels to all the state parks, there were about a dozen other places and sites that we visited that we feel are very important for readers of this book to know about. As I have said many times before, I have lived most of my life in this state and most of these sites that we found I had no idea they even existed.

The sites that I am talking about are a mix of waysides, national monuments, and two memorial sites which have been set aside to honor important Minnesotans from the past. Most of the waysides are located along the North Shore Drive, Hwy. 61, leading northeast out of Duluth. These waysides were created to help preserve natural features along the north shore and to create access points to the large system of hiking trails that are there for use by visitors to the area.

Also included here are two sites that can be found just inside the border with the state of Wisconsin. These two spots, one which is just south of Superior, Wisconsin, and the other is just a couple miles north of the bridge where Minnesota Highway 70 crosses the St. Croix River, west of the town of Grantsburg, Wisconsin.

(Scenic overlook at Good Harbor Bay, North Shore, Lake Superior.)

Caribou Falls State Wayside

- This state wayside is the trail head for many trails that lead up into the hills above North Shore Drive (Hwy. 61).

- Anyone traveling up to this wayside to use the trails should be warned that the parking lot is very small and it will not accommodate vehicles pulling trailers or large RV's.

- The trails that lead from the parking area will take you up into the hills and woods behind until you reach the base of Caribou Falls, on the Caribou River. You will also be able to see beautiful views of the Caribou River Gorge and Lake Superior from the trails. There is access to the Lake Superior Hiking Trail from the parking area.

- The Caribou River is a designated trout stream.

Cross River Wayside

- This wayside is not included in the listing of 'state waysides' like Flood Bay, Caribou Falls, and the others. I include it here with these other waysides because of the unique historical event that occurred here. The wayside has a nice large parking area next to a set of vault toilets along Hwy. 61, just outside the town of Schroeder, Minnesota.

- This wayside is dedicated to Father Fredrick Baraga. He was a missionary to the local Indians and during a large storm in October in 1846, he and his Indian guide were swept across the lake and made it to shore at the mouth of the small creek at the bottom of the hill. He erected a wooden cross at the side of the creek in a show of his appreciation for being so fortunate.

- Today, the wooden cross has been replaced with a granite cross. It sits on the same spot near the mouth of the river. A sign on the lake shore side of Hwy. 61 about ¼ mile past the parking area will guide visitors down to s mall parking lot near the mouth of the river.

- There is a plaque at the wayside on top of the hill near the parking area which relays the story. There is a heritage center and gift shop across the road from the wayside parking area.

Devils Track State Wayside

- This Wayside can be accessed at a location along the Gunflint Trail and the Lake Superior Hiking Trail. It is a remote site and is approximately a 2 mile hike to reach the wayside. From the wayside, hikers can follow the trails to a point referred to as – Pincushion Mountain. This is an elevated rock outcrop that will give visitors great views of Lake Superior.

- Northwest of Grand Marais is Devil Track Lake. Taking the Gunflint Trail to the top of the ridge above the city, visitors should take a left turn onto Devil Track Trail and follow the signs along the road. The lake access is about 8 miles down that road and the access is on the north side of the lake. The campground is just a little further down the road from the lake access.

- This State Wayside is a large wooded area located in the steep hills on the east and west side of the Gunflint Trail, north of Grand

Marais. There are several streams that run through the area and empty into Lake Superior below.

- The area that Devils Track State Wayside is located is remote in the extreme. Hikers, campers and visitors to the area should ensure that they have the proper skills and equipment necessary to tackle the rigorous requirements of hiking in this type of terrain.

Flood Bay State Wayside

- This is a small Wayside area located on the shore side of Hwy. 61, just north of the city of Two Harbors, Minnesota. There are no picnic tables to use at the wayside; but, there is one vault toilet.

- There is a very popular pebble beach that runs along the shore of Lake Superior there at the wayside and is a favorite spot for visitors to stop to look for Lake Superior agates.

- The bay is a wetland area used by many species during the year. Visitors can see ducks, geese, beavers, otters and many other animals and birds from the rest area and along the shore.

Grand Portage National Monument

- The National Monument is about three miles from the border checkpoint on Hwy. 61. There is a collection of buildings to include: the visitor's center and numerous buildings which have been rebuilt and are used to let visitors walk through a recreation of what the fort at the portage site looked like in the 16 and 1700's. The area at that time was operated by the North West Fur Trading Company.

- You can find a wonderful collection of artifacts, information, and souvenirs in the visitor's center. A walk through the stockade and the buildings at the fort site will allow your imagination to take you back to a time past when pioneers were first moving into this area. Staff working at the park work as re-enactors in order to give visitor's more detail about the site.

Inspiration Peak State Wayside

- This truly inspirational site is located about twelve miles west of Parkers Prairie, Minnesota. Drive west on Highway 38 through the little town of Urbank. The Wayside is located about 4 miles past Urbank, on the north side of the road.

- This spot is a tall hill, one of the tallest points along the glacial moraine left in the area about 10,000 years ago. The southern most part of the peak is clear of trees and allows for an unprecedented view of the area. Over 50 different lakes can be seen from the peak. Sites as far as 20 miles away can be viewed at the top of this hill.

- This is a tall hill and it is a steep climb up to the observation site. There is a paved path that leads all the way to the top. There are several benches along the way to allow for a brief rest. The climb to the top may be arduous; but, in the fall, when the leaves a changing the view is spectacular.

➢ This peak was a favorite spot for Sinclair Lewis, one of Minnesota's famous writers and a native of Sauk Center. The Ojibwe word for the area of Inspiration Peak was – Gaskibugwudjiwe – this was translated to mean 'Rustling Leaf Mountains.' After Sinclair Lewis wrote about the peak, people started to refer to it in the name it has today. This spot was made a state wayside in 1932.

➢ Visitors to the top of the peak will be able to view many species of native prairie wild flowers. The soil at the top of the peak has been left undisturbed for hundreds of years.

Joseph R. Brown State Monument

- This sign marks the area where the Joseph Renshaw Brown Memorial Wayside is located. This small wayside is located at the spot where Brown built a 3 story, stone home for his large family. In its day, this home was a real 'palace.' Brown went as far as to name the house – Farther and Gay Castle.

- The wayside is located 6 miles south of Sacred Heart. When taking Renville Cty. Rd. 9 south from Sacred Heart, just before you reach the Minnesota River, you will come to the intersection of Renville County. Rd. 15. Turn left and drive one mile and you will see the wayside on the left side of the road.

- All that is left of the house is the lower stone walls and foundation, the rest was destroyed when the house was set afire by Indians during the 1862 Dakota Uprising.

- There are a couple of picnic tables on the site for use. The wayside and the former home look out across an open field and a tree line that marks the north bank of the Minnesota River.

Kadunce River State Wayside

- This is a small rest area located off of Hwy. 61 as it travels north to the border. There is a small picnic area available for use.
- There is a short trail leading from the rest area that will take hikers to the Lake Superior Hiking Trail. Along this portion of the trails visitors can get great views of the Kadunce River Gorge.
- There is also access to the beachfront of the lake and the mouth of the river from the rest area parking lot.

Pipestone National Monument

- This locality in the southwestern corner of the state has been of importance to humans for thousands of years. The same layer of bed rock that comes to the surface 20 miles to the south at Blue Mound State Park is also exposed here and around the city of Pipestone, Minnesota. That rock formation is known as Sioux quartzite. Underneath the quartzite is another formation of rock called 'catlinite', also known as 'pipestone'.

- The native and prehistoric tribes that roamed the open plains before white settlement knew of the importance of this place. They mined this reddish colored rock and used it to fashion tools and pieces of art. This rock was the basis for trade among many of the different tribes that lived in North America and they would travel great distances to get here. The Sioux Indians have had a settlement at this site for as long as their history can be traced.

- The site of the monument came under the control of the National Park Service back in 1937. The Yankton Sioux set up special treaties with the federal government and to this day; they still mine the mineral from this location.

- The park entranced is located about ¼ mile north and ½ mile west of the intersection of MN Hwy. 23 and U.S. Hwy. 75 on the north side of the city. Besides the Interpretive Center at the site, there is a picnic area, a ¾ mile trail for hiking and visitors can walk over and see the beautiful Winnewissa Falls, created by the Pipestone Creek as it tumbles over the edge of the escarpment formed by the bedrock within the park.

Ray Berglund State Wayside

- This State Wayside allows visitors access to a trail that leads along the bluffs overlooking the Onion River. It is located about five miles northeast of Tofte, Minnesota, on Highway 61. The trail itself is about ½ mile long. There is also a public access to Lake Superior at the wayside.

- In 2009, the state reconstructed a large section of Hwy. 61 that was adjacent to this wayside. The state created a new parking lot on the north side of the road and there is a nice paved trail along side of the road for visitors to walk along and look down into the Onion River gorge.

- The Onion River is a designated trout stream.

Sam Brown State Monument

- This memorial park in Browns Valley, Minnesota, is dedicated to a frontiersman and soldier, son of Joseph R. Brown. Samuel Brown is known as the – Paul Revere of the Northwest Frontier. He made a harrowing ride of 55 miles in 5 hours on horseback to warn settlers of an impending Indian attack on April 19, 1866. The rumor of an impending attack turned out to be false.

- Sam Brown, one of numerous children born to Susan (Frenier) and Joe Brown, lived most of his long life in our state. He was renowned in his later life for being a very engaging public speaker and was invited to state functions and other important celebrations to regale the crowds with his stories of the frontier and life in rural Minnesota.

- There are several things to see and investigate while visiting this spot. There is a small museum that has been created in the building that is the actual log home of Sam Brown. Within the museum is a large collection of photos and artifacts concerning Sam Brown, his father Joseph Brown, the Brown family, Browns Valley, and the people and past of the area. There is a small one room school that has been moved to the memorial park and is now part of the exhibit.

Pattison State Park

(Big Manitou Falls)

- This park is located thirteen miles south of Superior, Wisconsin, on WI Highway 35. This small state park is one of my favorites in the state of Wisconsin.

- This park has the Black River running through it. Interfalls Lake is located near Highway 35 and the lake has a great sand beach. There are two separate waterfalls in the park – Little Manitou Falls and Big Manitou Falls.

- Big Manitou Falls is the fourth largest waterfall east of the Mississippi River.

- The campground has 59 sites, 18 of the sites have electric hookups available. There are flush toilets and showers available. There is a very nice picnic area, 9 miles of hiking trails and great scenic views of the waterfalls.

- The Ojibwe name for the Black River was 'Mucudewa' which means black or dark. The water of the river is very dark colored due to the tannins and other natural dyes that get into the river from the decay of vegetative material.

Sandrock Cliffs

("The Sandrock")

- If you find yourself traveling into Wisconsin and you are on Highway 70 traveling east, after you cross the bridge over the St. Croix River, you will be about six miles from this wonderful spot.
- The first paved road going north from Highway 70 is Soderbeck Road. Turn left onto this road and drive 2 miles north to the intersection with Benson Road. Turn left here and drive one mile to the 'T' intersection. Turn right onto Tennessee Road and follow it to the end. You will have arrived at the parking lot for the Sandrock Cliffs.
- There are two different channels of the St. Croix River at this spot. The west channel, on the Minnesota side, always has water flowing; but, the east channel is shallow and at times it is dry. Look at the

picture above, this photo was taken at mid summer and the channel was dry and you could walk across to a small island in the middle of the river without getting your feet wet.

- On top of these cliffs is a large stand of mature red pines. They stand tall and straight and help to give the area a very quiet, muffled feeling. My family and I have enjoyed canoeing down the St. Croix River since I was just a small boy and the Sandrock was one of several spots we used as an end point for our trips.
- There is a trail leading out to the cliffs from the parking lot. There are about a half dozen very basic campsites situated among the red pines. The sites have fire rings, there is a single vault toilet, and a water spigot located near the parking area.
- This small park is very lightly used, even by the people who live in the area. There are times that you would be the only people camping there. Again, I want to stress that this little camping area is remote and at night after you turn out the lights – it will be absolutely pitch black underneath the pines and so quiet you could hear the proverbial pin drop.

(Tall Red Pines)

- One last note, if you have driven all the way into Wisconsin to see the sights at the Sandrock and you are only 6 miles from Grantsburg, Wisconsin; then, you should take a drive up Burnett County Highway F. A short distance north, outside of town, you will enter the Crex Meadows Wildlife Area. Wildlife abounds in this preserve and you will see deer, badger and many other species of north woods mammals. However, the thing that draws most people to this wildlife area - the birds. There are hundreds of species of birds that can be found in the preserve. I strongly encourage you to visit this spot.

State Park List –

On the following pages you will find an alphabetical list of all of the state parks and the state waysides. A table is provided for you here to record the dates that you visited each of the parks and another space for you to record a favorite event or something about the park that made your visit special.

Park Name	Date	Special Event or What you liked best
Afton		
Banning		
Bear Head Lake		
Beaver Creek Valley		
Big Bog SRA		
Big Stone Lake		
Blue Mounds		
Buffalo River		
Camden		
Carley		
Cascade River		
Charles A. Lindbergh		
Crow Wing		
Cuyuna Country SRA		
Father Hennepin		
Flandrau		
Forestville/Mystery Cave		
Fort Ridgely		
Fort Snelling		

Park Name	Date	Special Event or What you liked best
Franz Jevne		
Frontenac		
Garden Island SRA		
George H. Crosby/Manitou		
Glacial Lakes		
Glendalough		
Gooseberry Falls		
Grand Portage		
Great River Bluffs		
Greenleaf Lake SRA		
Hayes Lake		
Hill Annex Mine		
Interstate		
Itasca		
Jay Cooke		
John A. Latsch		
Judge C.R. Magney		
Kilen Woods		
Lac Qui Parle		
Lake Bemidji		
Lake Bronson		
Lake Carlos		
Lake Louise		
Lake Maria		
Lake Shetek		
Lake Vermilion		
Maplewood		
McCarthy Beach		
Mille Lacs Kathio		
Minneopa		
Minnesota Valley SRA		
Monson Lake		
Moose Lake		
Myre-Big Island		

Park Name	Date	Special Event or What you liked best
Nerstrand Big Woods		
Old Mill		
Red River SRA		
Rice Lake		
St. Croix		
Sakatah Lake		
Savanna Portage		
Scenic		
Schoolcraft		
Sibley		
Soudan UndergroundMine		
Split Rock Creek		
Split Rock Lighthouse		
Temperance River		
Tettegouche		
Upper Sioux Agency		
Whitewater		
Wild River		
William O'Brien		
Zippel Bay		

State Waysides –

Wayside Name	Date	Special Event or What you liked best
Caribou Falls		
Devils Track		
Flood Bay		
Inspiration Peak		
Joseph R. Brown		
Kadunce River		
Ray Berglund		
Sam Brown		

The Parks Department in the state of Minnesota created their State

Park Passport program as a means to help encourage people to visit the state parks. Julie and I got one of the passport books and the rest of the material that came with it when the idea struck us to try and visit all of the parks. Contained within that material, the Parks Department had included a small book with pre-formatted pages that would allow campers to write down information on each page regarding the park they were visiting, when they were there, and a large area devoted to what they liked about each park.

We would like to offer you a similar opportunity to record that kind of information too. However, the small booklet the state put together was about 50 pages long and that would be much too long to be included here. We created a smaller table here to allow you to record similar information; you will just have to be brief with your comments.

- Citations -

> Minnesota Department of Natural Resources. 2010. The Minnesota Department of Natural Resources Website (online). Accessed August 2010 at http://www.dnr.state.mn.us/sitetools/copywrite.html

> Photograph of canoe on lake. Downloaded October 1, 2010 from stock.xchg VI. Website - http://www.sxc.hu

- References -

> Meyer, Ray W. (1991) *Everyone's Country Estates: A History of Minnesota State Parks*. St. Paul, MN. Minnesota Historical Society Press.

> Bogue, Margaret Beattie. (2007) *Around the Shores of Lake Superior: A Guide to Historic Sites,* 2nd edition. Madison, WI. University of Wisconsin Press.

> Lass, William E. (1998) *Minnesota: A History,* 2nd edition. New York, NY. W.W. Norton & Company

CPSIA information can be obtained
at www.ICGtesting.com
Printed in the USA
LVHW040150060623
748992LV00017B/67/J